REVEL enables students to read and interact with course material on the devices they use, **anywhere** and **anytime**. Responsive design allows students to access REVEL on their tablet devices, with content displayed clearly in both portrait and landscape view.

Highlighting, **note taking**, and a **glossary** personalize the learning experience. Educators can add **notes** for students, too, including reminders or study tips

REVEL's variety of **writing** activities and assignments develop and assess concept **mastery** and **critical thinking**.

Superior assignability and tracking

REVEL's assignability and tracking tools help educators make sure students are completing their reading and understanding core concepts.

REVEL allows educators to indicate precisely which readings must be completed on which dates. This clear, detailed schedule helps students stay on task and keeps them motivated throughout the course.

REVEL lets educators monitor class assignment completion and individual student achievement. It offers actionable information that helps educators intersect with their students in meaningful ways, such as points earned on quizzes and time on task.

Mastering Public Speaking

Ninth Edition

George L. Grice
Radford University, Professor Emeritus

John F. Skinner
San Antonio College

Daniel H. Mansson
Penn State Hazleton

Boston   Columbus   Indianapolis   New York   San Francisco
Amsterdam   Cape Town   Dubai   London   Madrid   Milan   Munich   Paris   Montreal   Toronto
Delhi   Mexico City   São Paulo   Sydney   Hong Kong   Seoul   Singapore   Taipei   Tokyo

Publisher, Communication: Karon Bowers
Editorial Assistant: Kieran Fleming
Director of Development: Sharon Geary
Senior Field Marketing Manager: Blair Zoe Tuckman
Program Product Marketing Manager: Becky Rowland
Program Team Lead: Maureen Richardson
Program Manager: Anne Riciglano
Project Team Lead: Linda Behrens
Project Manager: Raegan Keida Heerema
Project Coordination, Text Design, and Electronic Page Makeup: Cenveo® Publisher Services
Cover Design: Pentagram
Design Lead: Maria Lange
Digital Media Project Manager: Sean Silver
Operations Manager: Mary Fischer
Senior Manufacturing Buyer: Mary Ann Gloriande
Printer/Binder: RR Donnelley/Willard
Cover Printer: Phoenix Color/Hagerstown

Acknowledgments of third-party content appear on pages 323–324, which constitutes an extension of this copyright page.

Library of Congress Cataloging-in-Publication Data

Grice, George L.
   Mastering public speaking / George L. Grice, Radford University,
Professor Emeritus; John F. Skinner, San Antonio College; Daniel H.
Mansson, Penn State Hazleton. —Ninth edition.
         pages cm.
   Includes bibliographical references and index.
   ISBN 0-13-375383-2 (alk. paper)
 1. Public speaking.   I. Skinner, John F.   II. Mansson, Daniel H.   III.
Title.
   PN4129.15.G75 2015
   808.5'1—dc23

                                                                      2014048550

10 9 8 7 6 5 4 3 2 1

PEARSON

Student Edition: ISBN 13: 978-0-13-375383-7
                    ISBN 10:   0-13-375383-2
à la carte Edition: ISBN 13: 978-0-13-404736-2
                    ISBN 10:   0-13-404736-2
REVEL Edition: ISBN 13: 978-0-13-392254-7
                    ISBN 10:   0-13-392254-5

To Wrenn, Evelyn, Carol, and Leanne

To Ulla, Henric, and Vivian;
and the memory of
my father and role model, Hans-Uno Månsson;
my grandfather, Åke Svensson; and
my host-father, Ernest Domoney

and

To the memory of John F. Skinner,
author, teacher, colleague, and friend

Brief Contents

Contents

Appendix C: Developing and Delivering Team Presentations

Preface

In 1993, George Grice and John Skinner authored the first edition of *Mastering Public Speaking* to show students both the *hows* and the *whys* of public speaking. This was the first major public speaking textbook to devote an entire chapter to speaker and listener ethics and another chapter to managing speaker nervousness. It also introduced students to the 4 S's, a practical mnemonic device for organizing each major idea in a speech.

The text's instructional approach mirrored a view of the public speaking instructor as a "guide on the side" rather than a "sage on the stage." A primary goal was to empower students to take responsibility for their own learning by challenging them to make the decisions required of public speakers.

By incorporating into our text many credible examples, both actual and hypothetical, we hoped to inspire and encourage students to achieve the full potential of public speech.

To support our goals, we also wanted to help instructors shape the public speaking classroom into a community of caring, careful thinkers. We sought to improve the quality of feedback in the classroom by analyzing the elements of sound critiques and providing a helpful model for discussing speeches.

We live in a changed world in the early twenty-first century. New media have altered our expectations of what a public speech can accomplish, and new research tools have sent us scrambling to ensure that we know as much about these emerging technologies as do most of our students, but in our view, the fundamentals of public speaking remain the same. Sensitive audience analysis, adequate research, clear organization, and dynamic delivery remain the key ingredients for effective speeches. Therefore, our basic instructional approach in this text remains constant: We seek to engage students in the principles, practice, and ethics of public speaking—both as speakers and as listeners.

What's New in the Ninth Edition

REVEL™
Educational technology designed for the way today's students read, think, and learn

When students are engaged deeply, they learn more effectively and perform better in their courses. This simple fact inspired the creation of REVEL: an immersive learning experience designed for the way today's students read, think, and learn. Built in collaboration with educators and students nationwide, REVEL is the newest, fully digital way to deliver respected Pearson content.

REVEL enlivens course content with media interactives and assessments—integrated directly within the authors' narrative—that provide opportunities for students to read about and practice course material in tandem. This immersive educational technology boosts student engagement, which leads to better understanding of concepts and improved performance throughout the course.

Learn more about REVEL

http://www.pearsonhighered.com/revel/

Rather than simply offering opportunities to read about and study public speaking, REVEL facilitates deep, engaging interactions with the concepts that matter most. For example, when learning about public speaking anxiety, students are prompted to complete a self-assessment to gauge their own communication style and explore ways to improve their skills. By providing opportunities to read about and practice communication in tandem, REVEL engages students directly and immediately, which leads to a better understanding of course material. A wealth of student and instructor resources and interactive materials can be found within REVEL. Some of our favorites include:

- **Short Speech Excerpts**
  Abundant in-text speech excerpts let students listen to audio clips while they read, bringing examples to life in a way that a printed text cannot.

- **Videos and Video Quizzes**
  Video examples of sample speeches and expert advice throughout the narrative boost mastery, and many videos are bundled with correlating self-checks, enabling students to test their knowledge.

- **Animated Figures**
  Animated figures help students understand hard-to-grasp concepts through interactive visualizations.

- **Integrated Writing Opportunities**
  To help students connect chapter content with personal meaning, each chapter offers two varieties of writing prompts: the Journal prompt, which elicits free-form topic-specific responses addressing topics at the module level, and the Shared Writing prompt, which encourages students to share and respond to each other's brief responses to high-interest topics in the chapter.

For more information about all the tools and resources in REVEL and access to your own REVEL account for *Mastering Public Speaking,* Ninth Edition, go to www.pearsonhighered.com/revel

In addition to the immersive learning experience offered by REVEL, we've refined and updated the content in this new edition to create a powerful and contemporary resource for helping speakers connect to their audiences. We've added several new features and revised features that both instructors and students have praised.

As you read this new edition of *Mastering Public Speaking*, you will notice several structural changes. Drawing from suggestions of talented reviewers, colleagues, and students, as well as our own experience, we have switched the order of two chapters, retitled two chapters, deleted another, modified the internal structure of several chapters, and added two new appendices. In our opinion, these changes have enhanced the flow and cohesion of the textbook's content.

As with each new edition, we have replaced and updated many student and professional examples, using actual classroom and contest speakers for most of these.

We have inserted new learning objectives in all chapters and have incorporated changes specific to chapter content.

- Chapter 1, "An Introduction to Public Speaking," focuses more specifically on public speaking. For example, the discussion of "Levels of Communication" has been condensed and placed in Table 1.1. The "Communication Elements Model" has been renamed the "Communication Elements Model of Public Speaking" and is discussed from the perspectives of both public speakers and their listeners.

- Chapter 2, "The Ethics of Public Speaking," contains ethical guidelines that are now applied and illustrated more fully throughout the textbook.

- Chapter 3, now titled "Speaking with Confidence," places greater emphasis on how to *manage*, rather than control, speaker nervousness.

- Chapter 5, "Analyzing Your Audience," presents Maslow's hierarchy of needs as a "Theory Into Practice" feature. The discussion of using an audience questionnaire has been refined and placed in the new Appendix B, "Using an Audience Questionnaire."

- Chapter 7, "Researching Your Speech Topic," contains updated coverage of electronic research sources, databases, and academic search engines. It also introduces students to focus groups and primary, secondary, qualitative, and quantitative research, which are developed more in subsequent chapters.

- Chapter 9, "Supporting Your Speech," enhances our suggestions for orally citing sources in a speech.

- Chapter 10, "Introducing and Concluding Your Speech," revises the three functions of a conclusion. Two "Theory Into Practice" features have been added that annotate a sample speech introduction and conclusion.

- Chapter 11, "Outlining Your Speech," features a new extended example of the stages of outlining by a classroom public speaking student. The new "Theory Into Practice" shows his speaking notes and list of references.

- Chapter 12, "Wording Your Speech," is reorganized and revised to focus student attention on six strategies for using language effectively. Included is a "Theory Into Practice" feature that illustrates how to convert powerless language into powerful language.

- Chapter 13, "Delivering Your Speech," has a new "Speaking with Confidence" and a new "Theory Into Practice," with a bulleted list of speaking guidelines for impromptu speaking.

- Chapter 14, "Using Presentational Aids," includes a discussion about using Breeze presentations as a type of projected presentational aid.

- Chapter 15, "Speaking to Inform," places greater emphasis on guidelines that are more focused and specific to informative speaking.

- Chapter 16, "The Strategy of Persuasion," revises and extends the discussion of speaker credibility as a function of speaker competence, trustworthiness, and caring.

- Chapter 17, "Speaking to Persuade," has been renamed and presents a new student speech, which is annotated to illustrate the steps of Monroe's motivated sequence.

- New Appendix B, "Using an Audience Questionnaire," has been refined and moved from its previous location in Chapter 5. This new stand-alone topic allows instructors to assign it at the appropriate time in the semester or quarter.

- New Appendix C, "Developing Team Presentations," applies and expands what students have learned about giving individual speeches to preparing and delivering team presentations.

- Appendix D, "Sample Speeches," includes two new student speeches. Also included is a brief discussion of Oprah Winfrey's eulogy of Rosa Parks.

Special Features

There are many special features that are an integral part of the learning materials in this book. We've included these to help students understand and learn public speaking concepts. We have retained the following popular instructional features:

- **Learning Objectives** appear at the beginning of each chapter and are additionally highlighted in their related sections to help guide students' reading and learning.

- **Theory Into Practice** boxes, several of which have been newly revised and edited, reinforce the text's instructional approach and help students understand and apply communication concepts and strategies to enhance their public speaking competence. In REVEL, many include interactive opportunities that allow students to focus on one aspect at a time, listen to audio excerpts, or walk through an example that illustrates the concept.

Theory Into Practice TIP

HOW TO AVOID PLAGIARISM

To avoid plagiarizing, let the following five simple rules guide you:

- *Take clear and consistent notes while researching.* As you review your notes, you should be able to discern which words, ideas, examples, and organizational structures belong to which authors.
- *Record complete source citations.* Each sheet of notes, each photocopied article, and each printed page of a document you have accessed should indicate its source(s).
- *Clearly indicate in your speech any words, ideas, examples, or organizational structures that are not your own.* If you cite a source early in your speech and then use another idea from that author later, you must again give that author credit. You do not need to repeat the complete citation, however. Use an abbreviated citation, such as "Vance says that" in our earlier example, if you have provided the full citation earlier in your speech.
- *Use your own words, language style, and thought structure when paraphrasing.* Remember that both content and structure distinguish another person's statements. When paraphrasing what another person has written or said, you should use not just your own words but also your own language style and thought structure. Otherwise, you are "paraplaging."
- *When in doubt, cite the source.* If you are unsure whether you really need to acknowledge a source, it's always wise to err on the side of caution.

- **Key Points** boxes appear throughout the book to reinforce instruction and aid student review. They summarize important material and offer helpful guidelines throughout the public speaking process. REVEL takes them one step further as interactive quizzes that students can use to review and interpret concepts.

- **Ethical Decisions** boxes deepen students' understanding of the difficult choices speakers and listeners can face. These boxes present mini cases and ask students to choose between controversial courses of action. Thought-provoking questions follow each scenario, providing springboards for engaging in classroom debates and, in REVEL, writing online Journal entries.

Ethical Decisions

IS SEEING BELIEVING?

Jayden chose involvement in student government as the topic for his persuasive speech. In his research, he discovered a decrease in the percentage of students voting in Student Government Association elections. He chose to focus on the past six years. He compiled the voting percentages, drew a rough draft of his intended visual aid, and asked his friend Leah to prepare a line graph on her computer. She produced the following graph:

Figure 14A

- **Speaking with Confidence** boxes feature the stories of real students from public speaking classes throughout the country who explain how this text helped them build their confidence in public speaking. Additionally, REVEL offers audio versions of this feature.

Speaking with Confidence

Before presenting my speech on how to start a new small business, I began gathering and evaluating the supporting materials I would use to support my key ideas. Like most speakers, I searched online for information. I was careful to be selective and to avoid web pages that were based on personal opinion and bias. I supplemented the examples and statistics I found with my own expert testimony as a successful, self-employed businessman. I cited my sources to establish my credibility and let my listeners assess the quality of my data and documentation. Knowing that I had selected and tested my supporting materials allowed me to minimize my use of qualifiers such as "I think," "this might," and "maybe." I was confident with what I said, and the audience could be confident with what they heard.

JOVAN COKER
Radford University

- **Exploring Online** features sidebars that capture the creativity and commitment necessary to master public speaking, and direct students to a wealth of Internet information that we consider especially interesting or useful.

- **Sample Speeches** appear in selected chapters and in Appendix D as models for students to learn from or critique. In REVEL, some of the speeches include audio and/or video components.

Renaissance Fairs: The New Vaudeville[3]
Melissa Janoske, Radford University

1 Imagine you're walking down the street, minding your own business, about to go into a store, when suddenly, someone calls your name. You turn around, and the person advances toward you. Immediately, you find yourself in the middle of a sword fight—right in the middle of the street! As you fight for your life, a crowd gathers, watching and cheering. The fight is treacherous, and your opponent is worthy, but, finally, the fight ends when the gleaming edge of your sword pins your opponent onto the cobblestone path below him. Those who have gathered come up and congratulate you.

Melissa's opening comments arouse curiosity about her topic.

- **Journal** writing features in REVEL prompt students to write short answers to questions related to topics in each module, ranging from self-reflective questions to applications such as generating speech topics and responding to video clips.

- **Shared Writing** features in REVEL engage students in the routine of regular writing, collaboration, and critical thinking. Many of these features involve Practice Critiques, giving students the opportunity to learn how to provide helpful and thoughtful evaluations of others' speeches. Responses are shared in a discussion thread with the entire class, where students can comment on one another's posts.

Instructor and Student Resources

Key instructor resources include an Instructor's Manual (ISBN 0-13-386308-5), TestBank (ISBN 0-13-386307-7), and PowerPoint Presentation Package (ISBN 0-13-386306-9). These supplements are available at www.pearsonhighered.com/irc (instructor login required). MyTest online test-generating software (ISBN: 0-13-386309-3) is available at www.pearsonmytest.com (instructor login required). For a complete list of the instructor and student resources available with the text, please visit the Pearson Communication catalog, at www.pearsonhighered.com/communication

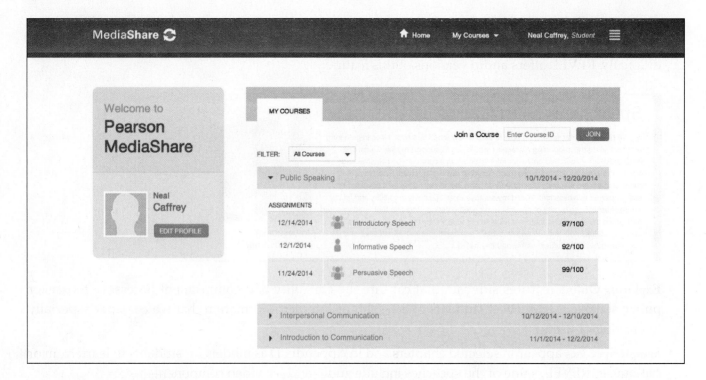

Pearson MediaShare

Pearson's comprehensive media upload tool allows students to post video, images, audio, or documents for instructor and peer viewing, time-stamped commenting, and assessment. MediaShare is an easy, mobile way for students and professors to interact and engage with speeches, presentation aids, group projects, and other files. MediaShare gives professors the tools to provide contextual feedback to demonstrate how students can improve their skills.

Structured like a social networking site, MediaShare helps promote a sense of community among students. In face-to-face and online course settings, MediaShare saves instructors valuable time and enriches the student learning experience by providing contextual feedback.

- Use MediaShare to assign or view speeches, outlines, presentation aids, video-based assignments, role plays, group projects, and more in a variety of formats including video, Word, PowerPoint, and Excel.
- Assess students using customizable, Pearson-provided rubrics or create your own around classroom goals, learning outcomes, or department initiatives.
- Set up assignments for students with options for full-class viewing and commenting, private comments between you and the student, peer groups for reviewing, or as collaborative group assignments.
- Record video directly from a tablet, phone, or other webcam (including a batch upload option for instructors) and tag submissions to a specific student or assignment.
- Embed video from YouTube via assignments to incorporate current events into the classroom experience.
- Set up quiz questions on video assignments to ensure students master concepts and interact and engage with the media.
- Import grades into most learning management systems.
- Ensure a secure learning environment for instructors and students through robust privacy settings.
- Upload videos, comment on submissions, and grade directly from our new MediaShare app, available free from the iTunes store and GooglePlay; search for Pearson MediaShare.

Pearson MediaShare is available as a standalone product, as part of MyCommunicationLab, or in a package with REVEL.

Acknowledgments

We are, first and foremost, grateful to the many university, college, and community college educators whose encouragement and support contributed to the success of previous editions of this textbook. The ninth edition of *Mastering Public Speaking* is the product of more than just the authors. Although we have tried to speak with one voice for the sake of our readers, the truth is that many voices resonate throughout this text: the voices of our teachers, our colleagues, our editors, and our students. Wherever possible, we have tried to acknowledge their contributions. For all their influence on this text we are thankful.

On the copyright page of this textbook is a list of Pearson professionals who have done the heavy lifting and guided this edition to completion. We thank the entire editorial, production, and marketing staffs for their time, talent, and contributions to this ninth edition.

We are indebted to five problem solvers extraordinaire: Karon Bowers, publisher; Raegan Heerema, project manager; Anne Ricigliano, program manager; Brenda Hadenfeldt, development editor; and Carol Alper, senior development editor. Thank you for your faith in this project, wise counsel, and responsiveness to our input, questions, and requests. Carol, what can we say? You've served as development editor for six of our nine editions and have been a wonderful part of the co-authors' lives. We wish you the best in your well-deserved retirement.

This is the first edition written or revised without our friend and co-author John F. Skinner. Yet, as we reviewed previous editions, we experienced, once again, his insights, scholarship, wit, and respect for language, and the conversational tone he established with readers. John, you will forever be a part of *Mastering Public Speaking* and a part of our lives.

Mastering Public Speaking has been shaped and refined by the close readings and thoughtful suggestions of a number of reviewers. We would like to thank the following reviewers for their comments on this edition:

Suzanne Atkin, *Portland State University*
Lana Becker, *Ivy Tech Community College*
Kathy Berggren, *Cornell University*
Chris McCollough, *Columbus State University*
Jeff Rhoads, *Estrella Mountain Community College*
E. Sue Weber, *University of Pennsylvania*

We would also like to acknowledge reviewers of previous editions:

Linda Anthon, *Valencia Community College*
Barbara L. Baker, *Central Missouri State University*
Elizabeth Bell, *University of South Florida*
Jim Benjamin, *University of Toledo*
Kathy Berggren, *Cornell University*
Tim Borchers, *Moorhead State University*
Sue E. Brilhart, *Southwest Missouri State University*
Gwendolyn Brown, *Professor Emerita, Radford University*
Carl R. Burgchardt, *Colorado State University*
Barbara Ruth Burke, *University of Minnesota, Morris*
Sharon Cline, *University of North Dakota*
Dolly Conner, *Radford University*
Pamela Cooper, *Northwestern University*
Michael Cronin, *Professor Emeritus, Radford University*
Sherry Dewald, *Red Rock Community College*

Thomas E. Diamond, *Montana State University*

Terrence Doyle, *Northern Virginia Community College*

Rebecca J. Franko, *California State Polytechnic University, Pomona*

Sandy French, *Radford University*

John Fritch, *Southwest Missouri State University*

Kristin Froemling, *Radford University*

Robert W. Glenn, *University of Tennessee*

Deborah Anne Gross, *Gwynedd Mercy College*

Trudy L. Hanson, *West Texas A&M University*

Dayle C. Hardy-Short, *Northern Arizona University*

Deborah Hatton, *Sam Houston State University*

Kimberly Batty Herbert, *Clovis Community College*

Susan Kilgard, *Ann Arundel Community College*

Leslie A. Klipper, *Miramar College*

Mary Kaye Krum, *formerly of Florence-Darlington Technical College*

Linda Kurz, *University of Missouri, Kansas City*

Nancy Legge, *Idaho State University*

Bruce Loebs, *Idaho State University*

Stacey M. Macchi, *Western Illinois University*

Sean McDevitt, *Lakeland College*

Patricia Palm McGillen, *Mankato State University*

David C. McLaughlin, *Montana State University*

David B. McLennan, *Peace College*

Dante E. Morelli, *Suffolk County Community College*

David Mrizek, *San Antonio College*

Eileen Oswald, *Valencia Community College*

Jolinda Ramsey, *San Antonio College*

Rosemarie Rossetti, *Ohio State University*

Jim Roux, *Horry-Georgetown Technical College*

Edward H. Sewell, *Virginia Polytechnic Institute and State University*

Suzanne Skinner, *San Antonio College*

Deborah Stieneker, *Arapahoe Community College*

Frances Swinny, *Professor Emerita, Trinity University*

Jason J. Teven, *California State University, Fullerton*

Cory Tomasson, *Illinois Valley Community College*

Beth M. Waggenspack, *Virginia Polytechnic Institute and State University*

Kimberly Warren-Cox, *Jackson State Community College*

Doris Werkman, *Portland State University*

Karin Wilking, *San Antonio College*

Dianna R. Wynn, *Midland College*

We also appreciate the many talented individuals who prepared the array of supplemental materials listed in the "Instructor and Student Resources" section in this preface. Their contributions to the effective teaching and learning of public speaking are immeasurable.

Finally, we are indebted to all our public speaking students who have crafted their messages, walked to the front of their classrooms, and informed, persuaded, entertained, and challenged us. Without their ideas and experiences, writing and revising this book would have been impossible, just as without tomorrow's students it would be unnecessary.

An Invitation

We welcome your feedback about the ninth edition of *Mastering Public Speaking.* Please contact us by email at the following addresses:

ggrice@radford.edu
dhm14@psu.edu

We look forward to hearing from you.

—George L. Grice and Daniel H. Mansson

Chapter 1
An Introduction to Public Speaking

 Learning Objectives

After studying this chapter text, you should be able to

1.1 Identify four benefits of studying public speaking.

1.2 Define communication, including its five basic levels.

1.3 Explain the model of communication in terms of the seven elements.

1.4 Use eight critical thinking skills in developing and evaluating speeches.

The word began as the spoken word. Long before anyone devised a way to record messages in writing, people told one another stories and taught one another lessons. Societies flourished and fell; battles were waged and won all on the basis of the spoken word. Ancient storytellers preserved their cultures' traditions and history by translating them orally to eager audiences. Crowds might wander away from unprepared, unskilled speakers, but the most competent, skilled storytellers received widespread attention and praise.

After the development of script and print, people continued to associate marks on the page with the human voice. Even today, linked as we are by Twitter, IMs, and Facebook updates, a speaker standing at the front of a hushed room makes a special claim on our attention and our imagination. As you develop and deliver speeches in class—and in future years as you deliver reports, sell products, present and accept awards, or campaign for candidates—you continue an ancient oral tradition.

Why Study Public Speaking?

1.1 Identify four benefits of studying public speaking.

More than 2,000 years ago, Aristotle argued that studying public speaking is beneficial to people. This claim has been supported in several recent research studies focusing on the benefits and impacts of studying public speaking.[1] These studies indicate that students who study public speaking enjoy academic, personal/social, professional, and public benefits. Our observations and feedback we've received from students and instructors also support the importance of developing and using the skills, principles, and arts that are the subject of this textbook.

Academic Benefits

Studying, practicing, and evaluating public speaking often leads to improved

- Classroom communication skills
- Critical thinking skills
- Group work skills
- Organization skills
- Research skills
- Writing skills

These are also *transferable* skills that can help you throughout your academic studies and in your chosen career.

Personal/Social Benefits

Research suggests that studying public speaking may also lead to personal and social benefits, such as enhanced

- Awareness and appreciation of other cultures
- Relationships with friends, family members, and romantic partners
- Self-awareness
- Self-esteem
- Understanding of social and environmental responsibilities

Mastering public speaking requires practice, but your efforts will reward you with increased knowledge, relational skills, and confidence.

Journal: Personal/Social Benefits

What is one personal or social benefit that you think developing your public speaking skills will help you with? How might it do that?

Professional Benefits

Although several studies suggest that studying public speaking may benefit you academically and personally/socially, even more studies indicate that this course may benefit you professionally, including improved

- Ability to obtain employment
- Career advancement (i.e., upward mobility in your workplace)
- Collaboration skills with coworkers
- Salary negotiation skills

Oral communication plays a critical role in your professional life. This course will instruct you in two of those vital skills: public speaking and listening.

Public Benefits

Finally, public speaking can help you play your role as a member of society. Public speaking is an important part of creating and sustaining a society of informed, active citizens. A democratic society is shaped in part by the public eloquence of its leaders:

- A philanthropist and former talk show host who encourages parents to jump-start a child's imagination through the power of reading.
- A young Pakistani woman and youngest recipient of the Nobel Peace Prize who eloquently advocates access to universal education for girls and women.

But a democratic society is also shaped by the quiet eloquence of everyday citizens:

- The police officer who informs residents of a crime-plagued area how to set up a Neighborhood Watch program.
- The social worker who addresses the city council and secures funding for a safe house for abused and runaway children.

In each of these instances, the speaker used the power of the spoken word to address a need and solicit an appropriate audience response. Active civic participation requires citizens to "speak out" about injustices and inequities. And though we increasingly use social media such as Facebook and Twitter to alert and quickly mobilize groups of people, activism will always involve one or more individuals stirring groups of people through public speech.

While we recognize effective speaking when we meet someone who always says just the right thing or who says things in funny and colorful ways, few of us have been trained to speak well. That's a shame in light of the academic, personal/social, professional, and public benefits public speaking can offer. To appreciate the power of communication, you must understand just what it is. That requires a look at some definitions of communication and at some of its essential components.

Key Points: Benefits of Studying Public Speaking

1. Academic benefits
2. Personal/social benefits
3. Professional benefits
4. Public benefits

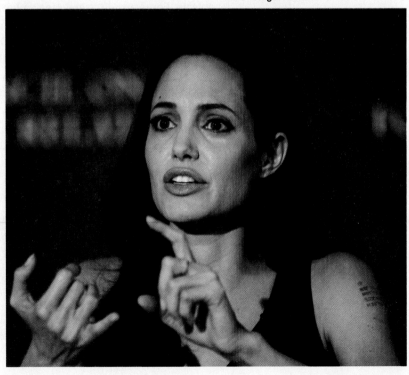

Angelina Jolie, a Special Envoy for the United Nations, uses her access to the media to urge the international community to address global poverty and refugee issues.

Definitions of Communication

1.2   Define communication, including its five basic levels.

The word *communicate* comes from the Latin verb *communicare*, meaning "to share." The concept of sharing is important in understanding communication and is implicit in our definition of the term. Simply stated, when you communicate, you share, or make common, your knowledge and ideas with someone else.

Some scholars view communication primarily as a *process*. For example, Thomas Scheidel provides a process perspective when he defines communication as "the transmission and reception of symbolic cues."[2] Other scholars see communication as an outcome or a *product* and define it simply as "shared meaning." We believe both perspectives are valid: communication is both a *process* and a *product*. **Communication**, then, is *the sharing of meaning by sending and receiving symbolic cues.*

Figure 1.1 represents Charles Ogden and I. A. Richards's triangle of meaning,[3] an illustration of the three elements necessary for communication: interpreter, symbol, and referent.

The word *interpreter* refers to both the sender and the receiver of a message. The **interpreter** is simply the person who is communicating, with words or other symbols.

The second element of this model, the **symbol**, is anything to which people attach or assign a meaning. Symbols can be pictures, drawings, or objects. Even colors can function as symbols; political pundits reduce us to living in blue or red states. Police officers' uniforms and squad cars are symbols of their authority. Facial expressions, posture, and gestures also convey messages of speakers and listeners. The most familiar symbols, however, are words. Many words refer to particular objects, places, and people: *chair*; *Wilmington, North Carolina*; *Long Beach, California*; *Chiwetel Ejiofor*; and *Eudora Welty*, for example. Some words refer to concepts, such as *freedom of expression*, *existentialism*, and *fair play*.

The third and final element of the triangle of meaning is the **referent**, the object or idea for which the symbol stands. Both the sender and the receiver of a message have a referent for the symbols used. This referent depends on each individual's knowledge and experience. People cannot exchange referents in the way they can exchange objects. For example, someone can hand you a paper clip, and that paper clip is the same in your hand as it is in your friend's hand. Your friends, however, cannot transfer their ideas or information to you. All they can do is to code their ideas into symbols and hope that the ideas you decode will be similar to the ones they intended. In short, as senders, we select a symbol based on our referent. That symbol, in turn, triggers the receiver's referent.

communication

The process of sharing meaning by sending and receiving symbolic cues.

interpreter

Any person using symbols to send or receive messages.

symbol

Anything to which people attach meaning.

referent

The object or idea each interpreter attaches to a symbol.

Figure 1.1 The Triangle of Meaning

Countless jokes and situation comedy plots revolve around interpreters who attach different referents to the same symbol. The *New Yorker* cartoon above illustrates one such outcome. However, miscommunication can sometimes be serious and divisive. Consider the experience of Muslim American Zayed M. Yasin, the Harvard student whose graduation speech was one of three the selection committee chose in the spring of 2002. A furor began when the campus newspaper, the *Harvard Crimson*, published the titles of the three student commencement speeches. Yasin's speech, to be delivered less than nine months after September 11, 2001, was titled "Of Faith and Citizenship: My American Jihad." His aim, he said, was to rescue the word *jihad* from extremists who had co-opted it to justify terrorism. He defined the term as a spiritual quest, "the determination to do right and justice even against your personal interests."[4] Among the definitions of the Arabic word are "striving," "effort," and "struggle," but many of those who protested the selection of Yasin's speech equated the term *jihad* with a "holy war." After the protests began on his campus, Yasin met with members of the selection committee, retitled his speech "Of Faith and Citizenship" for the printed program, and delivered the text of the speech without changing a word.[5]

As this example demonstrates, communication is clearest when all its interpreters attach similar referents to the message being communicated. You can, no doubt, think of experiences you have had when people misinterpreted what you said because they attached different referents to your words. The most important thing to remember about the triangle of meaning and the process of communication is this: *Words and other symbols have no inherent meaning. People create meaning; words do not.* A word takes on the meaning that each interpreter attaches to it.

What does the triangle of meaning have to do with public speaking? As you will discover throughout this book, this model applies to public speaking just as it does to all other forms of communication. If speakers and listeners always used specific symbols, interpreted them objectively, and attached similar referents to them, few communication problems would arise from the content of the message. As a result, your work in a public speaking class could be limited to improving your organization and polishing your style of delivery. Yet many of our communication problems can be traced directly to difficulties in the relationships between interpreters, the symbols they use, and the referents behind those symbols.

As a public speaker, you must try to ensure that the message your audience hears matches as closely as possible the message you intended. You do that by paying

Journal: Communication Breakdown

Think of an embarrassing experience that resulted from a breakdown in communication because you and someone else did not share similar referents. What referent(s) caused the confusion? Can you think of another example of miscommunication based on individuals having different referents for the same message?

Table 1.1 Levels of Communication

Communication can occur on five levels. Each level is distinguished by the number of people involved, the formality of the situation, and the opportunities for feedback. Public speaking, the subject of this book, incorporates elements of all these levels. A brief look at each will help you better understand public speaking.

Intrapersonal communication *is cognition or thought, in other words communication with yourself.* Much intrapersonal communication is geared toward a specific, conscious purpose: evaluating how you are doing in a particular situation, solving a problem, relieving stress, or planning for the near or distant future. You use intrapersonal communication when you give yourself a silent pep talk before you speak or, as you walk to the front of the room, you tell yourself to turn to the audience, pause, look at your listeners, and speak clearly.

Interpersonal communication, *sometimes called dyadic communication, occurs when you communicate with one other person.* Face-to-face or phone conversations between friends, colleagues, acquaintances, or strangers are common forms of interpersonal communication. You use interpersonal communication skills when you meet with your instructor to discuss your speech or when you interview an expert to gather information on your topic.

Group communication *generally takes place when three or more people interact and influence one another to pursue a common goal.* The important thing to remember is that the people involved have a sense of group identity. They believe and accept that they belong together for some reason, whether they face a common problem, share similar interests, or simply work in the same division of a company. You may practice your speech in front of friends and then follow that with a group discussion of the strengths and areas for improvement of your speech.

Public communication *occurs when one person speaks face to face with an audience.* Compared with the levels just discussed, public communication is a more one-directional flow of information. Whether the audience is 20 or 20,000, public communication always involves one person communicating to an audience that is physically present. Your public speaking class may be small enough that a question–answer period could follow your speech, or students could participate in a discussion of your topic and delivery.

Mass communication *occurs when a person or group communicates to an audience through some form of print or electronic medium.* This audience may be so large or so diffused that it cannot be gathered in one place; thus, some type of medium—newspaper, magazine, radio, television, or computer, among others— must be placed between the speaker or writer and the intended audience. One important characteristic of mass communication is that audience feedback is delayed. If an article inspires or angers you, you may write a letter to the editor or post a response. You have taken the opportunity to send feedback, but it is delayed. If you have the opportunity to record your practice speeches, you will gain experience with one of the media of mass communication.

particular attention to your content, organization, and delivery, all major subjects of this book. To understand the complexity of public speaking, you need to realize how it relates to other levels of communication. See Table 1.1 for a discussion of these levels.

You will develop public speaking skills more quickly and easily if you understand and use the connections between public communication and the four other levels of communication. You communicate intrapersonally when you brainstorm areas of expertise on which you can speak. You may use interpersonal and group communication to determine topics that interest your classmates. As you research and develop your speech, you will use mass communication to access information published electronically or in print. And as you deliver your public speeches, you will give yourself intrapersonal feedback about the job you are doing and the positive responses we hope you'll be receiving.

Elements of Communication

1.3 **Explain the model of communication in terms of the seven elements.**

Now let's look at the elements of communication to see how they apply, specifically, to the complex activity of public speaking. Remember, the better you understand how communication works in general, the better you will be able to make it work for you in specific speaking situations. Just as important, knowing these elements will let us see where some common communication problems arise.

Today, the most widely accepted model of communication has seven components, as illustrated in Figure 1.2, the communication elements model of public speaking. Although we can identify the individual elements of the communication process, we

Figure 1.2 The Communication Elements Model of Public Speaking

A speaker encodes a message and sends it through a channel to a listener, who decodes it. The listener provides feedback and sends it through a channel to a speaker. This interaction takes place in an environment with varying levels of internal and external noise.

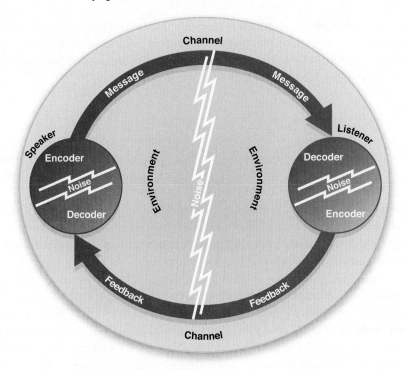

cannot assess them in isolation. Contemporary scholars emphasize the transactional, interactive nature of communication. Each element simultaneously influences, and is influenced by, the others.

Speaker

Human communication starts with a person, the **speaker**. We could also call this person the sender, the source, or the encoder. **Encoding** is the process of putting ideas into symbols. We encode so much and so well that we are aware of the process only when we find ourselves "at a loss for words" while either speaking or writing.

Message

Linked to the speaker is the **message**, the ideas actually communicated. Speech communication scholar Karlyn Kohrs Campbell captures the connection between messages and people when she writes:

> Ideas do not walk by themselves; they must be carried—expressed and voiced—by someone. As a result, we do not encounter ideas neutrally, objectively, or apart from a context; we meet them as someone's ideas.[6]

The ideas of the message originate with the speaker, who determines the form that the message will initially take. However, others who may participate in the communication process further shape that message.

Listener

The message is sent to a **listener**—the decoder or receiver. This person shapes the message by **decoding** it—that is, attaching meanings to the words, gestures, and

speaker
The sender, source, or encoder of the message.

encoding
The process of selecting symbols to carry a message.

message
Ideas communicated verbally and nonverbally.

listener
The receiver or decoder, of the message.

decoding
The process of attaching meanings to symbols received.

voice inflections received. Is every listener's decoded message identical to the one the speaker encoded? Remember our earlier discussion of the triangle of meaning; communication involves more than a single message. The truth is, there are as many messages as there are communicators involved. As long as these messages are similar, communication is usually effective.

Nor does the message stop as it is received. Instead, it is transformed—added to or diminished—as it is joined by other messages that originate with each listener. It is a mistake to assume that a person in the communication process is either a sender or a receiver of messages. We perform both roles simultaneously.

Feedback

The interactions between listeners and senders provide the fourth element in our model of communication—**feedback**. Feedback includes all messages, verbal and nonverbal, sent by listeners to speakers. If you tell a joke, your listeners will tell you through laughter and visual feedback whether they understood the joke and how they evaluated it. If you are paying attention, you will know who liked it, who disliked it, who didn't understand it, and who was offended by it. Note that "if you are paying attention" is the particularly important phrase. In order to be effective, feedback must be received and interpreted correctly.

Because public speaking is an audience-centered activity, you as a speaker must be sensitive to feedback from your audience. Some feedback is deliberate and conscious; some is unintentional and unconscious. But your audience will always provide you with feedback of some kind. If you are paying attention to it, you will know when they appreciate your humor, understand the point you are making, disagree with the position you advocate, or are momentarily confused by something you have said.

Channel

The fifth element of our model is the **channel**, or medium—the way the message is sent. Each speaker sending a message and each listener providing feedback uses a channel. In public speaking, the medium is vibrations in the air between speaker and listener, set in motion by the speaker's voice. Vocal elements such as rate, volume, and pitch also carry part of the message. Visual elements—another channel for the message—include eye contact, facial expression, gestures, movement, and presentational aids. As a public speaker, you must learn to use and control all these channels.

Environment

The sixth element of the communication model is the **environment**. Three factors shape an environment: (1) the occasion during which the communication occurs, (2) the larger social context in which the communication takes place, and (3) the physical setting where the communication occurs. The *occasion* refers to the reasons why people have assembled. Circumstances may be serious or festive, planned or spontaneous. Occasions for communication may be as relaxed and informal as a party with friends, as rule-bound as a college debate, or as formal and traditional as a commencement address.

The larger *social context* involves a variety of people and opinions that can vary by culture and affect the appropriateness of the messages that you communicate. For instance, if the members of your audience are from a collectivist culture (such as Latin America or Asia), they may be persuaded by cooperation more than by competition, which may play better in an individualistic culture such as the United States. However, although cultural tendencies do exist, a speaker would be advised to avoid stereotyping the audience; there will always be individual differences in any collected audience.

The *physical setting* for your classroom speeches is probably apparent to you. You know the size of the room and the number of people in the audience. You know

feedback

Verbal and nonverbal responses between communicators about the clarity or acceptability of messages.

channel

The way a message is sent.

environment

The occasion, social context, and physical setting for communication.

Effective public speakers adapt their speaking styles to the physical settings and the occasions for their speeches.

whether the seating arrangement is fixed or flexible. You know whether the room has a lectern or Internet access. You know, or may soon discover, potential problems with the setting: the table at the front of the room is wobbly, the air seems stuffy about halfway through each class meeting, one of the fluorescent lights flickers. Each of these distracting elements is a form of noise—the final element for which any accurate model of communication must account.

Noise

Noise is anything that distracts from effective communication and some form of noise is always present. Three forms of noise exist, distinguished by their sources. First, much noise is physical—that is, it occurs in the physical communication environment: the sounds of traffic, the loud *whoosh* of an air conditioner or a heater, the voices of people talking and laughing as they pass by a classroom. However, some physical noise may not involve a sound at all. If your classroom is so cold that you shiver or so hot that you fan yourself, then its temperature is a form of noise. If the room's lighting is poor, then that form of noise will certainly affect the communication occurring there. Anything in the immediate environment that interferes with communication is **physical noise**.

A second type of noise is **physiological noise**; a bad cold that affects your hearing and speech, a headache, and an empty growling stomach are examples. Each of these bodily conditions can shift your focus from communicating with others to thinking about how uncomfortable you feel, and creates a form of intrapersonal communication.

The third and final type of noise is **psychological noise**. This term refers to mental rather than bodily distractions. Anxiety, worry, daydreaming, anticipation, and even joy over some recent event can distract you from the message at hand.

Each form of noise—physical, physiological, and psychological—can occur independently or in combination. Some form of noise is always present, so as a speaker you must try to minimize its effects in public communication. For example, by varying your rate, volume, and pitch, or through lively physical delivery, you can combat noise and rivet the audience's attention to your message.

As you can see, public speaking is more complicated than just saying the right words. Communication is dynamic and transactional. Speaker, message, listener, feedback, channel, environment, and noise all interact to influence one another. Unlike that paper clip—the same in every hand that holds it—the message

Journal: Noise

What is one example of noise present around you right now? Is it physical, physiological, or psychological? How could you minimize any effects of this noise that might distract you from your reading?

noise
Anything that distracts from effective communication.

physical noise
Distractions originating in the physical environment.

physiological noise
Distractions originating in the bodies of communicators.

psychological noise
Distractions originating in the thoughts of communicators.

Key Points: Elements of Communication

1. Speaker
2. Message
3. Listener
4. Feedback
5. Channel
6. Environment
7. Noise

that emerges in communication will never be identical to what any one speaker intended.

Part of mastering public speaking begins with basic skills: organizing a presentation with an identifiable introduction, body, and conclusion; providing previews, summaries, and transitions; deciding whether the oral message needs the support of visual aids; and using appropriate grammar, pronunciation, and articulation.[7] However, to design, develop, and deliver a speech that is appropriate to you, your audience, and the communication context requires some higher-order thinking. Public speaking involves choices and, to choose appropriately, you must sharpen your thinking skills.

The Public Speaker as Critical Thinker

1.4   Use eight critical thinking skills in developing and evaluating speeches.

We began this chapter by discussing benefits you gain from studying and practicing public speaking. One of those benefits is that public speaking uses and develops your critical-thinking ability. **Critical thinking** is "reasonable reflective thinking that is focused on deciding what to believe or do."[8] If you have ever questioned the answers you were offered, looked for patterns you thought no one else had noticed, or followed a hunch to solve a problem in your own way, you have already begun to cultivate your critical-thinking ability.[9] You probably also recognize its importance to your personal and professional life. The authors of a national assessment of educational progress underscored the importance of developing critical thinking skills as follows:

> In a world overloaded with information, both a business and a personal advantage will go to those individuals who can sort the wheat from the chaff, the important from the trivial. . . . Quality of life is directly tied to our ability to think clearly amid the noise of modern life, to sift through all that competes for our attention until we find what we value, what will make our lives worth living.[10]

Drawing from the works of Stuart Rankin and Carolyn Hughes, Robert Marzano and his colleagues have identified eight categories of critical thinking skills (see Table 1.2). As a public speaker, you will exercise all of these skills, sometimes in a different order or in combination, as you develop and deliver your speech.

Journal: Critical Thinking

Write down one example of how you have used critical thinking skills in your personal life. Which of the eight categories of critical thinking skills did you employ?

Table 1.2 Eight Categories of Critical Thinking Skills

This Skill . . .	Enables the Public Speaker to . . .
Focusing	Define problems, set goals, and select pieces of information
Information gathering	Formulate questions and collect data
Remembering	Store information in long-term memory and retrieve it
Organizing	Arrange information so that it can be understood and presented more effectively
Analyzing	Clarify existing information by examining parts and relationships
Generating	Use prior knowledge to infer and elaborate new information and ideas
Integrating	Combine, summarize, and restructure information
Evaluating	Establish criteria and assess the quality of ideas

SOURCE: Adapted from Robert J. Marzano, Ronald S. Brandt, Carolyn Sue Hughes, Beau Fly Jones, Barbara Z. Presseisen, Stuart C. Rankin, and Charles Suhor, *Dimensions of Thinking: A Framework for Curriculum and Instruction*, Alexandria, VA: Association for Supervision and Curriculum Development (1988), 66, 70–112. Reprinted by permission. The Association for Supervision and Curriculum Development is a worldwide community of educators advocating sound policies and sharing best practices to achieve the success of each learner. To learn more, visit ASCD at www.ascd.org.

critical thinking

The logical, reflective examination of information and ideas to determine what to believe or do.

To see how one student used these eight critical thinking skills to develop, deliver, and evaluate her speech, read this chapter's "Theory Into Practice" feature.

Theory Into Practice TIP

THINKING ABOUT SPEAKING

Effective public speakers care about their topics and their audiences. As they research, construct, and deliver their speeches, they use the critical thinking skills discussed in this chapter. Consider how one student employed each of these skills in developing her speech.

- **Generating** Wanda's first assignment in her public speaking class was to prepare and deliver a speech about someone she admired. She immediately began generating a list of names: her mother, who held down two jobs to help raise five children; a high school teacher who inspired Wanda to go to college; Coretta Scott King, first lady of the Civil Rights Movement; and Thurgood Marshall, the first African American to serve on the U.S. Supreme Court.

- **Focusing** Wanda recalled how Marshall's commitment to justice for all was one of the reasons she decided to become a prelaw major. So she decided to focus her speech on Marshall.

- **Information gathering and remembering** She devised a research plan and began to gather her supporting materials. Remembering the moving tributes following Marshall's death, Wanda located some of these articles and also found several books about him.

- **Analyzing and focusing** She analyzed her audience, the occasion, and the information she had collected and began to focus her speech further. Wanda decided that a biography of Marshall's life was far too encompassing for a 3- to 5-minute speech. She also chose not to discuss his more controversial decisions on abortion and capital punishment.

- **Organizing, focusing, and integrating** Wanda organized her key ideas and integrated her supporting materials around two central images: closed doors and open doors. First, she would describe some of the doors closed to African Americans during much of Marshall's life: equal education, housing, public transportation, and voting. She would recount that Marshall, the great-grandson of a slave, was denied admission to the University of Maryland Law School. Second, she would tell how Marshall fought to open these doors by expanding access to housing, public transportation, and voting. And she would, of course, note that it was Marshall who successfully argued the case of *Brown v. Board of Education of Topeka* (1954), which declared racial segregation in public schools unconstitutional. She would conclude her story by observing that it was Marshall who litigated the admission of the first African American to graduate from the University of Maryland Law School.

- **Evaluating** Wanda evaluated each of these examples as she prepared her speech to ensure that her ideas were well supported.

- **Remembering** As she constructed her speaking notes, Wanda used only a brief outline to help her remember her ideas.

- **Evaluating** After delivering her speech, she evaluated her speaking strengths and weaknesses to improve her skills for her next speech.

Summary

Why Study Public Speaking?

1.1 Identify four benefits of studying public speaking.

- Public speaking teaches skills that can benefit you academically, personally/socially, professionally, and publicly.

Definitions of Communication

1.2 Define communication, including its five basic levels.

- Communication is the process of sharing meaning by sending and receiving symbolic cues.

- Communication involves individuals (interpreters) attaching referents (meanings) to a variety of symbols (words, gestures, and voice qualities).
- The five levels of communication are intrapersonal, interpersonal, group, public, and mass communication.

Elements of Communication

1.3 **Explain the model of communication in terms of the seven elements.**

- Communication involves seven key elements: speaker, message, listener, feedback, channel, environment, and noise.

The Public Speaker as Critical Thinker

1.4 **Use eight critical thinking skills in developing and evaluating speeches.**

- Developing and delivering a public speech exercises eight critical thinking skills: focusing, information gathering, remembering, organizing, analyzing, generating, integrating, and evaluating.

Chapter 2
The Ethics of Public Speaking

REWRITING THE BOOK
THE LIBRARY OF BIRMINGHAM

 ## Learning Objectives

After studying this chapter, you should be able to

2.1 Define ethics.

2.2 Describe how ethical principles should guide your actions as a speaker and a listener.

2.3 Apply six common ethical speaking guidelines.

2.4 Apply four common ethical listening guidelines.

2.5 Conduct secondary research in accordance with plagiarism and fair use principles.

2.6 Apply the principles of civility to your behavior in the classroom.

Commercial cartographers once produced maps containing small errors, such as non-existent streets or bodies of water with funny, fictitious names. Known as "copyright traps," these errors were used to establish ownership and to serve as grounds for legal action against anyone copying the maps without permission.[1]

Today, musicians, mapmakers, photographers, artists, and software creators are likely to place electronic watermarks or fingerprints in their original works using the techniques of steganography.[2] The ID tag hidden in an MP3 file and the electronic watermark on a DVD have the same purpose: to protect the value of the original works and the reputations of their creators.

As a classroom public speaker, you may create a product that leaves no permanent record, except possibly in the memories of some of your listeners. Nevertheless, the speeches you deliver will have a unique value, reflecting your originality, exercising your critical thinking, and building your credibility.

Ideas cannot be separated from the people who voice them. Everything you do or say affects the credibility your audience assigns you; that credibility in turn affects the believability of your ideas. Your personal credibility is as important as the perceived credibility you have with various audiences. One of your goals as a speaker should be to make choices that develop and maintain that integrity.

Effective and ethical public speakers understand and respect their audiences. They demonstrate this respect by honoring an unwritten contract with their listeners. Terms of this contract require that audience members expect to learn, listen without prejudging you or your ideas, and, ultimately, evaluate your message and give you feedback. As a speaker, you assume responsibility for being well prepared, communicating ideas clearly in order to benefit the audience, and remaining open to feedback that will improve your speaking. In this chapter, we focus on these mutual responsibilities as we examine ethical speaking, ethical listening, and plagiarism.

Definition of Ethics

2.1 Define ethics.

It is virtually impossible to read a newspaper or listen to a newscast today without encountering the topic of ethics. We hear of politicians selling out to special-interest groups, stockbrokers engaging in insider trading, accountants "cooking the books," and contractors taking shortcuts in construction projects. We read stories of people who agonized over the decision to allow—and in some cases help—a terminally ill loved one to die.

When we talk about **ethics**, we refer to the standards we use to determine right from wrong, or good from bad, in thought and behavior. Our sense of ethics guides the choices we make in all aspects of our professional and private lives. You should not be surprised that your academic studies include a discussion of ethics. You are, after all, educating yourself to function in a world where you will make ethical decisions daily. We will now examine why it is important for you to ensure that you communicate ethically.

Principles of Ethics

2.2 Describe how ethical principles should guide your actions as a speaker and a listener.

In discussing communication ethics, Donald Smith notes that communication is an ethically neutral instrument: "Speaking skill per se is neither good nor bad. The skill can be used by good persons or bad persons. It can be put to the service of good

ethics

Standards used to discriminate between right and wrong, good and bad, in thought and action.

© 1992 by P. S. Mueller. Reprinted by permission.

purposes [or] bad purposes. . . ."[3] In this course, you will learn fundamental communication skills that will empower you as both a speaker and a listener. How you exercise these skills will involve ethical choices and responsibilities.

Two principles frame our discussion of ethics.

- First, *all parties in the communication process have ethical responsibilities.* Assume, for example, that a classmate lets you know that he plans to argue in a persuasive speech that "hate speech"—such as protests at military funerals—should be constitutionally protected and is good for the country. Another classmate objects to that position and spreads false claims about what the speaker intends to argue. Students who knew the facts of this case might agree that both students acted unethically, or at least intemperately. As this example demonstrates, all parties involved in communication share ethical obligations.

- Second, *ethical speakers and listeners possess attitudes and standards that pervade their character and guide their actions before, during, and after their speaking and listening.* Ethical speakers and listeners do more than just abstain from unethical behaviors. Ethics is as much a frame of mind as it is a pattern of behavior. Ethics is a working philosophy you apply to your daily life and bring to all speaking situations.

Consider the actions of the speaker in the following incident:

> Lisa presented a persuasive speech on the need for recycling paper, plastic, and aluminum products. To illustrate the many types of recyclables and how overpackaged many grocery products are, she used as an effective visual aid a paper grocery bag filled with empty cans, paper products, and a variety of plastic bottles and containers. After listening to her well-researched, well-delivered speech, with its impassioned final appeal for us to help save the planet by recycling, the class watched in amazement as she put the empty containers back in the bag, walked to the corner of the room, and dropped the bag in the trash can! After a few seconds, someone finally asked, "You mean you're not going to take these home to recycle them?" "Nah," said Lisa. "I'm tired of lugging them around. I've done my job."

Journal: Principles of Ethics

Consider the following scenario. State representative Joan Richards is running for a seat in the state senate. She worked hard as a legislator and was voted the best representative by the Better Government League (BGL). The BGL voted her opponent, incumbent Mike Letner, one of the ten worst senators in the state. Many political analysts think Richards would be the superior senator. Letner has taken a "no new taxes" pledge and has challenged Richards to do the same. Richards personally thinks taxes may have to be raised in order to keep the state solvent. Nevertheless, she knows that unless she promises to oppose any new taxes, she will lose the election. What should Richards do?

EXPLORING ONLINE

Ethical Decision Making

Ethical speakers and listeners should consider the values that shape their decision making. The Markkula Center for Applied Ethics at Santa Clara University is devoted to the study of ethics. Access its site to view articles, case studies, and other resources relating to business, global, government, media, and technology ethics.

You may or may not believe that people have an ethical responsibility to recycle. But regardless of your views on that issue, you likely question the ethics of someone who insists, in effect, "Do as I say, not as I do." Lisa's actions made the entire class question her sincerity. Ethical standards cannot be turned on and off at an individual's convenience.

Ethical Speaking

2.3   Apply six common ethical speaking guidelines.

Maintaining strong ethical attitudes and standards requires sound decision making at every step in the speech-making process. In this section, we present six guidelines to help you with these decisions.

Speak to Benefit Your Listeners

First, *ethical public speakers communicate in order to benefit their listeners as well as themselves.* Speakers and listeners participate in a transactional relationship; both should benefit from their participation. Listeners give speakers their time; in return, speakers should provide information that is interesting or useful.

Informative speakers have an obligation to benefit their audiences. As in the following example, however, students sometimes lose sight of that responsibility.

> Assigned to give an informative speech demonstrating a process or procedure, plant lover Evelyn decided to show how to plant a seed in a pot. Her instructor was worried that this subject was something everyone already knew. Evelyn was, after all, speaking to college students who presumably could read the planting instructions on the back of a seed packet. The instructor did not want to discourage Evelyn but wanted the class to benefit from her speech.
>
> Without saying, "You cannot speak on this topic," the instructor shared her concerns with Evelyn. She found out that Evelyn had several other plant-related topics in mind. Evelyn agreed that a more unusual topic would be more interesting to the class and more challenging for her to deliver. On the day she was assigned to speak, Evelyn presented an interesting speech demonstrating how to propagate tropical plants by "air layering" them. Evelyn got a chance to demonstrate her green thumb, and her classmates learned something most had never heard of before.

You may often speak for personal benefit, and this is not necessarily unethical. You may, for instance, urge a group to support your candidacy or to buy your product. It is appropriate to pursue personal goals but not at the expense of your listeners. As one popular book on business ethics states, "There is no right way to do a wrong thing."[4] Speakers whose objective is to persuade should do so openly and with the goal of benefiting both the audience and themselves. A public speaker may try to inform, convince, persuade, direct, or even anger an audience. Ethical speakers, however, do not deceive their listeners. They are up front about their intentions, and those intentions include benefiting the audience.

Speak Up about Topics You Consider Important

Second, ethical public speakers make careful decisions about whether or not to speak. If an issue is trivial, silence is sometimes the best option. There are times, though, when people have an ethical obligation to convey information or when they feel strongly about an issue or an injustice. *Ethical communicators speak up about topics they consider important.* Our nation's history has been shaped by the voices of Thomas Jefferson, Frederick Douglass, Susan B. Anthony, Martin Luther King, Jr.,

Cesar Chavez, and other advocates. You may never have the sweeping historical impact of these famous speakers, but you do have an opportunity to better the communities of which you are a part. You have a chance to share information your classmates can use to help them get more from their college experience or function better in their careers and personal lives. You can educate others about problems you feel need to be confronted. This class provides a training ground to hone your skills as speaker and listener. Use these skills as you move from involvement in class and campus issues to improvement of your community.

Choose Topics That Promote Positive Ethical Values

All parties in the communication process—speakers and listeners—have ethical responsibilities.

Third, *ethical speakers choose topics that promote positive ethical values.* Unless you are assigned a topic, selecting a topic is one of the first ethical choices you will make. You give your topic credibility simply by selecting it. As an ethical speaker, your choice should reflect what you think is important for your audience.

In the course we teach, many student speeches have expanded our knowledge or moved us to act on significant issues. But consider this list of informative speech topics that some students chose.

> How to get a fake ID
> How to "walk" (avoid paying) a restaurant check
> How students can get a faculty parking permit
> How to get out of a speeding ticket

Even though they were informative rather than persuasive speeches, each of these how-to topics implies that its action is acceptable. We suggest that all these speakers disrespected their listeners, failed to consider the values they were promoting, and presented unethical speeches.

Use Truthful Supporting Material and Valid Reasoning

Fourth, *ethical speakers use truthful supporting materials and valid reasoning.* Listeners have a right to know both the speakers' ideas and the material supporting their claims. Ethical speakers are well informed and should test the truthfulness and validity of their ideas. They should not knowingly use false information or faulty reasoning.

One of our students gave his persuasive speech to urge his classmates to contact their state representatives to vote for a particular education bill. To help his audience with this task, he distributed a list of legislators with their phone numbers and addresses. After the speaker finished his speech, the instructor informed the speaker that the bill he supported had been passed by the legislature and signed by the governor the previous week. The premise that the bill had not yet been passed was false. Not getting caught in a factual or logical error does not free the speaker of the ethical responsibility to present complete, factual information. If you speak on a current topic, use the most recent information you can find and try to be as well informed as possible.

Consider the Consequences of Your Words and Actions

Fifth, *ethical speakers concern themselves with the consequences of their speaking.* Mary Cunningham observed, "Words are sacred things. They are also like hand grenades:

EXPLORING ONLINE

Checking Fairness in News Reporting

Conduct an Internet search for "Media Watchers and Activists" to access this excellent website sponsored by the University of Iowa's Department of Communication Studies. This site posts links to dozens of media watch organizations representing diverse political and journalistic perspectives.

Handled casually, they tend to go off."[5] Ethical speakers respect the power of language and the process of communication.

It is difficult to track, let alone to predict, the impact of any one message. Your audience interprets your statements and may communicate them to others. Individuals may form opinions and behave differently because of what you say or fail to say. Incorrect information and misinterpretations may have unintended and potentially harmful consequences. If you provide an audience with inaccurate information, you may contaminate the quality of their subsequent decisions. If you persuade someone to act in a particular way, you are partly responsible for the impact of the person's new action.

Strive to Improve Your Public Speaking

Finally, *ethical speakers strive to improve their public speaking.* Speakers who use the guidelines we have presented accept their obligation to communicate responsibly. Their ideas have value, are logically supported, and do not deceive their listeners. We would argue, however, that this is not enough.

Ethical speakers are concerned not only with *what* they say but also with *how* they say it. As a result, they work actively to become more effective communicators. This course provides you with an opportunity to begin mastering public speaking. You will learn how to select, support, evaluate, organize, and deliver your ideas. Your professional and public life beyond the classroom will extend your opportunities to speak publicly. Speakers have "the opportunity to learn to speak well, and to be eloquent [advocates of] truth and justice." If they fail to develop these abilities, they have not fulfilled their "ethical obligation in a free society."[6]

> **Key Points**
>
> **Responsibilities of an Ethical Speaker**
>
> 1. Speak to benefit your listeners.
> 2. Speak up about topics you consider important.
> 3. Choose topics that promote positive ethical values.
> 4. Use truthful supporting material and valid reasoning.
> 5. Consider the consequences of your words and actions.
> 6. Strive to improve your public speaking.

Ethical Listening

2.4 Apply four common ethical listening guidelines.

The guidelines for ethical speaking we've just discussed probably make perfect sense to you. If some seem intimidating, if you feel that the future of free expression in a democratic society rests squarely on your shoulders, remember that no individual bears such a responsibility alone. Members of your audience are obligated to adhere to four basic principles, and you share these ethical responsibilities as you listen to others' speeches.

Seek Exposure to Well-Informed Speakers

First, *ethical listeners seek out speakers who expand their knowledge and understanding, introduce them to new ideas, and challenge their beliefs.* These listeners reject the philosophy, "My mind's made up, so don't confuse me with the facts." A controversial speaker visiting your campus can expand your knowledge or intensify your feelings about a subject, whether you agree or disagree with the speaker's viewpoint. Even in situations in which you are a captive audience, such as this class, ethical listening should be the standard.

Avoid Prejudging Speakers or Their Ideas

Second, *ethical listeners listen openly without prejudging speakers or their ideas.* This may be difficult. Listening without bias may require that we temporarily suspend impressions we have formed based on the speaker's past actions. But the rewards of doing so can be great, as in this example:

Linda's first speech in class completely confused her classmates. She seemed nervous and unsure of herself and what she was going to say. The point of her speech eluded everyone. Class discussion after the speech focused primarily on Linda's delivery and some of the distracting mannerisms she exhibited and needed to control. When she went to the front of the room to begin her next speech weeks later, no one was really expecting to be impressed, but they were.

Linda's second speech dealt with the problem of homelessness. Her opening sentence told the class that three years before, she had been living on the street. She had their attention from that point on. In addition to citing recent newspaper and magazine articles, Linda had conducted a great deal of original research. She had interviewed the directors of local shelters and a number of the homeless people who took refuge there, and she quoted these individuals. Her speech was well organized and well delivered. It was both educational and inspiring.

When discussing the speech later, classmates kept referring to her first speech and noting the remarkable improvements Linda had made. One person was blunt, but apparently summed up the feelings of a number of listeners that day: "Linda, I wasn't expecting much from you because your first speech was so unclear to me, but today you had a topic that you obviously care about, and you made us understand and care about it, too. I can't get over the difference between those two speeches!"

When listening to your classmates, assume that you may learn something important from each speaker and therefore listen intently. Information and ideas are best shared in an atmosphere of civility and mutual respect.

Evaluate the Speaker's Logic and Credibility

Listening eagerly and openly does not imply a permanent suspension of judgment. The third standard is that *ethical listeners evaluate the messages presented to them.* A listener who accepts a premise without evaluating its foundation is like someone who buys a used car without looking under the hood. The warning "Let the buyer beware" is good advice not only for consumers of products but also for consumers of messages.

As a listener, you should critically evaluate a speaker's ideas. Is each idea logically constructed? Is each supported with evidence that is relevant, sufficient, and authoritative? In Chapter 9, Learning Objective 9.3, and Chapter 17, Learning Objective 17.2, you will learn specific strategies to help you answer these questions as you evaluate a speaker's evidence and logic.

Beware of the Consequences of Not Listening Carefully

Fourth, *ethical listeners concern themselves with the consequences of their listening.* As the following example illustrates, listeners who assimilate only part of a speaker's message because they fail to listen actively are responsible for the distorted message that results.

Speakers often present views that may be controversial. Whether or not we agree with them, we should withhold judgment until after listening to what they say.

Eduardo, a staff writer for the campus newspaper, mentioned in a speech that the online version of the paper was sponsoring a contest for best research suggestions. The student emailing the HTML page with the most useful research links, as judged by the publication staff, would win first prize: a new BlackBerry. Ted listened to his classmate Eduardo, but the only words that stood out were the name of the paper and the prize. At the next class meeting, Ted told Eduardo, "I called the paper yesterday asking how to get my free BlackBerry and they told me I had to develop a web page and enter some kind of contest." Eduardo replied, "I told you about that contest in my speech. Weren't you listening?"

Key Points

Responsibilities of an Ethical Listener

1. Seek exposure to well-informed speakers.
2. Avoid prejudging speakers or their ideas.
3. Evaluate the logic and credibility of the speaker's ideas.
4. Beware of the consequences of not listening carefully.

Journal: Careful Listening

Write down a personal example of a time when a lack of critical listening caused confusion or negative consequences, either because you did not listen carefully to someone or because someone did not listen carefully to you. Who was ethically responsible for the missed message—the speaker, the listener, or both? Explain.

Ted may have been embarrassed, but he didn't suffer greatly as a result of not listening to Eduardo. In other cases, however, the consequences of not listening are more serious. When you fail to listen to someone's directions and are late for an interview, you miss an employment opportunity. In both of these examples, the listener, not the speaker, bears responsibility for the breakdown in communication.

At other times, listener and speaker may share responsibility for unethical behavior. For example, audience members who become victims of scams because they did not listen critically share responsibility for their victimization with the speaker. Voters who tolerate exaggerated, vague, and inconsistent campaign statements from those who ask to represent them are similarly complicit in ethically lax political campaigns and partially responsible for the results of those campaigns.

In the past, views of communication ethics implied a dotted line across the front of a classroom, with ethics being solely the speaker's responsibility. In contrast, we view ethics as a shared responsibility of the speaker and each listener. An absence of ethical motives among speakers and listeners devalues the currency of communication.

Plagiarism and Copyright Law

2.5   **Conduct secondary research in accordance with plagiarism and fair use principles.**

Not only do ethical speakers carefully craft their own words to express their ideas, but they also care about how they use the words and ideas of others. Thus, two important aspects of ethics are avoiding plagiarism and understanding fair use guidelines. These topics deserve special attention.

Avoiding Plagiarism

The word *plagiarize* comes from a Latin word meaning "to kidnap," so in a sense a plagiarist is a kidnapper of ideas and words. A modern definition of **plagiarism** is "literary—or artistic or musical—theft. It is the false assumption of authorship: the wrongful act of taking the product of another person's mind, and presenting it as one's own."[7]

When you write a paper and submit it to a teacher, you are in effect publishing that work. If, in that paper, you copy something from another source and pass it off as your own work, you are plagiarizing. This act is such a serious offense that in most colleges and universities it is grounds for failing the course or dismissal from the school. Yet recent history has shown us numerous examples of politicians, educators, historians, and other public figures caught plagiarizing materials, either consciously or unconsciously. Plagiarism is an offense serious enough to derail a candidate's campaign for office, to force the resignation of a corporate officer, or to end a student's academic career. Students in a public speaking class should certainly understand what is and what is not plagiarism.

Plagiarism applies to more than simply the copying of another's words. You may also plagiarize another's ideas and organization of material. For example, if you presented a speech organized around the five stages of dying (denial, anger, bargaining, depression, and acceptance) and did not give credit to Elisabeth Kübler-Ross, you would be guilty of plagiarism. On the other hand, if your speech analyzed the political, economic, and social implications of a pending piece of legislation, you would probably not be guilty of plagiarism. Kübler-Ross developed, explained, and published her

plagiarism

The unattributed use of another's ideas, words, or pattern of organization.

framework, or model, in her book *On Death and Dying*, whereas the second example relies on a commonly accepted pattern of analyzing public policy initiatives. The line between legitimate appropriation of material and plagiarism is sometimes unclear. As a speaker, you must always be on guard to credit the source of your ideas and their structure.

Plagiarism can be intentional or unintentional. **Intentional plagiarism** occurs when speakers or writers knowingly present another person's words, ideas, or organization as their own. A related ethical issue is sometimes referred to as *double dipping*, *dual submission*, or *self-plagiarism*. This involves recycling your own work. Revisiting earlier research and extending, elaborating, rethinking, or updating it can be beneficial. But no one hearing you deliver a speech on "major themes in Thomas Pynchon's novel *Gravity's Rainbow*" is going to be tricked. You're recycling work you did for another class, and many schools have written policies prohibiting this practice. Check with your instructor about her or his policy regarding use of previous work or research you plan to use in a speech and for an assignment in another class.

Unintentional plagiarism is "the careless paraphrasing and citing of source material such that improper or misleading credit is given."[8] Intentional plagiarism is considered the more serious offense. Widespread use of the Internet for research may be blurring the distinction between deliberate and accidental plagiarism, however. Web pages are ephemeral; page content and design can change from one day to the next. That quality, together with the ease of browsing numerous sites in a short time, lets readers pick up phrases, ideas, or even organizational patterns almost unconsciously. If a researcher has not printed, bookmarked, or jotted down the URLs for key sites, retracing steps and finding those sites again may be difficult. Unintentional plagiarism may be committed due to ignorance or sloppy research methods, but the effect is still the same: one person is taking credit for the work of another.

To avoid plagiarism, always cite your sources. If you show even a portion of a YouTube video, tell your listeners that you found it on YouTube, the date you first accessed it, and mention the search terms you used to find it. If you want to use video or original writing available on a Facebook page, be sure to cite the source and the date you accessed it. Similarly, for information from an online reference work, newspaper, journal, magazine, or blog, simply cite the source and report when the information was posted or when you accessed it. Carefully citing your sources will help you avoid plagiarizing. Please refer to Chapter 9, Learning Objective 9.4.

Unintentional plagiarism sometimes occurs because of a common misconception that by simply changing a few words of another's writing, you have paraphrased the statement and need not cite it. Michael O'Neill refers to this "hybrid of half textual source, half original writing" as a **paraplage**.[9] Note the differences and similarities in the original and adapted passages of the following statement.

intentional plagiarism
The deliberate, unattributed use of another's ideas, words, or pattern of organization.

unintentional plagiarism
The careless or unconscious unattributed use of another's ideas, words, or pattern of organization.

paraplage
Plagiarism consisting of half original writing and half quotation from an unattributed source.

Statement by Erik Vance

In the mid-1940s, Norman Borlaug started the Green Revolution on a small farm in southern Mexico. His idea was simple. As the human population skyrocketed, he would grow a new kind of wheat with a thicker stem and bigger seed heads, thus increasing its yield and allowing farmers to grow more wheat—and feed more people—per acre.

The results were staggering. Within two decades, Mexico's wheat harvest had swollen six-fold, thanks to crops descended from Borlaug's original modified wheat. Borlaug then turned his talents toward rice in the Philippines, and high-yield crops spread into almost every major food staple. In all, Borlaug's revolution helped feed millions of people in poor and developing countries who would otherwise have starved—an achievement that earned him the 1970 Nobel Peace Prize.[10]

Speaker's Paraplage of Erik Vance

The Green Revolution started back in the 1940s as the human population skyrocketed. Working on a small farm in Mexico, Norman Borlaug developed a strain of wheat with thick stems and bigger seeds. As a result, farmers could increase their yields and feed more people.

Just two decades later, the Mexican wheat harvest had increased to six times what it was previously. Borlaug turned to genetically modifying rice, helping to feed millions of people. For his efforts, Borlaug earned the Nobel Peace Prize in 1970.

Speaker's Appropriate Citation of Erik Vance

As suspicious as some people are of "genetically modified" foods, the first such foods saved millions of lives. Freelance science writer Erik Vance tells the story of Norman Borlaug's experiments in the July/September 2010 issue of *Conservation Magazine*. Borlaug grew a new kind of wheat with thicker stems and bigger seed heads, which was therefore resistant to the effects of wind and water.

Vance calls the results "staggering" and says that "Within two decades, Mexico's wheat harvest had swollen six-fold." After Borlaug turned his attention to rice, he saved millions of people.

Notice that the appropriate citation above tells the listener something about Vance's credentials and explains exactly where his words appeared. With that information, any listener wanting to read the entire article could find it quickly.

The ability to paraphrase effectively tests your critical thinking skills of analyzing, integrating, and generating. To improve your paraphrasing, consider the following guidelines from the Purdue University Online Writing Lab:

1. Reread the original passage until you understand it fully.

2. Set the original aside; write your paraphrase on a notecard or on paper or type it into a computer file.

3. Below your paraphrase, write a few words to remind you later how you might use this material in your speech. Near your paraphrase, write a key word or phrase in all capital letters to indicate its subject.

4. Check your version against the original to make sure that your paraphrase accurately expresses all the essential information in a new form.

5. Use quotation marks to identify any unique terms or phrases you have borrowed exactly from the source.

6. Record the source on your notecard so that you can credit it easily if you incorporate the material in your speech.[11]

We have discussed some of the dangers of hiding the true authorship of words and ideas. There are also at least two benefits of crediting sources. First, speakers who cite their sources increase their credibility, or believability, with the audience. When you quote from a book, an article, or an interview and name the author or speaker of those words, you show the audience that you have researched the topic and that you know what you are talking about. Second, and far more important, acknowledging your sources is the right thing to do. It is honest. Good ideas and memorably worded thoughts are rare enough that the original writer or speaker deserves credit.

Fair Use Guidelines

If the person behind the counter in a copy shop has ever made you feel like a criminal for asking to copy a magazine or journal article—never mind a few pages or photographs from a book—you have experienced one of the quirks of copyright law. The

EXPLORING ONLINE

The Purdue Online Writing Lab

The Purdue Online Writing Lab offers a wealth of information for writers, including information on how to reference materials correctly.

Theory Into Practice TIP

HOW TO AVOID PLAGIARISM

To avoid plagiarizing, let the following five simple rules guide you:

- *Take clear and consistent notes while researching.* As you review your notes, you should be able to discern which words, ideas, examples, and organizational structures belong to which authors.

- *Record complete source citations.* Each sheet of notes, each photocopied article, and each printed page of a document you have accessed should indicate its source(s).

- *Clearly indicate in your speech any words, ideas, examples, or organizational structures that are not your own.* If you cite a source early in your speech and then use another idea from that author later, you must again give that author credit. You do not need to repeat the complete citation, however. Use an abbreviated citation, such as "Vance says that" in our earlier example, if you have provided the full citation earlier in your speech.

- *Use your own words, language style, and thought structure when paraphrasing.* Remember that both content and structure distinguish another person's statements. When paraphrasing what another person has written or said, you should use not just your own words but also your own language style and thought structure. Otherwise, you are "paraplaging."

- *When in doubt, cite the source.* If you are unsure whether you really need to acknowledge a source, it's always wise to err on the side of caution.

copy shop operates to make a profit; you probably don't have any commercial use for the material in mind. As a result, the copy shop employee may direct you to a self-service copy machine, where you assume full responsibility for respecting copyright law.

Copyright law applies to both print and electronic sources, including audio and video works. The "same copyright protections exist ... regardless of whether the work is in a database, on CD-ROM, on a bulletin board, or on the Internet."[12] Section 107 of the Copyright Law of the United States, commonly called the **fair use provision**, says that "the fair use of a copyrighted work ... is not an infringement of copyright."[13]

The law also specifies four factors to consider in determining whether your specific use of copyrighted material is fair. The law is ambiguous and can vary depending on the specific nature of the work you wish to use. We are not lawyers and cannot offer assurances that will apply to every case. However, Georgia Harper, copyright expert and Scholarly Communications Advisor for the University of Texas at Austin Libraries, has translated these four factors into rules of thumb that "describe a 'safe harbor' within the bounds of fair use."[14] If you plan to use any copyrighted material in a speech, ask the following four questions:

- *What is the purpose and character of the use?* If your intended use is personal, educational, or nonprofit, chances are it is fair use. Use of copyrighted material for purposes of research, scholarship, teaching, commentary, and news reporting usually falls under fair use.

- *What is the nature of the work to be used?* Use of published sources that report news and factual information weighs in favor of fair use. Fair use favors published works more than unpublished works, reinforcing the rationale "that authors should be able to decide when to publish their work."[15]

- *How much of the work will you use?* Noncommercial use of a small portion, excerpt, or clip of a copyrighted work likely qualifies as fair use. Commercial uses that exceed strict length limits, however, require permission.

- *What effect would your use have on the market value of the work?* Information from published sources for class speeches and papers are usually considered fair use.

fair use provision

Section 107 of U.S. copyright law allowing limited noncommercial use of copyrighted materials for teaching, criticism, scholarship, research, or commentary.

EXPLORING ONLINE

Fair Use and Copyright

These four websites provide a wealth of information related to copyright, fair use, and public domain.

- The U.S. Copyright Office website describes current copyright law and the fair use provision.
- Georgia Harper's "Copyright Crash Course" discusses clearly and in detail issues for instructors and students to consider, including liability for copyright infringement and applying the "four-factor use test."
- The Purdue University Copyright Office presents a series of charts and checklists to help you "make a good faith determination" that your use of copyrighted material is fair.
- The Stanford Copyright & Fair Use website links you to an entire chapter, with links, on fair use that includes summaries of fair use court cases.

Journal: Practice Paraphrasing

Paraphrase the following sentences from your textbook's discussion of fair use and include a citation: "We reiterate one final point. The fair use provision does *not* give you the right to use another's work without crediting that person, agency, or organization. Unattributed use—even fair use—of someone else's work leaves you open to charges of plagiarism, an issue that seems to grow more important in these days of cut-and-paste Internet research."

civility

Communication behaviors that reflect respect for others and foster harmonious and productive relationships.

Class assignments fall into the category of "one-time use;" speeches are seldom recorded and distributed.[16]

These guidelines seem to suggest that most copyrighted sources for classroom speeches and papers are covered by fair use. However, what if you publish your work beyond the classroom? What if you post your speech on the Internet, and it includes a clip from a popular movie? What if you include images from copyrighted sources on a blog or in an article you submit to a newspaper? What if you conduct a problem-solving workshop for an on-campus or off-campus organization and you draw heavily from suggestions in a copyrighted source? What if you get paid for the workshop? Be careful. You may be leaving that "safe harbor" of fair use.

Answering these questions requires an understanding of copyright law that is beyond the scope of this textbook. Fortunately, there are some excellent websites that offer more information, analysis, and guidelines. We introduce you to four of these sites in the "Exploring Online" feature "Fair Use and Copyright."

We reiterate one final point. The fair use provision does *not* give you the right to use another's work without crediting that person, agency, or organization. Unattributed use—even fair use—of someone else's work leaves you open to charges of plagiarism, an issue that seems to grow more important in these days of cut-and-paste Internet research.

Civility in the Classroom

2.6 Apply the principles of civility to your behavior in the classroom.

As Keith gave his first graded speech in his public speaking class, he thought, "This is going well." Then from the audience came a ringing sound. He stumbled over a few words as he noticed his classmate Eden reaching into her book bag to retrieve her cell phone. When the entire class heard Eden whisper, "I can't talk now. I'm in my speech class. I'll call you when it's over," the instructor asked Keith to stop until he regained the attention of all his listeners.

Sound familiar? We hope not, but we suspect that you and some of your instructors have had similar experiences. Unfortunately, examples of disrespectful and discourteous communication occur not only in classrooms but also in politics, in workplaces, in meetings, on blogs, and on Internet message boards. The Institute for Civility in Government laments "the lack of civility in our society in general and our public discourse in particular."[17] Communication professors Rod Troester and Cathy Sargent Mester define **civility** as a "set of verbal and nonverbal behaviors reflecting fundamental respect for others and generating harmonious and productive relationships."[18] Sometimes equated with courtesy and etiquette, civility is a more complex pattern of behavior that involves attitudes, such as respect, and behaviors, such as providing classmates feedback on their speeches.

We have argued that your public speaking class is a community of learners. You will be a part of that community for the rest of the semester or quarter, and the population will function best if all members exhibit respect and mutual support. The following guidelines, discussed more fully in subsequent chapters, will contribute to your enjoyment and success in this class as both a speaker and a listener.

Speaking with Civility

- *Have good motives.* Select topics that benefit your listeners and the communities to which they belong.
- *Prepare and assess what you will say.* Support your ideas with quality evidence and examples.

- *Respect your listeners.* Appreciate the diversity of your audience and adapt your messages to all your listeners.
- *Speak with conviction.* Believe in your topic and convey that commitment as you speak.
- *Encourage the other side to be heard.* Value public discussion and debate, and answer questions others may have about your topic.
- *Welcome feedback.* Appreciate and act on suggestions and criticisms to improve your speaking competence.

Listening with Civility

- *Give speakers your full attention.* Observe classroom courtesy. Don't text message, check your email, or walk into class when another student is speaking. And, of course, don't sleep or study for another class when your instructor or classmates are speaking.
- *Expect to learn something.* Don't prejudge speakers or their ideas. Value and learn from people's differences, believing with Malcolm Forbes that "education's purpose is to replace an empty mind with an open one."
- *Evaluate the merits of the speaker's ideas and supporting material.* Take responsibility for how you act on the information a speaker has presented.
- *Provide the speaker constructive feedback.* Contribute to the learning of others.

The civil classroom doesn't just happen; civility is a choice. It requires work on the part of the instructor and each student, but the results surely include more effective and enjoyable learning. Some advocates even assert that civility "reduces the literal and figurative costs of stress and leads to greater productivity, better health, and more happiness."[19]

Civility grows from mutual respect; it connects us with others. The attitudes and behaviors you develop and practice in this class can serve you well into the future. Civility is "the glue that holds us together and allows us as citizens of a representative democracy to dialogue with each other."[20]

> **Journal: Civility in the Classroom**
>
> Suppose a speaker in your class says something in a speech that you find offensive. How might you form a civil and constructive comment to give the speaker? What would *not* be a civil, constructive approach?

Summary

Definition of Ethics

2.1 Define ethics.

- *Ethics* refers to fundamental questions of right and wrong in thought and behavior.

Principles of Ethics

2.2 Describe how ethical principles should guide your actions as a speaker and a listener.

- All parties in communication—speakers and listeners—have ethical responsibilities.
- Ethical speakers and listeners possess attitudes and standards that pervade their character and guide their actions before, during, and after their speaking and listening.

Ethical Speaking

2.3 Apply six common ethical speaking guidelines.

- Ethical speakers speak to benefit their listeners, not merely to fulfill their own needs; they choose topics and issues they consider important; they choose topics that promote positive ethical values; and they present audiences with ideas backed by logical reasoning and authentic, up-to-date supporting materials. Ethical speakers care about the consequences their words and actions may have for their listeners, and they seek to improve their public speaking.

Ethical Listening

2.4 Apply four common ethical listening guidelines.

- Ethical listeners welcome challenges to their beliefs, just as they embrace learning; they listen openly, without prejudging the speaker or the speaker's ideas; they evaluate the speaker's ideas before acting on them; and they care about and accept responsibility for the consequences of their listening.

Plagiarism and Copyright Law

2.5 Conduct secondary research in accordance with plagiarism and fair use principles.

- Both speakers and listeners need to be aware of *plagiarism*, the unattributed use of another's ideas, words, or organization. Plagiarism may be either *intentional* or *unintentional*.

- Speakers planning to use copyrighted materials in their speeches need to be aware of the *fair use provision* of copyright law. Factors that determine whether a particular use is fair are the speaker's purpose, the nature of the work used, the proportion of the entire work that a speaker wants to use, and the effect that widespread use such as the speaker intends would have on the market value of the original work.

Civility in the Classroom

2.6 Apply the principles of civility to your behavior in the classroom.

- Civility in the classroom is a two-way street. Speakers should have good motives, prepare and assess what they will say, respect their listeners, speak with conviction, encourage the other side to be heard, and finally, welcome feedback.

- Listeners, on the other hand, should give speakers their full attention, expect to learn something, evaluate the merits of the speaker's ideas and supporting material, and, finally, provide the speaker constructive feedback.

Chapter 3
Speaking with Confidence

 ## Learning Objectives

After studying this chapter, you should be able to

3.1 Explain how speaker apprehension is normal and may even improve your ability to speak well.

3.2 Describe several concrete strategies that can help you manage your nervousness and build confidence.

3.3 Apply seven guidelines to help you develop a successful first speech.

Meryl Streep, one of America's most accomplished actors, said in a 1988 interview: "It's odd. I have this career that spans continents, but . . . I can't get up in front of people and speak. I get really, really nervous."[1] Despite her fear of public speaking, Streep has given dozens of acceptance speeches and has become a spokesperson to protect the environment, promote the creative arts, recognize the contributions of women, and improve the lives of children living in poverty.

Perhaps you experience some nervousness as you think about the speeches you will present in this class. This chapter and this class are designed to build your speaking confidence. First, you will learn what public speaking apprehension is and that it is normal. Most of your classmates are also nervous. Second, you will examine eleven strategies that can help you manage your nervous energy. Finally, you will study seven guidelines for preparing and presenting your first speech.

Recognize That Speaker Nervousness Is Normal

3.1 **Explain how speaker apprehension is normal and may even improve your ability to speak well.**

Communication apprehension is the "fear or anxiety associated with either real or anticipated communication with another person or persons," and one form, public speaking anxiety, is especially widespread.[2] A recent study by Kevin Dwyer and Marlina Davidson, published in 2012, "found that public speaking anxiety was selected by college students more often as a common fear than any other fear, including death." When asked to select their top fear from the common fears list, students chose "death as their top fear most often, followed by public speaking, and then financial problems."[3] So, if you are nervous about public speaking and experience what we sometimes call "platform panic," you are in good company.

As suggested by the above definition of communication apprehension, the origin of nervousness (or apprehension) is purely psychological in that it begins in your brain.[4] This nervousness may lead to a series of negative thoughts affecting your thought process and psychological well-being. In our review of communication apprehension and public speaking anxiety, we found that nervous speakers are often afraid of making mistakes and fearful of negative performance evaluations.[5] Other negative effects of communication apprehension and public speaking anxiety include lower levels of self-esteem,[6] cognitive flexibility,[7] self-perceived communication competence, and willingness to communicate in general.[8]

At this point you may think that taking this course was a terrible mistake. We assure you that it is not a mistake. In fact, it's quite the opposite. Research indicates that audience members want speakers to perform well. Other studies have proven that students' communication apprehension and public speaking anxiety decreases throughout the course. So, by applying the strategies presented in this chapter, you will be able to reduce and manage your nervousness. This also means that your self-esteem, self-perceived communication competence, cognitive flexibility, and other aspects of your psychological well-being are likely to improve throughout this course.

Our experience and research confirm the prevalence of this common fear among college students. When asked to list their communication weaknesses, a clear majority of students rank speaking before a group as their primary fear. James McCroskey has studied the anxieties of public speaking extensively. His Personal Report of Public Speaking Anxiety (PRPSA) assesses the fear college students have about giving public speeches. His data, collected from several thousand students, confirm that public

communication apprehension
The fear or anxiety associated with real or anticipated communication with another person or persons.

speaking generates greater apprehension than other forms of communication and that this fear spans several levels:

High anxiety 40%

Moderately high anxiety 30%

Moderate anxiety 20%

Moderately low anxiety 5%

Low anxiety 5%

Note that nearly three-fourths of college students fall into the moderately high to high anxiety range. This means that the person who always has the quick response, who can make others laugh, and who always looks "together" may be just as worried as you are about giving a speech. McCroskey and coauthor Virginia Richmond conclude, "What this suggests, then, is that it is 'normal' to experience a fairly high degree of anxiety about public speaking. Most people do. If you are highly anxious about public speaking, then you are 'normal.'"[9]

What is this platform panic and how does it affect us? Chemically and physiologically, we all experience stage fright in the same way. Adrenaline is suddenly pumped into the bloodstream. Respiration increases dramatically, and so do heart rate and perspiration. You may have heard stories of a 135-pound person lifting the front of a car to help rescue someone pinned under the car. Such incidents happen because the body is suddenly mobilized to do what must be done.

Yet the body can be similarly mobilized in stressful situations that are not life-threatening. Athletes waiting for the game to begin, actors for the curtain to go up, and speakers for their call to the lectern often feel their bodies marshaling all their resources either to perform to capacity or to get away from the threatening situation. This phenomenon is called, appropriately, the *fight-or-flight syndrome*.

As the time approaches for your first speech, you may experience any of several symptoms to varying degrees. Students tell us that their symptoms include blushing or redness, accelerated heart rate, perspiring, dry mouth, shaking, churning stomach, increased rate of speech, forgetfulness and broken speech, and nervous mannerisms such as playing with jewelry, tapping fingers, and clutching the lectern. Realize that these symptoms are typical of a public speaker. If you experience any of them, you have plenty of company.

Learn How to Manage Speaker Nervousness

3.2   Describe several concrete strategies that can help you manage your nervousness and build confidence.

Before discussing what your goal should be regarding speaker nervousness, it is important to note what it should not be. Do *not* make it your goal to eliminate nervousness. Such a goal is counterproductive for at least two reasons. First, nervousness is natural; attempting to eliminate it is unrealistic. Most experienced, successful public speakers still get nervous before they speak. In addition, focusing on eliminating your nervousness may make you more nervous.

A second reason why you should not try to eliminate nervousness is that some anxiety can actually benefit you as a speaker. Nervousness is energy, and it shows that you care about performing well. Use that nervous energy to enliven your delivery and to give your ideas impact. Instead of nervously tapping your fingers on the lectern, for example, you can gesture. Rather than shifting your body weight from foot to foot, incorporate motivated movement into your speech.

Nervous energy is a sign that you care about your speech performance. Try to channel that energy into gestures and body movement that will enhance your message.

Your goal, then, is to *manage* your nervousness. The coping strategies we suggest below will enable you to control the symptoms of nervousness and to channel that energy into dynamic, effective vocal and physical delivery. (See also Chapter 13, Learning Objective 13.2.)

James Belasco, professor and consultant to major corporations, describes how he uses nervousness as a transforming agent:

Fear is a wonderful stimulant. It quickens the mind, sharpens the senses, and heightens performance. I've learned to focus the stimulant on doing better, rather than worrying about doing worse. When fear runs through my system, I ask myself, "What can I do to remove the potential cause of failure?" "What can I do to ensure success?" I've evolved rituals to answer these questions constructively.[10]

The rituals Belasco then describes are quite practical and make a lot of sense. Get up early, practice saying the first part of each main point in the speech while in the shower, and get to the speech setting early to get the feel of the place.[11] Whether or not you develop your own "readiness rituals," the following eleven suggestions offer a systematic way to become a more confident communicator. If you consider and use these suggestions, you will control your nervousness and channel it into a dynamic and effective speaking style.

Know How You React to Stress

Nervousness affects people differently. Although nervousness is purely psychological, it affects our physical behaviors. Perhaps you feel that your hands or knees shake uncontrollably as you speak in public. The people sitting next to you may not experience those symptoms of nervousness but may have difficulty breathing comfortably and feel that their voices are shaky. Whatever your individual responses to stress are, don't wait until you are delivering a public speech to discover them.

Knowing your reactions to stressful situations helps you in two ways. First, it lets you predict and cope with these physical conditions. Your dry mouth or sweaty palms will not surprise you. Second, because you are anticipating these physical conditions, you will be better at masking them from the audience. How do you do this? Try these techniques.

If you know that your hands shake when you are nervous, don't hold a sheet of paper during the speech; the shaking paper will only amplify the movement of your hands and will telegraph your anxiety to your audience. If your voice is likely to be thin and quivery as you begin speaking, take several deep, slow breaths before you begin talking. If you get tense before speaking, try some muscle relaxation techniques: tense your hands, arms, and shoulders, and then slowly relax them. If you get flustered before speaking, make sure you arrive on time or even a little early—never late. If looking at an audience intimidates you, talk to audience members beforehand, and when you speak, look for friendly faces in the audience.

EXPLORING ONLINE

Relaxation Techniques

Conduct an Internet search for the WebMD Stress Management Center and link to "Ways to Relieve Stress" to learn techniques to relax your mind and body.

Know Your Strengths and Weaknesses

Surgeons spend many hours learning to use the equipment they need to perform operations. Each surgeon knows just what each instrument is capable of doing and strives to use it effectively. As a public speaker, your instruments are your voice, body, mind, and personality. Get to know these instruments, and you can use them effectively to create and communicate messages.

To know yourself, you must honestly assess both your strengths and your weaknesses. Use your strengths to communicate your message with force and impact. If you are a lively and enthusiastic person, channel that energy to reinforce your speech physically and enliven your listeners. If you have a talent for creating memorable phrases, use that creativity to help your listeners attend to and remember your ideas. Just as you can tap your strengths in these ways, you can minimize or avoid your weaknesses if you know them. If you are not effective in delivering humor, don't begin your speech with a joke. To do so would risk failure at this critical point in the speech, and that would make you even more nervous.

The more you understand your strengths and weaknesses, the better you will be able to craft your speech to your abilities. The more confident you are that you can accomplish what you set out to do, the less nervous you will be. One note of caution, however: Don't be too critical of yourself and construct a "safe" speech because you have exaggerated your weaknesses. Instead, expand your abilities by incorporating new strategies into your speech making. Only through thoughtful, measured risk taking will you develop as a public speaker.

Know Speech Principles

If you are confident that you have constructed an effective speech, you will be more confident as you step to the lectern. This textbook and your instructor will assist you in learning speech principles. What are the five functions of an effective speech introduction? How should you construct the body of your speech, and how should you develop each key idea? What strategies help you conclude your speech? How can you use your voice and body to communicate your ideas dynamically? What strategies help you word ideas correctly, clearly, and vividly? We address all these questions, and many others, in this book. As you begin to apply what you learn, you will feel more confident about the content, organization, and delivery of your ideas.

Know That It Always Looks Worse from the Inside

Remember that your audience cannot see your internal state. Because you feel nervous, you focus on your anxiety, exaggerate it, and become more nervous. Many times students have lamented their nervousness after concluding a speech, only to learn that classmates envied them for seeming so calm. In fact, a recent study indicated that the association between speakers' self-reported nervousness and audience members' perceived speaker nervousness is weak.[12] This means that even if you feel very nervous when speaking, the audience members are unlikely to perceive you that way. Even if you feel extremely nervous, your audience probably won't realize it. Knowing this should make you more secure and lessen your anxiety.

One of our students, Susan, wrote the following in her self-evaluation of her first graded classroom speech: "Too fast, too rushed. I forgot half of it. Yuck! Yuck! Yuck!" Yet here are a few of the comments from her classmates:

> "Wow! You seemed really relaxed! Your speech was organized, informative, and interesting."

> "She seemed to know what she was talking about."

> "Definitely the best speech given so far."

Susan obviously experienced her speech in a radically different way than her classmates and instructor. Asked about her listeners' written comments, Susan responded, "Wow! What you said is definitely true. It does look worse from the inside."

If you choose a subject you love, whether it is a favorite hobby, job, class, or poet, you will become deeply involved in developing your speech. This involvement, in turn, may reduce your inhibitions about speaking in public.

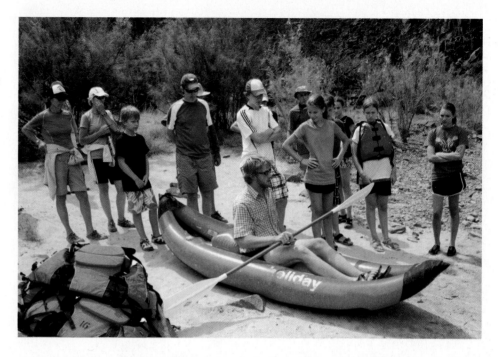

If Susan had not received feedback from her audience, she would probably have retained her high level of public speaking fear, perhaps even avoiding future opportunities to share her ideas with others. By offering honest evaluation, her classmates let Susan see her speech from "the other side," lessened her anxieties, and motivated her to continue improving her public speaking skills.

Know Your Speech

Knowing your strengths and weaknesses, speech principles, and your audience gains you little if you don't know your speech. If you don't know what you want to say, you won't say it. If you think you will forget, you probably will. The more confident you are about your message, the less nervous you will be.

You certainly don't need to memorize the entire speech. Yet to be well prepared, you should know the outline of your major points and the order in which you want to present them. If you forget your notes or drop them and cannot get them back into proper order, you should still be able to deliver your speech. Take a minute to number your notecards, and you have one less worry.

Believe in Your Topic

If you are giving an informative speech, you must believe that what you say will benefit your listeners. If you are giving a persuasive speech, be committed to the belief you are attempting to initiate in your audience. Convincing your audience that they should listen to your speech is easier if you believe that the topic is important. The more you believe in your topic, the more earnestly you will want to inform or convince your listeners. In short, if you doubt the importance of the topic, you will feel and seem tentative.

View Speech Making Positively

More and more we are discovering and investigating the mind's ability to affect behavior. Doctors have learned, for example, that patients' attitudes about their illnesses significantly affect their speeds of recuperation or their chances for recovery. One method for reducing communication anxiety is called **cognitive restructuring**.

This approach recognizes that nervousness is, in part, caused by illogical beliefs. If speakers can restructure their thinking and focus on positive rather than negative self-statements, they reduce their anxiety. Cognitive restructuring involves two steps. First, identify your negative self-statements ("Everyone will laugh at me when I give my speech"). Second, replace the negative thoughts with positive ones ("My classmates understand what it's like to be nervous and will support my speaking efforts").

If you view public speaking as a tedious chore, your audience will sense it from your vocal and physical delivery and perhaps even from your choice of speech topic. On the other hand, if you look at public speaking as an opportunity, your positive attitude will help you manage your nervousness. The following examples illustrate how you can replace negative thoughts with positive ones.

Replace the negative thought . . .	**With a positive thought.**
"My audience will probably be bored with my speech."	"I found the topic of how music affects our moods interesting, and my audience will, too."
"When I get up to speak, my mind will probably go blank, and I'll have nothing to say."	"I've rehearsed my speech, and I have a good set of speaking notes. If I momentarily forget a point, I'll just look at my notecards and then continue."

Thinking positively can help turn anxiety into anticipation. Genuine enthusiasm about the chance to speak in public will guide your choice of topic and will reveal itself to the audience through your lively delivery. Seek out opportunities to test and develop your communication skills. Volunteer for oral reports in classes, speak up at organizational meetings, or offer to introduce a guest speaker at your club's banquets. This positive attitude, coupled with practice and experience, will help make you less apprehensive and more confident.

Visualize Success

If you have ever watched golf on television, you may have seen a player taking a practice swing before a shot and then looking down the fairway or toward the green for several seconds. During that time, the player is visualizing the golf ball flying and landing perfectly as intended by the player. As the player mentally watches the ball end up in the desired place, he or she hears the applause from the audience members in recognition of the perfect shot. This process enhances the player's confidence and likelihood of executing the shot as planned.

Like athletes, public speakers can also use **visualization** to reduce their nervousness and improve their performance. A study of 430 college speech students revealed lowered speech anxiety among those who visualized themselves delivering an effective presentation.[13] Rodney describes how he used positive visualization to build his confidence:

> The week before I gave my speech, I found quiet spots where I could relax. I closed my eyes and visualized myself giving an effective presentation. I saw myself arriving at my classroom on the day I was to speak. Calmly, I would walk to my seat. I'd sit down, check my speaking notes to see that they were in order, and collect my thoughts. When Dr. Conner called my name, I got up from my seat and walked confidently to the front of the room. I put my notes on the lectern, looked at my classmates, and smiled. I paused, took a breath, and then began. I visualized myself being relaxed and delivering my speech as I had planned, with clarity and poise. I felt good talking about a topic that was so important to me. I visualized my classmates smiling at my humor and nodding in agreement as I explained my ideas. I concluded with a dramatic story that

Journal: Turning Negative into Positive

What is one negative thought you have about public speaking? Write it down. Then write a second version, turning the negative into a positive thought.

cognitive restructuring

A strategy for reducing communication anxiety by replacing negative thoughts and statements with positive ones.

visualization

A strategy for reducing communication anxiety by picturing yourself delivering a successful speech.

EXPLORING ONLINE

Reducing Anxiety

Do an Internet search for the article "Overcoming Speaking Anxiety in Meetings and Presentations" by Lenny Laskowski, a Connecticut speech consultant, to learn his ten steps for reducing speech anxiety.

really drove home my point. I paused, then walked to my seat. My classmates applauded, and one of them even whispered to me, "Great speech, Rod!"

Project Confidence

Daryl Bem's theory of self-perception states that if you perceive yourself acting a particular way, you will assume that you feel that way.[14] Thus, if you want to feel confident, act confident. Begin by identifying characteristics of speakers who seem confident; then incorporate those behaviors into your speaking. For example, instead of walking tentatively to the lectern, approach it confidently. Instead of avoiding eye contact with your listeners, look directly at them. Instead of leaning on the lectern or shifting your weight from foot to foot, stand erect and still. Instead of tapping your fingers on the lectern or jingling change in your pocket, use your hands to gesture emphatically. Displaying confident behaviors such as these will make you *appear* and *feel* more confident.

Test Your Message

Confident speakers must believe that their speech content will interest listeners or satisfy an audience need. If your listeners are bored with your topic, you will sense it, and that will make you more nervous. If the audience is interested in the content of your speech, they will be attentive.

As a speaker, you can test your message by practicing your speech in front of friends. Can they restate your main points after listening to you? Do they find your supporting material believable? Does your delivery detract from or reinforce your message? Answers to these questions will guide your subsequent practice sessions. The more confident you are that your message will achieve the desired effect on your audience, the less nervous you will be.

Practice Your Delivery

The previous coping strategies have implied the importance of practice. Practicing your speech is so important that it deserves its own discussion. The late Jack Valenti, former presidential speechwriter, correctly observed, "The most effective antidote to stage fright and other calamities of speech making is total, slavish, and monkish preparation."[15]

Your approach to practice sessions will vary, depending on how your presentation develops. Sometimes you may practice specific sections of your speech that give you difficulty. But you should also practice your speech several times from start to finish without stopping. Too often when students make mistakes while practicing, they stop and

Speaking with Confidence

I love to talk, so I never thought that speaking in front of a crowd, big or small, could place my nerves on a roller coaster. However, I found myself breathing so hard even before I arrived at my public speaking class. It was such a relief to learn that nervousness is quite common and that others are just as nervous as I am. Some methods I use to boost my public speaking confidence are to prepare (practicing in front of a mirror helps me), to take deep breaths before I get up to speak, and, finally, to just do it! When I stood in front of my classmates and began to speak, I scanned the audience and became familiar with some friendly faces, and this put me more at ease. Also, moving my hands for appropriate gestures helped me relax. With practice, you can keep nervousness from having a negative effect on your speech. All of these techniques have helped me build confidence in my public speaking ability.

MARIELY SANCHEZ-MORONTA
Marymount Manhattan College

begin again. This is not a luxury you have when you address an audience. As you rehearse your speech, you should practice recovering from mistakes. Knowing that you can make it through your speech despite blunders should make you more confident.

You should also occasionally practice your speech in an environment laden with distractions. Students who practice only in the silence of an empty classroom may not be prepared for distractions that arise when they actually deliver their speeches—for example, a student coming into the classroom during the speech, a lawn mower passing by the window, or two students talking in the back of the room. These distractions, especially those stemming from rudeness, should not occur; in reality, though, they sometimes do. Practicing with the television on in the background or in your room with noise in the hallway forces you to concentrate on what you are saying, not on what you are hearing. You develop poise as a speaker only through practice.

The eleven coping strategies we've discussed will help you channel your nervous energy into dynamic confident delivery. After each speech, reflect on the experience and gauge your success using the suggestions in this chapter's "Theory Into Practice" feature. In addition, the "Speaking with Confidence" boxes throughout this book reveal how other public speaking students developed their self-assurance using some of

> **Key Points**
> **Guidelines for Building Speaker Confidence**
> 1. Know how you react to stress.
> 2. Know your strengths and weaknesses.
> 3. Know speech principles.
> 4. Know that it always looks worse from the inside.
> 5. Know your speech.
> 6. Believe in your topic.
> 7. View speech making positively.
> 8. Visualize success.
> 9. Project confidence.
> 10. Test your message.
> 11. Practice your delivery.

Theory Into Practice TIP

GAINING PERSPECTIVE

In this chapter, we present eleven strategies for building your speaking confidence. You incorporate these suggestions as you prepare and deliver your speeches. However, what should you do *after* your speech? You've heard the expression, "Experience is the best teacher." Well, there's some truth in that folk wisdom; you can use your public speaking experiences to build your confidence.

After each speech, assess your performance by asking and answering important questions. Your instructor will give you feedback for some of these questions; others you will need to answer for yourself because you alone know the true answers.

- How did you react when you walked to the front of the room, turned, and looked at the audience looking at you?
- Did you remember what you planned to say?
- Did you have trouble finding your place in your notes?
- What techniques did you try in your speech that worked? What didn't work?
- Did you get less or more nervous as the speech progressed?
- How did your audience respond to your speech? What did their nonverbal communication convey as you delivered your speech? What feedback did you receive from your classmates and instructor following the speech?

Remember, don't be too critical as you evaluate your performance. You will do some things well, and this should build your confidence. Focus on other aspects of your speech that you can improve.

Suppose that you encounter a serious problem: You lose your place, your mind goes blank, and you bury your head in your notes and race to the end of your speech. Use this as a learning experience. Ask yourself *why* you forgot: Did you try to memorize your speech instead of speaking from notes? Were your notes disorganized, or did they contain too little or too much information? Did you focus too little on the audience?

Once you face a problem and determine its cause, you will be better able to plan so that it does not occur again. You don't *discover* confidence; you build it. Each public speech provides an opportunity to improve and enhance your confidence for your next speech.

these principles. For now, however, you can begin training those butterflies to fly in formation as you prepare your first speech in this class.

Prepare Your First Speech

3.3   Apply seven guidelines to help you develop a successful first speech.

This class may require you to give your first speech before you have read much of this textbook. What is absolutely necessary to know, then, in order to deliver that first speech successfully? Preparing your first speech will be easier if you keep in mind two principles of public speaking. First, the more effectively you prepare, the better the speech you will deliver and the more confident you will feel. Only then can you recognize what you already do competently and begin to identify skills you want to improve.

The second principle is that every public speech is a blend of *content*, *organization*, and *delivery*. Each of these aspects affects the others. The more you know about these principles, the better your speech will be. The following seven guidelines will help you toward that goal.

Understand the Assignment

An essential requirement for preparing any speech is to know exactly what you are expected to do. The following questions can help you identify your goals for the speech:

- What am I supposed to do in this speech: inform, persuade, or entertain?
- What are my minimum and maximum time limits for the speech?
- Are there are special requirements for the organization of the speech? If so, what are they?
- Are there special requirements for the content of the speech? If so, what are they?
- Are there special requirements for the delivery of the speech? If so, what are they?

Develop Your Speech Content

If your assignment is to introduce yourself, begin by jotting down as many aspects of your life as you can. Audit your history, assess your current circumstances, and project your future goals. Among others, topics that apply to your life and the lives of all your listeners include accomplishments, aspirations, career plans, educational backgrounds, heroes, hobbies, personal values, pet peeves, prized possessions, skills, special interests, and unusual life events. You could decide to limit your speech to one of the preceding areas or to combine several that you think your listeners will find most interesting.

If your first speech topic is not assigned, brainstorm for topics that interest you and those that you think would benefit or interest your audience. Don't settle for the first topic that comes to mind. Consider subjects that you discover as you conduct research. If you generate many possible topics and spend some time reflecting on them, the subject you finally choose will probably be more satisfying for you and more interesting to your listeners.

To ensure you have a clear grasp of your speech topic, answer questions such as these:

- What is my speech topic, and why have I chosen this topic?
- Who are the people in my audience?
- What do I want my listeners to know or remember when I'm finished speaking?

The best way to answer that last question is to ask, "What aspects of my topic interest me and are likely to interest my audience?" Limit the number of main ideas to give you enough time to develop them with adequate supporting material. Once you have done this preliminary work, you are ready to assess your speech content by asking questions such as the following:

- Have I selected a few key points that I can develop in the time allowed?
- Is everything that I say relevant to my topic?
- Do I use a variety of specific supporting materials, such as examples and stories, to develop my key points?
- Will my supporting materials be clear and interesting to my audience?
- Do I acknowledge sources for everything I quote or paraphrase from other speakers or writers?

Organize Your Speech

A coherent speech has three divisions: an introduction, a body, and a conclusion. To determine whether your ideas are clearly organized and easy to follow, you must consider the organization of each of these three parts of your speech.

ORGANIZE YOUR SPEECH INTRODUCTION.   Though usually brief, your speech introduction serves five vital functions. First, it focuses the audience's attention on your message. You want to command their attention with your first words. How can you do this? Question your audience, arouse their curiosity about your subject, or stimulate their imaginations. (See also Chapter 10, Learning Objective 10.1)

Second, your introduction should clarify your topic or your purpose in speaking. State your purpose clearly in a well-worded sentence. A third function is to establish the importance of your topic or to explain your interest in it. Fourth, use your introduction to establish your credibility on that topic. Reveal any special qualifications you have for speaking on the topic, and use your words, voice, and body to instill confidence in your listeners that you have prepared thoroughly. Finally, your introduction should highlight or preview the aspects of your subject that you will discuss in the body.

Well-planned and well-delivered opening remarks will make the audience want to listen and will prepare them for what comes next. To check the integrity of your speech introduction, answer the following questions:

What are the parts of my introduction?
- What is my attention getter?
- What is my statement of purpose?
- What rationale do I provide for speaking about this topic?
- How do I establish my credibility to speak on this topic?
- What are the main points I will cover in my speech?

ORGANIZE THE BODY OF YOUR SPEECH.   The body of your speech is its longest, most substantial section. Though it follows your introduction, you should prepare the body of your speech first. Your organizational goal in the body is to structure your main points so clearly that they are both distinct and unmistakable to your listeners.

We recommend a four-step sequence—the 4 S's—for organizing each of your main ideas. First, *signpost* each main idea. Typical signposts are numbers ("first" or "one") and words such as *initially* and *finally*. Second, *state* the idea clearly. Third, *support*, or explain, the idea; this step will take you the most time. Finally, *summarize* the idea before moving to your next one. These four steps will help you highlight and develop each of your main ideas in a logical, orderly way. The following questions should help you determine whether the body of your speech is well organized. (See also Chapter 8, Learning Objective 8.3.)

Have I organized the body of my speech clearly?

- What are my main ideas?
- What will I say about each main idea?
- How will I summarize each main idea?

ORGANIZE YOUR SPEECH CONCLUSION.   Your speech conclusion is a brief final step with three main functions. The first is to restate your key ideas, a final review of the main points you have covered. Restating may be as simple as listing the key ideas you discussed in the body of the speech. You should not introduce and develop any new ideas in the conclusion. When you summarize, you bring your speech to a logical close.

The conclusion's second function is to activate an audience response by letting your listeners know whether you want them to accept, use, believe, or act on the content of your speech. Whether your speech is informative or persuasive, you want the audience to have been involved with your information and ideas. This is your last opportunity to highlight what you want your listeners to take away from your speech.

Finally, your conclusion should provide your speech with a strong sense of closure. To do this, end on a positive, forceful note. You can use many of the same techniques here that you used to get the audience's attention at the speech's beginning: question the audience, amuse them, stimulate their imaginations, and so forth. Your final remarks should be carefully thought out and extremely well worded. Ask and answer these questions to test your speech conclusion:

What are the parts of my conclusion?

- How do I restate the key ideas?
- What am I asking my audience to remember or do?
- What is my closing statement?

If you answer each of the questions we've posed so far, you should have an interesting, well-developed speech that is easy to follow. Both your content and your organization are in good shape.

So far, you have spent most of your time thinking about the speech and jotting down ideas. Now you have to word those ideas and practice getting them across to your audience through your vocal and physical delivery. (See also Chapter 10, Learning Objective 10.1.)

Word Your Speech

Unless your instructor requests that you do so, avoid writing out your first speech word for word. Even though having the text of your speech in front of you may make you feel more secure, students who deliver speeches from manuscripts often suffer two consequences. The first is that what they say tends to sound like writing rather than speech. (See Chapter 12, Learning Objective 12.6, to learn more about differences between oral and written styles.)

A second problem is a lack of eye contact. Effective speakers make eye contact with their listeners. If you are reading, you can't do this. Therefore, if you have a choice, speak from just a few notes rather than from a prepared manuscript.

The language of your speech should be correct, clear, and vivid. To illustrate this, assume that you have been assigned a practice speech of self-introduction early in the course. Assume, too, that you have decided to make your travels one of your main points. "I've traveled to other countries" is a vague, general statement. Without supporting materials, the statement is also superficial. Instead, suppose you said:

> When I was seven, my father worked in the booming oil business, and my family got a chance to live in Venezuela. Instruction in Spanish started in the first grade, and by the time we returned to the States, I was bilingual. I have vivid memories of picking mangoes and papayas off the trees and swimming outdoors on Christmas day.

The second statement is more specific and vivid than the first. The language is personal, conversational, and crisp. The following questions should help you test the language of your speech:

- Does my speech sound conversational?
- Do I use language correctly?
- Will the language of my speech be clear to my listeners?
- Will the language of my speech be vivid for my listeners?

Practice Your Speech

Mental rehearsal is no substitute for oral and physical practice. Merely thinking about what you plan to say will never adequately ready you to deliver a prepared speech. As we said earlier in this chapter, speech making is an active process. You gain a heightened knowledge of what you plan to say and increased confidence in your abilities just by practicing your speech out loud. Before you can do that, however, you must create the notes you will use to practice and deliver the speech.

PREPARE YOUR NOTES. Make certain that your speaking notes are in the form of key words or phrases, rather than complete sentences. Remember, you want your listeners to recall your main ideas, not necessarily your exact wording. You should need only a word or phrase to remind you of the order of your ideas. Make sure that your notes are easy to read. If your speaking notes are on notecards, be certain to number the cards and have them in the correct order before each practice session.

Preparing thoroughly, practicing often, and wanting to communicate with your audience are keys to any successful speech.

PRACTICE PRODUCTIVELY. Most of your practice will probably be done in seclusion. Practice any way that will help you, being sure to stand as you rehearse. Visualize your audience, and gesture to them as you hope to when giving your speech. You may even want to record and listen to your speech or watch it on video if you have access to that equipment. Give yourself the opportunity to stop for intensive practice of rough spots. Just make sure that you also practice the speech from beginning to end without stopping.

As valuable as solitary practice is, you should also try your speech out on at least a few

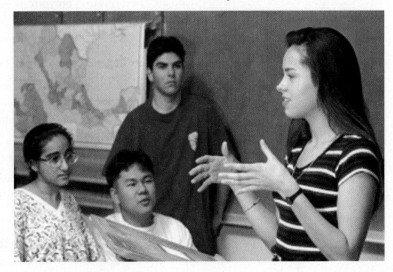

listeners, if possible. Enlist roommates and friends to listen to your speech and help you time it. The presence of listeners should make it easier to practice the way that you approach your speaking position before you speak and the way you leave it after finishing. Your rehearsal audience can tell you if there are parts of your speech that are too complex and difficult to grasp. They may also be able to suggest clearer, more colorful, or more powerful ways of wording certain statements. A practice audience can point out strengths of your delivery and help you eliminate distractions. Most important, serious practice in front of others should focus your attention on the important interaction involved in delivering a speech to an audience. The following questions make up a checklist for your speech practice:

- Have I practiced my speech as I intend to deliver it in class?
- Have I made my speaking notes concise and easy to use and read?
- Have I recorded my speech and made changes after listening to or viewing it?
- How many times have others listened to my speech, and what suggestions have they offered for improving it?
- Have I timed my speech? Is the average time within my overall time limit?
- What adjustments can I make in my speech if it is too long or too short?

Deliver Your Speech

Your speech delivery is made up of your language, your voice, and your body. Speaking in public should feel natural to you and seem natural to your audience. You want to be conversational and to talk *with* your listeners, not *at* them.

Effective vocal delivery is energetic, easily heard, and understandable. Your voice should also show that you are thinking about what you are saying as you deliver your speech. With practice, your voice can communicate humor, seriousness, sarcasm, anger, and a range of other possible emotions. Check your vocal delivery by answering the following questions:

- Do I speak with enough volume to be heard easily?
- Do I change the pitch of my voice enough to create a lively vocal delivery?
- Do I vary my rate of speaking to match my audience's comprehension of what I am saying?

Effective physical delivery is direct and immediate. You demonstrate your involvement in your topic and in the speaking situation by interacting with your audience. If you are concentrating on your message and your audience's nonverbal feedback, your physical delivery will most likely seem natural. To gauge your directness, immediacy, and involvement, answer the following questions about your physical delivery:

- Are my clothing and other elements of my appearance appropriate to my topic, my audience, and the speaking occasion?
- Do I look at members of my audience most of the time I am speaking? Do I look at listeners in all parts of the room?
- Do my gestures add emphasis to appropriate parts of the speech? Do my gestures look and feel natural and spontaneous?
- Do my facial expressions show that I am thinking about what I am saying rather than about how I look or sound?
- If I include place-to-place movement, does it serve a purpose?

Your goal should be delivery that looks and sounds effortless. Yet ironically, that will require significant practice and attention to the vocal and physical elements of your delivery.

Evaluate Your Speech

Don't forget your speech as soon as you deliver your final words and return to your seat. While the experience is fresh in your memory, evaluate your content, your organization, and your delivery. What sorts of feedback did you get from your listeners? To evaluate the kind of speaker you are now and the kind of speaker you can become, answer the following questions:

- What did I do well?

- What areas can I target for improvement in this class?

- What specific efforts do I need to make in order to improve my next speech?

No matter what your level of public speaking experience, you will benefit from recognizing two concerns that you probably share with everyone in class. First, most of your classmates are probably as apprehensive as you are about their first speech. Your nervousness is natural, typical, and healthy. In fact, your anxiety is a sign that you have reasonably high expectations of yourself and that you care about doing well.

Second, you should know that public speaking is a teachable skill, much like math, reading, and writing. So, yes, you can *learn* to speak well. We share responsibility for part of that learning with your instructor. You are also responsible for much of your learning through your own effort and initiative.

We began this chapter by focusing on speaker nervousness, because we know that it is a real worry for most people. We have suggested some techniques to help manage and channel your anxiety into a lively, enthusiastic speech. We have also sketched in broad strokes the process of developing and delivering an effective speech. Your audience is made up of peers. They are pulling for you. Use this friendly atmosphere as a training ground to become a more effective speaker.

Summary

Recognize That Speaker Nervousness Is Normal

3.1 Explain how speaker apprehension is normal and may even improve your ability to speak well.

- Speaker nervousness is natural.

- Your goal should be not to eliminate, but rather to control and channel, your nervousness.

Learn How to Manage Your Nervousness

3.2 Describe several concrete strategies that can help you manage your nervousness and build confidence.

- To manage nervousness: (1) know how you react to stress, (2) know your strengths and weaknesses, (3) know basic speech principles, (4) know that it always looks worse from the inside, (5) know what you plan to say without memorizing your speech,

(6) believe in your topic, (7) have a positive attitude about speech making, (8) visualize yourself speaking successfully, (9) project confidence, (10) test your message prior to delivering it in class, and (11) practice as much as possible in a variety of situations.

Prepare Your First Speech

3.3 Apply seven guidelines to help you develop a successful first speech.

- Prepare thoroughly for your first speech by (1) understanding the speaking assignment, (2) developing adequate content on a narrow topic, (3) organizing the various sections of the speech, (4) wording your ideas effectively, (5) practicing productively, (6) delivering the speech, and (7) evaluating your performance.

Chapter 4
Listening

 Learning Objectives

After studying this chapter, you should be able to

4.1 Explain the importance of listening, using examples.

4.2 Distinguish between listening and hearing.

4.3 Apply the six steps of the listening process.

4.4 Describe five common obstacles to effective listening, using examples.

4.5 Apply eight strategies to improve your ability to listen effectively.

Effective public communication occurs in the charged space between a speaker and an audience, with each party leaning slightly toward the other. Within that space, for the duration of a speech, each speaker and each listener bears ethical responsibilities. Ethical speakers must be well prepared, communicate information and ideas clearly in order to benefit the audience, and remain open to feedback that will improve future speeches. Ethical listeners should listen openly and critically, and provide feedback to assist speakers' thinking on the topic and to help them improve as public speakers. Mutual respect and civility are essential components for a community of learners.

The Importance of Listening

4.1   Explain the importance of listening, using examples.

You probably remember playing the game of telephone when you were a child. Someone whispered a phrase or sentence to another person, who whispered it to the next one, and so on. The last person to receive the message then said it aloud. Usually, the final message bore little resemblance to what the first person whispered, and the group laughed at the outcome.

You can probably think of several examples of problems, or at least embarrassing situations, caused by your own ineffective listening. For example, you asked a question the teacher had just answered. You didn't realize that a complete sentence outline of your informative speech was due a week before you were scheduled to speak. You arrived at a party dressed in jeans, a T-shirt, and flip-flops only to find everyone else dressed formally.

Each day, you send and receive both oral and written messages. Of the four roles you perform—speaker, listener, writer, and reader—you spend the most time as a listener. College students, for example, spend approximately 53 percent of their communication time listening.[1] Yet you probably know less about this activity than about other forms of communication. While you have taken several courses teaching you to read and write, you have probably never taken one in listening. In short, you have received the least training in what you do the most!

It will probably not surprise you, then, to learn that most of us are inefficient listeners. This doesn't surprise listening expert Robert Montgomery, who says:

> Listening is the most neglected and the least understood of the communication arts. It has become the weakest link in today's communications system. Poor listening is a result of bad habits that develop because we haven't been trained to listen.
>
> But there is good news, as Montgomery adds, "Fortunately, it is a skill that can be learned."[2]

In this chapter, we focus on the topic of listening. As we look at the process, problems, and potential of listening, we will provide you with the tools you need to improve your listening skills.

Listening versus Hearing

4.2   Distinguish between listening and hearing.

Does the following situation sound familiar? You're watching *The Daily Show with Jon Stewart*, listening to an iPod®, or doing economics homework when your friend walks by and tells you she will be back to take you to the library. Twenty minutes later, she walks in and finds you still preoccupied with television, music, or homework, and not ready to go. She asks, "Didn't you hear me?" Well, of course you did. You heard her

listening

The intermittent, learned, and active process of giving attention to aural stimuli.

hearing

The continuous, natural, and passive process of receiving aural stimuli.

just as you heard Stewart joking with Samantha Bee, Stevie Ray Vaughan playing a riff, and the air conditioner clicking on in the hall. You *heard* all these things, but you might not have been *listening* to any of them.

What is the difference between **listening** and **hearing**? The two activities differ in at least four important ways.

Listening Is Intermittent

Listening is not a continuous activity but occurs only from time to time when we choose to focus and respond to stimuli around us. Hearing, on the other hand, is a continuous function for a person with normal hearing.

Listening Is a Learned Skill

Hearing means simply receiving an aural stimulus. Unless you have a hearing loss, you don't need training to hear. We hear sounds before we are born, and throughout our lives we hear sounds even as we sleep. Listening, however, must be taught and learned.

Listening Is Active

The act of hearing is passive; it requires no work. Listening, in contrast, is active. It requires you to concentrate, interpret, and respond—in short, to be involved. You can hear the sound of a fire engine as you sit at your desk working on your psychology paper. You listen to the sound of the fire engine if you concentrate on it, identify it as a fire engine rather than an ambulance, wonder if it is coming in your direction, and then turn back to your work as you hear the sound fade away.

Listening Implies Using the Message Received

Audiences assemble for many reasons. We choose to listen to gain new information; to learn new uses for existing information; to discover arguments for beliefs or actions; to laugh and be entertained; to celebrate a person, place, object, or idea; and to be inspired. There are literally thousands of topics you could listen to—for example, regulating the Internet, the history of blue jeans, crimes of ethnic intimidation, preparing lemon-grass chicken, digital photography, and the life of Nelson Mandela. Some of these topics might induce you to listen carefully. Others might not interest you, so you choose not to listen. The perceived usefulness of the topic helps determine how actively you will listen to a speaker. Listening implies a choice; you must choose to participate in the process of listening.

The Process of Listening

4.3 **Apply the six steps of the listening process.**

Any time two people communicate, two messages are involved: the one the sender intends and the one the listener actually receives. These messages will never be identical because people operate from different frames of reference and with different perceptions. To better understand this concept, examine the six steps in the process of listening shown in Figure 4.1.

Receive

The first step in listening is to **receive** sounds, the auditory stimuli. In other words, hearing is the first step toward effective listening. Some people, such as those with a hearing loss, unintentionally filter or leave out part of the stimulus. Whenever we filter, parts of the messages available to us will be lost.

Select

Individuals **select** different stimuli from those competing for their attention, a phenomenon sometimes called *selective perception*. When the police gather reports from various witnesses to a traffic accident, they often find conflicting information. Each bystander's report will be shaped by where the person was standing or sitting, what the person was focusing on at the moment of impact, how the person was feeling, and a host of other factors. Each witness has a selective perception of the event.

In public speaking situations, the audience reacts in a similar way. One person may focus primarily on what speakers are saying, another on their voices or gestures, still another on what they are wearing or even on the distracting hum of the heating system. If you are intrigued by the speaker's accent, you have selected to focus on that element of speech delivery, and you will probably hear a slightly different speech than will the person sitting next to you. You may even be distracted by psychological noise, such as worrying about an upcoming exam or trying to resolve a conflict with your roommate. Our perception of a speech is shaped by what we decide to heed.

Interpret

Individuals not only choose differently among stimuli competing for their attention, they also **interpret** those stimuli differently. Interpreting is the process of decoding the message. When you interpret, you attach meanings to the cluster of verbal and nonverbal symbols the speaker provides—words, tone of voice, and facial expression, for example. The speaker's knowledge and experience must be similar to the listener's if communication is to be clear and effective. (See Figure 1.1 in Chapter 1, Learning Objective 1.2.)

receive
Getting auditory stimuli.

select
Choosing which stimuli to focus on.

interpret
Decoding, or attaching meaning to the stimuli.

Figure 4.1 The Process of Listening

Receive	Select	Interpret	Understand	Evaluate	Resolve
You get the stimuli.	You focus on stimuli.	You attach meanings to stimuli.	You integrate the message into your frame of reference.	You judge the merits of the information.	You decide what to do with the information.

Understand

Once you have decoded, or attached meanings to, a speaker's symbols, you begin fitting the message into your framework of knowledge and beliefs. To **understand** a speaker, you must consider both the content and context of a message. Is the speaker attempting to inform or persuade you? Is the speaker serious or joking? In short, what is the speaker trying to do? As you learn more about speakers, you can understand their messages more accurately.

Evaluate

Before acting on the message you have decoded and understood, you **evaluate** it. Evaluating is the process of judging the speaker's reliability and the quality and consistency of her or his information. Is the speaker making eye contact with you? Does he or she speak fluently, without unnecessary pauses or filler words? Do the speaker's gestures and other body language seem relaxed and spontaneous? In short, does the person seem well prepared, confident, and sincere? If the answer to any of these questions is no, you may wonder whether the speaker has ulterior motives. As you evaluate the speaker's message, you decide whether you believe the data presented and whether you agree or disagree with the position the speaker advocates.

Resolve

The final step in listening, resolving, involves deciding what to do with the information you have received. As listeners, you can **resolve** to accept the information, reject it, take action on it, investigate it further, or just try to remember the information so that you can resolve it later.

Obviously, we do not consciously think about each of these six steps every time we listen to someone. As the significance of the message increases for us, we become more involved in the process of listening—a point every speaker should remember.

Obstacles to Effective Listening

4.4   Describe five common obstacles to effective listening, using examples.

Speakers and audience members should recognize some of the reasons why effective listening is so difficult. Learning to listen better is easier if you know what you're up against. For this reason, you need to identify the major obstacles to effective listening. We list and discuss five of them in this section.

Physical Distractions

Have you ever told someone that he or she was being so loud that you couldn't hear yourself think? If so, you were commenting on one obstacle to effective listening: physical distraction. **Physical distractions** are interferences coming to you through any of your senses, and they may take many forms: glare from a sunny window, chill from an air-conditioner vent, or the smell of formaldehyde in your anatomy and physiology lab. You may have trouble focusing on the message of a speech if you concentrate on the speaker's outlandish clothing, on a vigorous game of touch football outside, or on the overpowering smell of cologne on the person near you.

Journal: Selective Perception

Think of a recent speech or class lecture that you listened to. What are some specific verbal and nonverbal cues of the speaker that still stand out to you now? How have these affected your lasting perception of the speaker and the message?

---

understand

Integrating the stimuli into your frame of reference by considering both the content and context of the stimuli.

evaluate

Judging the merits of the stimuli you received.

resolve

Deciding what to do with the stimuli you received or how to respond.

physical distractions

Listening disturbances that originate in the physical environment and are perceived by the listener's senses.

Physiological Distractions

Physiological distractions have to do with the body. Any illness or unusual physiological condition is a potential distraction to effective listening. A bout of flu, a painful earache, or fatigue after a sleepless night will place limitations on your willingness and ability to listen.

Psychological Distractions

Your attitudes also affect your listening behavior. **Psychological distractions**, such as a negative attitude toward the speaker or the topic, or your reason for attending a speech, can affect how you listen. If you are antagonistic toward the speaker or the point of view he or she is advocating, you may resist or mentally debate the statements you hear. If you are coerced to be in the audience, you may also be more critical and less open-minded about what is being said. In short, if you are concentrating on thoughts unrelated to what the speaker is saying, you will receive less of the intended message.

Factual Distractions

College students are often hampered by **factual distractions**, listening disturbances caused by the flood of facts presented to them in lectures. You may be tempted to treat each fact as a potential test question, but this way of listening can pose problems. For example, have you ever taken copious notes in one of your classes only to realize later that, although you have lots of facts, you missed the key ideas? Students and other victims of factual distractions sometimes listen for details but miss the speaker's overall point.

Semantic Distractions

Semantic distractions are those caused by confusion over the meanings of words. Listeners may be confused by a word that they have never heard before or that is mispronounced. If a student gave a speech about her native country, Eritrea, without showing that word on a visual aid, most listeners would probably begin wondering, "How do I spell that?" "Have I ever seen that word on a map before?" "Is this a new name for an established country?" "Is the speaker pronouncing correctly a word I've always heard mispronounced?" These thoughts divert them from the serious business of listening to a speech filled with new and interesting information.

Promoting Better Listening

4.5 **Apply eight strategies to improve your ability to listen effectively.**

A major theme of this book is that each party in the communication process has a responsibility to promote effective communication. Promoting better listening should be a goal of both the sender and the receiver of the message. How can you encourage better listening?

As a speaker, you can enhance your audience's retention when you select your ideas carefully, organize them clearly, support them convincingly, word them vividly, and deliver them forcefully.

As a listener, you must work hard to understand and remember the speaker's message. The following suggestions will help you become a more effective listener. As you master these suggestions, you will find yourself understanding and remembering more of what you hear.

EXPLORING ONLINE

Listening Habits

Visit the International Listening Association's website. Click on "Resources," then on "Education," and then on "Irritating and Poor Listening Habits." Read and reflect on these habits compiled by four noted listening researchers and scholars.

Key Points

Obstacles to Effective Listening
1. Physical distractions
2. Physiological distractions
3. Psychological distractions
4. Factual distractions
5. Semantic distractions

Journal: Obstacles to Listening

Think of a time you had difficulty listening effectively to a speech, lecture, or message from a friend or relative. What was one of the distractions? Which of the categories of distractions does this fit into? What did you do or could you have done to help overcome the distraction?

physiological distractions
Listening disturbances that originate in a listener's illness, fatigue, or unusual bodily stress.

psychological distractions
Listening disturbances that originate in the listener's attitudes, preoccupations, or worries.

factual distractions
Listening disturbances caused by attempts to recall minute details of what is being communicated.

semantic distractions
Listening disturbances caused by confusion over the meanings of words.

Speaking with Confidence

While preparing my persuasive speech to convince my classmates to use lower viscosity synthetic motor oil, I realized the topic would challenge their listening skills. Although I could do very little to control physical and physiological distractions my audience might experience, I considered ways to address other possible distractions. I tried to overcome psychological distractions by stressing the importance of the topic: they would save money on fuel costs and car repairs. To minimize semantic noise, I defined viscosity as oil thickness and explained how oil flows through motor parts. To reduce factual distractions, I supported my ideas with key facts and expert opinions that I cited in my speech. As I spoke, I could see audience members becoming involved in my topic. I had helped make it easier for them to listen to my speech, and I was rewarded with a stronger feeling of confidence as a speaker with an intrigued—dare I say persuaded—audience.

JODIE MOODY
Radford University

Desire to Listen

Your attitude will determine, in part, your listening effectiveness. Good listeners begin by assuming that each speech might benefit them. You may not find a speech on how financial institutions determine a person's credit rating of great interest right now. The first time you apply for a loan you may be happy that you paid attention.

Good listeners can learn something from any speech, even if it is poorly prepared and awkwardly delivered. For example, you can determine what the speaker could have done to improve the poorly developed speech. Thus, listening to others' speeches enables you to apply speech principles you have learned and improve your own speaking.

You may also have the opportunity to offer helpful suggestions to speakers. Listen carefully so that you can help them improve. If you have a genuine desire to listen to a speaker, you will understand and remember more.

Speakers can promote better listening by demonstrating early in their speeches how the information will benefit their listeners. Let your audience know quickly why it is in their interest to listen carefully to your speech.

Focus on the Message

Your first responsibility as a listener is to pay attention to the speaker's message. Yet a speaker's message competes with other, often quite powerful, stimuli for your attention. Often speakers themselves create distractions. They may play with change or keys in their pockets, dress inappropriately, sway nervously from side to side, use offensive language, or say "um" throughout their speeches. These quirks can be distracting. We have had students, for example, who actually counted the number of "ums" in a speech. After a classmate's speech, they would write in their critiques, "You said 'um' 31 times in your speech." While this may have provided the speaker with some valuable feedback, we suspect these listeners learned little else from the speaker's message. You may not be able to ignore distractions completely as you listen, but you should try to minimize them.

Effective speakers can help listeners focus on the message by eliminating distracting mannerisms and by incorporating nonverbal behaviors that reinforce rather than contradict their ideas. For example, appropriate gestures that describe objects, provide directions, and illustrate dimensions can make a speech easier to remember.

Listen for Main Ideas

You are familiar with the cliché that sometimes you can't see the forest for the trees; well, that saying applies to listening. A person who listens for facts often misses the main point of the message. While it is important to attend to the supporting material of a speech, you should be able to relate it to the major point being developed.

When listening to a speech, pay close attention to the speaker's organization. A speech's structure provides a framework for both speakers and listeners to organize the supporting points and materials. Speakers who clearly enumerate key ideas and repeat them at several points in their speeches give their audience a better opportunity to listen attentively. (We discuss organizational techniques in Chapters 8 and 10.)

Understand the Speaker's Perspective

Each of us has different referents for the words we hear or speak because we have different life experiences that affect how we view our world.

Speaking in favor of agricultural programs that would preserve the family farm, Cathy tried to involve her audience in her speech by tapping their memories. She asked her classmates to think of the houses they grew up in and the memories created there.

> Think of Thanksgiving and family gatherings. Think of slumber parties and birthday celebrations. Of how you changed your room as you moved from child to teenager to young adult. Think of your feelings as you left home to come to college, and of your feelings when you return to those comfortable confines.

After the speech, several students said they were moved by Cathy's eloquence and passion. She had sparked memories that were important to them. Others in the audience, however, said they were unable to relate to the topic in the way Cathy intended. Several had grown up in more than one house. Some were in military families and had moved often. Still others said they had lived in rented townhomes or apartments. And a few commented that their childhood memories were not fond ones. Both speakers and listeners need to remember that different experiences shape and limit our understanding of another's message.

When speakers and listeners come from different cultures, the chances for misunderstanding increase. Differences in language, education, and customs challenge listeners to work especially hard at understanding the speaker's message and intent. These differences are often evident in today's multicultural classroom. Some foreign students, for example, come from educational environments that are more structured and formal than the typical American college classroom. They may interpret a speaker's casual dress and use of humor as an indication that the speaker is not serious about the speech. On the other hand, some American students may perceive the more formal presentations of some of their foreign classmates as stiff and indicating a lack of interest in the topic. Understanding one another's frame of reference minimizes this distortion.

Speakers should do two things to clarify their points of view. First, explain early in the speech if you have some particular reason for selecting your topic or some special qualifications to speak on it. If you choose to speak on radio formats because you work at your campus radio station or because you are a media studies major, tell the audience a little about your background. Second, try to relate your subject to your listeners' frames of reference.

What are some of the listening skills these travelers can use to make the communication experience a positive one for both the speaker and audience?

Rather than using technical jargon or complex explanations that may limit the audience's ability to listen effectively, use examples and language your listeners will understand.

Provide Feedback

A listener can enhance the communication process by providing feedback to the speaker. Although there is greater opportunity for *verbal* feedback in interpersonal and group environments, it is nevertheless also possible in public speaking contexts. The effective speaker will especially read the audience's *nonverbal* cues to assist in the speech's presentation. If listeners understand and accept the speaker's point and nod in agreement, the speaker can move to the next idea. If listeners appear perplexed, that signal should prompt the speaker to explain the idea fully before moving to the next point.

Theory Into Practice TIP

REINFORCING THE MESSAGE

Most Americans speak at rates between 125 and 190 words per minute. Yet as listeners, we can process 400 to 500 words per minute.[3] This means that, depending on the situation, we can listen at a rate up to four times faster than a person speaks! As a result, we may get bored and move our attention back and forth between what the speaker is saying and some extraneous message, perhaps a personal problem that concerns us. Sometimes, the unrelated thought takes over and psychological noise, which we discussed earlier, drowns out the speaker's message. To be a better listener, you must make better use of this extra time. You can increase your listening accuracy and retention by mentally repeating, paraphrasing, and summarizing what the speaker is saying.

Repeat the Message

You use repetition when you state exactly what the speaker has said. Consider, for example, a speaker who argues that a tuition increase is necessary to preserve educational excellence at your college or university. The first reason she offers is this: "A tuition increase will enable us to expand our library." If, after the speaker makes this claim, you mentally repeat her argument, you are using repetition to help you remember her message.

Paraphrase the Message

Using paraphrase is a second way to help remember the message. By putting the speaker's ideas into your own words, you become actively involved in message transmission. Suppose the same speaker offers this statement to justify one benefit of a tuition increase:

> A tuition increase would generate funds that could be used to enhance our library facilities and resources. In the chancellor's budget proposal, one-third of the tuition increase would go directly to the library. The chancellor estimates that this would enable us to increase our database subscriptions and electronic resources by 10 percent. Also, projected construction would create at least twelve new study rooms.

Obviously, it would be difficult to restate the speaker's explanation word for word. Yet you could paraphrase and summarize her message this way:

> A tuition hike would increase our library holdings by 10 percent and expand the number of study rooms by twelve.

Summarize the Message

You use summary when you condense what a speaker says. The above paraphrase includes summary, as it leaves out some of the specific information the speaker presented. As a speaker concludes her or his message, you should recollect the key points of the speech. Your summary might be, for example, "A tuition increase will help us expand the library, increase the number of faculty, and renovate some of the older dormitories."

By getting you actively involved in the communication process, repetition, paraphrase, and summary increase your chances of understanding and remembering the message.

Listen with the Body

We listen with more than our ears. In a sense, we listen with our entire bodies. If, as your instructor lectures, you lean back, stretch your legs, cross your arms, and glance at a fellow classmate, you detract from your listening effectiveness. Part of listening is simply being physically ready to listen.

You can ready yourself for listening if you sit erect, lean slightly forward, and place both feet flat on the floor. As you listen, look at the speaker. As important as the message you hear is the message you see. For example, by looking at a person who gestures while giving directions, you are more likely to remember the information. Similarly, focusing on the speaker's facial expressions may provide information about how the speaker really feels. Remember, you want to detect any nonverbal messages that intensify or contradict the speaker's verbal message.

Withhold Judgment

You filter what you hear through your own set of beliefs and values. Many of us have a problem withholding judgment. We hear something and immediately label it as right or wrong, good or bad. The problem is that once we do that, we cease to listen objectively to the rest of the message.

It is difficult to withhold judgment, of course, when you listen to a speech advocating a position you strongly oppose. The following are topics student speakers sometimes discuss: abortion, capital punishment, genetic engineering, gun control, Internet censorship, legalization of drugs, minimum wage laws, racial profiling, standardized tests, and voluntary euthanasia. We suspect you may have some fairly strong opinions on several of these issues. You may even find it difficult to listen to a speech opposing your view without silently debating the speaker. Yet as you mentally challenge these arguments, you miss much of what the speaker is saying. If you can suspend judgment until after speakers have presented and supported their arguments, you will be a better listener.

Listen Critically

Even though listeners should understand a speaker's point of view and withhold judgment, they should nevertheless test the merits of what they hear. If you accept ideas and information without questioning them, you are in part responsible for the consequences. If the speaker advocating a tuition increase quotes from the chancellor's budget proposal before it has even been submitted, you have every right to be skeptical. "Will the final budget actually earmark one-third of the tuition increase for library use? Will the board of regents accept the chancellor's proposal? Or is this all speculation?" Decisions based on incorrect or incomplete data are seldom prudent and are sometimes disastrous.

Critical listeners examine what they hear by asking several questions: Is the speech factually correct? Are sources clearly identified, and are they unbiased and credible? Does the speaker draw logical conclusions from the data presented? Has the speaker overlooked or omitted important information? Speakers help listeners answer those questions by presenting credible information, identifying their sources, and using valid reasoning.

John Marshall, chief justice of the United States from 1801 to 1835, once stated, "To listen well is as powerful a means of communication and influence as to talk well." If you use these eight suggestions, you will become a better listener.

> **Key Points**
> **Guidelines to Promote Better Listening**
> 1. Desire to listen.
> 2. Focus on the message.
> 3. Listen for main ideas.
> 4. Understand the speaker's perspective.
> 5. Provide feedback.
> 6. Listen with the body.
> 7. Withhold judgment.
> 8. Listen critically.

> **Journal: Improving Your Listening Skills**
> List what you perceive to be some of your listening strengths and weaknesses. For each weakness, indicate specific strategies that could minimize this problem.

Summary

The Importance of Listening

4.1 Explain the importance of listening, using examples.

- The personal costs of poor listening include lost opportunities, embarrassment, financial losses, and lost time.

Listening vs. Hearing

4.2 Distinguish between listening and hearing.

- *Listening* differs from *hearing* in four ways: (1) Listening is intermittent, while hearing is continuous; (2) listening is a learned behavior, while hearing is natural for most people; (3) listening is active while hearing is passive; and (4) listening implies doing something with the message received.

The Process of Listening

4.3 Apply the six steps of the listening process.

- Listening involves six steps. The listener *receives* sound stimuli, *selects* particular parts of the total stimulus field for attention, *interprets* or decodes the message, *understands* by matching the speaker's message with the listener's frame of reference, *evaluates* the reliability of the speaker and the speaker's message, and *resolves*, or decides, what to do with the information received.

Obstacles to Effective Listening

4.4 Describe five common obstacles to effective listening, using examples.

- *Physical distractions* are listening obstacles that originate in the physical environment. *Physiological distractions* arise from conditions in the listener's body. *Psychological distractions* include worry, distraction, or preconceived attitudes toward the speaker or the message. *Factual distractions* are caused by our tendency to listen for small supporting details, even when we miss the speaker's main point. *Semantic distractions* are confusion over the meanings of words.

Promoting Better Listening

4.5 Apply eight strategies to improve your ability to listen effectively.

- Both speakers and listeners can contribute to effective listening.

- Listeners should develop a genuine desire to listen; focus on the speaker's message; listen for the speaker's main ideas; understand the speaker's perspective; provide the speaker with feedback; listen with the whole body; withhold judgment about the speaker and the message until after hearing and considering both; and listen critically.

- Listeners can also reinforce a speaker's message by using repetition, paraphrase, and summary.

- Speakers should express a sincere desire to communicate; minimize distracting behaviors and use forceful delivery to underscore their messages; organize their speeches carefully to highlight their key ideas; reveal their credentials and motives for speaking on a particular topic; adapt to feedback from listeners; and present logically supported ideas and cite credible sources.

Chapter 5
Analyzing Your Audience

 ## Learning Objectives

After studying this chapter, you should be able to

5.1 Explain with examples how a diverse audience can enrich the speaking experience for speakers and listeners.

5.2 Apply your analysis of audience demographics, psychographics, needs, and specific situations before your speech.

5.3 Apply your analysis of your audience's attention, understanding, and evaluation of you as you speak.

5.4 Conduct a post-speech analysis.

EXPLORING ONLINE

Speech Texts

To compare the texts of Abraham Lincoln's and Edward Everett's speeches at Gettysburg, do an Internet search for American Rhetoric. This site has thousands of speeches available in print, audio, and occasionally video formats. The list of speakers includes some international figures, as well as Americans from all walks of life.

Today we would call it an urban legend—the tale about Abraham Lincoln and how he wrote the Gettysburg Address. As the story goes, Lincoln was such a great thinker and accomplished speaker that he wrote his now-famous speech on some scraps of paper while on the train to Gettysburg, Pennsylvania.[1] Repeated for many years, the story seemed plausible because the speech is only 272 words long. Today, we have a better picture of how Lincoln composed the Gettysburg Address.

Lincoln had anticipated for some time an occasion for an important speech on the same theme. The words of the speech began to take shape in his mind long before he wrote them on paper. Thomas Scheidel points out that in informal remarks four months before delivering the Gettysburg Address Lincoln had said,

> How long ago is it?—eighty-odd years since, on the Fourth of July for the first time in the history of the world a nation by its representatives, assembled and declared as a self-evident truth, that "all men are created equal." . . . Gentlemen, this is a glorious theme, and the occasion for a speech; but I am not prepared to make one worthy of the occasion.[2]

Lincoln was asked to speak at a ceremony dedicating a memorial cemetery for soldiers who had died in the Civil War battle at Gettysburg. He was not the main speaker on this occasion, however; Edward Everett, the most famous orator of his day, had top billing. Everett spoke for 1 hour and 57 minutes to an audience estimated at between 15,000 and 50,000 people seated and standing outdoors.[3] On November 19, 1863, Lincoln rose and, holding two pieces of paper, spoke ten sentences in less than 3 minutes.[4] He began his speech:

> Four score and seven years ago our fathers brought forth on this continent a new nation, conceived in liberty and dedicated to the proposition that all men are created equal.

In those intervening months Lincoln had done an excellent analysis of his audience and the occasion, polishing his ideas and distilling them to their essence.

Making speeches "worthy of the occasion" requires meticulous audience analysis today, just as it did in Lincoln's time.

Recognize the Value of Audience Diversity

5.1 Explain with examples how a diverse audience can enrich the speaking experience for speakers and listeners.

In interpersonal communication, you adapt your message to one other person. Your task as a public speaker is more challenging, however, for each added person increases the diversity of any audience. Each audience member is unique.

Today's college classroom, like most segments of American life, is increasingly diverse. Your classmates may differ from one another in terms of age, sex, ethnicity, educational background, beliefs, values, attitudes, and numerous other characteristics. Talking about those differences can reveal what you have in common and build your sense of community. Your challenge is to recognize how your listeners differ from one another and to understand, respect, and adapt to this diversity as you develop and deliver your speeches. Evidence shows that it's a challenge worth taking.

Based on his research and his review of other scholars' studies, education professor Jeffrey Milem concludes that students benefit when they interact with peers of different backgrounds. Specifically, these students

- become more engaged in their own learning,
- improve their critical thinking skills,
- enhance their interpersonal and social competence,

- are more satisfied with their college experience,

- are more likely to engage in community service, and

- demonstrate greater acceptance of people from other cultures.

Milem argues that diverse environments provide students "opportunities to develop the skills and competencies they will need to function effectively as citizens of an increasingly diverse democracy."[5]

If you value your listeners and want to communicate successfully, then you must consider their diversity and view public speaking as an audience-centered activity. You can accomplish this in three ways:

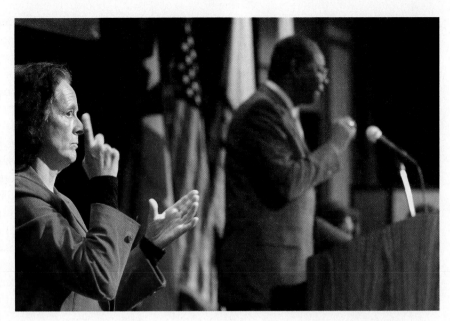

Ethical public speakers consider the diversity of their audiences and use appropriate channels to communicate with as many of them as possible. Here, an interpreter uses American Sign Language to make the speaker's message accessible to members of the deaf community.

1. *Recognize your own place as part of the audience.* You must admit that you are only one part of the total audience, a fact that should make you want to learn as much as possible about the other parts.

2. *Respect your listeners.* Respect and care for the audience means wanting to enhance their knowledge and understanding by providing interesting or useful information. To do this, you must recognize and appreciate their beliefs, values, attitudes, and behaviors.

3. *Recognize and act on audience feedback,* whether it's verbal or nonverbal. Speakers who are attuned to their audience will try to discover and cultivate interests their listeners already have, as well as challenge them with new, useful topics.

To discover who your audience members are and what motivates them, you will exercise at least five critical thinking skills. You will engage in information gathering as you collect data to develop an increasingly clearer picture of who your listeners are. As you exercise the skill of remembering, you'll tap your memories of what your listeners have said and done. You will focus on elements of the picture that seem most relevant to topic areas you are considering for your speeches. As you combine, summarize, and restructure pieces of information about your listeners, you will exercise the critical thinking skill of integrating. Finally, you will analyze the information you have collected by examining individual characteristics of your listeners and the relationships among those characteristics.

Audience analysis is a process that shapes and molds the preparation, delivery, and evaluation of any well-planned public speech. In other words, audience analysis occurs *before*, *during*, and *after* the act of speaking. Let's consider more closely how this process works.

> **Journal: Thinking about Your Audience**
>
> Based on what you have learned in this section, what are a few diverse characteristics of your classroom audience that you anticipate will affect how you develop a speech for them?

Analyze Your Audience *before* the Speech

5.2 **Apply your analysis of audience demographics, psychographics, needs, and specific situations before your speech.**

You will spend more time analyzing your audience before you speak than during or after. Your speech may last less than 10 minutes, for example. Yet, if you care about doing well, your audience analysis before the speech will take considerably more time.

Audience analysis in an online public speaking class poses special challenges. You may or may not have a chance to meet some classmates at a face-to-face orientation session or at other scheduled meetings. Your instructor may invite you to post a message introducing yourself to the class listserv or bulletin board as the class begins. You may be able to administer a questionnaire online to collect student input on a topic area you are considering. Aside from those opportunities, you will have to analyze your classmates based on the messages you read or hear from them.

A traditional face-to-face class provides you the rare opportunity to "live" with your audience for the duration of the course. From the comments they make in and outside class, from the questions they ask other student speakers or your instructor, and from their nonverbal feedback while listening to classroom speeches, you will gradually assemble an increasingly accurate portrait of these people. They will disclose, or you will deduce, information about their beliefs, values, interests, likes, and dislikes. Your audience analysis will be a semester- or quarter-long process, and by the time you deliver your final speech in the class, your audience analysis should be both easier and more accurate than it was at the term's beginning.

Analyze Audience Demographics

Your first step as a speaker is to discover and evaluate audience demographics. **Demographics** are characteristics of the audience, such as age, sex, ethnicity, education, religion, economic status, and group membership. Demographic analysis helps you tailor a message to a specific audience by helping you answer the question, "Who is my target audience?"

Part of your audience analysis will involve discovering what you can about the various divisions or subgroups that constitute your listeners. Advertisers and public relations people call this process **audience segmentation**. You might then choose a topic that you believe can relate to all segments of your audience. However, sometimes speakers choose to address only one or more segments of a larger audience, a strategy called **audience targeting**.

For example, if you know that some of your listeners love to travel but are on tight budgets, you could inform them about the option of becoming airline couriers. An informative speech on the dangers of heatstroke and heat exhaustion might be appropriate for athletes in your audience or for those who work outdoors. Of course, you must be sure that your target audience does exist and that it is sufficient in size to justify giving them your primary focus.

You will never know everything about your listeners and will therefore make generalizations from what you do know. One note of caution, however: be careful not to turn these generalizations into stereotypes. This will undermine your speech-making efforts. However, the more you know, the better prepared you will be to present a successful speech.

AGE. One of the most obvious concerns you have is the age of your listeners. Your public speaking class may include first-year college students, people returning to college to change careers, and others pursuing interests after retirement. People who are 18 to 20 years old today relate to the fall of the Berlin Wall, the Rwanda Genocide, and Nelson Mandela's release from the Victor Verster Prison only as important topics of history. While they may be eager to learn more about those topics, it also means they may not understand most casual references to them. To make sure your speech on any topic is understandable, you must use supporting materials that are familiar to your listeners, and age is one of the most obvious influences on the audience's frame of reference.

SEX. It is obviously easier to determine the sex of your listeners than their age. However, don't fall into the trap of stereotyping based on sex. What seems to be sensitivity

demographics
Characteristics of the audience, such as age, sex, ethnicity, education, religion, economic status, and group membership.

audience segmentation
The strategy of dividing an audience into various subgroups based on their demographic and psychographic profiles.

audience targeting
The strategy of directing a speech primarily toward one or more portions of the entire audience.

to sex may be disguised sexism: "I'm going to inform you girls about the rules of football," or "This recipe is so easy that even you guys should be able to make it." It's important to understand that all men aren't alike and all women aren't alike. Additionally, both men and women can be—and are—assertive, caring, competitive, independent, nurturing, sensitive, and supportive.

Obviously, some speech topics will resonate more with listeners of one sex. An informative speech on the risks of estrogen replacement therapy has more immediate interest for women than men; a speech on prostate cancer, more obvious importance for men than women. But couldn't either of these topics benefit both female and male listeners? You can make virtually every topic relevant to both females and males. Rather than using sex to select or eliminate topics, approach any topic so that everyone can benefit from your speech. For example, a few years ago, a male student asked to give an informative speech about "how to be a perfect gentleman." When his instructor told him that his topic seemed to focus primarily on the male audience members, the student said: "Not really, because by listening to my speech, the female students will know what to look for in a man." When establishing importance of his topic in the introduction, the student specifically noted that both female and male audience members could benefit from his speech.

ETHNICITY.   Ethnicity is the classification of a subgroup of people who have a common cultural heritage with shared customs, characteristics, language, history, and so on. As with sex, avoid ethnic stereotypes. Never assume that because individuals are of the same ethnicity they also share similar experiences and attitudes. Two people of the same ethnicity may have diverse attitudes, interests, and experiences because of differences in their ages, education, income levels, and religion.

EDUCATION.   Your audience's educational level affects what subjects you choose, how you approach them, and the language you use in your speech. Students in your class may have attended private schools, had homeschooling, or earned graduate equivalency degrees after interruptions in their high school educations. Others may have lived and studied overseas. Prepared speakers will find out as much as they can about their listeners' levels and types of education.

Also remember that education can be informal as well as formal. Listeners who have not completed high school or college are not necessarily uneducated. They may have a wealth of "book" knowledge as well as specialized practical knowledge and training. If you can, find out what your audience knows about a potential speech topic and whether they have experience relevant to your topic. Then tailor your speech to build upon the knowledge they already have. When possible, try to avoid jargon and complex language with which your audience members may not be familiar. If you have to use jargon or complex language, make sure you define each term clearly.

RELIGION.   Your audience may include agnostics, atheists, and members of various religious groups. People from other countries may practice religions you do not know about, or they may practice familiar religions in a different way. Religion will be very important to some listeners and relatively unimportant to others. If your audience's religious views are important to a topic you are considering, you need to find out more about their beliefs than the denominational labels they prefer. Religious beliefs are often deeply ingrained in people's lives and if you're not careful,

Effective speakers need to consider the individual life experiences of their audience members to avoid stereotyping and offending some individuals.

you may offend your audience members if you overlook their religious beliefs. For example, it may be offensive to Muslim students if you gave a persuasive speech about why we should eat pork rather than beef or lamb.

ECONOMIC STATUS.   Economic status is another key factor affecting audience attitudes and behaviors. Discovering the range of incomes of your classmates' families may be difficult. Certainly, it would be impolite to ask. However, you can probably locate or construct several general profiles of the typical students at your college. Your school's Office of Institutional Research or Office of Student Life may compile and publish student fact books on their websites.

Overall, be realistic, be fair, and be sensitive when choosing topics dealing with economic issues. We have observed student speakers generate lively audience interest on topics such as summer employment opportunities at national parks and historic sites and how to negotiate the price of a new or used car. Although money may be of greater concern to some people than to others, few people want to spend money needlessly.

GROUP MEMBERSHIP.   We join groups in order to spend time with others who enjoy our hobbies and pastimes, to learn more about subjects that can help us, or to further our educational, political, and social goals. Many of these groups are voluntary, such as clubs, honor societies, political parties, environmental groups, and social fraternities or sororities. We may also be required to belong to professional associations and labor unions in order to get or keep jobs or special licenses.

Knowing your listeners' group membership can be particularly helpful as you prepare persuasive speeches. How you develop your persuasive appeal and select supporting material will reflect assumptions you have made about your audience. If you are speaking to an organization, research the nature of that group as thoroughly as you can.

Analyze Audience Psychographics

Just as you should develop a demographic profile of your audience, you should also generate a psychological profile. **Psychographics** is a term for audience characteristics such as values, beliefs, and attitudes, which often influence our behaviors. These elements help you understand how your listeners think, feel, and behave. Figure 5.1 illustrates how our behavior is typically shaped by our attitudes, which are based on beliefs, which are validated by values. To better understand the interaction among these elements, we will look at each level of the pyramid, beginning with values and moving upward.

psychographics

Characteristics of the audience, such as values, beliefs, and attitudes, which influence behaviors.

value

Judgment of what is right or wrong, desirable or undesirable, usually expressed as words or phrases.

belief

A statement that people accept as true.

VALUES.   A **value** expresses a judgment of what is important and unimportant, desirable and undesirable, right and wrong, or good and evil. Values are usually stated in the form of a word or phrase. For example, most of us probably share the values of equality, freedom, honesty, fairness, justice, good health, and family. These values compose the principles or standards we use to judge and develop our beliefs, attitudes, and behaviors.

If we value honesty, for example, we are probably offended when we learn that a political leader has lied to us. If we value equality and fairness, we will no doubt oppose employment practices that discriminate on the basis of sex, ethnicity, religion, or age. While our actions may not always be consistent with our values, those standards guide what we believe and how we act. When we act contrary to our values, we may experience conflict or even guilt. That perceived inconsistency or dissonance will often motivate us either to change our behavior to match our beliefs and values or to change our beliefs by rationalizing our behavior.

BELIEFS.   A **belief** is something we accept as true, and it can usually be stated as a declarative sentence. We probably do not think about many of our beliefs because

Figure 5.1 Levels of Influence

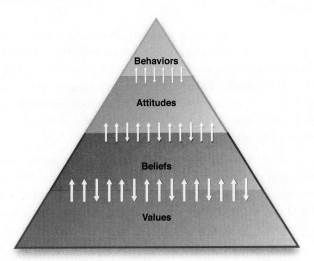

they are seldom challenged: observing speed limits saves lives, sexual abuse is psychologically and physically harmful to children, illiteracy in the United States undermines economic productivity, and so on.

Other beliefs are more controversial, and we often find ourselves defending them. Each of the following statements is debatable:

- Colleges place too much emphasis on athletics
- The benefits of surveillance technology in the workplace outweigh its risks
- Use of the Internet improves the quality of student research

Those statements you accept as true are part of your beliefs

ATTITUDES. An **attitude** is an expression of approval or disapproval, our likes and dislikes. A statement of an attitude makes a judgment about the desirability of an individual, object, idea, or action. Examples include the following: "I support capping enrollment at our college," "I prefer classical music to jazz," "I favor a pass-fail grading system."

Attitudes usually evolve from our values and beliefs. When two values or beliefs collide, the stronger one will generally predominate and determine attitudes. You may value both airline safety and the right to privacy. If a speaker convinces you that a proposed government action will diminish the right to privacy, you may oppose the action. If another speaker demonstrates that the plan is necessary to increase airline passenger safety, you may support the proposal. A single belief in and of itself is not a reliable predictor of a person's attitude.

BEHAVIORS. A **behavior** is an overt action; it is how we act. Unlike values, beliefs, and attitudes, which are all psychological principles, behaviors are observable. You may feel that giving blood is important (attitude) because an adequate blood supply is necessary to save lives (belief) and because you respect human life (value). Your behavior as you participate in a blood drive and donate blood is a logical and observable extension of your outlook. As such, people's attitudes, values, and beliefs are intertwined, which often influence our behaviors. If Adrian likes to jog (an attitude) and she thinks that it's important to remain healthy (a value) and that physical exercise improves her health (a belief), she is very likely to jog (a behavior).

Your knowledge of the foregoing principles will help you analyze your audience and develop its psychological profile. How do you obtain information about your

attitude
A statement expressing an individual's approval or disapproval, like or dislike.

behavior
An individual's observable action.

audience's values, beliefs, attitudes, and behaviors? You have two options, both requiring some work.

- The first option is to use your powers of observation and deduction. You can make educated guesses about people's values, beliefs, and attitudes by observing their behaviors. For example, what do your classmates talk about before and after class? What subjects do they choose for classroom speeches? How do they respond to various speeches they hear? How do they dress? What books do they carry with them to class? The answers to these and many other questions help you infer a psychological profile of your audience.

- The second way is to conduct interviews or administer questionnaires. These may be informal or, if you have the time and resources, formal. You could interview classmates informally during conversation before or after class. Questionnaires administered during class may be as simple as asking for a show of hands to answer a question ("How many of you have broadband Internet access?") or as formal as asking classmates to answer a written questionnaire. Most often you will not have the luxury of using audience interviews and questionnaires for presentations outside the college classroom. Still, if you are addressing a group of strangers, ask your contact person lots of questions about the audience. (See Appendix B.)

Analyze Audience Needs

Once you have considered your audience's demographic and psychographic profiles, you will be in a better position to determine their needs or what motivates them. One particular model, Maslow's hierarchy, will get you thinking about audience needs in an organized way.

MASLOW'S HIERARCHY.   Sociologist and psychologist Abraham Maslow is best remembered for a model of human needs commonly referred to as **Maslow's hierarchy**.[6] A hierarchy is an arrangement of items according to their importance, power, or dominance. Maslow's thesis was that all human needs can be grouped into five categories, based on the order in which they are ordinarily filled.[7] As a public speaker, you should be aware of the needs dominating any particular audience you address. Maslow's categories are as follows:

1. *Physiological, or physical, needs*—basic human requirements for water, food, and sleep. As Maslow and others have observed, hungry people don't play.

2. *Safety needs*—everything that contributes to the "safe, orderly, predictable, lawful, organized world" on which we depend.[8] Having roofs over our heads and reliable transportation are typical safety needs.

3. *Belongingness and love needs*—our relationships with people around us. Giving affection to and receiving affection from other people provides us a sense of community.

4. *Esteem needs*—feelings of individual self-worth and reasonably high self-evaluation that other people confirm and validate as they recognize what we do well. Everyone has certain talents, and we all need a pat on the back from time to time.

5. *Self-actualization needs*—goals we must achieve in order to feel we have reached our potential or fulfilled our destiny. Our cluster of highly individual self-actualization needs can change at different points in our lives.

Note that we all fill our physiological needs in the same way (when it's possible to get those needs met): by taking nutrition and getting rest. The needs at the top of Maslow's model, in contrast, can be both personally distinctive and temporary. The physical needs also are different from the other needs in that the absence of physical

Maslow's hierarchy

A model of five basic human needs—physiological, safety, belongingness, esteem, and self-actualization—in an ordered arrangement.

Theory Into Practice TIP

APPLYING MASLOW'S HIERARCHY OF NEEDS

What does Maslow's hierarchy mean for you in public speaking? Does this model apply to your listeners, and if so, how? We suggest several ways to make the hierarchy work for you.

- *Physiological and safety needs.* The people sitting around you in class probably have most of their physiological and safety needs met. This does not mean that you cannot appeal to them on the levels of physiological or safety needs. If you alert listeners to the harms of aggressive driving, dangerous food additives, or potentially deadly drug interactions, for example, you move them to focus on basic issues of survival.

- *Belongingness and love needs.* If many of your classmates entered college directly from high school, they are probably interested in being well liked and fitting in. In other words, Maslow's third category, belongingness and love needs, is extremely important at this point in their lives. If many or most of the people in your class are in their first year of college, their self-esteem may depend partly on whether they succeed or fail in college, and speeches on scholastic success may easily hold their attention.

- *Self-actualization needs.* Although many college students are unsure of the careers they will undertake after graduation, most people have formed, or are forming, self-actualization needs by the time they are in their teens or twenties. Older students may be reassessing and reformulating their self-actualization needs. Those goals are changeable and will adapt as individuals discover new talents, interests, and abilities. For that reason, a college-age audience is likely to be quite receptive to speeches showing how various pursuits can provide personal rewards or self-fulfillment.

- *The relevance of needs.* It is important to understand that you cannot easily assign all your listeners a specific set of needs. In fact, as Maslow admits, all of us probably have unmet needs at each of the five levels of his hierarchy. We move from one level to another more frequently than we suspect. *Your challenge as a speaker is to identify and emphasize audience needs that are relevant to your topic.*

  For example, if you feel secure in your surroundings, you may take your safety needs for granted. However, if you read in your school newspaper reports of several attacks on campus, your concern for your own and others' safety will increase. If you choose to address this issue in a persuasive speech, you will want to stress this need for safety, bringing it to the front of your listeners' awareness. Once the situation is evident to them, you can point out ways to satisfy that need. You might advocate for better campus lighting, more security patrols, or personal escort services.

Figure 5.2 Maslow's Hierarchy of Needs

From *Motivation and Personality*, 1st ed., by Abraham H. Maslow, © 1954. Electronically reproduced by permission of Pearson Education, Inc., Upper Saddle River, New Jersey.

The VALS™ Survey

Advertisers and other persuaders segment their audiences. The VALS (values and lifestyle) typology, originally developed by the Stanford Research Institute, classifies U.S. consumers according to eight types. Strategic Business Insights offers you the opportunity to discover how you're classified. Conduct an Internet search for the *VALS™ Survey*, take the survey, and get an immediate report of your primary and secondary types. How do you think these categories could help you in analyzing your audience?

needs (e.g., food, water, air) has an immediate negative impact on us. However, if we don't have time to socialize with our friends one week due to our school work, we will not suffer any immediate and serious consequences.

Successful speakers identify the unmet needs of their listeners and respond appropriately in informative and persuasive speeches.

Analyze Specific Speaking Situations

Demographic and psychographic analyses give you an arm's-length view of the people who will make up your audience. But who, specifically, is going to be sitting in the audience you will face? Finding this out requires you to analyze your listeners' dispositions, the size of your audience, the occasion, the physical environment, and the time of day that your speech will occur.

AUDIENCE DISPOSITION. **Audience disposition** describes how listeners are inclined to react to speakers and their ideas. After gathering information regarding audience beliefs and attitudes, you must assess if your listeners are favorable, unfavorable, or neutral toward you and your topic.

The greater your speaker credibility, the more likely your audience is to believe you. Thus, if some of your listeners have a neutral or even unfavorable view of you, you will need to work to enhance your image. (Also, see Chapter 16, Learning Objective 16.5 for a discussion of the importance of speaker credibility, its three components, and strategies to enhance your perceived competence, trustworthiness, and caring.)

A second component of audience disposition is your listeners' attitudes toward your topic. Your audience can be slightly, moderately, or strongly favorable or unfavorable toward your topic, and you should try to determine this level of intensity. A listener who only slightly opposes your position will probably be easier to persuade than one who strongly opposes it.

If you sense that some of your listeners are neutral toward your topic, try to uncover the reasons for their neutrality. Some may be *uninterested,* and you will want to convince these listeners of the topic's importance. Other listeners may be *uninformed,* and your strategy should be to introduce them to the data they need to understand and believe your ideas. Still other listeners may simply be *undecided* about your topic. They may be interested, informed, and aware of the pros and cons of your position. However, they may not have decided which position they support. Your strategy in this instance should be to bolster your arguments and point out weaknesses in the opposition's case.

As you can see, evaluating your audience's disposition is a complex activity. The more you know about your listeners, the easier this process becomes.

audience disposition

Listeners' feelings of like, dislike, or neutrality toward a speaker, the speaker's topic, or the occasion for a speech.

Ethical Decisions

GHOSTING 101

Listening to a speaker, we usually expect to hear the authentic thoughts of that individual. That seems to be a basic principle of the speaker-audience contract. Yet politicians often do not write the speeches they deliver. Instead they rely on speechwriters, sometimes called "ghostwriters." Journalist Ari Posner laments this tradition, observing, "If college or high school students relied on ghosts the way most public figures do, they'd be expelled on charges of plagiarism."[9]

Is it ever ethical for political leaders to deliver speeches they did not write? Why or why not? If so, what principles of audience analysis should guide the use of these speeches?

Frank and Ernest, by Bob Thaves

SIZE OF THE AUDIENCE. When speaking to a small group, a speaker may be frequently interrupted with questions. The situation may be so informal that the speaker sits in a chair or on the edge of a table during the presentation. A speaker in such a situation may use jargon and colloquial language, presentational aids, and a conversational style of delivery.

As the audience grows larger, however, the speaker must make adjustments. The language of the speech may become more formal, especially if the speaker knows that the speech will be published or recorded. As the distance between the speaker and the last row of audience members increases, the speaker's volume must increase, gestures and facial expressions must be exaggerated slightly, and presentational aids must be projected in order to be seen. Unless the audience is encouraged to ask questions after the speech, they will likely remain silent. As you can see, the size of your audience affects both the type of speech you deliver and your manner of presentation.

OCCASION. The occasion—or the reason for the speaking event—is a critical factor in determining what type of audience you will face. You need to ask yourself (and maybe even some members of the group), "Why is this audience gathering? What special circumstances bring them together?" A class, an annual convention, a banquet, a party, a competition, a reunion, and a regular meeting of an organization are all examples of occasions. These can be formal or informal, serious or fun, planned or spontaneous, closed to the public or open to all.

In addition to a simple description of the occasion, speakers may need to know about the history of the occasion or about the recent history of the group they will address. Say, for example, that the officers of an organization have invited you to speak to their entire membership. If there has been recent conflict between the members and the officers, the majority of your audience may look upon you and your speech skeptically. To understand any occasion, you must know both the purpose and the circumstances of the gathering.

PHYSICAL ENVIRONMENT. The physical environment or setting can affect the messages sent by the speaker and received by the audience. For example, the size of the room itself may impede communication. You may be speaking to a large audience through an inadequate or defective public address system. Or, you may compete with a variety of physical noise sources: the sounds of another meeting next door, a room that is too warm, and interruptions from caterers bringing in carts of ice water. Discovering these challenges before you speak will help you prepare your speech and adapt to your audience.

TIME. The time at which you deliver your speech is an important part of analyzing the speaking occasion. An address given at 4:00 p.m. on Friday will almost surely find an audience more fatigued and restless than will one given Tuesday at 9:30 a.m. If you are scheduled to speak first in a class that meets at 8:00 a.m., your audience may be half asleep, so you may need to boost your own energy to enliven them.

audience profile

A descriptive sketch of listeners' characteristics, values, beliefs, attitudes, and/or actions.

The placement of your speech in a program may also affect how your audience receives it. If you follow several other speakers, you may need to work harder at getting and keeping your listeners' attention. In short, if your listeners are not at their best, plan on working extra hard to enliven your delivery.

When you use the techniques discussed in this chapter to analyze your audience's demographics, psychographics, and the specific speaking situation, you will be able to construct an **audience profile**, a sketch of the relevant characteristics of your listeners. Keep in mind that your understanding of the audience will never be complete. You may have to make educated guesses based on incomplete data. Remember, too, that some information you collect may be irrelevant to your speech topic. Finally, bear in mind that your audience is not a uniform mass but a collection of individuals with varying experiences, values, beliefs, attitudes, behaviors, and personalities.

Analyze Your Audience *during* the Speech

5.3 Apply your analysis of your audience's attention, understanding, and evaluation of you as you speak.

Careful audience analysis before your speech will guide your topic selection, how you focus and develop your subject, the language you use, how you plan to deliver your speech, and even your use of humor. However, even the most thorough, conscientious audience analysis will not guarantee a compelling, effectively delivered speech. Speakers do not perform for audiences; they interact with them. The physical presence of listeners transforms and shapes each public speaking experience. To make that vital connection with your listeners, your audience analysis must continue during the delivery of your speech. Communication scholars suggest that, as you speak, you must be aware of three characteristics of your listeners—their attention, understanding, and evaluation.

Audience Attention

First, you must be aware of the audience's *attention* or interest. Do their eye contact, posture, and other body language indicate that they are concentrating on you and your message? Are there physical distractions in the speech setting that are competing with you for the audience's attention? Do you seem to have the audience's attention throughout some parts of the speech, only to lose it during other parts? If you are concentrating on your message and on your listeners rather than on how you sound and look, you will know the answers to these questions.

If you detect a lapse of audience attention during your speech, how can you recapture it? You could address some of your listeners by name or make a connection between your speech and another one that the audience has already heard. You can also recapture your audience's attention with statements such as "The most important point to remember is. . . ." You may also be able simply to change some aspect of your delivery: speaking more loudly or softly, for example, or moving from the lectern for part of the speech so that you are closer to the audience. Any change in your established pattern of delivery will likely rekindle audience attention and interest. In addition, changing your usual style of delivery may be essential to overcome the distractions of a stuffy room, a noisy heater, or the coughs and other audience noise.

Audience Understanding

A second characteristic of your audience that you must try to assess is their *understanding* or comprehension of your message. If you have ever produced a false laugh when you didn't really understand a joke, you know how difficult it is to fake comprehension.

Journal: Body Language

Give two specific examples of body language that may indicate an audience member is listening to your speech with interest. Give two specific examples that could mean an audience member is not paying attention to you.

Speaking with Confidence

Audience analysis is important for all public speakers. The more I learned about my classmates, the easier it was to choose a topic that would affect them, to avoid sensitive issues, and to relate to their life experiences. Although I did most of my analysis before my speech, it didn't stop there. I continued to analyze my audience as I spoke. Reading my listeners' expressions and body language helped me determine how my speech was going. For example, if students at the back of the room were having trouble hearing me, I would speak louder. If someone looked confused, I would give an example to clarify my point. If a couple of audience members seemed bored, I might use some humor or walk slightly toward them. And when my classmates smiled approvingly, I was confident that I was getting through to them. Audience analysis during a speech requires quick thinking, but it shows your listeners that you care about them.

KRYSTAL GRAVES
West Texas A&M University

No matter how hard most of us try to cover up a lack of understanding, something about our voices or our bodies signals to others that we didn't really get it.

Of course, your audience may not try to hide their incomprehension. Members may deliberately tell you with puzzled expressions and other nonverbal cues that they are confused. The worst thing a speaker can do under such circumstances is to continue as if there were no problems. Clarifying something for the audience may be as simple as repeating or rephrasing the problem statement. If a particular word seems to be the source of confusion, defining the word or displaying it may solve the problem.

Audience Evaluation

The third component of audience analysis during the speech is your listeners' *evaluation* of you and your message. Sensitive speakers attuned to their audiences are able to gauge the reactions of those listeners. Do members of the audience seem to agree with what you are saying? Do they approve of the suggestions you are making? Answers to these questions are particularly important when you are seeking to persuade your audience.

Sometimes the answer to such questions will be no. You may be delivering bad news or taking what you know will be an unpopular stand on an issue. Having the audience disagree with the content of your message doesn't necessarily mean that your speech has been a failure. Simply knowing that many listeners agree or disagree with you at the end of a persuasive speech shows that you are an audience-centered speaker.

Analyze Your Audience *after* the Speech

5.4 **Conduct a post-speech analysis.**

Too often, speakers assume that the speech-making process concludes as you utter your final statement and walk to your seat. However, your influence on audience members can continue for some time. We encourage you to add one additional step: *post-speech analysis.* Part of this step should be self-reflection as you analyze your performance. Did you accomplish what you hoped you would? What do you sense were the strongest aspects of your speech? What were the weakest? How would you rate the content, organization, and delivery of the speech? How can you improve these aspects of your next speech?

Your answers to these questions provide subjective evaluation of your speech efforts. You may be much more critical than your listeners were because only you know how you planned to deliver the speech. For that reason, you should also consider your audience's assessment of your speech content, organization, and delivery.

In this class, that information may come from oral or written critiques from your peers or from comments some of them give you after class. If you deliver a good speech on an interesting topic, one pleasant reward is having audience members ask questions. The tone and content of those questions will tell you a great deal about how the audience received your message. You will also receive helpful suggestions from your instructor. If you expect to improve as a public speaker, pay attention to the feedback from all your listeners and act on the comments that are particularly relevant.

Summary

Recognize the Value of Audience Diversity

5.1   Explain with examples how a diverse audience can enrich the speaking experience for speakers and listeners.

- Your challenge as a speaker is to recognize how your listeners differ from one another and to understand, respect, and adapt to this diversity as you develop and deliver your speeches.

Analyze Your Audience *before* the Speech

5.2   Apply your analysis of audience demographics, psychographics, needs, and specific situations before your speech.

- Before the speech, you should consider your audience's demographics, psychographics, and needs. Information you gather about these characteristics can help you select a topic and then develop and support it for a particular group of listeners.

- Demographics refer to characteristics of the audience, such as age, sex, ethnicity, education, religion, economic status, and group membership.

- Psychographics is a term for audience psychology and how listeners' thoughts influence their actions. Three key components of audience psychology are values, beliefs, and attitudes, which ultimately influence audience members' behaviors.

- *Maslow's hierarchy* of needs is a useful tool for analyzing audience motivation by ranking five human needs in terms of their predominance: physiological needs, safety needs, belongingness and love needs, esteem needs, and self-actualization needs.

- Speakers should analyze specific speaking situations by considering the type, disposition, and size of the audience; the occasion and physical environment for the speech; and when the speech is given.

- Gathering information about your audience can be formal or informal. You can observe their behaviors or you can administer a questionnaire and analyze its results.

Analyze Your Audience *during* the Speech

5.3   Apply your analysis of your audience's attention, understanding, and evaluation of you as you speak.

- During the speech, you should focus on your listeners' attention, comprehension, and evaluation of the speech.

Analyze Your Audience *after* the Speech

5.4   Conduct a post-speech analysis.

- After delivering the speech you should continue to analyze the audience for signals about their evaluation of the message. Anyone who is serious about improving public speaking must be aware of and act on audience feedback after a speech.

Chapter 6
Selecting Your Speech Topic

 ## Learning Objectives

After studying this chapter, you should be able to

6.1 Apply the four brainstorming strategies to generate potential speech topics.

6.2 Select an appropriate speech topic based on four topic criteria.

6.3 Focus your topic into the main ideas you will cover.

6.4 Identify the general purpose of your speech.

6.5 Construct the three parts of your specific purpose statement.

6.6 Word a one-sentence thesis statement, or synopsis of your speech.

The successful writer begins with a blank sheet of paper or a clear computer screen. The successful director begins with an empty stage. To achieve a finished product—a book or a play—both must go through several complicated steps. Directors must study the literary form, understand its dynamics, research the script, generate ideas, focus and organize those ideas, and then translate them into performance. In so doing, they give the finished product their individual signatures. Writers follow a similar process to complete a project.

As a public speaker, you are both author and director. And you seek to fill two voids: a blank sheet of paper and an empty space in front of an audience. However, before you can exercise your artistry with language, your persistence as a researcher, or any other talents you possess, you must have a topic. Choosing an excellent speech topic involves six steps, as shown in Figure 6.1. You should (1) generate a list of possible topics, (2) select a topic, (3) focus the topic, (4) determine your general purpose, (5) formulate your specific purpose, and (6) word your thesis statement.

Generate Ideas

6.1   Apply the four brainstorming strategies to generate potential speech topics.

The first step in the process of selecting a speech topic is **brainstorming**. This technique involves listing all the ideas that come to mind without evaluating or censoring any of them. As a rule, the larger your list of possible topics, the better the topic you will finally select. What may seem silly to you at first can turn out to be an unusual speech subject with a lot of potential to interest your audience.

> Angelita brainstormed topics for her informative speech by listing her interests and activities. She had played the saxophone in her high school band, so she decided to inform her classmates how to play the saxophone. When she shared this idea with her instructor, however, the teacher cautioned her that such a goal was unrealistic within the 5- to 7-minute time limits. Hadn't it taken her years to learn how to play the sax? Still interested in this topic area, Angelita consulted encyclopedias and found that this hybrid instrument was popular in military and American jazz bands. She began researching military bands and found the topic fascinating.
>
> She learned that in the early 1600s, when European nations began to create standing armies, those troops needed to march together. Composers wrote marches for this purpose. Military bands played at outdoor celebrations and demonstrations, requiring instruments, such as the saxophone, that were louder than many string instruments. What began as a speech on how to play the saxophone eventually became a very interesting speech on the history of military bands. The topic expanded Angelita's knowledge and also taught her listeners something new.

You can turn brainstorming into productive work toward your speech by asking and answering four questions:

brainstorming
Noncritical free association to generate as many ideas as possible in a short time.

1. What topics interest *you*?
2. What topics interest your *listeners*?

Figure 6.1 The Steps in Choosing a Topic for a Speech

3. What topics develop from the *occasion*?

4. What topics develop from your *research*?

Your answers will help you devise a list of many topics from which you can select the most appropriate.

self-generated topics

Speech subjects based on the speaker's interests, experiences, and knowledge.

Self-Generated Topics

Self-generated topics come from you—your memory, your notes, your interests, and your experiences. Jot down your hobbies, your favorite courses, books you have read, your pet peeves, names of people who intrigue you, and issues and events that excite you. What are your likes and dislikes? On what topics do you consider yourself knowledgeable? Review your list and beside each item write possible speech topics. If you are irritated by people who are late, you could inform your audience about why people procrastinate or about how to set and meet goals. If you are nearing graduation and have been reading books on how to land your first job, a speech on the dos and don'ts for the employment interview may be fitting.

Self-generated topics may also include subjects you *need* to know. If, for example, you expect to travel soon, you may find yourself riding in taxis, staying in hotels, and dining in restaurants. Are you familiar with tipping etiquette for cabdrivers, baggage carriers, and wait staff? Researching and delivering a speech on tipping will serve your needs and be interesting and informative for your listeners.

Consider the following topics generated by students, using only their personal interests and knowledge:

Black history in textbooks	Great Barrier Reef
Cyberbullying	Photograph restoration
Deaf culture	Reducing your carbon footprint
Exercise safety	Writing a cover letter

Use what you know as a starting point in your selection process. Don't worry that you don't know enough about each topic at this stage to construct a speech. What is important is that you have a list of topics that interest you. Because these topics come from *your* knowledge, experience, and interests, your commitment to them is usually strong. Your interest and knowledge will motivate you in preparing your speech. In addition, your enthusiasm for your topic will enliven and enhance your speech delivery.

Self-generated topics can provide you with interesting ideas, but they can also pose some difficulties. One potential pitfall is the use of overly technical language and jargon. If your topic is technical, be especially attentive to the language you choose to convey your meaning.

A second potential problem with self-generated topics is a lack of objectivity about the subject. Researching your subject is a process of discovery. When you begin with rigid preconceptions, you may disregard important information that doesn't match your preconceived ideas. To avoid limiting your thinking about a subject, gather some good supporting data before you commit yourself to a specific focus for your topic.

A lack of objectivity about a self-generated topic can take a second form: excessive devotion

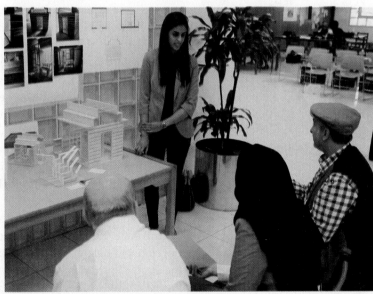

Thinking about your own hobbies and interests is one way to brainstorm for speech topics.

to the subject. You may choose an interest or a hobby that is a passion of yours. You are enthusiastic about the topic, you already have a wealth of information on it, and doing further research will seem more like a pleasure than a chore. What could possibly go wrong?

"The audience will love this topic," you think. Be careful. Your audience may not share your enthusiasm for aardvarks or restoring Studebaker cars. Your interest in a topic is just one criterion in the selection process. For most speech topics, you must work to generate audience interest. Your audience may not initially share your enthusiasm for aardvarks (or Bob Marley or the history of fireworks or optical illusions), but if you *work* at it, you can *make* them interested.

In addition, be prepared to listen openly to others' speeches. Remember that ethical listeners do not prejudge either a speaker or that speaker's ideas. Granted, some topics seem so narrow or so offbeat that you think, "Who cares?" But a speech might be terrific if the speaker is genuinely interested and has lots of vivid supporting material. Much of the value of education is that it makes you a better (smarter, happier, more well-rounded) person. Some information is intrinsically rewarding and just plain fun to know. Don't dismiss information presented in a speech (or anywhere else) just because it won't make you more money, save you time, or whiten your teeth.

Audience-Generated Topics

Pursuing **audience-generated topics** is a second way of coming up with speech ideas. What topics interest or seem important to your listeners? If you are asked to speak to a group, it may be because you have expertise in a particular area. In such a case, the topic may be predetermined.

On other occasions, such as in this class, you may not be provided with topics or topic areas. How can you find out what interests your classmates? There are three ways to do this. First, *ask them.* Ask some of your classmates in casual conversation about topics they would like to hear discussed. If possible, you could use a questionnaire to seek topic suggestions from the entire class. When you speak to an organization, ask the person who contacted you about issues of probable interest to the group.

Second, *listen and read.* What do your classmates discuss before and after class? Articles in your campus or local paper or letters to the editor may suggest issues of concern. Finally, *use the audience analysis strategies* to generate topics. Consider your listeners' needs. If your class is composed primarily of students just entering college, a speech on the history of your school could be interesting, informative, and appropriate. If your class is composed primarily of seniors, a speech on establishing a good credit history may be timely. (See also Chapter 5, Learning Objective 5.2.)

If you are lucky enough to be in a class with a lot of student diversity, you can tap your classmates' lack of knowledge about various topics. Our student Zoljargal surely had this in mind when she chose to inform her listeners about the clothing and cultural festivals of her native Mongolia. Chantal, a doctor and director of the blood bank at an area university hospital, gave her classmates an insider's view of liver transplants. Another student older than her classmates informed them about great blues musician Robert Johnson and his influence on guitarists like Eric Clapton. In each case, these students chose topics by considering both their own knowledge and their peers' lack of knowledge.

You may even find that most of your audience seems to feel one way about a controversial topic while you take the opposite view. You could use this situation to develop and deliver a persuasive speech aimed at winning support for your view of the issue.

audience-generated topics

Speech subjects geared to the interests and needs of a speaker's listeners.

The following topics were generated by our students using an audience-centered approach:

Cult movie classics	Mnemonic (memory) devices
Ethereal music	Online scholarship searches
Hazing on college campuses	Taking online classes
Interviews, dressing for	Test anxiety, how to control

Occasion-Generated Topics

Occasion-generated topics are a third source of speech subjects. When and where a speech is given may guide you in selecting a topic. A speech on setting goals may benefit your classmates more at the beginning of the term, whereas a speech on stress management may have more impact before exams.

If you are scheduled to speak near a holiday, a speech on the history or importance of that holiday may be appropriate. A speech on a culture different from yours would seem appropriately timed during Diversity Awareness Month, while Banned Books Week may be the ideal occasion for a speech on censorship. To find examples of other holidays, look at your calendar or examine different calendars at a bookstore or online. Specialty calendars or almanacs list unusual but interesting holidays, birth dates of notable and notorious people, or anniversaries of important historical events.

Our students generated the following topics as they focused on different occasions for speeches:

Barcelona bullfighting	Golden Globes Awards, history of
Chinese New Year	Halloween
Festival of the lanterns	Swedish midsummer celebrations
Fireworks, designing displays	World Laughter Day

An occasion-generated topic can often lead you to other interesting topics. Drought conditions in your area may make you consider the subjects of cloud seeding or desalting seawater. The National Day of Unplugging—sometimes referred to as a "tech-free Sabbath"—may be an occasion to urge your audience to take a 24-hour break from their "always on" digital world and to re-connect with things that really matter.

Research-Generated Topics

Research-generated topics, a fourth strategy for sparking speech ideas, require you to explore a variety of sources. First, you could consult some databases and indexes. Look at the list of subjects and jot down those that interest you. A second research strategy is to browse through magazines or journals in your library, at a local newsstand, or online. Just remember that this exploration is the first step in selecting a speech topic. Don't leap at the first interesting topic you find. A third research strategy is to peruse book titles at a good bookstore or library, noting those that interest you. Bookstores are convenient places to discover speech topics because the books are grouped by general subject area and are arranged to catch your eye. By using these three research tools—databases and indexes, magazines and journals, and books—you may not only discover a speech topic but also locate your first source of information.

Rituals and special occasions can provide excellent speech topics. Here guests arrive in traditional dress for a Lapp wedding.

occasion-generated topics

Speech subjects derived from particular circumstances, seasons, holidays, or life events.

research-generated topics

Speech subjects discovered by investigating a variety of sources.

EXPLORING ONLINE

Occasion-Generated Topics

With just a few mouse clicks, you can search for occasion-generated speech topics at the AnyDay-In-History and BrainyHistory websites. These pages let you discover events that occurred on any day and month you select. They also list names of people who were born or died on that date, along with holidays and religious observances.

Researching World News

Conduct an Internet search for "Online Newspaper Directory" for access to thousands of newspapers throughout the world. Newspapers are often searchable by name and geographical location.

Journal: Generating Topic Ideas

Using the four strategies, list one topic idea each for self-, audience-, occasion-, and research-generated categories.

visual brainstorming

Informal written outline achieved by free associating around a key word or idea.

Effective speaking and learning occur when both the speaker and audience are genuinely interested in the topic.

Consider the following topics. You might not have thought of these on your own, but all have the potential to be excellent subjects and all came from resources our students found.

Autism spectrum disorder	Marley, Bob
Color's effects on moods	Nuclear medicine, future of
Cryobiology	Obsessive-compulsive disorder
Fingerprints, features of	Racial profiling

It is important that you use all four of these strategies to generate possible speech topics. If you end the topic-generation process too quickly, you limit your options. A substantive list of self-, audience-, occasion-, and research-generated topics gives you maximum flexibility in selecting a subject.

Select Your Topic

6.2   Select an appropriate speech topic based on four topic criteria.

Once you have selected your topic area, use a technique called **visual brainstorming**, described in this chapter's "Theory Into Practice" box, to investigate the range of possibilities within that topic.

You can incorporate research into your discovery and focusing process. For example, if you are interested in learning about humor in organizations, your research would reveal that there are workshops that teach how to use humor to improve workplace morale, enthusiasm, and productivity. There are humor coaches and even a Humor University. Any one or a combination of these subjects could provide the topic for an excellent speech.

Once you have generated a list of possible speech topics, you must select the best one. Asking and answering four questions will help you make a wise decision.

1. *Am I interested in the topic?* The more enthusiastic you are about a topic, the more time and attention you will give to researching, constructing, and practicing your speech. When you enjoy learning, you learn better. As a result, speakers motivated

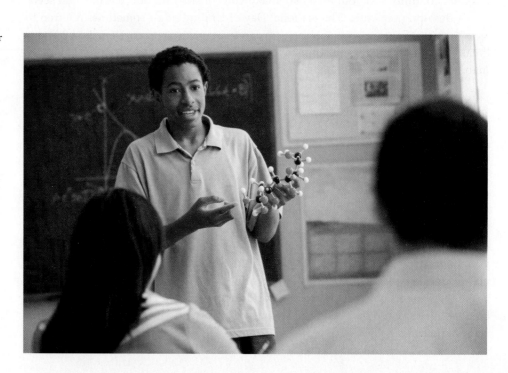

Theory Into Practice TIP

VISUAL BRAINSTORMING

Visual brainstorming uses free association around a key word or idea to reveal possible topic areas or clusters of subtopics for speeches. As your thinking suggests additional topics, you will probably be surprised at the web of possible speech topics you have created just from your brainstorming.

Take out a sheet of paper and write your topic in the center or at the top. Now, think of how you could divide and narrow that topic. It may help you to think of some generic categories such as "causes," "types," and "solutions" that are appropriate to numerous topics. As you think of subtopics, draw a line from your initial topic in any direction and write the narrower topic.

Figure 6.2 illustrates the end product of a visual brainstorming exercise on the topic of pet therapy. Notice how Luis used creative thinking and research to select his topic of service alert dogs—a topic that may not have occurred to him without this brainstorming exercise.

Figure 6.2 Visual Brainstorming

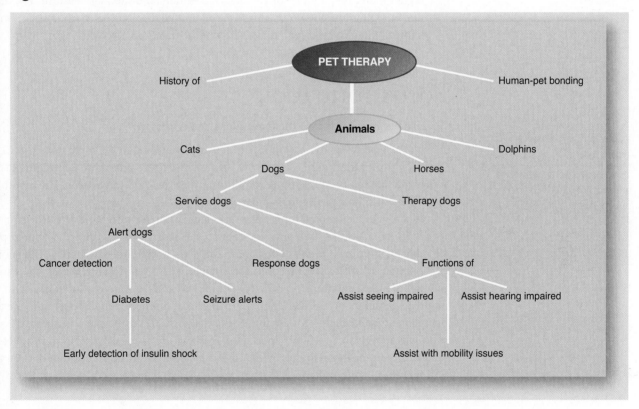

by their topics are almost always more productive than those bored with their topics.

2. *Is the topic of interest or importance to my audience?* This question helps you avoid choosing a topic that you love but that your audience will never care about. Speech making is easier when your listeners are potentially interested in what you have to say. When your audience is more attentive and receptive, you can relax and make your delivery livelier. Sometimes topics seem to be of little initial interest to an audience but may, nevertheless, be important to their personal or career success. As long as you can demonstrate the importance and relevance of the topic, you will motivate your audience to listen.

3. *Am I likely to find sufficient authoritative supporting material in the time allotted for researching and developing the speech?* Unless your topic is truly offbeat or brand new, your answer to this question will likely be yes. Even if the topic is so new that it has not yet appeared in articles, chances are good that you'll find information about it on the Internet. In that case, you'll have to judge whether the information you find is authoritative. If your best sources are items you have to order through interlibrary loan or purchase by mail order, do you have the time? You obviously cannot wait until the week before your speech to order such items. Remember the adage that if something can go wrong, it will. Build some flexibility into your schedule so that you can adapt to any crisis that may arise.

4. *Do I understand the topic enough to undertake and interpret my research?* A speaker arguing the merits of a tax increase must understand economics in order to assess research data. When you inform the audience about music therapy, you need some understanding of psychological treatment techniques and procedures. A speaker may misinterpret the reasons that violent crime in the United States is higher than in Japan if he or she does not understand Japanese culture. You don't need to know much about your topic as you begin your research, but you must know enough to be able to make sense of the data you discover.

Focus Your Topic

6.3   Focus your topic into the main ideas you will cover.

After you select your topic, you must focus it. Even though we have heard students speak on topics that were too narrow, this is rare. More commonly, students tackle topics that are too broad, leaving too little time to develop their ideas. The result is a speech that is more surface than substance.

When you decide on a topic area, use visual brainstorming to determine some of its divisions, or subtopics. For his speech on service alert dogs, Luis discovered possible benefits for individuals with cancer, diabetes, and frequent seizures. The subject of "loneliness," for example, could focus on any of the following topics: the causes of loneliness, the relationship between loneliness and depression, loneliness and the elderly, characteristics of the lonely person, the differences between being alone and being lonely, or strategies for coping with loneliness. You could never discuss all these topics meaningfully in a short speech. Narrowing the scope of your inquiry gives direction to your research and provides sufficient time to support the limited ideas you will present to your audience.

Journal: Eliminating Topic Areas

Of the topic areas you have brainstormed so far, what are two or three that you would eliminate? Describe how you came to the decision to drop these.

Speaking with Confidence

Topic selection can be the most important step of the entire speech. When I brainstormed for topics, I would think about things that really interested me. If you choose something that doesn't excite you, you won't be comfortable speaking about it. Interesting topics, however, make the whole experience more enjoyable. During the past election, I really wanted my classmates to register and vote, so I made this my purpose for speaking. My commitment to this topic motivated me to research and practice my speech. I wanted my audience to share my enthusiasm for voting. Public speaking doesn't have to be boring. You can be creative and have fun with your topic. Knowing that I had something important and interesting for my classmates to hear made me feel more confident delivering my speech.

BRYAN McCLURE
Virginia Tech University

Visual brainstorming is an excellent way of focusing your topic. A second way is through research. The more you read about your subject, the more likely you will discover its many aspects. Some may be too narrow for a complete speech, but others may be suitable for an entire speech or may be combined to form a speech.

For a 5- to 7-minute informative speech assignment, Rob developed three main points in the body of his speech on baseball:

I. The history of baseball
II. How the game is played
III. The uniform and equipment used

As you might guess, Rob found himself rushing through the speech, and he still did not finish it within the time limit. Each of his main points was too broad; he needed to focus his topic further.

Rob could have concentrated on the history of baseball and focused on a specific era that interested him. For example, he could have discussed baseball during the Civil War or focused on the all-black leagues from the 1920s until the integration of baseball during the 1950s. Rob could have spoken about the All-American Girls Professional Baseball League formed during World War II when many professional baseball players were being drafted. Each of these topics would probably have interested and informed Rob's listeners. Notice, too, that each of these narrower topics places baseball in a sociological context. Rob's speech on the sport's history could have become a lesson about a particular period of American social history, having appeal even for listeners with no interest in baseball.

Determine Your General Purpose

6.4   Identify the general purpose of your speech.

Broadly speaking, a speech may have one of three general purposes: to inform, to persuade, or to entertain. The general purpose of your speech defines your relationship with the audience. You play the role of mentor when you provide information. You are an advocate when you seek to change beliefs, attitudes, values, or behaviors through a persuasive speech. Your speech to entertain is meant to amuse your audience. As the entertainer, you set a mood to relax your audience using your delivery style, tone, and content.

You may sometimes find it difficult to distinguish these purposes. Because information may affect both what we believe and how we act, the distinction between informative speaking and persuasive speaking is sometimes blurred. A speech meant to entertain is frequently persuasive because it may make a serious point through the use of humor. Despite the overlap between these general purposes, you must be secure about your primary purpose any time you speak in public. A closer look at the objectives and intended outcomes of each general purpose will help you distinguish them.

Speeches to Inform

The objective of a **speech to inform** is to impart knowledge to an audience. You convey this information in an objective and unbiased manner. Your goal is not to alter the listeners' attitudes or behaviors but to facilitate their understanding of your subject and their ability to retain this new information. A speech on any of the following topics could be informative: Appalachian culture, the history of science-fiction movies, the middle child syndrome, music software, and vertical ice climbing. (See also Chapter 15, Learning Objective 15.3.)

speech to inform

A speech designed to convey new or useful information in a balanced, objective way.

Journal: Distinguishing Purposes

The text notes that it can be difficult to distinguish among the general purposes. What are some reasons for why this is?

Speeches to Persuade

A **speech to persuade** seeks to influence beliefs or actions. The former, sometimes called a **speech to convince**, focuses on audience beliefs and attitudes. A speech designed to persuade audience members to embrace a belief stops short of advocating specific action. Without suggesting a plan of action, a speaker may argue, for example, that polygraph testing is unreliable. Another speaker may try to convince listeners that women have been neglected in medical research without offering a plan to solve the problem.

A speech designed to persuade to action, or a **speech to actuate**, attempts to change not only the listeners' beliefs and attitudes but also their behavior. A speech to actuate could move the audience to boycott a controversial art exhibit, to contribute money to a charity, or to urge their elected officials to increase funding for women's health research. In each case, the speaker's goal would be first to intensify or alter the audience's beliefs and then to show how easy and beneficial taking action could be. (We discuss persuasive speeches in Chapter 16, Learning Objective 16.4, and Chapter 17, Learning Objective 17.4.)

Speeches to Entertain

A third general purpose of a speech is to entertain. A speech to entertain differs from speaking to entertain. *Speaking to entertain* includes humorous monologues, stand-up comedy routines, and storytelling, for example. When you tell your friends jokes or recount a humorous anecdote, you are trying to entertain them. You are probably not trying to develop a key point in an organized, methodical way.

A **speech to entertain** is more formal than speaking to entertain because it is more highly organized and its development is more detailed. Speeches to entertain are often delivered on occasions when people are in a festive mood, such as after a banquet or as part of an awards ceremony. Remember that all speeches, including those to entertain, should develop a central thought through organized supporting material and ideas. Though the ideas in a speech to entertain will be illustrated and highlighted by humor, a mere collection of jokes does not qualify as a speech. We agree with the communication scholars who contend that a speech to entertain is actually either a speech to inform or a speech to persuade, usually the latter. (We discuss the speech to entertain in more detail in Chapter 18, Learning Objective 18.5.)

Formulate Your Specific Purpose

6.5   Construct the three parts of your specific purpose statement.

When you are asked to state the **general purpose** of your speech, you will respond with two words from among the following: *to inform*, *to persuade* (or *to convince* or *to actuate*), or *to entertain*. When asked to state your specific purpose, however, you must be more descriptive. A **specific purpose** statement has three parts.

First, you begin with the speech's general purpose, stated as an infinitive—for example, "to convince." Second, you name the individuals to whom the speech is addressed, usually phrased simply as "the audience" or "my listeners." Third, you state what you want your speech to accomplish. What should the audience know, believe, or do as a result of your speech? You may want to establish the belief that alcoholism is hereditary. In this case, then, your complete specific purpose statement would be "To convince the audience that alcoholism is hereditary." Other examples of specific purpose statements are:

- To inform the audience on how to communicate constructive criticism
- To inform the audience on celebrity worship syndrome

speech to persuade

A speech designed to influence listeners' beliefs or actions.

speech to convince

A persuasive speech designed to influence audience beliefs and attitudes rather than behaviors.

speech to actuate

A persuasive speech designed to influence audience behaviors.

speech to entertain

A speech designed to make a point through the creative, organized use of humorous supporting materials.

general purpose

The broad goal of a speech, such as to inform, to persuade, or to entertain.

specific purpose

A statement of the general purpose of the speech, the speaker's intended audience, and the limited goal or outcome.

Ethical Decisions

SHOULD INSTRUCTORS CENSOR?

A colleague of ours had a long and distinguished career teaching communication. After class one day, she returned to her office visibly upset. When questioned by her colleagues, she said one of her students had announced in his speech introduction that his purpose was to teach the class how to make a lethal poison using ingredients people already had in their homes or could easily buy. "Moreover," she said, "to stress the significance of the topic, he assured us that this substance would kill any living animal, certainly even the heaviest human being."

"What did you do?" her colleagues asked. "I sat there thinking of the rash of teenage suicides, even copycat suicides, we've been hearing about lately, and all the other meanness in the world," she replied. "I wrestled with my conscience for about a minute and a half, and then, for the first time since I started teaching, I interrupted a speaker. I told the student I didn't think we needed to hear this information, and asked him to be seated."

Was this teacher's action justified? Did she violate the student's freedom of speech? Placed in that teacher's position, what would you have done?

- To convince the audience that text messaging while driving is a serious problem
- To convince the audience that laughter is medically therapeutic
- To move the audience to draft and sign a living will
- To move the audience to spend their spring break building a house for Habitat for Humanity

Word Your Thesis Statement

6.6   Word a one-sentence thesis statement, or synopsis of your speech.

A **thesis statement** presents the speech's central idea in one sentence. The thesis statement of a persuasive speech on compulsory national service could be, "Compulsory national service would benefit the nation by promoting the national spirit, the national defense, and the national welfare." This statement is the speech's central idea, a proposition the speaker will support with evidence and argument.

Notice that the process of topic selection has, up to this point, enabled you to focus your subject on something specific and manageable. You are now ready to construct a *working thesis*: a statement that, based on your current research and thinking, summarizes what you will say in your speech.[1] Although a thesis statement is designed to keep you focused, it may change as you continue to work on and develop your speech. It gives you a handle on your subject and, as you begin to develop your key ideas, will help you determine whether you can support your thesis statement. In organizing the body of the speech, you may realize that your ideas are not balanced or that two of your main points should be collapsed into one. As you research your speech, you may discover additional ideas that are more important than some you had planned to present. That was the experience of our student who spoke on compulsory national service.

> **Key Points**
>
> **To Develop Your Specific Purpose Statement**
> 1. State your general purpose.
> 2. Name your intended audience.
> 3. State the goal of your speech.

Stuart was developing a persuasive speech advocating a system of compulsory national service (CNS). As he began his research, he planned to focus only on the national security that compulsory military service would provide. His working thesis was, "Compulsory national service would benefit the nation by ensuring its military readiness." Yet his research quickly revealed many other benefits of CNS: domestic conservation and recycling, rural health care, and in-home assistance to the elderly.

By the time he had completed his research, Stuart had broadened the focus of his speech and felt he had developed a much stronger case for instituting a CNS program. When he delivered his speech, he presented three main arguments:

thesis statement

A one-sentence synopsis of a speaker's message.

I. CNS would promote the national spirit.

II. CNS would promote the national defense.

III. CNS would promote the national welfare.

Stuart revised his thesis statement to reflect his new organization.

The following examples illustrate how you can narrow a topic's focus from a general area to the speech's thesis statement.

Topic Area: Sculpture

Topic: Works by Andy Goldsworthy

General Purpose: To inform

Specific Purpose: To inform the audience about Andy Goldsworthy's sculptures

Thesis Statement: Andy Goldsworthy sculpts wood, ice, and leaves into intricate works in their natural settings.

Topic Area: Police oversight

Topic: Mandatory videotaping of police

General Purpose: To persuade

Specific Purpose: To persuade the audience that all police actions in police stations should be videotaped

Thesis Statement: Videotaping all police actions in police stations will deter police misconduct, discourage false charges of police misconduct, and restore public confidence in police work.

Summary

Generate Ideas

6.1 Apply the four brainstorming strategies to generate potential speech topics.

- To choose an appropriate speech topic, brainstorm a list of subjects focused around your interests, the needs and interests of your audience, the occasion for your speech, or the subjects you have researched.

Select Your Topic

6.2 Select an appropriate speech topic based on four topic criteria.

- Select your topic after assessing your interest in it; the topic's interest or importance to your audience; your ability to find adequate, quality supporting materials on the topic in the time you have; and your ability to understand what your research reveals about the topic.

Focus Your Topic

6.3 Focus your topic into the main ideas you will cover.

- Focus or narrow the topic you've selected by using visual brainstorming and initial research on the subject.

Determine Your General Purpose

6.4 Identify the general purpose of your speech.

- Understand the general purpose of your speech—to inform, to persuade, or to entertain—before moving on to the details of your speech.

Formulate Your Specific Purpose

6.5 Construct the three parts of your specific purpose statement.

- Decide what you want your speech to accomplish: what the audience should know, believe, or do as a result of hearing your speech.

Word Your Thesis Statement

6.6 Word a one-sentence thesis statement, or synopsis of your speech.

- State the central purpose of the speech in one sentence.

Chapter 7
Researching Your Speech Topic

 Learning Objectives

After studying this chapter, you should be able to

7.1 Assess your knowledge of your speech topic.

7.2 Construct a plan for accessing information.

7.3 Collect and evaluate information from appropriate sources.

7.4 Record relevant information systematically.

7.5 Identify the appropriate time to conclude your research.

Research scholar Patricia Breivik summarizes the snowballing accumulation of information as follows:

> The sum total of humankind's knowledge doubled from 1750–1900. It doubled again from 1900–1950. Again from 1960–1965. It has been estimated that the sum of humankind's knowledge has doubled at least once every 5 years since then. . . . It has been further projected that by the year 2020, knowledge will double every 73 days![1]

In light of these circumstances, it is surely smarter to think of being educated as *knowing how to access and analyze* information, rather than *possessing* it.

For public speakers, the challenge is selecting from the wide range of available data the information most appropriate for their speeches. That requires knowing how to research—how to scratch "an intellectual itch."[2]

Research is the gathering of evidence and arguments you will need to understand, develop, and explain your subject. Research is not one step of the speech construction process but should occur throughout that process. First, research can help you select your topic. Once you have chosen a topic, additional research helps you focus and determine your specific purpose. As you begin to construct the body of your speech, you may need to develop some of your ideas further with additional research. Your research continues even as you consult dictionaries, thesauruses, and collections of quotations to help you word your ideas before delivering your speech.

Research is not necessarily a linear process. As a result, you may be exercising and developing a number of critical thinking skills simultaneously. If you have some experience with or knowledge about the topic area, you'll begin by *remembering* and assessing your knowledge. You'll be *gathering information* as you formulate questions you want your research to answer and then collect your data. You will use your *generating* skills to develop new lines of inquiry based on the research you have completed. Throughout the process, you'll be *analyzing* whether and how information from different sources fits together. As you connect items of information, you'll be *integrating* and *organizing*. As you measure the quality and quantity of your research results, you'll be *evaluating*. And because you will often find more information than you can use, your entire research process will have you *focusing* your speech topic more and more narrowly.

The following five-step sequence can help you generate excellent ideas and supporting material regardless of your speech topic.

1. Assess your knowledge of the topic.
2. Develop your research plan.
3. Collect your information.
4. Record your information.
5. Conclude your search.

Assess Your Knowledge

7.1 **Assess your knowledge of your speech topic.**

The first question you should ask and answer is, "What do I know that will help me develop my topic?" Your memory has been shaped by what you have read, heard, observed, and experienced. Use that knowledge as a starting point for researching your topic.

For example, a student who worked as a plainclothes security guard for a major department store drew from personal experience in his speech on detecting and apprehending shoplifters. A student who helped her father administer polygraph tests

research

The process of gathering evidence and arguments to understand, develop, and explain a speech topic.

chose as her speech topic the use and misuse of lie detectors. These speakers used their knowledge and experiences as starting points for their research. Both students developed and delivered interesting speeches.

Upon being asked how long he had prepared for one of his speeches, Winston Churchill replied, "For forty years." Communication scholars Robert Jeffrey and Owen Peterson observe, "In a sense, a speaker spends his or her entire life preparing for a speech. Everything we have learned and experienced, as well as the attitudes we have developed, shapes and influences our speech."[3] Your knowledge and experience give you a head start in selecting and developing your topic.

Develop Your Research Plan

7.2 Construct a plan for accessing information.

Once you have developed your idea for a topic, developing your research plan is the next important step in the research process. Your research plan begins as you answer several questions:

1. What information do I need?
2. Where am I most likely to find information about my topic?
3. How can I obtain this information?
4. How will time constraints affect my research options?

Your topic and specific purpose clearly help determine your research plan. If you see a news report about deep brain stimulation to treat Parkinson's disease and you select that topic for a speech, you will obviously need to find and read medical materials. If you decide to speak about the upcoming Oktoberfest celebration or about a new sleep clinic in your area, your best information may not be in print. You will likely spend time talking to people.

Don't assume that all relevant information for a given topic can be found online. Different topics demand different research strategies and a good research plan accounts for these variations. Keep a running list of what you need and where you can obtain that information.

You should also prepare a timetable for constructing your speech. If you will be speaking in two weeks, you still have time for a lot of online or library research. You may even have time to arrange, conduct, and transcribe interviews. However, two weeks is not enough time to order transcripts or recordings and be assured they will arrive by surface mail in time to analyze them and integrate them into your speech.

Collect Your Information

7.3 Collect and evaluate information from appropriate sources.

Once you have developed a research plan, begin collecting the information you need to understand and develop your topic.

The Internet

If you research primarily online, be aware that URLs (uniform resource locators)—or website addresses and the routes you use to retrieve information—can change quickly. Thus, we recommend downloading or printing copies of any Web-based information you intend to use in your research. In addition, you may find more information than you can possibly read in the time you have for research. Approximately 25 percent of

Journal: Starting to Plan

Select a topic for one of your speeches. What are at least two types of information you will need to research?

college students report finding too much information.[4] How can you determine which information is most useful and which resources are reliable?

While there are a multitude of **search engines** available to conduct online research, such as Yahoo!, Bing, and Ask.com, the most widely used is Google. In 2010, Google held 71.6 percent of the market share for search engines, with Yahoo! a distant second at 14.3 percent. One feature that makes Google such an attractive search engine for students is its Google Scholar search engine, which specifically targets academic resources. This allows students to use a search engine with which they are likely very familiar without having to go through the library databases. Instead, Google Scholar provides links directly to articles in the school's library databases. However, keep in mind that this feature works best when you are using your school's computers or Internet service on your personal computer. Academic opinions regarding Google Scholar appear to be split, however, with one librarian arguing that Google Scholar "is easy to use, saves them [students] time in writing essays, and links to a vast amount of information,"[5] while one university website cautions students, "It is in no way comprehensive, and has limited field searching."[6] We encourage students, therefore, to use Google Scholar as a starting point into a topic, realizing that the most effective next step is to move to academic search engines for full-text and better searching and indexing capabilities. Academic search engines filter the extraneous from the essential and are a key component of serious, targeted searches. Here are four academic search engines and their addresses:

Academic Index	www.academicindex.net
EbscoHost	http://search.ebscohost.com
INFOMINE	infomine.ucr.edu
ipl2	www.ipl.org

Information from academic search engines is more focused and of higher quality than what you may find via general search engines such as Google, Bing, Yahoo!, and others.

The **deep Web**, sometimes called the *invisible Web*, contains public, government, corporate, and private information. The "content in the deep Web is massive—approximately 500 times greater than that visible to conventional search engines—with much higher quality throughout."[7] Deep Web information often exists in topic-specific databases as multimedia files, graphic files, or in portable document file (PDF) formats.[8] "A full 95 percent of the deep Web is publicly accessible information—not subject to fees or subscriptions."[9] In contrast to static web pages, information in the deep Web is "dynamic"—that is, the pages form only in response to specific research queries.

To explore the deep Web, try the following portals:

- InfoPlease (www.infoplease.com/index.html): a free search engine with access to numerous encyclopedias, almanacs, and atlases.
- DeeperWeb (www.deeperweb.com): a free search engine option that uses tag cloud methods to explore Google search results.
- Zuula (www.zuula.com): "With Zuula, it is quick and convenient to get results from all the top search engines."

A popular Internet resource is *Wikipedia*. Once students have selected their speech topics, many turn first to this Web-based, free online encyclopedia with access to more than 3.7 million articles in English and many more in other languages. A recent study revealed that students often begin and end their research at *Wikipedia*.[10] One criticism of *Wikipedia* is that it operates on an "openly editable" model, allowing virtually anyone with an Internet connection to write or edit its entries. This

search engine

A tool for locating information on the Internet by matching items in a search string with pages that the engine indexes.

deep Web

Huge databases of Internet information posted by public, government, corporate, and private agencies and available only by specific queries.

presents problems for students seeking accurate and timely information on their topics. *Wikipedia* acknowledges its limitations as a trusted academic source, stating "Students should never use information in *Wikipedia* (or any other online encyclopedia) for formal purposes (such as school essays) until they have verified and evaluated the information based on external sources."[11] Similar to Google Scholar, we suggest that *Wikipedia* should only be used to get started with your research and it should not be your only source of information. Once you have found a useful *Wikipedia* page, scroll down to the bottom of the page and review the references used to compile the *Wikipedia* Webpage information. Next, locate the most appropriate sources using your library's databases or consult a librarian.

See the "Theory Into Practice" feature below for recommendations about evaluating information you find on the Internet.

Theory Into Practice TIP

EVALUATING INTERNET RESOURCES

When you use the Internet for research, your critical thinking skills may get not just exercise but a full-tilt workout. This is because anything can get posted and quickly communicated to millions of people online. For all the convenience it provides, the Internet forces us to evaluate information. What should you ask about sites that you are considering using to support your speech? Basic questions you may need to ask are listed below.

Purpose

- What seems to be the purpose of this site? To provide information? To promote a position? To sell a product or service?
- What type of site is it? aviation (.aero), commercial (.com, .coop, or .biz), educational (.edu), governmental (.gov), information business (.info), military (.mil), nonprofit organization (.org), personal (.name), or professional (.pro)?
- Is there an institution, agency, or organization identified as sponsoring the site?
- Does the site contain advertisements? If so, by whom?
- Who is the author's apparent audience, as reflected by the vocabulary, writing style, and point of view? Students? Professionals? Consumers? Advocates?

Expertise

- Is the author, compiler, or webmaster identified?
- Does the author have verifiable expertise on the subject?
- Are the author's or compiler's credentials provided?
- Do you know the author's occupation?
- Do you know the author's educational background?
- Do you know the author's organizational affiliation?
- Does the author provide contact information, such as an email address, phone number, or mailing address?
- If the site is a compilation, are sources and authors of individual works identified?
- If the site is a research project, does the author explain data, methodology, and interpretation of results? Does the author refer to other works? Provide notes?
- If links to other works are provided, are they evaluated in any way?
- Is the site linked to another site that you already trust or value?
- Are sources or viewpoints missing that you would expect to be present?
- What does this page offer that you could not find elsewhere?

Objectivity

- Does the author's affiliation with an organization, institution, or agency suggest a bias?
- Does the site's sponsorship by an organization or institution suggest an inherent bias?
- Are opposing views represented or acknowledged?
- Are editorial comments or opinions clearly distinguished from facts?

Accuracy

- Can you corroborate the facts using other Internet or library resources (reference works or indexed publications)?
- Is the site inward-focused (providing links only to other parts of the site) or outward-focused (providing links to other websites)?
- Has the author expended the effort to write well, with correct spelling and proper grammar?
- Does the author solicit corrections or updates by email?

Timeliness

- Is the publication date important to this subject matter?
- Can you tell when the site was created?
- Can you tell when the site was last updated?
- Are links from this site current or broken?[12]

Library Resources

Though it's certainly not necessary to start your research from your school library these days, that facility contains many resources that you won't find anywhere else. One of the most helpful sources of information is the library staff, particularly reference librarians. A good reference librarian can (1) acquaint you with the library's services and holdings, (2) guide you to particularly helpful sources of information, and (3) instruct you in the use of library equipment. He or she can also guide you to your library's areas of strength, making your research more efficient and your life easier.

Ethical Decisions

THE PRIVACY OF PUBLIC INFORMATION

Jeanine was researching a speech on the problem of child sexual abuse. While she was searching the Internet, she discovered a series of forums devoted to this topic, including a newsgroup and a live chat group. She found thought-provoking and useful discussions in the newsgroup, but the chat discussions were the most intimate and revealing. There, sexual abuse survivors described their memories of actual incidents and talked about how the trauma affected their adult lives. Jeanine took notes on some of the most remarkable stories and decided to recount one in her speech to vivify her speech.

Is this a legitimate way for Jeanine to use her research? Should stories told on the Internet be considered public property, available for anyone to write or speak about? Should Jeanine try to find out whether the speaker would feel comfortable about having the story repeated in a speech? Should she try to verify that the story is true?

Magazines and Journals

Magazine and journal articles are probably the most common source of information for student speeches. With more than 218,000 magazines from which to choose, however, it's helpful to use an index to filter useful from extraneous information.[13] Hundreds of excellent indexes of periodicals exist, and many standard indexes are now available online. These can guide you as you focus your search even more.

College libraries provide computer terminals to help you research your speech topic. With a few keystrokes you can unlock a wealth of information in and beyond the library.

The true monster trucks of academic research in periodicals today are full-text **databases**. These databases are powerful because each gives you access to articles in hundreds or even thousands of periodicals and scholarly journals. You can print useful articles or email them to another address. Moreover, if you are a registered college or university student, you have already paid to use these research tools from any computer with Internet access through your school's library website.

Some of the general full-text databases likely available to you are listed in Table 7.1. In addition, specialized indexes exist for almost every academic field. Subject-specific computer databases include *Alternative Health Watch, Biography in Context, Contemporary Women's Issues,* and so on. Similar print indexes in the reference section of your library may include titles such as *Education Index, Hispanic American Periodicals Index,* and *Music Index.* Because these indexes are so specialized, the periodicals and journals they lead you to will likely be written for a specific audience; they may use jargon and technical language familiar only to people in that field. Even if you understand these articles easily, you may have to simplify their language and ideas for a more diverse listening audience.

If you have particular magazines and journals in mind at any stage in your research, you can also check the online versions of these publications. Some magazines provide the full text of current issues along with searchable archives; others give you only sample articles and subscription information. Though browsing individual magazines is not an efficient use of limited research time, searchable online periodicals can be useful.

To find online magazines and journals in your school's library, you need to:

1. Navigate to your school's library website

2. Click on e-journals or e-magazines

3. Type the name of the journal or magazine in the search box and click find/search/OK

4. One or more hyperlinks will appear that take you directly to the online version of the magazine or journal for which you searched

The above steps can also be used if you want to search a specific database. Instead of clicking e-journals or e-magazines in step 2, click on databases. Then follow the same steps.

Newspapers

Newspapers offer abundant information—local, national, or international in scope. Large newspapers such as the *New York Times,* the *Washington Post,* and the *Christian Science Monitor* have been indexed individually in the past. The computer index to the *New York Times,* for example, provides full text of all articles from 1851 to the present.

database

A huge collection of information arranged for quick retrieval by computer using key words stipulated by a researcher.

Table 7.1 Examples of Subscription Databases and Indexes

Database/Index	What It Provides
Academic Search Complete	The world's most comprehensive full-text database for multidisciplinary research, includes full coverage of multidisciplinary, full-text academic journals, reports, books, and much more.
AccuNet/AP Multimedia Archive	Searchable archive of Associated Press (AP) photos, charts, logos, maps, and other graphics produced for AP, nineteenth century to present. Brief stories accompany most photos 48 hours after publication.
Communication & Mass Media Complete (CMMC)	CMMC is the most comprehensive database related to communication and mass media. It includes the content of *CommSearch* (formerly produced by the National Communication Association) and *Mass Media Articles Index* (formerly produced by The Pennsylvania State University) along with numerous other journals in communication, mass media, and closely related fields of study.
ERIC	An online digital library with access to more than 1.3 million bibliographic records of journal articles and other education-related materials.
General OneFile	Approximately 80 million articles and records in refereed journals, general interest magazines, newspapers, National Public Radio transcripts, subject-specific collections, and other sources. From this website you can also access InfoTrac Student Edition with access to nearly 9 million articles, updated daily.
LexisNexis Academic	International business, health, law, news, and reference articles, most in full text. Updated continually.
Opposing Viewpoints in Context	Pro–con essays on controversial topics. Includes text of reference works, magazine and newspaper articles, websites, statistics, and images.
Project Muse	Full-text articles from nearly 500 scholarly journals published by scholarly presses in the arts, humanities, social sciences, and mathematics.
ProQuest Education Journals	Includes more than 1,000 educational publications, such as *Childhood Education, College Teaching, Harvard Educational Review, Journal of Athletic Training,* and *Educational Theory.*
Science in Context	Full-text articles from more than 200 magazines, scholarly journals, and links to quality websites. Includes biographies, experiment descriptions, pictures, illustrations, topic overviews, and news of recent scientific discoveries.

Today, however, your campus library is more likely to subscribe to powerful databases such as *LexisNexis Academic* that contain full-text newspaper articles in addition to other sources.

Most newspapers now have websites and provide indexes to their own archives. If you have selected a localized topic, you may want to research specific newspapers using a search engine like Google. If you're unsure about newspaper titles, *Newslink* (http://newslink.org) lets you browse lists of U.S. newspapers by state as well as world newspapers by continent or country; click on links to specific papers.

Government Documents

The most prolific publisher in the United States is the federal government. Much of our bureaucracy is devoted to collecting, cataloguing, and disseminating information. Luckily, most of what's available is accessible online: presidential speeches and transcripts of press conferences, pending legislation, contact information for senators and representatives, agency reports, and ordering information for documents not available online in full text. Online, you can take a virtual tour of the White House, listen to audio files of unedited arguments before the Supreme Court, and see digital photographs of historical documents. In short, almost every federal agency has a website.

Your library probably subscribes to several government databases, among them *LexisNexis Government Periodicals Index*, *Federal Register Online*, and *MarciveWeb DOCS*. Searchable by keyword, these databases save you time.

With just a couple of Web addresses, you can access virtually any area of the government. The Library of Congress maintains THOMAS: Legislative Information on the Internet at http://thomas.loc.gov. The Government Printing Office maintains a list of links to government information products at www.access.gpo.gov. At those two sites, you can get any information you need from the legislative, executive, or judicial branches of the government.

Books

Books are excellent sources of information. Because they are longer than magazine and newspaper articles, books allow authors to discuss topics in greater depth and often provide an index to key ideas and a list of sources consulted. However, if your speech topic requires the most up-to-date data you can find, information in magazines and newspapers may be more current and accessible than what you find in books. Despite this limitation, books can be an integral part of your research plan. Today the online catalog in most academic libraries permits you to search by subject, title, author, and key word.

Additionally, books you need may be available as ebooks that you can access—"check out"—in your choice of formats after you establish a library account. On the Internet, full-text literary works are also well represented by Literature Online (*LION*, http://lion.chadwyck.com), a searchable subscription database of more than 350,000 British and American works.

Reference Works

Reference works include many types of collections to aid you in your research. Whether you use hard-copy versions in the library, access databases through your library's web page, or log on to the Internet, a few of the reference works you will find most helpful are dictionaries, encyclopedias, almanacs, and books of quotations.

Dictionaries help you clarify the meanings, spellings, and pronunciations of words. Online dictionaries often provide audio pronunciation of words, terms, and names. For example, search for "mischievous pronunciation," "Alzheimer's pronunciation," and "Ryukyu Islands pronunciation" to hear correct ways to say these words.

Encyclopedias are multivolume sets of books that organize information on many branches of knowledge. Some electronic encyclopedias are free; for others you may have to pay a subscription fee unless you access them from a library or through a library website.

Almanacs contain a wide range of specific and statistical information about topics such as education, politics, sports, entertainment, and significant events of a particular year. Almanacs are excellent sources when you need specific facts and background information.

Captivating quotations, both serious and funny, can enliven the language of your speech. Quoting another person also may add credibility to your comments and strengthen the development of your ideas. Fortunately, many excellent *books of quotations* are available in bookstores, libraries, and online. These collections of quotations are organized alphabetically by author or subject, with handy indexes or search functions.

Television and Radio

You can find ideas for excellent speech topics and materials to support them among the investigative reports on television and radio. Many programs provide transcripts

---

EXPLORING ONLINE

Government Documents

Do an Internet search for the Library of Congress website THOMAS, which helps you obtain information from the U.S. Congress. You can download House and Senate committee reports, summaries of bills being considered and notes about their status, copies of laws enacted, and even remarks recorded in the *Congressional Record*. Click on "Help" and access the FAQ (frequently asked questions) feature that provides information that will enhance your research skills as well as instructions on how to conduct a search in THOMAS. Download a bill or committee report, contact your representative or senators, and cite the documents.

for purchase, with ordering information given at the show's conclusion. Networks now offer transcripts of many of these shows for print or download at their websites. If you require older transcripts, you may have to order them online for a fee. Many National Public Radio programs are archived for downloading as podcasts after their initial broadcast.

Your library or DVD rental service may have copies of special televised broadcasts such as the PBS documentary series *Lewis and Clark* or Martin Scorsese's *Bob Dylan: No Direction Home*. Through informational videos, you can research topics such as military battles, McCarthyism, and space exploration, to name just a few. Commercial videos (as well as websites) can take you on tours of museums such as the Louvre or the Museum of Modern Art and of distant places such as Australia and Italy. Instructional DVDs can teach you how to garden, refinish furniture, and make a sales presentation.

Interviews

So far, you have learned how to conduct *secondary research*, which means that you have gathered existing information. Sometimes, however, you may need to conduct *primary research*, which means that you generate new information about your topic. Most primary research is either qualitative or quantitative. *Qualitative research* refers to gathering descriptive, non-numerical information, which can be done by conducting interviews or focus groups. *Quantitative research*, as the name implies, focuses on numerical information, which can be gathered by administering a questionnaire.

Depending on your topic, an interview may be the best source of firsthand information. Today you can interview people by email, instant messaging, Skype, telephone, or in person. The personal interview can aid you in four ways. First, if published sources are inaccessible, the personal interview may be your only option. The topic you have chosen may be so recent that sufficient information is not yet in print or online. Your topic may also be so localized as to receive little or no coverage by area media.

A second advantage of the personal interview is that it permits you to adapt your topic to your specific audience. Take, for example, the topic of recycling. If you interview the director of your school's physical plant to find out how much trash custodians collect and dispose of each day, you give your speech a personal touch. You could take your speech one step further by figuring out how much your college could contribute to resource conservation. This shows your audience how this topic affects them directly. You will grab their attention.

Third, personal interviews provide opportunities for you to secure expert evaluation of your research and suggestions for further study. The experts you interview may challenge some of your assumptions or data. If this happens, encourage their feedback and don't get defensive. Knowing all the angles can only help you give a more thoughtful speech. Near the end of your interview, ask your interviewee to suggest additional sources that will help you better research and understand your topic.

Finally, personal interviews can enhance your image as a speaker. Listeners are usually impressed that you went beyond library research in preparing your message for them.

PREPARE FOR THE INTERVIEW.   Once you decide to conduct a personal interview, you must take several steps in preparation.

1. *Determine whom you want to interview.* Your interviewee should be someone who is both knowledgeable on the topic and willing to speak with you.

2. *Decide on the format for the interview.* Will you conduct it face to face, by phone, or online? A face-to-face interview may give you the most information. People tend to open up more when they interact both verbally and nonverbally. In a

face-to-face interview, you can listen to what the interviewee says and also observe the nonverbal messages. A phone interview is another possibility when you cannot travel to the expert. A third option, conducting an interview by email or Skype, has both advantages and disadvantages. The email interview is time-consuming because you must prepare a set of questions, send it to the interviewee, and wait for a response. It has the added disadvantage of not allowing for immediate follow-up questions. If something needs clarification, you must email another question. An interview via Skype or by instant messaging eliminates this time lag. However, the email interview often results in more thoughtful and better worded responses than face-to-face, telephone, or Skype interviews.

3. *Schedule the interview.* When requesting an interview, identify yourself and the topic on which you seek information. Let the person know how you intend to use that information, the amount of time needed for the interview, and any recording procedures you plan to use. Some people may object to being quoted or recorded. You are likely to discover that most people you seek to interview are flattered that you selected them as experts and are therefore happy to cooperate.

4. *Research the person to be interviewed.* Research the interviewee beforehand. Obviously, your selection of this person suggests that you already know something about him or her. In addition, read any articles the interviewee has published on your topic. This enables you to conduct the interview efficiently. You won't ask questions that the person has already answered in print, and your prior reading may prompt some specific questions on points you would like clarified. Also, your research will show that you are prepared. The interviewee will take you and the interview seriously.

5. *Prepare a list of questions.* Always have more questions than you think you will be able to ask, just in case you are mistaken. Mark those that are most important to your research, and ask them first. You may want to have some closed and some open questions, as Joel did when he interviewed a professor of recreation for his speech on how American adults spend their leisure time. *Closed questions* are those that can be answered with a yes, a no, or a short answer. For example, Joel asked, "Do American adults have more time for leisure activities today than they did a generation ago?" and "How many hours per week does the typical adult spend watching TV?" The first question can be answered by a yes or a no, the second with a specific figure.

    Open questions invite longer answers and can produce a great deal of information. Joel asked this open question: "How do American adults typically spend their leisure time?" When you ask open questions, sit back and prepare to listen for a while! The less time you have for the interview, the fewer open questions you should ask. Open questions can sometimes result in rambling responses. At times, the interviewee's rambling will trigger questions you would not have thought of otherwise. Joel was surprised to learn that American adults spend approximately two hours a week in adult education, a venture he had not included on his initial list of adult leisure activities. When you and the interviewee have plenty of time, and particularly if you are recording the interview, open questions can provide the richest information.

Open questions, such as those that begin with the phrase, "How do you feel about," can elicit more substantive responses from interviewees than do closed yes or no questions.

CONDUCT THE INTERVIEW.   The face-to-face interview is an excellent opportunity to practice your interpersonal communication skills. Specifically, you should follow these guidelines:

1. Introduce yourself when you arrive, thank the person for giving you time, and restate the purpose of the interview.

2. Conduct the interview in a professional manner. Make sure you arrive appropriately dressed. Be ready and able to set up and handle any recording equipment with a minimum of distractions. Try to relax the interviewee—establish a professional atmosphere, pose questions that are clear and direct, listen actively, take notes efficiently, and follow up when necessary. You should control the interview without appearing to be pushy or abrupt.

3. When you have finished, thank the person again for the interview.

FOLLOW UP ON THE INTERVIEW.   After the interview, review your notes or listen to your recording. Do this as soon as possible after the interview, when your memory is still fresh. If you are unclear about something that was said, do not use that information in your speech. You should contact your interviewee to clarify the point if you think it will be important to the audience's understanding of the topic.

As a matter of courtesy, you should write to the people you interviewed, thanking them for the time and help they gave you. You may even want to send them a copy of your finished speech if it is in manuscript form.

In addition to conducting individual interviews to gather information about your speech topic, you can also conduct focus groups, which in some cases provide even more information than interviews.

Focus Groups

A focus group is a type of group interview in which you can collect information from multiple people simultaneously by facilitating a group discussion. Generally, it's recommended to have 5–10 participants when conducting focus groups.[14] Therefore, focus groups have three primary advantages compared to personal interviews. First, focus groups are time efficient. Instead of conducting multiple personal interviews with one person at the time, you can interview several people simultaneously. Second, focus groups may provide more information than personal one-on-one interviews. In focus groups, the interviewees often feed off one another's comments, which results in deeper and more detailed information. Third, information gathered in a focus group is more reliable than information from a single one-on-one interview. In a personal interview, you cannot be sure that other people have similar experiences. In focus groups, however, you may be able to identify common themes among the participants and you will notice if the participants seem to have similar or different opinions and experiences.[15]

Speaking with Confidence

Once I choose my speech topic, the fun begins. Sometimes I already know the main points I want to discuss in my speech; sometimes I don't. Either way, what really builds my speech are the interesting and credible supporting materials I find in my research. Of course, it's great to have an informative source like the Internet at my fingertips, but it's also rewarding to use sources that may take a little more time and effort to obtain.

A trip to the library, for example, puts books, newspapers, and journals at my disposal. My favorite source, however, is the interview. Asking an expert specific questions on my topic can yield lots of really helpful information. The person can also direct me to other sources I may not know about. The more I research, the more confident I feel about my speech. So, remember to start researching early and use all the resources available.

MATTHEW WILLIAMS
Radford University

Similar to personal interviews, focus groups can be conducted electronically, such as using a group chat room, or they can be conducted face to face. If you do decide to gather information using a focus group, follow the same guidelines for preparing, conducting, and following up your focus group as you would in a personal one-on-one interview.

Questionnaires

A questionnaire is a series of written questions given to people in order to gather information. When you administer a questionnaire, you engage in *survey research*. As with other research methodologies, there as both advantages and disadvantages of using questionnaires. One advantage is that they are time-efficient. You may be able to ask all of your classmates to complete your questionnaire at the end of class. This would give you information from 20–25 students in just a few minutes. The main disadvantage is the possibility that the participants' answers are influenced by their own biases. Oftentimes, we inflate our responses to positive questions and deflate our responses to negative questions. For example, as a student you are expected to study hard and not to skip class. So, if asked how many hours per week you study, your answer may be 20 hours even if the correct answer is 15 hours. On the other hand, if you are asked how many times per semester you skip class, you may answer 2–3 times even though the true answer may be 4–5 times. This is known as *social desirability bias*.[16]

To develop your questionnaire, you should first look for existing questionnaires that can be used. For example, if you want to explore if female and male students experience different levels of anxiety when speaking in public, the Personal Report of Public Speaking Anxiety would be a suitable questionnaire for you to use. Sometimes, however, you may need to develop your own questionnaire. (See Appendix B, where you will find sample questions and guidelines for how to develop your questionnaire.)

Calling, Writing, and Emailing for Information

Some years ago, one of our students, Lindahl, wanted to develop an informative speech on the savant syndrome. This was before the film *Rain Man* made many people aware of the special talents and disabilities of savants. Lindahl had seen a *60 Minutes* segment on the syndrome but could not find recent written sources. Her best source, she said, was an article from a 3-year-old issue of *Time*. Others might have abandoned their research and switched topics, but Lindahl followed a hunch that paid off.

The *Time* article quoted several university professors and medical doctors who were engaged in ongoing research on the savant syndrome. Lindahl got their office telephone numbers and called these experts to see if they could recommend new sources she had been unable to locate. The people Lindahl called were flattered by her attention and complimented her perseverance as a researcher. One psychologist mailed her a photocopy of a book chapter she had written on the savant syndrome; a medical doctor mailed Lindahl a packet of journal articles, including the galleys of an article he was about to publish; a psychology professor sent her a tape of savants playing piano concertos they had heard for the first time only moments before. In short, Lindahl received a gold mine of new, expert research as a result of her few long-distance calls. If Lindahl were to conduct such a search today, she might find that email would be a quicker, although less personal, way to contact the experts.

Lindahl was lucky that she began her research more than a month before her speech was due. To take advantage of pamphlets and brochures available through the mail, you will need to plan ahead as well. Thousands of organizations, such as the American Cancer Society and United Way, publish their own informational literature. Political parties and lobbying groups prepare position papers on issues that affect them. Corporations distribute annual reports to their stockholders and will share these on request. You can write to or email any of these organizations. Most post contact information on their websites. You can locate URLs for companies or groups through search indexes available online. Another source that can be helpful is the three-volume *Encyclopedia of Associations*. Each volume lists names, addresses, telephone numbers, email addresses, and URLs for websites, along with descriptions of the organizations. If time permits and research warrants, writing, calling, or emailing these organizations to request information can add relevant primary research to your speech.

Record Your Information

7.4 Record relevant information systematically.

Once you have located information, you must determine what to record and how to record it.

What to Record

When in doubt, record more rather than less. Certainly, it is possible to copy too much information. If you find everything potentially important, your topic probably needs better focus. Without some focus, you risk becoming so bogged down in research that you leave little time for organizing and practicing your speech.

On the other hand, if you are too selective, you may be inefficient. As you research your speech, you may shift your topic focus; hence the supporting material you previously thought was irrelevant becomes important. Discarding unnecessary information is easier than trying to remember a source, retracing your steps, hoping that the information is still on the library shelves or that the Internet source is still live, and then recording that information. (See Chapter 9, Learning Objective 9.4.)

How to Record Information

Traditional advice to researchers is to record each piece of information on a separate notecard, along with the source citation, as you find it. With this strategy, you can organize your speech visually and experiment with different structures. The disadvantage of this method is that it consumes a great deal of library time that might be better devoted to searching for other sources. In addition, much of what you record on notecards may not be used in your speech at all.

Another, more common, method is to photocopy material at the library or to print articles you find online. Later, you can review, evaluate, and select from the materials. However, be aware that photocopies or printed articles may lull you into a false sense of accomplishment. What you have copied may turn out to be of little or no use. To avoid this problem, read your material before or very shortly after copying it. Don't wait until the night before your speech to read the information you have been collecting.

Also, remember to note your sources on the copied pages. If the web page URL does not appear as a header or footer on printed pages, be sure to write it down. Copy the page or pages containing publication information for each book you use. If you follow these simple directions, photocopying and printing have two additional advantages over using notecards. First, you may not know what you want to use from an article at the time you first find it. If the focus of your speech changes, a different part of the article may become important (indeed, sometimes your research forces you to refocus the speech topic). Second, if you are quoting from or paraphrasing one specific part of an article, you may need to check to make sure that you are not quoting the author out of context. Having a copy of the book chapter, the journal article, or the encyclopedia entry lets you check the context and the accuracy of your quotation.

If you are gathering information from the Internet, be sure to print the pages you will need or download the information to a disk or flash drive. Remember that what appears on the Internet disappears quickly. If you do not capture it in print or store it in a file when you find it, you may have to forgo using the information in your speech. If you do not know how to create a storage file for Internet material, ask your librarian or computer lab instructor for help.

It is important to record full citations of sources you have consulted in your research in your list of works cited at the end of your speech. Most writer's handbooks recommend a particular form. Three popular forms are presented in the *Publication Manual of the American Psychological Association,* sixth edition (APA); the *Modern Language Association Handbook for Writers of Research Papers,* seventh edition (MLA), and the *Chicago Manual of Style,* sixteenth edition (CMS). Be sure to check with your instructor, who may prefer one of these or some other bibliographic form.

Copies of the three style manuals we just listed are probably in your library's reference section. Whether you want to cite a segment of National Public Radio's *All Things Considered*, a memory-training DVD, or lecture notes you took in an anthropology class, the most recent editions of these reference books are likely to give you a pattern to follow. College and university libraries often have online guides for citing print and online resources. One of our favorites is the Purdue University Online Writing Lab (OWL).

Conclude Your Search

7.5 **Identify the appropriate time to conclude your research.**

As you prepare your speech, you must make choices. Your goal is to support your ideas with the most compelling evidence and arguments you can find. The more you know about your topic, the greater your flexibility in determining its content and, subsequently, its impact. This concept of choice can make your task more complex, but it will also produce a more effective speech.

There is a limit, however, to the time you can spend researching. An important part of effective research is knowing when to stop accumulating materials and when to start using them. In his book *Finding Facts Fast*, Alden Todd provides the following guideline for research projects:

> If the last 10 percent of your planned research time has brought excellent results, you are doubtless on a productive new track and should extend the project. But if the last 25 percent of your scheduled time has brought greatly diminished results, this fact is a signal to wind up your research.[17]

Although Todd's 10/25 formula may not be wholly applicable to your researching a speech for this class, it does highlight an important issue: at some point you must stop researching and start structuring your speech.

In Chapter 9, Learning Objectives 9.1 and 9.2 we discuss the purposes and types of supporting material. Understanding these topics will help you evaluate your research and select the best information to support the ideas of your speech.

Summary

Assess Your Knowledge

7.1 **Assess your knowledge of your speech topic.**

- Thorough research of a subject begins with assessing your knowledge of your topic and organizing that knowledge.

Develop Your Research Plan

7.2 **Construct a plan for accessing information.**

- Your research plan begins with your answers to four questions: (1) What information do I need? (2) Where am I most likely to find it? (3) How can I get this information? (4) How will time constraints affect my research options?

- Keep a list of what you need and a timetable for obtaining it.

Collect Your Information

7.3 Collect and evaluate information from appropriate sources.

- Gather information from the Internet; your library; magazines and journals; newspapers; government documents; books; reference works; television and radio; interviews; focus groups; questionnaires; and experts and organizations you may contact by mail or email.

- Productive online research requires you to be able to use available databases and to launch out onto the Internet using appropriate search engines.

- As you assemble your information, be sure to assess its purpose, expertise, objectivity, accuracy, and timeliness.

Record Your Information

7.4 Record relevant information systematically.

- The fourth step in research is to record the information you consider important and useful. You may choose to take notes, photocopy, or print your information.

- Being sure to record the source of the information using a current bibliography form.

Conclude Your Search

7.5 Identify the appropriate time to conclude your research.

- The quality and quantity of the information you collect will not only help you focus and organize your topic, but should also signal when you have exhausted your research efforts.

Chapter 8

Organizing the Body of Your Speech

 Learning Objectives

After studying this chapter, you should be able to

8.1 Construct an organizing question to identify relevant information.

8.2 Select an organizational pattern appropriate for your topic and purpose.

8.3 Develop your key ideas using the "4 S" strategy.

8.4 Construct four types of transitions to connect the key ideas in your speech.

The seventeenth-century mathematician and philosopher Blaise Pascal once wrote to a friend, "I have made this letter longer than usual, because I lack the time to make it short."[1] If you've ever furiously written several pages to answer an essay question only to discover that the answer requires just one brief paragraph, Pascal's comments

Organization: Why and How

Conduct an Internet search to access the essay, "Principles of Organization," by Professor John Friedlander of Southwest Tennessee Community College. It is an excellent explanation of the importance of organization to effective writing, thinking, and speaking. Friedlander also discusses various patterns of organization.

probably make a great deal of sense to you. It takes time to organize your thoughts to write a coherent letter or give a succinct answer to an essay question. Investing the time to organize simplifies the task in the end. Getting organized will also simplify your speech preparation and make your speech more vivid and memorable for your listeners.

A coherent speech has a beginning, a middle, and an end—what we call the *introduction*, *body*, and *conclusion*. Many speech textbooks and instructors summarize the overall strategy of a speech as follows: "Tell us what you are going to tell us. Tell us. Then, tell us what you told us." Use this organizational perspective in every speech.

In this chapter, we teach you how to organize the body of your speech. Although you deliver it after the introduction, organize the body of your speech first, for in order to "tell us what you are going to tell us," you must first determine what to tell us. In constructing the body of a speech, your best strategy is to formulate an organizing question, divide the speech into key ideas, and then develop each idea. (See also Chapter 10, Learning Objectives 10.1 and 10.2.)

Formulate an Organizing Question

8.1   Construct an organizing question to identify relevant information.

If your research is productive, you'll gather more information than you can use in your speech. Some of that information will be relevant to your topic; some of it will not. You may also be missing some information that you need to develop your topic fully. Deciding what is relevant, irrelevant, or missing requires your critical thinking skill of *analyzing* as you examine items of information and the relationships among them. You will also be *integrating* as you combine and restructure the pieces of information and *organizing* as you arrange your information so that you can present it effectively, in a way your listeners can understand.

How can you start assessing the information you have, how it fits together, and what you still need? Begin by constructing an organizing question. An **organizing question** is one that, when answered, indicates the ideas and information necessary to develop your topic. The way your question is worded will shape the structure of your speech. For example, if you wanted to speak on the process of selecting a baby's sex, you could ask any of the following organizing questions:

- What issues are involved in sex selection?
- What are the methods of sex selection?
- What are the benefits of sex selection?
- What are the problems with sex selection?

Each of these questions will lead you to a different set of answers—and thus to a different speech. The first two questions are appropriate for an informative speech, the latter two for persuasive speeches.

Suppose you selected the first organizing question: What issues are involved in sex selection? To answer this question, you would probably study the opinions and research of ethicists and medical experts, among others. From the information you collected, you might construct the following thesis statement: "Before deciding on the process of sex selection, parents should consider the ethical, medical, and social issues involved." Constructing, researching, and answering your organizing question helps you focus your speech and determine what information you will need to support it.

Write your organizing question on a notecard or a sheet of paper, and keep it in view as you sift through your research. Ask yourself periodically, "What information helps answer this question?" As you continue working, you may change your organizing question; usually it will become more specific, helping you focus your speech further.

organizing question

A question that, when answered, indicates the ideas and information necessary to develop your topic.

What does the National Holocaust Memorial Museum contain? Researching and answering this organizing question will help a speaker focus the speech and determine the information needed to support it.

You should find that your organizing question suggests a pattern, perhaps several possible patterns, of organization. Consider these examples:

- What does it take to brew a great cup of coffee?
- What does the U.S. National Holocaust Memorial Museum contain?
- Why do some people favor and others oppose the medical use of marijuana for terminally ill patients?

Answering the first question will probably require you to discover and discuss a formula or procedure (chronological organization). The second question calls for a description of the physical areas of the museum (spatial organization). The third question will require you to study and explain the arguments for and against (pro–con organization) the medical use of marijuana.

Journal: Construct an Organizing Question

Choose one of the following topics: yoga, NASCAR, Memorial Day, health-care policy, motorcycle safety, Keystone XL Pipeline. Construct two different organizing questions that you could use to develop a speech on this topic.

Divide the Speech into Key Ideas

8.2   Select an organizational pattern appropriate for your topic and purpose.

In the body of the speech, you develop your key ideas according to a specific organizational pattern or strategy. Public speakers employ a wide variety of organizational structures. We will discuss seven strategies and patterns most commonly used: (1) topical, (2) chronological, (3) spatial, (4) causal, (5) pro–con, (6) problem–solution, and (7) need–plan. The first five patterns are appropriate for either informative or persuasive speeches. Problem–solution and need–plan patterns are appropriate only for persuasive speeches.

As you consider these patterns, keep in mind that no single pattern is best. To be effective, you must select a structure that accomplishes the purpose of your speech. In other words, fit the organization to your topic rather than your topic to the organization.

Topical Division

Topical division is the most common organizational pattern for public speeches. This is a pattern, not a strategy, because it does not require you to arrange your key

topical division
Organization of a speech according to aspects, or subtopics, of the subject.

ideas in a specific order. Instead, the topical division pattern creates subtopics, or categories, that constitute the larger topic. For example, a speech on graffiti is divided topically if it focuses on graffiti as artistic expression, as political expression, and as vandalism. Note, though, that the order in which these key ideas are presented will not affect the audience members' ability to follow your speech. Similarly, a speech about the positive influence of the Hispanic/Latino culture on U.S. culture can be divided into three key points: food, language, and dance styles. However, the speech would be equally easy to follow if the key ideas were presented in any other order because they do not build on one another, they are simply subtopics, or categories, of the larger topic.

Coffee-lover Rowena organized her informative speech to cover the following points:

Specific Purpose: To inform the audience on the types and tastes of coffee
Key Ideas: I. Types of coffee
                   A. Dark roasts
                   B. Blends
                   C Decaffeinated
                   D. Specialties
              II. Tastes of coffee
                   A. Acidity
                   B. Body
                   C. Flavor

An example of topical division for a persuasive speech is as follows:

Specific Purpose: To persuade the audience to adopt a pet
Key Ideas: I. Caring for a pet reduces anxiety and stress.
              II. Caring for a pet increases exercise and physical health.
             III. Caring for a pet decreases loneliness and depression.
              IV. Caring for a pet enhances empathy and self-esteem.

As these examples suggest, topical organization is particularly appropriate as a method of narrowing broad topics, and that may explain its popularity and widespread use.

Chronological Division

Chronological division is considered a strategy because your key ideas are arranged to follow a time sequence. This organization is especially appropriate if you are explaining procedures or processes. A simple and familiar example of chronological organization is a recipe. Any well-written recipe is organized in a time sequence: First, make sure that you have these ingredients; second, preheat the oven; and so forth. Topics that begin with phrases such as "the steps to" or "the history of" may be developed chronologically. Examples of such topics include the history of your university, the biography of author Toni Morrison, the stages of intoxication, steps to getting your first job, and how a product is marketed.

The following ideas are developed chronologically:

Specific Purpose: To inform the audience of Elisabeth Kübler-Ross's five stages of dying
Key Ideas: I. Denial
              II. Anger
             III. Bargaining
              IV. Depression
               V. Acceptance

chronological division
Organization of a speech according to a time sequence.

Specific Purpose: To inform the audience about the history of garage rock
Key Ideas: I. The 1960s: The "British Invasion" Inspiration
          II. The 1980s: The Garage Rock Revival
          III. Today: The Garage Band Academy

Spatial Division

Spatial division is a strategy in which you organize your main points according to their physical proximity or geography. This pattern is appropriate for a speech discussing the parts of an object or a place. Examples of spatial division are the following:

Specific Purpose: To inform the audience about the halls and palaces of the Forbidden City in Beijing, China
Key Ideas: I. The Halls of Harmony
          II. The Palace of Heavenly Purity
          III. The Palace of Earthly Tranquility
          IV. The Hall of the Cultivation of the Mind

Specific Purpose: To inform the audience of the parts of the U.S. National Holocaust Memorial Museum
Key Ideas: I. Four classrooms, two auditoriums, and two galleries for temporary exhibits occupy the lower level.
          II. The permanent exhibit occupies four floors of the main building.
          III. The library and archives of the U.S. Holocaust Research Institute occupy the top floor.

Causal Division

Causal division is a strategy as it is used to trace a condition or action from its causes to its effects, or from effects back to causes. Medical topics in which a speaker discusses the symptoms and causes of a disease can easily be organized using this method of

spatial division

Organization of a speech according to the geography or physical structure of the subject.

causal division

Organization of a speech from cause to effect, or from effect to cause.

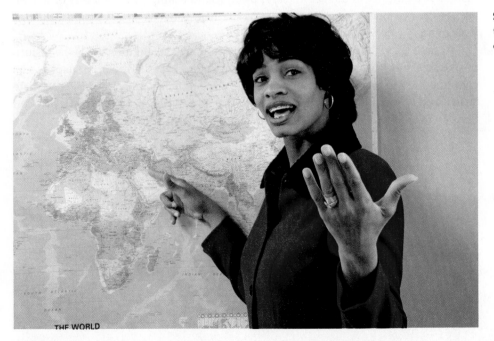

Speakers often use maps and diagrams to organize their topics spatially and to discuss the parts of places.

division. Informative speeches on topics such as hurricanes, lightning, earthquakes, and other natural phenomena may also be organized using this pattern. The following speech outline illustrates the causal pattern:

Specific Purpose: To inform the audience about the effects and causes of sports-victory riots

Key Ideas: I. Effects
      A. Death and injuries
      B. Vandalism
      C. Law enforcement costs
  II. Causes
      A. The competitive nature of sports
      B. Mob psychology
      C. Unfavorable economic conditions
      D. Inadequate police presence

Because the causal pattern may be used any time a speaker attributes causes for a particular condition, it is suitable for persuasive as well as informative speeches. A speaker could attempt to prove that certain prescription drugs are partly responsible for violent behavior among those who use them; that televising executions would lead to a call for an end to capital punishment; or that new antibiotic-resistant bacteria are promoting the incidence of infections once thought to be under control.

Pro–Con Division

Pro–con division is a strategy in which you present the arguments for and against a position. Thus, it informs you specifically of how to arrange your key ideas. Because it is balanced in perspective, this pattern is more appropriate for an informative speech than a persuasive one. After discussing each side of an issue, however, you could choose to defend the stronger position. In this case, your division becomes *pro–con-assessment*, a pattern appropriate for a persuasive speech.

Brian decided to inform his classmates on "snapping." Also known as "cracking," "dissing," and "playing the dozens," this game of insults is part of African-American history and culture. In the book *Snaps*, Brian found examples of this war of words, such as Quincy Jones's snap "Your house is so small, you have to go outside to change your mind."

At first, Brian thought he would use a topical division and discuss (1) the history of snaps, (2) how the game is played, (3) common topics, and (4) sample snaps. As he continued to research his topic, however, he discovered that there is a lively debate as to whether snapping is constructive or destructive. Brian decided to use a pro–con division to tell his listeners about the debate:

Specific Purpose: To inform the audience about the arguments for and against snapping

Key Ideas: I. Snapping should be encouraged.
      A. It is part of African-American history and culture.
      B. It is a nonviolent way of expressing hostility.
      C. It encourages imagination and creative wordplay.
  II. Snapping should be discouraged.
      A. It is demeaning.
      B. It can provoke violence.
      C. It is not an effective way to express anger.

pro–con division

Organization of a speech according to arguments for and against some policy, position, or action.

The following outline also demonstrates a pro–con analysis of a controversial issue:

Specific Purpose: To inform the audience of the arguments for and against an increase in the minimum wage

Key Ideas: I. Increasing the minimum wage would be beneficial.
   A. The number of poor people would decrease.
   B. The number of people on welfare would decrease.
   C. The concept of social justice would be affirmed.
II. Increasing the minimum wage would be harmful.
   A. Unemployment would increase.
   B. Inflation would increase.
   C. Business bankruptcies would increase.

An advantage of the pro–con pattern is that it places an issue in its broader context and provides balance and objectivity. A disadvantage, however, is the time required to do this. You need plenty of time to discuss both sides of an issue in sufficient detail. Therefore, you will probably want to use this strategy only in one of your longer speeches. If you do not devote sufficient time to each idea, a pro–con or pro–con-assessment development may seem simplistic or superficial to your audience.

Problem–Solution Division

The **problem–solution division** is a simple, rigid, organizational approach for a persuasive speech. In this approach, the major divisions of your speech and their order are predetermined: you first establish a compelling problem and then present a convincing solution. Therefore, the key ideas build on one another (problem-solution), making it a strategy. Because you advocate a plan of action, this pattern is by nature persuasive.

Speeches that call for a law or some action often use a problem–solution format, as in the following example:

Specific Purpose: To persuade the audience to support reform of our national park system

Key Ideas: I. Our national parks are threatened.
   A. Political influence is a threat.
   B. Environmental pollution is a threat.
   C. Inadequate staffing is a threat.
II. Our national parks can be saved.
   A. The National Park Service should have greater independence.
   B. Environmental laws should be stricter.
   C. Funding should be increased.

A common alternative to the problem–solution division is to divide the speech into a discussion of problems, causes, and solutions. Notice how Matthew uses this approach:

Specific Purpose: To persuade the audience that involuntary psychiatric commitment laws should be reformed

Key Ideas: I. The problems caused by involuntary commitment laws are serious.
   A. Many are potential victims of being wrongfully committed.
      1. The elderly are especially at risk.
      2. The poor are at risk.
      3. All of us are at risk.
   B. Victims face physical and financial dangers.

Problem–solution division

A rigid organizational pattern that establishes a compelling problem and offers one or more convincing solutions.

need–plan division

A variation of problem–solution organization that (1) establishes a need or deficiency, (2) offers a proposal to meet the need, (3) shows how the plan satisfies the need, and (4) suggests a plan for implementing the proposal.

II. Two factors perpetuate these problems.
   A. Medicare policies indirectly encourage hospitals to commit patients regardless of their actual health.
   B. Involuntary commitment laws are too vague.
III. To remedy this problem, we must act on three levels.
   A. The federal government must reform involuntary commitment procedures.
   B. The psychiatric industry must establish greater control over mental hospitals.
   C. We, as individuals, must take action as well.[2]

Need–Plan Division

The **need–plan division** is a variation of the problem–solution division. This fourfold approach (1) establishes a need or deficiency in the present system, (2) presents a proposal to meet the need, (3) demonstrates how the proposal satisfies the need, and (4) suggests a plan for implementing the proposal. Because it requires a specific order of your key ideas, it is considered a strategy.

Salespeople often use the need–plan strategy. They demonstrate or create a need, supply the product or service to meet that need, demonstrate or describe how well it will work, and often even arrange an easy payment plan to help guarantee your purchase. This fundamental sales approach is prevalent for one simple reason: it works! You can use this strategy when you want to prompt an audience to action.

Suppose the specific purpose of your speech is to persuade your audience that employers should provide health promotion programs for their employees. Using the need–plan pattern, you could make four arguments. First, employee illness results in absenteeism, lost productivity, and increased health care costs. Second, employers should establish on-site health and fitness centers for their employees. Third, when health promotion programs have been tried, they have reduced absenteeism, increased productivity, and capped health care costs. As your final step, you could suggest an implementation strategy to include exercise and conditioning programs, alcohol- and drug-awareness education, stress-management workshops, antismoking clinics, and health status testing and evaluation.

As previously suggested, your best approach to organizing your key ideas is to formulate an organizing question, divide the speech into key ideas, and then develop each idea. Ask yourself, *"If I heard a speech about this topic for the first time, what division strategy or pattern would make it easiest for me to follow and understand?"* Keep in mind, however, that most speeches can be organized in several ways. A speech about golf courses, for example, can be organized spatially by talking about the one closest to campus, second closest to campus, and the one farthest away from campus. These three golf courses could also be discussed chronologically by first talking about the most recently built course, the second most recently built course, and finally the oldest course. Additionally, you could organize this speech topically by arranging the three golf courses into different types, such as links, parkland, and resort courses.

> **Key Points**
>
> **Patterns for Dividing Your Speech into Key Ideas**
>
> 1. Topical division
> 2. Chronological division
> 3. Spatial division
> 4. Causal division
> 5. Pro–con division
> 6. Problem–solution division
> 7. Need–plan division

> **Journal: Selecting an Organizational Pattern**
>
> Select an organizational pattern you think would be appropriate for a speech with the specific purpose "to inform the audience about relaxation techniques." Could the specific purpose be achieved using other patterns? If so, which ones?

Develop the Key Ideas

8.3   **Develop your key ideas using the "4 S" strategy.**

Assume that your speech is divided into key ideas, that you have selected the most appropriate pattern to organize them, and that you have decided their order in the speech.

Figure 8.1 The "4 S" Strategy of Speaking

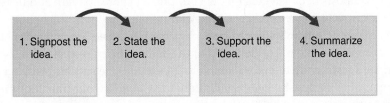

1. Signpost the idea.
2. State the idea.
3. Support the idea.
4. Summarize the idea.

Now you need to develop each major point. Obviously, the number of major points you can develop in a speech depends on the time you have been given to speak, the topic's complexity, and the audience's level of education and knowledge of the subject. There is no fixed rule, but we recommend that you develop at least two, but not more than five, main points. Many speakers find that a three-point structure works best.

Regardless of the number of points you select, your responsibility is to explain and support each one sufficiently. The organizational strategy we suggest is one we call the 4 S's; see Figure 8.1. Your listeners will better comprehend and remember your speech if you *signpost*, *state*, *support*, and *summarize* each idea.

Signpost the Idea

It's Monday morning and you're sitting in your introductory psychology class. You take notes as Dr. Potter lectures on factors that influence interpersonal attraction. In which scenario will you likely understand and remember more of what she says?

1. Dr. Potter presents her material using words and phrases such as "also," "another factor," and "moving on to similarity."

2. Dr. Potter introduces her ideas with statements such as "a third factor of attraction is proximity" and "similarity is a fourth component of attraction."

If you're like most students, you chose the second scenario. In fact, one experiment tested this and found that "students are able to process information more effectively when lecturers use obvious organizational cues." The researcher's advice to teachers is: "Incorporating organizational cues appears to pay substantial dividends. . . ."[3]

That same advice is equally important for public speakers. Because your audience may not consist of note takers, your task is even more challenging. One "obvious organizational cue" you can use is signposting. A **signpost** is a word such as *initially*, *first*, *second*, and *finally*. Just as a highway milepost tells travelers where they are in their

signpost
Numbers (*one, two, and three*) or words (*initially, second, or finally*) that signal the listener of the speaker's place in the speech.

Speaking with Confidence

Having never spoken in public before, giving a speech to a room full of strangers was quite unnerving. Not to mention that constructing a strong speech can be overwhelming for anyone who lacks the proper tools. By using the 4 S's to properly structure my speeches I was able to create a solid foundation to give me the confidence I needed. I was able to express my thoughts concisely, in a way that benefited both the audience and me. Even writing and organizing my speech became easier by using this simple but powerful framework. Oftentimes I have found myself referring back to the 4 S's, not only when developing speeches but also when writing papers. The 4 S's makes structuring key points for any topic an effective process.

MELISSA GILBERT
San Antonio College

journey, so a signpost in a speech tells the audience where they are in the speaker's message. Signposts help listeners follow your organizational pattern and increase the likelihood that they will remember your key ideas.

Take a look at Austin's speech about chewing gum. (See Appendix D.) Not only did he signpost the two major divisions of the body of his speech, he also used signposts in the substructure to make it easier to understand the specific pros and cons of chewing gum. A signpost serves as a "safety net." Even if your transition from one key idea to another isn't clear, it will become obvious that you are starting a new idea when you signpost the next point.

State the Idea

Each major idea needs to be worded precisely and with impact. In her persuasive speech, Esperanza argued the benefits of a multicultural college experience. Her specific purpose was to persuade the audience that ethnic studies (ES) courses should be required for all students. Her organizing question was:

> Why should all students be required to take ES courses?

Using a topical organization, Esperanza presented three reasons to support her proposal. Before we tell you how she actually worded those ideas, let's look at how a less experienced student might have stated them:

1. ES courses promote cultural awareness.
2. I would like to discuss ES courses and what research and expert opinion say about the way they affect conflict that may be ethnic or racial.
3. Third, social skills.

Do these points seem related? Are they easy to remember? No, they're a mess! To avoid clutter, keep the following suggestions in mind when wording your key ideas:

1. *Main headings should clearly state the points you will develop.* The first statement ("ES courses promote cultural awareness") does that; the others do not.
2. *Main headings should usually be worded as complete sentences.* Think of the main heading as a statement that you will prove with your supporting materials. Listeners would probably remember the wording of statement 1 in the previous list. As a result, they would remember the point of the speaker's evidence. That is not true for the other two statements.
3. *Main headings should be concise.* You want listeners to remember your key ideas. The first statement is easier to remember than the second. The third statement is the shortest but it isn't a complete sentence. Remembering it doesn't help you understand the point the speaker made.
4. *Main ideas should be parallel to other main ideas.* Parallel wording gives your speech rhythm and repetition, two qualities that help listeners remember your points.
5. *Main ideas should summarize the speech.* When you state your main points, listeners should see how those points answer the organizing question and achieve your specific purpose.

Now let's see how Esperanza worded each of her key ideas:

1. ES courses promote cultural awareness.
2. ES courses reduce ethnic and racial conflict.
3. ES courses improve social skills.

Each of these main headings clearly states a distinct point that Esperanza will argue. Each statement is a concise, complete sentence. All three sentences are grammatically parallel. Notice, too, that each of the three key ideas directly answers Esperanza's organizing question:

> Why should ES courses be required for all students?

An alternative to introducing your key idea as a declarative sentence is to ask a question. For example, the specific purpose of Evan's speech was:

> To inform the audience on the civil rights Freedom Rides of 1961

He organized his supporting materials to answer three questions:

1. What were the goals of the Freedom Riders?
2. What resistance did they confront?
3. What were their successes?

He introduced each of these ideas with a signpost, for example:

> The *first* question we must answer to understand this chapter in the Civil Rights Movement is: What were the goals of the Freedom Riders?

He was then ready to answer this question using various types of supporting materials.

You can usually accomplish the first two S's, signposting and stating your idea, in one sentence. For an informative speech assignment requiring the use of visual aids, our student Jennifer decided to speak about Victorian homes—America's "painted ladies." Using spatial organization, she focused her speech on interior details and decoration, taking her listeners on a virtual tour of a Victorian home she called Conglomeration House. Jennifer introduced her first key idea as follows:

> The first room we will visit on our tour of a Victorian home is the parlor, the woman's domain.

That sentence clearly signposts and states Jennifer's initial main point.

In Austin's speech about chewing gum, he stated each key idea clearly. After his first signpost, he stated the key idea by saying, "let's uncover the positive effects of chewing gum." Similarly, he stated his second key idea by saying "let's discuss the negative implications of chewing gum." (See Appendix D.)

Support the Idea

This third S is the meat of the 4 S's. Once you have signposted and stated the idea, you must support it. Several categories of supporting materials are at your disposal, limited only by the amount of research you have done and by time limits on your speech. (See Chapter 9, Learning Objective 9.2 for a discussion of examples, definitions, comparisons, and statistics.)

In her speech on Victorian homes, Jennifer combined specific language with visual aids to depict a different style of each room. For example, as part of her support for the first room, the parlor, she stated the following:

> The parlor in Conglomeration House is done in the Rococo revival style, which is almost exclusively used in interior design. In their book *The Secret Lives of Victorian Homes,* Elan and Susan Zingman-Leith, who restore Victorian houses, give us this wonderful example of this style. [Jennifer showed an enlarged photograph.] Typical of the Rococo theme, the walls are painted white or a pastel color and are broken into panels decorated with wooden molding or even artwork painted directly onto the wall. Around the windows and ceiling are intricately carved wooden details that are influenced by botanical or seashell designs. These are painted to match the color of the walls, but are heavily accented with gilt, or gold-colored paint. Following the pale color scheme, the mantel is made of marble. It is also intricately carved in a botanically inspired design and has cherubs worked into it as well.

Summarize the Idea

A summary at the end of a key idea reinforces the gist of that key idea by drawing attention to the main point discussed within that key idea. These periodic summaries may be as brief as one sentence. Early in the course, our students sometimes summarize a point by saying, "So I've told you a little about. . . ." What you say in these internal summaries within the body needs to be more substantial and more varied than that. An effective summary should reinforce the point you have just developed and also provide a note of closure for that key idea. Keep in mind, however, that your summary statements should only focus on one key idea. So, if you talked about bottled water in your first key idea and bottled soft drinks in your second idea, your second summary should only reinforce the gist of your soft drinks key idea without referencing bottled water.

If you introduced your idea as a question, your summary should provide the answer. Remember, your point is lost if the audience remembers only your question; they must remember your answer as well.

To summarize his second key idea, Austin stated,

> Researchers are continually attempting to discover connections between chewing gum and maintaining our memory. However, the phenomenon of gum chewing is very robust and it is unclear to determine whether or not chewing gum is actually beneficial.

Jennifer summarized her first key idea with the following statement:

> So the parlor gives us a wonderful example of the Rococo revival architectural style: very feminine, very ornate, and very French.

Such a summary not only clued her audience that she had finished discussing this first room but alerted them that they were about to move to the second room on the tour.

We believe that the use of the 4 S's is fundamental to effective organization within the body of any speech. As you begin to master and apply this four-step strategy, it may seem to be a cookie-cutter approach to public speaking. It is exactly that. The 4 S's are to speech organization what the required movements are to gymnastics—basics that you must learn before you can develop your own style or flair. As you master the 4 S's and gain confidence in public speaking, clear organization will become almost a reflex reaction performed without conscious effort. As your ability to organize ideas clearly becomes second nature, you will find that the structure of your thinking, writing, and speaking has greatly improved.

Ethical Decisions

CRUNCH TIME

Rosa has delayed working on her speech until the night before it is due. She logs on to the Internet and begins downloading articles related to her topic: how to avoid harming yourself with prescription drugs. The next morning, she sorts through the material, jotting down examples, statistics, and testimony she finds interesting. However, by the time she needs to leave for class, Rosa's speech is still not well organized, and she admits that her listeners may not be able to follow some of the information she plans to present. Rosa is torn between two courses of action. She does not want to get a failing grade on the speech, and she'd like to get some practice speaking in front of a group, so she is tempted to "wing it" and see what happens. "I can always clear up any confusion by answering questions later," she thinks. "After all, I have done the research." However, because she knows that some people in the audience may get lost and even misinterpret the information she presents, Rosa considers telling her instructor that she is not prepared and is willing to accept the consequences of delivering her speech late.

What would you do if you were Rosa? Would she be violating any ethical standards if she were to forge ahead and deliver her speech? Do you think that delivering a disorganized speech is an abuse of the power a speaker wields over an audience?

Theory Into Practice TIP

APPLYING THE 4 S's

Assigned to deliver an informative speech about something that originated or that exists outside of the United States, our student Alex developed the first main point in the body of his speech as follows:

> *First,* I'd like to *describe the Itsukushima Shrine's Grand O-Torii Gate* as I experienced it for the first time. Along the way I'll give you some specific details about the structure. During 1991 and halfway into 1992, I was still in the military and living in Japan. On one of our off weekends, we decided to visit the shrine in Miyajima-guchi, a small town south of the military base where we were stationed. We boarded a train and enjoyed the 30- to 45-minute ride to the small town. From the train station, we walked a short distance to a pier. There we boarded a ferry that took us to Miyajima Island, where the shrine was located. We got off the ferry and walked toward the shrine location, not knowing that it was really close. The tide was in. Suddenly, there appeared this big red Japanese gate in the water about half a football field away from where we were standing near the shore.

Signpost of key idea
Statement of key idea
Support for key idea

(narration)

(comparison)

> I was already excited from the train ride and the ferry ride. Seeing the Grand O-Torii Gate was kind of like seeing Sleeping Beauty's Castle at Disneyland for the first time. You see it in pictures and movies all the time. But seeing it for real, well, if you've been to Disneyland you know the feeling. This is what the Grand O-Torii Gate looks like when the tide is in. [Alex shows a photograph of the Grand O-Torii Gate.] It really looks like it's floating in the water, especially if you have never seen it when the tide is out.

(visual example)

> I promised you some specific details about the structure and I won't let you down. On the 3rd of June 2005, I found a website, www.hiroshima-cdas.or.jp, sponsored by a Japanese Internet service provider. The site mentions that the gate is almost 52½ feet tall and that each pillar is about 44 feet tall and at least 24½ feet around. The gate is constructed entirely of wood from the camphor tree, which is native to the area. Concrete beams and pillars support the O-Torii gate, and it's covered with vermillion, or deep red, lacquer. Because it is out at sea, partially submerged in the water, shipworms and barnacles encrust and slowly deteriorate the wood at the base. I've seen the barnacles but I had no clue of the damage that was going on. Fortunately, plastic resin has been found to be effective in preserving the wood.

(citation, source)

(statistics)

(definition)

> You can now imagine the impression the Grand O-Torii gate made on me even from a distance, but it can be even more awe-inspiring when you get a chance to stand as close to it as I did.

Summary of key idea

> Japan is, unfortunately, subject to destructive typhoons. That's why governments and organizations have banded together to help preserve this shrine for future generations. So, second, let's examine some of the work required to preserve the gate.

(transition to second key idea)

To clarify the look of the Grand O-Torii Gate for his listeners, Alex showed them this view he had seen as he stood on the shore of Miyajima Island at high tide looking out at the Sea of Japan.

Connect the Key Ideas

8.4 **Construct four types of transitions to connect the key ideas in your speech.**

A speech is composed of key ideas—the building blocks of your speech—and you have just seen how to develop each according to the "4 S" approach. For your speech to hang together, you must connect those ideas, just as a mason joins bricks and stones with mortar. A speaker moves from one idea to the next—puts mortar between the units—with the aid of a transition. A **transition** is a statement connecting one thought to another. Without transitions, the ideas of a speech are introduced abruptly. As a result, the speech lacks a smooth flow of ideas and sounds choppy.

A transition not only connects two ideas but also indicates the nature of their connection. Transitions are usually indicated by *markers*, words or phrases near the beginning of a sentence that indicate how that sentence relates to the previous one.[4] You will use some transitions *within* each of your main points to offer illustrations (*for example*), indicate place or position (*above, nearby*), or make concessions (*although, of course*).[5] However, the transitions you use *between* the main points of your speech will indicate four basic types of connections: complementary, causal, contrasting, and chronological.

A **complementary transition** adds one idea to another, thus reinforcing the major point of the speech. Typical transitional markers for complementary transitions include *also*, *and*, *in addition*, *just as important*, *likewise*, *next*, and *not only*.

Each of the following transitions uses the complementary approach to reinforce the speaker's thesis:

> It is clear, then, that golf courses have sociological effects on communities where they are located. Just as important, however, are their environmental effects.

> Vocal cues, however, are not the only source of information that may help you determine if someone is lying. You may also look for body cues.

You can also review Austin's speech. He used a complementary transition between the first and second key idea.

> In addition to the positive effects of chewing gum, it should be noted that chewing gum has also been found to have negative effects on people, or even no effects at all.

A **causal transition** emphasizes a cause–effect relationship between two ideas. Words and phrases that mark a causal relationship include *as a result, because, consequently*, and *therefore*.

In his speech, Victor documented problems resulting from excessive noise. As he shifted his focus from cause to effect, he used the following transition:

> We can see, then, that we live, work, and play in a noisy world. An unfortunate result of this clamor and cacophony is illustrated in my second point: excessive noise harms interpersonal interaction.

A **contrasting transition** shows how two ideas differ. These transitions often use markers such as *although, but, in contrast, in spite of, nevertheless, on the contrary*, and *on the other hand*.

In her tour of Conglomeration House, Jennifer moved her audience from her first to her second main idea with the following clear contrasting transition:

> In sharp contrast to the parlor is the library, the man's retreat in the home. This is the second room we will visit on our tour.

A **chronological transition** shows the time relationships between ideas and uses words or phrases such as *after, as soon as, at last, at the same time, before, later*, and *while*.

Will informed his classmates on the SQ3R system of studying and remembering written material. He organized his five main points around five key words: *survey,*

---

transition

A statement that connects parts of the speech and indicates the nature of their connection.

complementary transition

Adds one idea to another.

causal transition

Establishes a cause-effect relationship between two ideas.

contrasting transition

Shows how two ideas differ.

chronological transition

Shows how one idea precedes or follows another in time.

question, *read*, *recite*, and *review*. His transitions emphasized the natural sequence of these stages:

> After surveying, or overviewing, what you are about to read, you are ready for the second stage of the SQ3R system: to question.

A second example of a chronological transition is the following:

> If thorough preparation is the first step in a successful job interview, the second step is to arrive on time.

A good transition serves as a bridge, highlighting the idea you have just presented and preparing your listeners for the one to come. It smoothes the rough edges of the speech and enhances the cohesiveness of your ideas. Note, however, that transitions alone cannot impose order on a speech. The main ideas and their natural links must exist before you can underscore their connections with transitions.[6] Developing and pursuing an organizing question can help ensure that you know your main ideas and their connections in the first place.

Effective transitions require more than just inserting a word or phrase between two ideas. If you find yourself always using a single word such as *now*, *next*, or *okay* to introduce your ideas, you need to work on your transitions. Avoid using weak and pedestrian phrases as transitions, such as "Moving on to my next point" or "The next thing I would like to discuss." Instead, work on composing smooth, functional transition statements as Bonnie did in the following example.

In her persuasive speech, Bonnie advocated voluntary school uniforms for students in kindergarten through high school. She previewed her ideas in her introduction by stating that pilot programs demonstrate that "voluntary uniforms would help create a safer school environment, enhance academic achievement, and promote a positive social climate." In the body of her speech, Bonnie explained and supported each of these points, connecting them by using smooth transitions. Bonnie used the following excellent transition as she moved from her first to her second idea:

> Every student has a right to learn in a safe environment, and school uniforms help eliminate one cause of school violence. But schools should do more than ensure safety; they should promote learning. A second benefit of school uniforms is that they enhance academic achievement.

If you follow the guidelines and examples in this chapter, the body of your speech will be well organized. You should now know how to generate an organizing question and use it to select an organizational pattern that is appropriate to your topic, your purpose, and your audience. You should also know how to develop each main idea in the body of your speech according to the 4 S's and how to connect those main ideas with appropriate transitions. (See Chapter 10, Learning Objectives 10.1 and 10.2, for discussions of extending this excellent organization to the introduction and conclusion of your speech.)

> **Journal: Assessing Transitions**
>
> Which of the following transitions is more effective: (1) "Now that you have heard arguments supporting the pipeline, let's look at key arguments against it" or (2) "Now that you have heard these arguments, let's explore different ones." Explain why. What type of transition is it?

> **Key Points**
> **Transitions**
>
> 1. Complementary transition
> 2. Causal transition
> 3. Contrasting transition
> 4. Chronological transition

Summary

Formulate an Organizing Question

8.1 **Construct an organizing question to identify relevant information.**

- Answering an organizing question will help you determine the main ideas and information you need in order to develop your topic. Your answer should also suggest possible ways of organizing the body of your speech.

Divide the Speech into Key Ideas

8.2 **Select an organizational pattern appropriate for your topic and purpose.**

- There are seven organizational patterns for the body of the speech. Five are appropriate for both informative and persuasive speeches: *topical division, chronological division, spatial division, causal division,* and *pro–con division*.

- Two organizational patterns are appropriate only for persuasive speeches: *problem–solution division* and *need–plan division*.

Develop the Key Ideas

8.3 Develop your key ideas using the "4 S" strategy.

- To organize the presentation of each major idea in the body of your speech, we recommend the memory device we call the 4 S's: *signpost* the idea, *state* the idea, *support* the idea, and *summarize* the idea. Apply these four steps to each major idea in the speech.

Connect the Key Ideas

8.4 Construct four types of transitions to connect the key ideas in your speech.

- Each of the main points you develop needs to be connected to the next main point using a transition. Effective transitions indicate the nature of the relation between the ideas: *complementary, causal, contrasting,* or *chronological.*

Chapter 9
Supporting Your Speech

 Learning Objectives

After studying this chapter, you should be able to

9.1 Explain the four purposes of supporting materials.

9.2 Develop supporting materials that are appropriate to your topic, your audience, and yourself (the speaker).

9.3 Apply the seven guidelines for evaluating the validity and strength of your evidence.

9.4 Cite sources while delivering your speech.

A fact in itself is nothing. It is valuable only for the idea attached to it, or for the proof which it furnishes.

—Claude Bernard

When you think of argument, you likely think of two people trying to persuade each other. In a real sense, however, all public speaking is argument. We should speak and accept ideas only if they are supported with sufficient evidence and reasoning. Speakers must prove what they assert in both informative and persuasive speeches. Listeners should think critically and evaluate the merits of any statement based on evidence the speaker offers for its support.

In this text, we recommend applying a formula for structuring each major idea in your speech. This pattern, called the "4 S" Strategy, consists of *signposting*, *stating*, *supporting*, and *summarizing* each key idea. In this chapter, we focus on the third of these four S's: *supporting* your major ideas. You will learn more about the purposes of supporting materials, and we will discuss seven types you can use. Finally, we'll suggest ways to evaluate evidence and how to cite it to ensure that you communicate your ideas clearly, memorably, and authoritatively (see Figure 9.1). (See Chapter 8, Learning Objective 8.3.)

Figure 9.1 Supporting Your Speech in the "4 S" Strategy of Speaking

1. Signpost the idea.   2. State the idea.   **3. Support the idea.**   4. Summarize the idea.

Purposes of Supporting Materials

9.1   **Explain the four purposes of supporting materials.**

You will use supporting materials in your speeches to provide specific points of reference for your audience. Effective supporting materials help you anchor your ideas in the minds of your listeners. They do so by giving your ideas clarity, vividness, relevance, and credibility.

Clarity

A sign in an Austrian ski hotel says, "Not to perambulate the corridors in the hours of repose in the boots of ascension."[1] Translation (we assume): "Don't tramp down the halls in ski boots while guests are sleeping." You have no doubt seen other examples of what happens when well-meaning people try to translate something into an unfamiliar language. Yet people can send unclear messages even in their first language. Thus we have an advertisement on a bag of chips: "You may be a winner! Details inside! No purchase necessary."

As a speaker, your first goal is to communicate clearly. *Clarity* refers to the exactness of a message. The clarity of any message you send results partly from your language. In addition, the supporting material you choose should make your message clear. As you develop a speech, ask yourself, "Does my supporting material really explain, amplify, or illustrate the point I'm trying to make?" If it does not, disregard it and continue your search for relevant material. Clear supporting materials help listeners understand your ideas.

Vividness

Which of the following sentences makes a stronger impression?

> An online practice test program is a helpful teaching tool in the classroom.

or

> An online practice test program is a wise and genial tutor, giving immediate feedback and waiting patiently until the student masters the task at hand.

If you are typical, you chose the second sentence. The first statement seems flat, generic. The second personalizes the technology, gives it human qualities, and creates an image that remains with you for a while.

In this chapter, we use several excerpts from speeches to illustrate various types of supporting materials. Once you finish reading this chapter, you will no doubt remember some of the examples and forget others. Those you remember will be ones you found particularly vivid. *Vivid* supporting materials are striking, graphic, intense, and memorable. A major purpose of supporting materials, then, is to help your audience remember the key points in your speech. You will accomplish this best by using vivid forms of support chosen with your unique audience in mind.

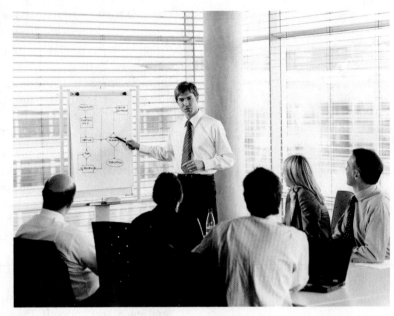

Supporting materials clarify, enliven, and add credibility to your speech. When you prepare your speech, ensure accuracy by recording in complete form any quotations and definitions you plan to use.

Relevance

When you listen to your professors in class, you probably appreciate their efforts to make the course content relevant and applicable to you. In fact, this often motivates students to learn more in class. Audience members of relevant speakers also develop positive attitudes toward the speakers and they generally follow the speakers' recommendations. So, relevance means that speakers structure both their verbal and the nonverbal messages in a way that establishes a connection with the audience.[2]

You can enhance your perceived topic relevance verbally by using examples with which the audience members are familiar. For instance, if you are a Penn State student, you can make a speech about student athletes more relevant to your audience by using examples of athletic teams on your Penn State campus. Nonverbally, you enhance your perceived topic relevance by using illustrators to accompany various types of supporting materials, such as using a definition by visual example. If you are giving a speech about boxing, you can illustrate how a boxer "throws" an uppercut while you orally define that particular method of hitting the opponent. Illustrate how a boxer initiates an uppercut by lowering her or his hand below the waist and then moves it upward rapidly. By doing this, your audience members can see how they can use an uppercut if ever in a boxing match.

Credibility

You gasp as you see the headline "Scientists Discover Microbial Life on Mars." Would it make a difference whether you saw this on the cover of *Scientific American* or the *National Enquirer*? Of course it would. A scientific article reviewed and selected for publication by a panel of experts is significantly more believable than an article from any weekly tabloid. **Credibility** refers to the dependability or believability of a speaker or that speaker's sources.

Many ideas in the speeches you prepare will require simple supporting materials: short definitions, brief examples, or quick comparisons, for example. In other instances, you may present complex or controversial ideas that require several types of supporting materials. Whether your supporting materials are simple or complex, they must be accurate and their sources clearly cited if they are to reinforce your ethos, or credibility. A speech with all its ideas and support taken from a single source is too limited. Using several sources to corroborate your ideas and facts can be a valuable and persuasive tool. Your main points will be more credible if you show that these ideas are shared by several experts.

credibility

The believability or dependability of speakers and their sources.

You establish clarity by explaining your idea so that listeners *understand* it. You establish vividness by presenting your idea so that listeners will *remember* it. You establish topic relevance by *relating* your topic to some aspect of your audience members' lives. Finally, you establish credibility by presenting the idea so that listeners *believe* it. If the supporting materials in your speech make the audience understand, remember, and believe what you say, you have done a good job selecting them.

Accomplishing these goals will require you to use four critical thinking skills. *Focus* on and *evaluate* specific pieces of information and measure their quality. *Analyze* the different supporting materials to see how they fit together to clarify your message. Finally, *integrate* as you combine and restructure your information in a way that is both appropriate to your listeners and uniquely your own.

Types of Supporting Materials

9.2 **Develop supporting materials that are appropriate to your topic, your audience, and yourself (the speaker).**

To help you achieve clarity, vividness, relevance, and credibility in your speaking, consider seven types of supporting materials available to you: example, definition, narration, comparison, contrast, statistics, and testimony. Keep in mind that there is no best type of support for your ideas. Select what is most appropriate to your topic, your audience, and yourself.

Example

An **example** is a specific illustration of a category of people, places, objects, actions, experiences, or conditions. In other words, examples are specimens or representations of a general group. The sound of the word itself gives perhaps the easiest definition to remember: An *example* is a *sample* of something. Measles, mumps, and chicken pox are examples of common childhood illnesses. *The Kids are All Right* and *Laurel Canyon* are examples of Lisa Cholodenko movies. Using examples that are familiar to listeners is an excellent way to make your points clear, relevant, and memorable. This, of course, requires you to have done some good audience analysis.

Our student, Ashkan, provided examples of Turkish empires in his speech about the Turkish culture by stating that "Some of those empires include the Great Hun, Uygar, Avar, and many more."

BRIEF EXAMPLES. Brief examples are short, specific instances of the general category you are discussing. They may be used individually but are often grouped together. Notice how Jocelyn combined several brief examples early in her speech on the attractions of New York City:

> Your walking tour of midtown Manhattan could take you to places as diverse as St. Patrick's Cathedral, Rockefeller Center, and the Museum of Modern Art. Try not to gawk as you look at some of the most famous architecture in the world—the Chrysler Building, the Empire State Building, and Grand Central Station. Tired of pounding the pavement? Slip into a chair in the Algonquin Hotel's dim lobby, soak up the literary history, ring the bell on your table, and order something to drink. Hungry? You've got the world's table to choose from—everything from four-star restaurants to little holes-in-the-wall serving the best ethnic dishes: Chinese, Vietnamese, Indian, Mexican, Thai.

example

A sample or illustration of a category of people, places, objects, actions, experiences, or conditions.

EXTENDED EXAMPLES. Extended examples are lengthier and more elaborate than brief examples. They allow you to create more detailed pictures of a person, place, object, experience, or condition. Later in her speech, Jocelyn developed an extended example of one of her favorite New York City attractions:

> Beginning with my second visit to New York, one of my first stops has usually been the Museum of Modern Art. If you're like me, you'll need to give yourself at least a couple of hours here, because for a small admission price you're going to get a chance to see up close art that you've only seen before as photographs in books. Upstairs on my last visit, I saw works such as Vincent Van Gogh's *Starry Night* and Roy Lichtenstein's huge pop art paintings of comic strip panels. On a wall with a number of other paintings was a canvas so small that I almost missed it. I'm glad I didn't. It was Salvador Dali's famous surrealist work, *The Persistence of Memory*, with its melting clock and watch faces. Then over in a corner is a special room that holds only one painting. As you walk in, you see an expanse of gray carpet and several upholstered benches. One wall is glass, two others are white and bare, but the fourth one holds the three panels of Claude Monet's massive painting, *Water Lilies*.

Notice how vividly this extended example suggests a scene and re-creates an experience. But whether your examples are brief or extended, they can be of two further types: actual and hypothetical.

ACTUAL EXAMPLES.   An **actual example** is real or true. Each of the examples we've used so far is an actual example. Lisa Cholodenko did direct the two films listed. The Chrysler Building and the Empire State Building are famous New York landmarks.

Notice how Kyle tells a real story in his speech on the health of 9/11 recovery workers:

> Upon graduating as an NYPD detective, Michael Valentin took an oath to have utmost "loyalty, bravery, and fidelity." So on the morning of 9/11, Valentin could do nothing else than selflessly and heroically put his fears second and head straight to downtown Manhattan. For 2 months he searched for the bodies, but within weeks of working at the site, Valentin began feeling numbness in his hands, coughing up blood, and developed a cancer mass the size of a lemon outside his lung. Now every breath he takes is a choice between a life of pain and no life at all.[3]

Later in this chapter, we'll show how Kyle combined this one example with statistics, another type of supporting material, to develop a compelling case for helping 9/11 recovery workers.

HYPOTHETICAL EXAMPLES.   A **hypothetical example** is imaginary or fictitious. A speaker often signals hypothetical examples with phrases such as "Suppose that," "Imagine yourself," or "What if." Hypothetical examples clarify and vivify the point you are making, but they do not prove the point.

Notice how the following introduction mentions actual products but places them in a hypothetical situation. The speaker chose this method knowing that not all listeners would have all the products listed. The speaker then generalizes from these examples to support the claim that we live in an electronic world.

> We wake up in the morning to soothing music coming from our AM-FM digital clock radio equipped with a gentle wake-up feature. We stumble downstairs, enticed by the aroma of coffee brewed by a preset coffee maker with 24-hour digital clock timer and automatic shut-off function. We zap on our 37-inch wide-screen HDTV with on-screen display of current time and channel. As we sit in our six-way action recliner, we use our 26-function wireless remote to perform the ritual of the morning channel check. Finding nothing that captures our interest, we decide instead to watch the video of last week's family reunion recorded with our 12X power zoom, fully automatic digital camcorder with self-timer, electronic viewfinder, and "flying erase head for 'rainbow'-free edits." Oh dear! What would our grandparents think? Certainly, we live in an electronic world!

actual example

A true instance or illustration.

hypothetical example

An imaginary or fictitious instance or illustration.

Definition

A **definition** tells us the meaning of a word, a phrase, or a concept. Definitions are essential if your audience is unfamiliar with the vocabulary you use or if there are multiple definitions of a particular term. In her speech on the protection of animals, Paris used the terms *animal welfare* and *animal rights* interchangeably. Her speech confused and misled her listeners. You want to clarify terms early in your speech so you don't confuse your listeners and lose their attention. For instance, in his second key idea, Ashkan noted that in Turkey, the "father is the head of the household, meaning he holds all authority in the house." In the second part of this statement, Ashkan defined what it means to be the "head of the household" in Turkey.

Definitions can take several forms. Four of the most common are definition by synonym, definition by etymology, definition by example, and definition by operation. Choose the form most appropriate to your audience and to the term you want to clarify.

DEFINITION BY SYNONYM. The first type of definition is **definition by synonym**. Synonyms are words that have similar meanings. Consider these pairs of words:

mendacity and *dishonesty*	*pariah* and *outcast*
obviate and *prevent*	*anathema* and *curse*
mitigate and *lessen*	*surreptitious* and *secret*

Each word is coupled with one of its synonyms. The first word of each pair may not be a part of your listeners' working vocabularies. As a speaker, you would want to use the second word in each pair; because those words are more familiar, they communicate more clearly. As the joke goes, never use a big word when a diminutive one will do.

DEFINITION BY ETYMOLOGY. A second type of definition is **definition by etymology**. Etymology is the study of word origins. Describing how a word has developed may clarify its meaning. You can use this type of definition to highlight the unusual nature of a familiar term. The reference section of your library and a variety of websites have several dictionaries of word origins and histories of word usage that may be useful as you prepare your speeches.

DEFINITION BY EXAMPLE. An example is a specific instance or illustration of a larger group or classification. **Definition by example** uses a specific instance to clarify a general category or concept. In his informative speech on violent crimes, Jacob presented two definitions to help his audience understand the distinction between "assault" and "battery."

> According to the Chicago Police Department website, accessed last Saturday, "In Illinois assault is a threat, while battery is an actual attack." The New York Public Library Desk Reference provides a more vivid explanation. Their 2002 calendar draws this distinction: "If you angrily shake your fist at someone, it's legally considered assault. If you follow up your actions by punching the person in the nose, the offense is assault and battery."

Jacob first used definition by synonym and then definition by example to clarify the distinction between these two terms.

You need not confine your definitions by example to language, however. Often audible and visual examples can be the quickest and most vivid ways to define a term or concept.

Audible examples are those you let your audience hear. Speeches on types of music, voice patterns, or speech dialects could define key terms by audible examples. For instance, if you used the word *scat* in a speech on jazz, you could offer a dictionary definition of the term: "jazz singing that uses nonsense syllables."[4] But wouldn't a taped example be more memorable to your audience?

definition

An explanation of the meaning of a word, phrase, or concept.

definition by synonym

Substitution of a word having similar meaning for the word being defined.

definition by etymology

Explanation of the origin of the word being defined.

definition by example

Providing an instance or illustration of the word being defined.

Visual examples define a term by letting the audience see a form of what you are describing. If you're using the term *krumping* in a speech on contemporary dance, you could construct a definition, using phrases that describe the term, for example: a style of urban street dance that integrates elaborate face painting and facial expressions with exaggerated movements of arms and legs to suggest the expressive style of hip-hop. But a more vivid way to define the term might be to show a video clip of dancers *krumping*.

DEFINITION BY OPERATION.   Sometimes the quickest and liveliest way to define a term is to explain how it is used. **Definition by operation** clarifies a word or phrase by explaining how an object or concept works, what it does, or what it was designed to do. The terms radar detector, MP3 player, and laser scalpel are but a few of the physical objects best defined by explaining their operation.

You can also define concepts, actions, or processes by operation. To define magnetic resonance imaging, you would have to explain how that technology operates. Notice how the following speaker defines an unfamiliar term by explaining its function:

> Humpback whales feed themselves by the technique of "bubble netting." A group of four or five whales will locate a school of krill or other small fish. The whales dive deep, encircling the fish and releasing a curtain of rising bubbles. The bubbles confuse the krill and force them into a tight column. The humpbacks then surface through the middle of the column with their mouths wide open, enjoying the feast.

Definition by operation is often livelier and clearer than many dictionary definitions. It can also be especially useful in the case of new technologies whose dictionary definitions have yet to be written.

Narration

Narration is storytelling, the process of describing an action or a series of occurrences. If you come to school on Monday and tell a friend about something you did during the weekend, you are narrating those events.

PERSONAL NARRATIVE.   As a participant in the events, you will probably speak in first person at least part of the time, using the pronouns *I* or *we*. Such a story is called a **personal narrative**. We have suggested that you draw on your own experiences as you select and develop a speech topic, and personal narratives can be rich and interesting supporting materials.

Let's pretend that Henric, an international student from Croatia, wants to deliver a speech to actuate in which he attempts to persuade his audience to visit his native country. To enhance his speech, Henric could use a personal narrative by stating, "When I visit Croatia during the summer, I go snorkeling in the clear Adriatic Sea water. I also travel to the many beautiful islands, and I enjoy their amazing pizzas."

THIRD-PERSON NARRATIVE.   Narratives need not be personal but may relate incidents in the lives of others. When you speak from someone else's point of view and use the pronouns *he, she,* or *they,* you are telling a **third-person narrative**.

In the following example, notice how Chiwoneso used third-person narrative to illustrate the need for improved global food aid policies.

> Muna is an eight-year-old girl from Mulonda, Zambia. Every morning she walks to a food distribution point set up by the World Food Program at a nearby hospital. She holds tightly to her battered tin cup as she waits in line for hours to receive the mixture of corn and soy powder, but the stocks are running low and like every other day, she walks home empty-handed. Muna's reality is that she is an AIDS orphan who struggles to stay alive, but she will not die from AIDS; more than likely she will die of hunger.[5]

Journal: Using Definitions

Discuss a method of definition you could use for each of the following terms:

a. Palpable
b. Ballistic fingerprinting
c. Speed dating

definition by operation

Explanation of how the object or concept being defined works, what it does, or what it was designed to do.

narration

The process of describing an action or series of occurrences; storytelling.

personal narrative

A story told from the viewpoint of a participant in the action and using the pronouns *I* or *we*.

third-person narrative

A story told from the viewpoint of a witness and using the pronouns *he, she,* or *they.*

comparison

The process of associating two items by pointing out their similarities.

literal comparison

Associations between two items that share actual similarities.

figurative comparison

Associations between two items that do not share actual similarities.

contrast

The process of distinguishing two items by pointing out their differences.

literal contrast

Distinctions between two items that share actual differences.

figurative contrast

Distinctions between two items that do not have actual differences.

Comparison

Comparison is the process of depicting one item—a person, place, object, or concept—by pointing out its similarities to another, more familiar item. Just as examples can be actual or hypothetical, comparisons can be literal or figurative.

LITERAL COMPARISON.   A **literal comparison** associates items that share actual similarities. Roger spoke on the need for a national high-speed rail network. He framed his speech using a comparison with the Interstate Highway System, developed in the 1950s through 1970s. Roger argued that the interstate system significantly promoted economic growth, decreased travel time, and increased travel safety and mobility. The challenge, he noted, was that it required a strong national commitment of vision, patience, and resources. Roger used literal comparison as he presented these same arguments for a high-speed rail system.

FIGURATIVE COMPARISON.   When you draw a **figurative comparison**, you associate two items that do not necessarily share actual similarities. The purpose of figurative comparisons is to surprise the listener into seeing or considering one person, place, object, or concept in a new way.

Effective figurative comparisons must contain an element of surprise, as well as a spark of recognition. Katherine highlighted the enormous popularity of the social-networking site Facebook when she quoted from the May 2011 issue of *Success*: "If Facebook were a nation, it would be the world's third largest nation, behind only China and India."

Contrast

Contrast links two items by showing their differences. A **literal contrast** distinguishes items that do share some similarities. A **figurative contrast**, on the other hand, distinguishes items that share no similarities. In a persuasive speech on the dangers of overexposure to the sun, our student Patricia effectively used the following literal contrast:

> Sunblocks are either chemical or physical. Oils, lotions, and creams that claim a certain SPF factor all contain chemical blocks. On the other hand, zinc oxide, the white or colored clay-looking material you see some people wearing, usually on their noses, is a physical block.

You can use comparison and contrast together in your speech. If you clarify a term by showing how it is similar to something the audience knows, you can often make the term even clearer by showing how it differs from something the audience also knows.

Another student, Paul, used a variety of supporting materials to document problems of exercise anorexia, an addiction to exercise:

Supporting materials, such as visual aids, can help make complicated concepts clearer and easier for an audience to grasp.

> According to *Psychology Today*, June 2005, this disorder can affect 35 percent of those who work out three to five times a week for more than an hour each time. Specific symptoms can be when someone exercises even when ill, or withdraws from others to exercise, or becomes upset if unable to work out. Just like alcoholics, exercise anorexics are literally addicted to their behavior. But unlike alcoholism, exercise anorexia is an even bigger epidemic because people don't recognize that there is a problem.[6]

Paul explained exercise anorexia by comparing and contrasting it with alcoholism. He also demonstrated the dimension of this problem by using statistics, the next type of supporting material we discuss.

Statistics

Statistics are collections of data. Broadly speaking, any number used as supporting material is a statistic. Think of how much trust politicians and the general public put in preference polls gathered before elections. Statistics can predict certain events in our daily lives, such as price increases or decreases on certain goods and services. Used appropriately, statistics can make your ideas clear and vivid, can increase your credibility, and can prove your point. For instance, in his speech about gum chewers, Austin claimed that "In a survey consisting of American undergraduate students, 'nearly 87 percent confirmed that they chew gum at least occasionally.'" He also stated that chewing gum has "even become a billion dollar industry." These statements clarify the widespread use of chewing gum.

Used inappropriately, however, statistics may baffle, bore, or even mislead your audience. The following five suggestions should guide you in presenting statistical material.

DO NOT RELY EXCLUSIVELY ON STATISTICS.   If statistics are your only form of supporting material, your audience will likely feel bombarded by numbers. Since your listening audience has only one chance to hear and assimilate your statistics, use statistics judiciously and in combination with other forms of support.

Remember Kyle's speech on the health of 9/11 recovery workers? He used a real example, NYPD detective Michael Valentin, to illustrate serious health consequences and to tap listeners' emotions. Kyle then introduced statistics to demonstrate the breadth of this problem:

> But, Valentine is not alone in his illness. A September 5, 2006, CBS News article reveals an astonishing 70 percent of the 40,000 recovery workers who responded to the attack on the World Trade Center are suffering lung problems.[7]

ROUND OFF STATISTICS.   A statistic of 74.6 percent has less impact and is more difficult for your audience to remember than "nearly three-fourths." No one in your audience will remember the statistic of $1,497,568.42; many, however, may be able to remember "a million and a half dollars." Rounding off statistics for your listeners is neither deceptive nor unethical. Instead, it reflects your concern for helping your audience understand and retain key statistical information.

USE UNITS OF MEASURE THAT ARE FAMILIAR TO YOUR AUDIENCE.   In her speech on London tourist attractions, Veronica described the London Eye as being "135 meters high—equivalent to 64 red telephone boxes stacked on top of one another." If she had stopped there, listeners unfamiliar with the metric system or with British phone boxes would have had only a vague idea of the height Veronica was describing. However, she wisely converted meters to feet, adding that the London Eye is 443 feet tall.

USE PRESENTATIONAL AIDS TO REPRESENT OR CLARIFY RELATIONSHIPS AMONG STATISTICS.   In his first informative speech of the semester, Alec discussed U.S. college study-abroad programs. He accessed a report by the Institute of International Education listing the percentages of students studying in various host countries: 20.4 percent in the United Kingdom, 9.7 percent in Spain, 9 percent in Italy, 8.3 percent in France, and so forth. Alec decided that his classmates would remember more of this information if he presented it orally and visually. So he constructed a chart that ranked these nations according to the percentage of U.S. students studying there. Listeners were able to see the rankings and focus on the particular countries where they would like to study.

EXPLORING ONLINE

Locating Statistics

Need a statistic to document the extent of a condition or problem? Access the Statistic Brain website, with information and statistics divided into categories ranging from crimes, to food, to sports.

statistics

Data collected in the form of numbers

STRESS THE IMPACT OF LARGE NUMBERS. Former U.S. Surgeon General C. Everett Koop used statistics effectively to make his point that tobacco-related diseases cause significant deaths. Notice how he used repetition and helped his audience visualize the enormity of these deaths:

> Let's start with a factual description of the problem. Based on the calculations of the finest statistical minds in the world and the World Health Organization, they have predicted that by 2025, . . . 500 million people worldwide will die of tobacco-related disease. That's a numbing figure. It is too large to take in, so let me put it in other terms for you. That's a Vietnam War every day for 27 years. That's a Bhopal every 2 hours for 27 years. That's a Titanic every 43 minutes for 27 years.
>
> If we were to build for those tobacco victims a memorial such as the Vietnam Wall, it would stretch from here [Washington, D.C.] 1,000 miles across seven states to Kansas City. And, if you want to put it in terms per minute, there's a death [every] 1.7 seconds, or about 250 to 300 people since I began to speak to you this afternoon.[8]

Testimony

Examples, definition, narration, comparison, contrast, and statistics are discrete types of supporting materials. Each is a different strategy for validating the ideas of a speech. Speakers sometimes generate these types of support themselves. Other times, they glean them from their research, citing their sources but justifying the point in their own words. Still other times, speakers find the words and structure of the original source so compelling that they quote directly or paraphrase the source. This latter strategy is known as **testimony**, or quotation.

Testimony is a commonly used supporting material. It is therefore not surprising that both of our students, Ashkan and Austin, used testimony to support their arguments. In his last key idea, Ashkan noted that "Hande Bozdagan, a famous Turkish chef has said, 'Turkish food is amongst the top three greatest cuisines in the world.'" Similarly, in his first key idea, Austin stated that "in 2011, Tucha and Simpson reported that chewing gum has a positive effect on healthy adults' abilities in maintaining focus during extended periods of time."

In his speech "Ribbons: Function or Fashion," Tony discussed how wearing an awareness ribbon can inform and connect communities. To give his ideas credibility, he used the testimony of a communication professor and an animal welfare website:

> Dr. Judith Trent, a communication professor at the University of Cincinnati, states in the *Cincinnati Enquirer* of September 18, 2001, that wearing a ribbon "shows you're a part of something that's larger than yourself. It helps to unify and support the cause. It's a public signal about a private thought." By wearing ribbons, people can easily give support and find comfort in people around them. The Purple Ribbon Campaign website, last updated July 15, 2003, states, "Wearing a ribbon allows a person to represent their hopes and drive for a better day to come. It also provides support to others in letting them know that they are not suffering alone."[9]

Tony clearly identified two sources and quoted them directly, trusting their credibility and their words to persuade his listeners. Testimony relies largely on the reputation of the source being quoted or paraphrased.

Expert testimony is not limited to the statements of other people, however. As a speaker, you use *personal testimony* when you support your ideas with your own experiences and observations. Many students select a speech topic because they have some special knowledge or experience with the subject. One student, for example, gave a speech comparing retail prices at large supermarkets to those at convenience stores. He was careful to explain his credentials and establish his expertise in the subject. Not

testimony

Quotations or paraphrases of an authoritative source to clarify or prove a point.

Speaking with Confidence

Before presenting my speech on how to start a new small business, I began gathering and evaluating the supporting materials I would use to support my key ideas. Like most speakers, I searched online for information. I was careful to be selective and to avoid web pages that were based on personal opinion and bias. I supplemented the examples and statistics I found with my own expert testimony as a successful, self-employed businessman. I cited my sources to establish my credibility and let my listeners assess the quality of my data and documentation. Knowing that I had selected and tested my supporting materials allowed me to minimize my use of qualifiers such as "I think," "this might," and "maybe." I was confident with what I said, and the audience could be confident with what they heard.

JOVAN COKER
Radford University

only did he wear his store apron and manager's name tag, but he also said early in his introduction, "As a former receiving control manager, I was in charge of purchasing products for the store, so I have some knowledge of how wholesale prices are translated into the retail prices you and I pay." The speaker enhanced his credibility both verbally and nonverbally. Speakers should choose supporting materials carefully and ethically.

Tests of Evidence

9.3   **Apply the seven guidelines for evaluating the validity and strength of your evidence.**

The positions you develop in your speech will be only as strong as the evidence supporting them. Seven guidelines will help you evaluate the validity and strength of your supporting materials. These suggestions will also help you evaluate evidence you hear others present in their speeches.

Is the Evidence Quoted in Context?

Evidence is quoted *in context* if it accurately reflects the source's statement on the topic. Evidence is quoted *out of context* if it distorts the source's position on the topic. For example, suppose Joyce was preparing a speech on hate crimes on campus. She read in the campus paper the following statement by the president of her college:

> We've been fortunate that our campus has been relatively free of bias-motivated crimes. In fact, last year, only two such incidents were reported—the lowest figure in the past 5 years. Yet no matter how small the number is, any hate crime constitutes a serious problem on this campus. We will not be satisfied until our campus is completely free from all bias-motivated intimidation.

Now, suppose Joyce used the following statement to support her position that hate crimes are prevalent on campus:

> We need to be concerned about a widespread and growing problem on our campus: the prevalence of hate crimes. Just this past week, for example, our president argued that hate crimes constitute, and I quote, "a serious problem on this campus."

The president did say those words, but Joyce failed to mention the president's position that hate crimes on campus are few and decreasing. By omitting this fact, she has distorted the president's message. Joyce has presented the evidence out of context.

The evidence you cite in your speech should accurately represent each source's position on the topic.

Is the Source of the Evidence an Expert?

If you delivered a speech advocating the licensing of law clerks to draft wills and conduct other routine legal business, would you rather quote a first-year lawyer or a senior law partner of a major legal corporation? Of course, it would depend on the specific individuals and what they said, but you would probably place more trust in the more experienced person.

An expert is a person qualified to speak on a particular topic. We trust the opinions and observations of others based on their position, education, training, or experience. The chairperson of a committee that has studied the effects of a community-based sentencing program is knowledgeable about that issue. A person completing graduate study on the effects of a local Head Start program on literacy has also developed an area of expertise. As a speaker, select the most qualified sources to support your position.

Our student who compared the pricing policies of large supermarkets and convenience stores was careful to establish his own credibility both verbally and nonverbally. When you fail to present your qualifications or the qualifications of those you quote, you give listeners little reason to believe you.

Is the Source of the Evidence Unbiased?

When Markdown Marty of Marty's Used Cars tells you he has the best deals in town, do you accept that claim without questioning it? Probably not. Marty may be an expert on used cars, but he's understandably biased. When individuals have a vested interest in a product, a service, or an issue, they are often less objective.

You expect representatives of political parties, special-interest groups, business corporations, labor unions, and so forth to make statements advancing their interests. For example, the supermarket receiving control manager we quoted earlier concluded his speech by stating that it is more economical to shop at large supermarkets than at convenience stores. When you include testimony and quotations in your speeches, try to rely on objective experts who do not have a vested interest in sustaining the positions they voice.

Ethical Decisions

BIASED SOURCES: TO USE OR NOT TO USE

You probably wouldn't be surprised that a Gallup study sponsored by Motorola found that people who use cellular phones are more successful in business than those who don't or that a Gallup poll sponsored by the zinc industry revealed that 62 percent of Americans want to keep the penny. These are just two examples that *Wall Street Journal* writer and editor Cynthia Crossen uses in her book *Tainted Truth: The Manipulation of Fact in America* to illustrate the difficulty of distinguishing between neutral research and commercially sponsored studies.

Assume that you are preparing to give a speech about how college students' use of iPads® for note-taking impacts their academic performance. While researching your topic, you find a study that suggests that students who use iPads for note-taking earn higher grades than students who take notes using traditional notebooks. When you look for the source, you see that the study was sponsored by Apple—the iPad manufacturer.

What course of action should you follow? Should you disregard the findings because the study was sponsored by Apple, use the findings without mentioning the study's sponsor, mention the findings and acknowledge that the study was sponsored by Apple, or treat the findings in some other way?

Is the Evidence Relevant?

Evidence should relate to the speaker's claim. Sounds pretty obvious, doesn't it? However, both speakers and listeners often fail to apply this guideline in evaluating evidence. A speaker who contends that amateur boxing is dangerous but presents only evidence of injuries to professional boxers has clearly violated the relevance criterion. However, many times irrelevant evidence is difficult to detect.

Ryan's speech called for increased funding of medical trauma centers. Throughout his speech, he cited the need for the specialized care provided in these facilities. Yet when he estimated the demand for this care, he used statistics of emergency room use. Trauma centers are not the same as emergency rooms. Therefore, Ryan's evidence was irrelevant to his argument. As you construct your speech, make certain your evidence relates specifically to your key points.

Is the Evidence Specific?

Which of the following statements is more informative?

> The new convention center will increase tourism a lot.

> The new convention center will increase tourism by 40 percent.

What does "a lot" mean in the first statement? 20 percent? 50 percent? 80 percent? We don't know. The second statement is more precise. Because it is specific, we are better able to assess the impact of the new convention center. Words such as *lots*, *many*, *numerous*, and *very* are vague. When possible, replace them with specific or precise words or phrases.

Notice how Tasha used specific evidence to document her assertion that there is a need for organ donors.

> As of April 22, 2009, at 8 p.m., 101,719 people wait hopefully for an organ, cited by the OPTN, Organ Procurement and Transplantation Network's website. To put this growing number into perspective, The *Saturday Evening Post* of December 1989 reported that at that time, 17,000 names were on the list. That's a 590 percent increase in the past 20 years.[10]

Is the Evidence Sufficient?

In her speech on rap music, Lea played excerpts from two rap songs, one of which she characterized as antiwoman and the other as antipolice. She encouraged her listeners to boycott rap music because "it demeans women and law enforcement officers." Lea did not apply this sixth guideline to her evidence. Two examples do not justify a blanket indictment of rap music.

In considering the guideline of sufficiency, ask yourself, "Is there enough evidence to prove the point?" Three examples of college athletes graduating without acquiring basic writing skills are insufficient to prove that athletes are failing to get a good education. One example may illustrate a claim, but it will rarely prove it. Make certain you have sufficient evidence to support your points.

Is the Evidence Timely?

If you were preparing a travel budget for a trip overseas, which would you find more helpful: an airline ticket pricing schedule you had from last year or one you printed from a travel website this week? Of course you would want to rely on more recent information. The timeliness of information is especially important if you are speaking about constantly changing issues, conditions, or events. What you read today may already be dated by the time you give your speech.

Key Points

Tests of Evidence

1. Is the evidence quoted in context?
2. Is the source of the evidence an expert?
3. Is the source of the evidence unbiased?
4. Is the evidence relevant?
5. Is the evidence specific?
6. Is the evidence sufficient?
7. Is the evidence timely?

Some speech topics, however, are timeless. If you speak about the gods of Mount Olympus, no one would question your use of Robert Graves's *Greek Gods and Heroes*, published in 1960. As a scholar of mythology, Graves earned a reputation that time is not likely to diminish. Similarly, if you deliver a speech on the ancient Olympic Games, your most authoritative sources may be history textbooks. If, however, your topic concerns current drug-testing procedures in Olympic competition, it would be vital for you to use the most recent sources of the best quality you can find. The date of your evidence must be appropriate to your specific argument.

Supporting Materials and Sources

So far, you have learned about several different types of supporting materials and how to evaluate the quality of your supporting materials. It is important, however, to understand the difference between supporting materials and sources. Sources refer to where you obtained your information whereas supporting materials refer to what type of information you extracted from a source. A source can contain several types of supporting materials. In this book, for example, we provide definitions of various terms, such as communication; we use testimony when reporting specific research findings; and we use statistics when discussing the prevalence of communication apprehension among college students. Thus, you can often find many different types of supporting materials in any given source. But to boost the effectiveness of your supporting materials, you need to cite your sources.

Citing Your Sources

9.4   Cite sources while delivering your speech.

A bibliography of quality sources you consulted in researching your speech will build your credibility with your instructor. However, most of your listeners will not have an opportunity to see it. To acknowledge your sources and to take credit for the research you have done, you will need to provide "oral footnotes" for ideas and supporting materials in your speech that are not your own. Doing so accomplishes two goals. First, clear source citations enhance the credibility of what you say by demonstrating that experts and data support your position. Second, clear source citations help interested listeners find published sources that they might wish to read or study.

How do you "orally footnote" sources as you deliver your speech? Your instructor may require more or less information in oral source citations than we do, so be sure to check. Our rule of thumb is this: give only the information necessary to build the credibility of the source but enough information to help listeners find your source if they wish.

Do you need to include *all* the information that was in your bibliographic entry for the source? No. Only the most active listener would remember the title and page numbers of a journal article or the publisher of a book that you cite, for example. Is there any information not in your bibliography that you *should* mention as you cite a source? Yes. To establish the credibility of any source you name, you need to explain at least briefly that individual's qualifications. You can usually find such information somewhere in the book, magazine, journal, or website you are using. If not, check a biographical database.

If the author is a newspaper or magazine staff writer, however, you do not need to name that individual. If the publication has a corporate author (a group, committee, or organization), just mentioning the name of the group or organization is probably sufficient. The date of publication may be extremely important to building credibility on a current topic. For periodicals published weekly or for online magazines that are frequently updated, specify the date, month, and year that the material was published or that you accessed the source.

Orally footnoting Internet sources poses special challenges. Though it is never acceptable just to say, "I found a web page that said . . ." or "I found this on Yahoo!," most listeners will not remember a long URL. If the URL is simple and easily recognizable, mention it: "pbs.org," "cnn.com," or "espn.com," for example. Identifying the sponsor of a website is important. If you cannot identify the group or individual who published and maintains the site, you may need to look for a better source.

Compare the following source citations:

Instead of saying:	Say this:
"Studs Terkel says in his book *Will the Circle Be Unbroken?* . . ."	Studs Terkel, Pulitzer Prize–winning oral historian, says in his 2001 book *Will the Circle Be Unbroken?* . . ."
"In an article I found online . . ."	"Senior reporter Sandra Garcia's article titled "Math Education" in the July 16, 2014, issue of the *Wilmington Star News* indicates that . . ."
"Leigh T. Hollins says in his article in the journal *Fire Engineering* . . ."	"Leigh T. Hollins, a certified EMT and battalion chief in the Manatee County, Florida, fire department, says in his article in the June 2005 issue of the journal *Fire Engineering* . . ."
"Based on the Bureau of Labor Statistics . . ."	"Based on the March 3, 2014, updates of U.S. Department of Labor's Bureau of Labor Statistics website . . ."
"I found an article at memory.loc .gov/ammem/jrhtml/jr1940.html . . ."	"On March 12 of this year, I found an article entitled 'Breaking the Color Line: 1940–1946.' It's a link from the Recreation and Sports collection of the Library of Congress's website American Memory . . ."

In each case, the oral footnote that takes a few more words identifies the source more clearly and more specifically, and would reinforce the speaker's credibility. Note that oral citations can be phrased in several different ways. To avoid redundancy, try to avoid citing all sources in a similar manner, such as "According to . . ." The "Theory Into Practice" feature summarizes our advice for citing books, articles, and other types of sources.

Theory Into Practice TIP

INFORMATION FOR ORAL FOOTNOTES

If you are citing:	Tell us:
A magazine/journal article	That it is an article, the title of the magazine or journal, the author's name and credentials (if other than a staff writer), and the date of publication
A newspaper article	That it is an article, the name of the newspaper, the author's name and credentials (if other than a staff writer), and the date of the issue you are citing
A website	The title of the web page; the name of the individual, agency, association, group, or company sponsoring the site; and the date of publication, last update, or the date you accessed it
A book	That it is a book, the author's name(s) and credentials, the book's title, and the date of publication

An interview you conducted	That you interviewed the person, the person's name, and her or his position or title
A television or radio program	The title of the show, the channel or network airing it, and the date of broadcast
A videotape or DVD	The title of the tape or disk and the date of publication
A reference work	The title of the work and the date of publication
A government document	The title of the document, the name of the agency or government branch that published it, and the date of publication
A brochure or pamphlet	That it is a brochure; its title; the name of the agency, association, group, or company that published it; and the date of publication (if available)

Summary

Purposes of Supporting Materials

9.1 Explain the four purposes of supporting materials.

- Supporting materials in a speech achieve four purposes: *clarity, vividness, relevance,* and *credibility.* Clarity helps the audience understand your ideas. Vividness assists them in remembering your ideas. Relevance enables the audience members to make a personal connection with the topic. Credible supporting materials make your ideas believable.

Types of Supporting Materials

9.2 Develop supporting materials that are appropriate to your topic, your audience, and yourself (the speaker).

- Types of material you can use to support the main ideas of your speech include example, definition, narration, comparison, contrast, statistics, and testimony.

- *Examples* are samples or illustrations of a category.

- *Definitions* are explanations of an unfamiliar term or of a word having several possible meanings. We can define terms by synonym, etymology, example, or operation.

- *Narration* is storytelling. Narratives may be personal or third person.

- *Comparisons* associate two or more items to show the similarities between or among them. Comparisons can be either literal or figurative.

- *Contrasts* function like comparisons except that their purpose is to distinguish or show differences between or among two or more items. Contrasts can be either literal or figurative.

- *Statistics* are data collected in the form of numbers. Used properly, they can bolster a speaker's credibility and lend vivid support to the ideas of the speech.

- You use *testimony* when you cite, quote, or paraphrase authoritative sources. The authorities you cite may employ examples, definitions, narration, comparison, contrast, or statistics. *Personal testimony* comes from your own experience.

Tests of Evidence

9.3 Apply the seven guidelines for evaluating the validity and strength of your evidence.

- To ensure that your supporting materials are credible, answer seven questions about each piece of evidence you consider using: Is the evidence quoted in context? Is the source of the evidence an expert? Is the source of the evidence unbiased? Is the evidence relevant to the point you are making? Is the evidence specific? Is the evidence sufficient to prove your point? Is the evidence timely?

Citing Your Sources

9.4 Cite sources while delivering your speech.

- If you use supporting materials that others have developed, you must cite them in your speech by providing "oral footnotes." You should offer enough information to establish the credibility of the source without overwhelming the listener.

Chapter 10
Introducing and Concluding Your Speech

 Learning Objectives

After studying this chapter, you should be able to

10.1 Construct an introduction that achieves the five objectives of effective speech introductions.

10.2 Construct a conclusion that achieves the three objectives of effective speech conclusions.

Although famed Southern writer Eudora Welty refers specifically to beginning and ending a short story or novel, her quotation also applies to public speaking. As a speaker, your first words can make a positive impression on your audience, capture

I think the end is implicit in the beginning. It must be. If that isn't there in the beginning, you don't know what you're working toward. You should have a sense of a story's shape and form and its destination, all of which is like a flower inside a seed.

—Eudora Welty

their attention, prepare them to listen more effectively, and enlist their support. These first words are crucial, of course, because they can occur only once in a given speech.

In Chapter 8, Learning Objectives 8.2 and 8.3, you learned how to organize the most substantial part of your speech, the body. In this chapter, we examine how you frame the body of your speech by discussing the objectives of speech introductions and conclusions, as well as specific strategies you can use at these important points.

Introducing Your Speech

10.1 Construct an introduction that achieves the five objectives of effective speech introductions.

After you work on the body of your speech, you are ready to focus on the introduction and conclusion. An introduction should achieve five objectives: (1) get the attention of your audience, (2) state your topic, (3) establish the importance of your topic, (4) establish your credibility to speak on your topic, and (5) preview the key ideas of your speech. Studying these objectives and the ways to achieve them will enable you to get your speech off to a clear, interesting start.

Get the Attention of Your Audience

Your first objective as a speaker is to secure the audience's attention. The way you get the audience involved in your speech will depend on your personality, your purpose, your topic, your audience, and the occasion. Your options include the following seven possible techniques.

QUESTION YOUR AUDIENCE.   A speaker can get an audience involved through the use of questions, either rhetorical or direct. A **rhetorical question** stimulates thought but is not intended to elicit an overt response. For example, consider the following opening questions:

- How did you spend last weekend? Watching television? Going to a movie? Sleeping late?
- What would you do if you saw your best friend copying another student's answers during a test?
- Do you remember what first attracted you to this school?

A speaker who asks any of the above questions does not expect an overt audience response. In fact, it would probably disrupt the rhythm of the presentation if someone answered orally. A question is rhetorical if it is designed to get the audience thinking about the topic.

A **direct question** seeks a public response. Audience members may be asked to respond vocally or physically. For example, in Austin's speech about "gum chewers," he gets the audience members' attention by asking, "By a show of hands, how many of you in this room chew gum?" Other examples of questions that could be answered by a show of hands are:

- How many of you have worked as a volunteer for some charitable group within the last year? The last 6 months?
- Last week the Student Government Association sponsored a blood drive. Raise your hand if you donated blood.

Like the rhetorical question, a direct question gets the audience thinking about your topic. However, the direct question has the additional advantage of getting your listeners physically involved in your speech and, consequently, making them more

rhetorical question
A question designed to stimulate thought without demanding an overt response.

direct question
A question that asks for an overt response from listeners.

alert. This strategy may be especially appropriate if you are the first or final speaker, or if you give your speech when your listeners are especially tired.

When you ask a direct question and you want oral responses, you need to pause, look at your listeners, and give them sufficient time to respond. If you want a direct question answered by a show of hands, raise your hand as you end the question. In this way, you indicate nonverbally how you want the question answered. If you seek and get oral responses, however, make sure that you neither lose control nor turn your public speech into a group discussion. Practice these techniques as you rehearse in front of friends before making them part of your speech.

There are two final cautions about using a question to get the audience's attention. First, avoid asking embarrassing questions. "How many of you are on scholastic probation?" "Has anyone in here ever spent a night in jail?" Common sense should tell you that most people would be reluctant to answer direct questions such as these. Second, don't use a question without first considering its usefulness to your speech. Don't rely on a question just because you have not developed or found a more creative attention getter. Asking a relevant question that listeners answer either openly or to themselves gets them immediately involved and thinking about your speech topic.

AROUSE YOUR AUDIENCE'S CURIOSITY.   A lively way to engage the minds of your listeners is through suspense. Get them wondering what is to come. Ashkan began his speech, "They were once part of the Ottoman Empire. Their country is filled with rich influences left and right, and the capital is known as Ankara." Ashkan aroused the audience's curiosity by providing this information before he identified his topic of Turkish culture.

Angela chose to keep her audience in suspense in her attention-getting step as she described an arrest scene.

> On a dark and stormy night in May 2008 outside Chicago's O'Hare International Airport, Stefanie Giesselbach and Magnus von Buddenbrock thought they had gotten away with the perfect crime. Unfortunately for them, it wasn't their families waiting for them at the gate. After six years of investigations that began in Australia when imports from Singapore were intercepted, they were arrested for their involvement in an 80-million-dollar laundering scheme. Fifteen more people and six companies worldwide were stung with indictments in a scheme to avoid $80 million in anti-dumping duties.

Angela paused and then resolved the suspense by stating the topic of her speech: "The crime: honey laundering."[1]

STIMULATE YOUR AUDIENCE'S IMAGINATION.   Another way to engage the minds of your listeners is to stimulate their imaginations. To do this, you must know what referents they share, and this requires some good audience analysis on your part. Notice in the following example how Shanika began her speech by relating her topic to an experience with which her audience would be familiar:

> Imagine yourself on a white sandy beach. The sun is shining and the clear blue water is only 25–30 feet away. You have a freshly squeezed orange drink in your hand and your best friend is next to you. As you enjoy this amazing moment you think about all the fun adventures and experiences you have ahead of you.

Notice Shanika's use of visualization and sensory appeal. In the rest of her speech, she provided four compelling reasons for why college students should visit Jamaica during their spring break.

In Chapter 12, we discuss the use of language to create these and other sensory impressions in your audience.

EXPLORING ONLINE

Quotations

If you want to find a profound or funny quotation to get your listeners' attention, search the Internet for Bartleby quotations. This site offers a searchable database that provides thousands of entries from multiple sources, including the venerable *Bartlett's Familiar Quotations.*

PROMISE YOUR AUDIENCE SOMETHING BENEFICIAL.   We listen more carefully to messages that are in our self-interest. If you can promise your audience members something that meets one or more of their needs, you secure their attention very quickly. Remember that audience members who perceive the speaker's topic to be relevant are motivated to listen to the speaker. For example, beginning your speech with the statement "Every person in this room can find a satisfying summer internship related to your major field of study" immediately secures the attention of your listeners— at least those not currently working in their dream jobs. Other effective examples are ones in which a speaker promises that her information can save audience members hundreds of dollars in income tax next April, or in which a speaker says, "The information I will give you in the next 10 minutes will help you buy an excellent used car with complete confidence." Job satisfaction, savings, and consumer confidence—the promises of these three attention getters—are directly related to the interests of many audience members.

AMUSE YOUR AUDIENCE.   The use of humor can be one of a speaker's most effective attention-getting strategies. Getting the audience to laugh with you makes them alert and relaxed. You can use humor to emphasize key ideas in your speech, to show a favorable self-image, or to defuse audience hostility. However, any humor you use should be tasteful and relevant to your topic or the speaking occasion. As a speaker, you must be able to make a smooth and logical transition between your humorous opening and your speech topic. Telling a joke or a funny story and then switching abruptly to a serious topic trivializes the topic and may offend your listeners.

Stacey encouraged her classmates to study a foreign language, introducing her classroom speech with the following attention-getting riddle:

> What do you call someone who is fluent in many languages? A polylingual. What do you call someone who is fluent in two languages? A bilingual. What do you call someone who is fluent in only one language? An American!
>
> This is a joke commonly told among the Japanese. Behind the apparent humor of this joke are some embarrassing truths.

Stacey combined humor and rhetorical questions to get her listeners' attention. She then discussed those "embarrassing truths" and the price we pay for speaking only one language.

Tasteful and relevant humor can capture your audience's attention and prepare them to listen to the rest of your speech.

ENERGIZE YOUR AUDIENCE. Sometimes speakers can command attention simply by their presence. Martin Luther King, Jr., had that ability. Although few people can achieve such dynamism, most speakers can work to enliven their delivery. A positive attitude, appropriate dress, a confident walk to the platform, direct eye contact, a friendly smile, erect posture, a strong voice, and forceful gestures give an introduction as much impact as any of the preceding strategies. Conversely, the absence of these elements can destroy the effect of even the best-worded opening statement. Remember that an energized delivery is not a stand-alone strategy. It cannot substitute for a well-worded opening statement, but rather it is best used in combination with one of the other attention-getting strategies. Not only can an "energized" presence get your audience's attention as you begin your speech, it can help keep their attention throughout your speech.

ACKNOWLEDGE AND COMPLIMENT YOUR AUDIENCE. At some point in your life, you will probably be called on to deliver a formal, public speech to an assembled group. Perhaps you will be the keynote speaker for a convention, or maybe you will accept an award from a civic group. Such an occasion usually requires that you begin by acknowledging the audience and key dignitaries. On July 20, 2011, U.S. Secretary of State Hillary Clinton, addressed the Working Women's Forum in Chennai, India. She began by acknowledging its founder and president, Dr. Jaya Arunachalam. Notice how Clinton praised the organization's mission of improving the "economic, social, and cultural status of poor working women" in India.

> I want to thank my friend and your friend, a wonderful woman who is viewed as a leader around the world, Jaya. [Applause] I want you to know that I have admired the work of the Working Women's Forum for many years. [Applause] In 1978, there were only 800 women members. Today, there are more than one million of you. I am honored to be here with you to celebrate your accomplishments in bringing micro-credit to women, in bringing healthcare and other services to women so that they could have a better life for themselves and their children. [Applause][2]

Secretary Clinton complimented her audience on their accomplishments and used words such as *I*, *my*, *you*, and *your* to demonstrate a shared commitment.

In this class, your classmates make up your audience. You have interacted with them and by now probably know them pretty well. To begin your speech formally by acknowledging and complimenting them would seem stiff and insincere. You should not have to compliment fellow classmates; in fact, if you have prepared well, they

> **Key Points**
> **Strategies for Getting Your Audience's Attention**
> 1. Question your audience.
> 2. Arouse curiosity.
> 3. Stimulate imagination.
> 4. Promise something beneficial.
> 5. Amuse your audience.
> 6. Energize your audience.
> 7. Acknowledge and compliment your audience.

Speaking with Confidence

AMANDA GIPSON
Pennsylvania State
University Hazleton

If you fail to attain your audience's attention in the introduction, you won't have it in the rest of your speech. My introduction's success in my speech on Virtual Cyber Charter Schools was important not only for the rest of my speech but also because it would become the audience's first impression of me. I asked the audience members to close their eyes and picture a classroom, not one of rows of desks, but one with a computer and headset that existed in virtual space. By starting off with this place I knew well and wanted to share, I felt confident in my ability to deliver an effective introduction.

When I asked my audience to open their eyes, I could see that their imaginations were stimulated. Their genuine interest allowed me to be confident throughout the entire speech, especially in the parts that were complicated, like explaining the nuances between curriculum choices available to cyber students. By asking my audience to close their eyes for the briefest of moments, my own were opened to a whole new facet of myself: self-assurance.

should be thanking you for providing excellent information. For your assigned speeches, therefore, choose one of the other attention-getting strategies we have discussed.

State Your Topic

Once you have your audience's attention, state the topic or purpose of your speech directly and succinctly. For an informative speech, your statement of purpose typically takes the form of a simple declarative sentence. "Today, I will show you how you can improve your study skills" clearly informs the audience of your topic.

This second goal of a speech introduction is vitally important, even though the actual statement of purpose will take only a few seconds for you to say. Consider the following beginning section of a speech introduction:

> How many of you have had a cholesterol count taken in the last year? Do you know what your numbers are and what they mean? It seems like we have all recently become much more aware of good cholesterol and bad, high-density lipoproteins and low-density ones, the dangers of high-fat diets and how difficult they can be to avoid in these fast-food, nuke-it-till-it's-hot times. People who never really considered exercising are spending a lot of money to join health clubs and work out. They know that a high cholesterol count can mean you are in danger of developing arteriosclerosis and finding yourself a candidate for surgery. Even if you don't have a heart attack, you may be hospitalized for one of several new procedures to clean out arteries clogged with plaque.

Now answer the following question: What was the speaker's purpose?

a. To discuss the interpretation of cholesterol tests.

b. To explain sources of cholesterol in popular food.

c. To encourage exercise as a key to reducing serum cholesterol.

d. To explain new nonsurgical procedures for opening clogged arteries.

e. I can't tell what the speaker's purpose was.

Unfortunately, in this case, the correct answer is e. What went wrong? The speaker started off well enough by using two legitimate questions—the first direct, the second rhetorical—as an attention getter. But then things got out of control; for almost a minute of speaking time, the speaker lapsed into a series of generalizations without ever stating the purpose of the speech. This excerpt represents a minute of wasted time! In a 5- to 7-minute speech, that minute represents one-fifth to one-seventh of total speaking time. The speaker

Ethical Decisions

REVEALING VERSUS CONCEALING YOUR PURPOSE

Yvonne has decided on a specific purpose for her persuasive speech: to convince her classmates that same-sex couples should have equal access to adopt children. As she analyzes her audience's attitudes, she concludes that some of her classmates disagree with her position, a few quite strongly. She is fearful that if she reveals her specific purpose in the introduction, some audience members will stop listening to her speech objectively and will either begin formulating counterarguments or simply tune her out. She decides that, instead, she will delay the announcement of her purpose and present some basic criteria for a good family. After securing agreement on these criteria, she will then reveal her purpose for speaking—to an audience that is primed to listen.

Is Yvonne's strategy ethical? Is it acceptable for speakers to conceal their purposes in an introduction in order to keep their audiences' attention? If you think this strategy is legitimate, write an example of a situation in which it would be justifiable. Try to list and explain the ethical guidelines speakers should follow in making decisions about this strategy.

has confused the audience with vague statements and has lost their confidence. The real shame is that any of the four purposes just listed could be the goal of a good speech. Prepare properly and you will know your purpose. Then, state that purpose clearly as the second step of your introduction.

Establish the Importance of Your Topic

The third goal in organizing the introduction to your speech should be to convince the listeners that the topic is important to them. You want to motivate them to listen further. In his speech titled "The New Catch-22: Unemployment Discrimination," Michael stated:

> This [unemployment discrimination] should alarm us for several reasons. Now even though the economy is beginning to show signs of recovery, the Bureau of Labor Statistics of April 6, 2012, still points out there are 5.3 million Americans who have been unemployed for seven months or more because of the recession. It's not fair to discriminate against them. Second, many of us at this tournament will soon be looking for jobs in the "real world." And I'm guessing we won't have an employment track record either--unless you count the fast food industry.[3]

(You can read Michael's full speech in Appendix D.)

In the introduction of his speech about heart disease in women, Jake provided statistics and examples to establish the importance of his topic for the women and men in his audience:

> "[T]he truth," as stated in the *Pittsburgh Post Gazette* of December 12, 2000, "is that heart disease kills more women every year than all forms of cancer, chronic lung disease, pneumonia, diabetes, accidents, and AIDS combined." Whereas one in twenty-eight women will die of breast cancer, one in five will die of heart disease. And guys, before you take the next nine minutes to decide what you'll eat for lunch, ask yourself one question, "What would my life be like if the women who make it meaningful are not there?" Clearly, this is an issue that concerns us all.[4]

Speakers can motivate audience members to listen by explaining how the topic affects them.

Establish Your Credibility to Speak on Your Topic

The fourth goal of a speech introduction is to establish your credibility to speak on your topic. Your listeners should understand why you selected your topic and should believe that you are qualified to speak on your topic. Establishing your credibility begins in the introduction and should continue throughout your speech. Introducing relevant supporting materials and citing sources are two ways to demonstrate that you have carefully researched and considered your topic.

You can also enhance your credibility by drawing on your experience with your topic. In the introduction of his speech about the Turkish culture, our student Ashkan mentioned that he lived in Turkey for two years. Therefore, the audience members were aware of Ashkan's first-hand experience with the Turkish culture, which

preview
A statement that orients the audience by revealing how the speaker has organized the body of a speech.

enhanced his credibility. However, Ashkan also mentioned that he had conducted research about the Turkish culture, which enhanced his credibility further.

In his speech about gum chewers, Austin referenced two sources in his introduction, which indicated that he had conducted research on his speech topic. Not only did this help establish the topic's importance for his listeners, it also established his credibility to speak on his topic. Austin stated, "In a survey consisting of American undergraduate students, 'nearly 87 percent confirmed that they chew gum at least occasionally.'" He added, "Chewing gum has grown into being one of the world's oldest candies [and] has even become a billion dollar industry."

Preview Your Key Ideas

A final objective in organizing your introduction is the **preview**, in which you "tell us what you're going to tell us." The preview, working like a map, shows a final destination and reveals how the speaker intends to get there. As a result, the audience can travel more easily through the body of the speech. A speaker addressing the issue of urban decay could preview her speech by saying, "To better understand the scope of this problem, we must look at four measurable conditions: the unemployment rate, housing starts, the poverty level, and the crime rate." That preview lists the four topics to be covered in the body of the speech and prepares the audience to listen more intelligently.

Preview statements are usually only one sentence, but they can also be two or three sentences. Rarely do they need to be longer. Each of the following examples is appropriately brief and specific.

- Ashkan previewed his key ideas by stating, "[The most important aspects of the Turkish culture that I will share with you today are its historical background, family structure, and foods."

- Austin previewed his key ideas by stating, "Today, I will inform you first on the positive effects of chewing gum, and second, I will inform you on the negative effects of gum chewing."

- Michael previewed his key ideas by stating, "In order to do so, we must first reveal the damage created by this discrimination, second refute its reasoning, and finally provide the specific steps to solve for what the National Employment Law Project's executive director Christine Owens fears "'is becoming business as usual.'"

Preview statements, however, are often bland and predictable. Use your creativity to accent the ideas that will follow. For example, Jayme could have used the following preview statement in her speech on e-paper: "To understand the potential impact of e-paper, we must look first at what it is and how it works; next, at its advantages and disadvantages; and finally, at its future." Although this statement previews the key ideas of the speech, it conveys little creativity. Instead, Jayme opted for a longer statement to reinforce the ideas of her speech:

> In order to understand why the impact of e-paper could be of Gutenberg proportions, we must first start with a blank sheet as we explore what e-paper is and how it works; next, fill up the page with its advantages and disadvantages; and finally, widen the margins to discuss future directions of this amazing new technology.[5]

If you achieve the five objectives we have outlined for a speech introduction, your audience should be attentive, know the purpose of your speech, be motivated to listen, trust your qualifications to speak on the topic, and know the major ideas you will discuss. To see how one student achieved these goals, read the "Theory Into Practice: Annotated Sample Introduction."

Key Points

Functions of a Speech Introduction

1. Get the attention of your audience.
2. State your topic.
3. Establish the importance of your topic.
4. Establish your credibility to speak on your topic.
5. Preview the key ideas of your speech.

Theory Into Practice TIP

ANNOTATED SAMPLE INTRODUCTION

Tess Drager of South Central College in Minnesota was a semi-finalist at the 2013 Interstate Oratorical Association contest. Notice how she developed a complete and effective introduction using the five steps we've discussed.[6]

Minnesota native and loving mother of five, Marilyn Joyce Moulds died at the age of 76. Marilyn dealt with severe uncontrollable diarrhea, dehydration, debilitating abdominal cramping, and an inability to keep foods or liquids down. Doctors removed parts of her colon to help stem the infection, but she only lived a few months after her routine abdominal surgery.

Tess uses description and visualization to arouse her listeners' curiosity.

Marilyn died due to a dangerous *Clostridium difficile* infection. *Clostridium difficile*, also known as C-Diff. It is a deadly bacterium that infects the human colon, causing a person to become extremely ill.

Tess introduces her topic and defines C-Diff infection.

But death from this deadly disease is not uncommon. In fact, according to the *Federal Agency for Health Care Research and Quality* more than 9 percent of C-Diff-related hospitalizations end in death—nearly five times the rate for other hospital stays. This equates to 30,000 deaths a year. When you consider automobile accidents take 32,000 lives a year, one can see how serious this condition is. This deadly bacterium is running rampant and is not just costing human lives, but also costing us over $1 billion in extra in health care costs each year according to the Centers for Disease Control.

Tess uses statistics to establish her topic's importance and to reinforce her knowledge of the topic.

I work in a nursing home and I am exposed to C-Diff on a daily basis. This is a very serious bacterium, which very few of us know anything about. This bacterium causes serious problems and we cannot ignore it any longer.

Tess enhances her credibility by mentioning her work experience.

Today we are going to look at this resilient bacterium by first exploring some of the harms associated with C-Diff. Second, I will elaborate on the causes of this spread before finally providing some simple suggestions on how to slow down C-Diff so people like Marilyn won't have to die anymore.

Tess previews the key ideas she will develop in the body of her speech.

Concluding Your Speech

10.2 Construct a conclusion that achieves the three objectives of effective speech conclusions.

The final part of the speech is the conclusion. Although it is often briefer than the introduction, your conclusion is vitally important to achieving your desired response. The conclusion is the last section your listeners hear and see and must be well planned and carefully organized. It will be easier to develop if you work to achieve three goals: restate your key ideas, activate audience response to your speech, and provide closure.

Restate Your Key Ideas

When you **restate your key ideas**, you "tell us what you told us." Of all the steps in the process of organization, this should be the easiest to construct. You have already organized the body of the speech and, from it, constructed a preview statement. Restatement parallels your preview. If your speech develops three key ideas, you reiterate them. If your speech is on self-concept enhancement, for example, you may simply say, "A good self-concept, therefore, benefits us in three ways. It enhances our social interaction, our academic achievement, and our career success." A speech on dying might be phrased: "Denial. Anger. Bargaining. Depression. Acceptance. These are the five stages of dying described by Kübler-Ross."

Restating your key ideas is more than simply repeating key words. The goal is to show how those ideas support the goal of your speech. Remember that Ashkan said he was going to talk about three aspects of the Turkish culture when he previewed his key ideas. In his conclusion he restating those ideas and connected them to his topic by stating, "Today I talked about Turkey's historical background, family structure, and foods. Hopefully what you have learned today has given you a better understanding of the basic components of the Turkish culture." By adding one more sentence after merely reiterating his key ideas, he effectively connected the key points to the overall purpose of his speech, which was to provide a general understanding of the Turkish culture.

Therefore, when you restate your key ideas, you should also strive to give the listener one last chance to hear and remember the main points of your presentation and how they reinforce the purpose of your speech. As such, it reinforces the ideas of the speech and brings it to a logical conclusion.

Activate Audience Response

What do you want your audience to do with the information you have provided or the arguments you have proved? The second function of a speech conclusion is to activate an audience response by letting your listeners know whether you want them to accept, remember, use, believe, or act on the content of your speech. Whether your speech is informative or persuasive, you want your audience to be involved with your information and ideas. The conclusion is your last opportunity to ensure this. If you have provided practical information that can make your listeners smarter, healthier, happier, or wealthier, challenge them to remember and use what they learned. If you have educated them about a problem and proposed a solution to it, remind them of the significance of not acting. If you have spoken on a topic that you find inherently interesting, hoping to generate audience interest by communicating your enthusiasm as well as your information, this is your last opportunity to invigorate or animate your listeners about the subject.

Rather than saying, "I hope you'll find what I've said about the film scores of Philip Glass useful," you might say something like this: "The next time you find your attention drawn to a movie's sound track because you like the music or feel that it could stand on its own, think about the painstaking process of matching sight and sound that an acclaimed composer like Philip Glass has to go through."

This function of the conclusion is generally easier to fulfill in a persuasive speech than an informative speech. In persuasive speeches, your goal is to influence your listeners' attitudes, beliefs, values, or behaviors. So, when you activate audience response in a persuasive speech, you should emphasize how you want your audience to think, feel, or act. For instance, if you have given a persuasive speech in which your goal was to reduce your audience members' caffeine consumption, you may activate audience response by saying: Considering the health risks associated with excessive caffeine consumption, I encourage you to alternate between caffeinated and caffeine-free drinks every other day to reduce the risk of caffeine-related health implications.

In an informative speech, however, you act like a teacher in that you provide information. It is then up to the audience to decide what to do with that information. Therefore, you should not tell your audience how to think, feel, or act when you activate audience response in your informative speeches. Instead, you have to approach this function objectively. Let's assume that you have given a speech about Germany. Rather than encouraging your audience members to visit Germany, which would be persuasive, you may want to say: The information I have shared with you today about Germany may be useful to you in the future. If you are ever considering a trip to Europe, you may want to review this information, as it will help you plan your vacation.

In her speech, Kimberly discussed an often overlooked problem: motorists who run red lights. Using vivid examples, expert testimony, and compelling statistics, she documented the problem: More than "200,000 people are injured and more than 800 people die every year in the United States due to motorists running red lights."[7] She called for individual, community, and government action to combat the problem.

After reiterating the key ideas in her speech's conclusion, Kimberly sought to activate personal responsibility in her listeners:

> On your way home tonight, when you approach that traffic light, think of the facts we have talked about today. These facts apply to you every time you approach a traffic signal. Don't run red lights! When we take an extra minute or two to stop for the light, we are helping to protect hundreds of innocent people. The lives you save could be your neighbor's, your mother's, or your own.[8]

Provide Closure

When you restate your key ideas, you conclude your speech *logically*, but your activation and closure statements end the speech *psychologically*. An effective final statement ties the speech together and provides a strong note of closure. You should not have to tell your listeners that the speech is finished. Your wording, as well as your delivery, should make this clear. Without resorting to saying, "In conclusion," or "To conclude," you should mark the end of your speech by slowing your rate, maintaining direct eye contact with your listeners, and pausing briefly before and after your final sentence.

Sometimes a speaker employs what is called a **circular conclusion**, in which the final statement echoes or refers to the attention-getting step of the introduction. Remember Ashkan's speech about the Turkish culture in which he aroused curiosity to get his audience members' attention in the introduction. He provided facts about Turkey without disclosing his topic. At the end of his speech, he brought his listeners back to the opening statements of his introduction by saying: "So if anybody ever asks you 'hey, what country was known for being the Ottoman Empire?' Or 'hey, what country is known for having rich influences?' You will know that it is, indeed, the country of Turkey."

Your final statement does not have to allude to your attention-getting step. Any of the specific techniques we discussed for gaining audience attention can help bring your speech to a psychologically satisfying conclusion. You can ask a question, even the same one you began with or a variation of it. Or you can answer the question you initially asked. Once you arouse your audience's curiosity in your speech, you must satisfy it in order to provide closure. You could stimulate their imaginations through vivid imagery or promise them that the information you have provided can benefit them. You could conclude with a joke or humorous story relevant to your topic. Through lively delivery, you could energize the audience to act on the information you have provided. In a speech presented on more formal occasions than a classroom assignment, you may end by complimenting and thanking the audience.

All three functions of the conclusion are important. Restating your key ideas reinforces the *ideas* of your speech. Activating an audience response and providing closure reinforce the *impact* of your speech. To see how one student achieved these goals, read "Theory Into Practice: A Sample Speech Conclusion."

In earlier chapters you learned how to organize and develop the body of a speech. In this chapter you have learned the five functions of a speech introduction and the three functions of a speech conclusion. Take a moment to review the individual steps in a well-organized speech.

1. Attention-getting step
2. Statement of topic
3. Emphasis on topic's importance
4. Emphasis on speaker's credibility
5. Preview of key ideas
6. Body of speech
7. Restatement of key ideas
8. Activation of audience's response
9. Closure

This is the correct sequence to follow as you *deliver* a speech. It is not, however, how you should *develop* your speech. There are several approaches to developing a speech; your instructor may offer her or his own.

circular conclusion

A conclusion that repeats or refers to material used in the attention-getting step of the introduction.

Journal: Writing the Closure Statement

Rewrite the closure statement of Jennell Chu's speech in Appendix D using a strategy other than the one Chu uses. Which closure strategy—hers or yours—do you prefer? Why?

Key Points

Functions of a Speech Conclusion

1. Restate your key ideas.
2. Activate audience response.
3. Provide closure.

Theory Into Practice TIP

A SAMPLE SPEECH CONCLUSION

In the introduction of his speech on breaking the silence about ovarian cancer, Viqar presented a startling statistic: "According to the National Cancer Coalition, every 9 minutes in the United States a woman is diagnosed with ovarian cancer."[9] Notice how Viqar used this statistic to frame his three-step conclusion.

> In the last 9 minutes we've explored ovarian cancer and the deadly problems associated with the disease, and analyzed a solution to break the silence.
>
> In the last 9 minutes, a woman has been diagnosed with ovarian cancer. Women like the mother of Rene Rossi, who in the last 9 months of her life told her daughter, "You must do something about this disease." In the last 9 minutes, you have been given the power to do just that. Do it for the women in our lives—our mothers, our daughters, our loved ones.
>
> Shout out this silent killer.[10]

Viqar restates his key ideas.

Using a statistic and an example, Viqar urges audience action.

Viqar provides closure with a direct, five-word sentence.

One approach is to prepare the body of the speech first, the introduction second, and the conclusion last. Some instructors suggest developing the body first, the conclusion second, and the introduction third.

We suggest a sequence we have named the Outward Method of Speech Development (see Figure 10.1). In Stage 1 you construct the body of your speech, determining your key ideas and developing them using the 4 S's. After completing this stage, you then work outward.

Figure 10.1 The Outward Method of Speech Development

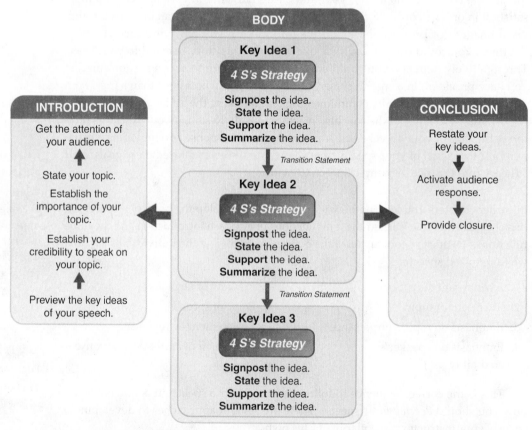

In the remaining stages, work on the introduction and conclusion simultaneously, focusing on elements that have similar purposes. In Stage 2 you word your preview and your restatement of key ideas. These two steps are similar because they highlight the speech's key ideas. As you complete Stage 2, you have fulfilled the overall strategy of a well-organized speech: You are ready to "tell us what you're going to tell us," "tell us," and "tell us what you told us."

In Stage 3 you work on the remaining elements of the introduction and conclusion. You decide how you will state your topic, explain its importance, build your credibility, and active audience response. You may develop the attention getter and closure statement at the same time to enhance the unity of your speech.

Summary

Organize the Introduction of the Speech

10.1 Construct an introduction that achieves the five objectives of effective speech introductions.

- The introduction should achieve five goals: (1) get the attention of your audience; (2) state your topic or purpose; (3) stress the importance or relevance of your topic; (4) establish your credibility to speak on your topic; and (5) preview the key ideas you will develop in the body of the speech.

- To get your audience's attention, you can question your listeners, arouse their curiosity, stimulate their imaginations, promise them something beneficial, amuse them, energize them, or acknowledge and compliment them.

Organize the Conclusion of the Speech

10.2 Construct a conclusion that achieves the three objectives of effective speech conclusions.

- An effective conclusion does the following: (1) restate your key ideas; (2) secure your listeners' commitment to your information and ideas; and (3) provide closure, bringing your speech to a satisfying psychological conclusion.

Chapter 11
Outlining Your Speech

 ## Learning Objectives

After studying this chapter, you should be able to

11.1 Apply the five functions of outlining a speech.

11.2 Apply the five principles of outlining a speech.

11.3 Construct working, formal, and speaking outlines.

How long would it take you to memorize and repeat the following 26 letters: *c-p-s-y-n-i-r-t-y-m-v-i-e-m-r-t-o-i-p-o-e-m-o-m-e-m*? A typical learner would need a good deal of practice to remember more than the first four to seven letters.[1] Would it help if the letters were rearranged as follows: *y-m-c-o-i-t-p-s-i-p-t-y-m-m-v-e-n-e-o-i-r-r-m-e-o-m*? Unless you have a photographic memory, such a shuffling of letters is likely no help at all. But what if the letters were scrambled again: *m-y-t-o-p-i-c-i-s-m-e-m-o-r-y-i-m-p-r-o-v-e-m-e-n-t*? Those letters are more recognizable and even more obvious if we eliminated the dashes and used a familiar pattern of grouping and spacing: *my topic is memory improvement*. You could now master the entire sequence of 26 letters in correct order, orally or in writing, without much effort.

Notice that we did not add or delete any letters. We merely reorganized them until they formed a pattern that is easy to recognize and repeat. When you outline, you perform essentially the same task. You organize and reorganize material into a pattern easy to recognize and remember.

Previously, we discussed the importance of organization to the delivered speech and suggested some ways of achieving a well-organized presentation. Outlining your speech is the preliminary written work necessary to foster clear organization of your oral message. In this chapter, you will learn why outlines are important to your speech, examine some different types of outlines, and learn how to write an excellent outline.

Functions of Outlining

11.1 Apply the five functions of outlining a speech.

A well-prepared outline serves five important functions for a speaker:

1. It tests the scope of the speaker's content.
2. It tests the logical relations among parts of the speech.
3. It tests the relevance of supporting ideas.
4. It checks the balance or proportion of the speech.
5. It serves as notes during the delivery of the speech.

Tests Scope of Content

The first purpose of outlining is to test the scope of the speaker's content. Have you narrowed the topic sufficiently to cover your key ideas in some depth? Or are you trying to cover too much material and consequently skimming the surface of the subject, repeating things your audience already knows? Outlining allows you to organize your main ideas and then add, delete, regroup, shuffle, condense, or expand these ideas so you approach your topic in a manageable way. Thus, outlining is a process of setting goals for the speech.

Tests Logical Relation of Parts

Second, outlining allows speakers to test the logical relations among the various parts of the speech. Does one idea in the outline lead to the next in a meaningful way? Do the arguments or subtopics under each of your main points really develop that point? To answer these questions, you must understand the concepts of coordination and subordination. **Coordinate ideas** are those of equal value or importance in the overall pattern of the speech. **Subordinate ideas** are those that support more general or more important points in a speech. The following example illustrates the relation between coordinate and subordinate ideas.

coordinate ideas

Ideas that have equal value in a speech.

subordinate ideas

Ideas that support more general or more important points in a speech.

If you delivered an informative speech on the functions of service dogs, you might arrange your speech topically and focus on just these two areas:

I. Search functions

II. Protection functions

These two topics are coordinate because they seem to be of equal value. You might have more information on one of them than on the other and thus spend more time in the speech discussing that topic. However, neither is a subtopic of the other. Under that first main topic, you would then list subordinate ideas, or subtopics, that support particular topics.

I. Search functions
   A. Narcotics detection
   B. Bomb detection
   C. Arson detection
   D. Cadaver location
   E. Disease detection

Notice that points A through E are not only subordinate to the main idea—search functions—but also coordinate with one another since they seem to be equally important. Subordinate points for the second main point could include the following:

II. Protection functions
   A. Seeing-eye dogs
   B. Guard dogs
   C. Attack dogs
   D. Seizure-alert dogs

Your outline is not yet complete, but you can begin to ask yourself the following questions: Are my main points different enough to qualify as separate points? Do my subordinate points really support the main ideas? At this stage, the answers to both of these questions seem to be yes. The visual form of the outline helps you test the logical connections among parts of your speech. You continue this process to further refine and add to the outline.

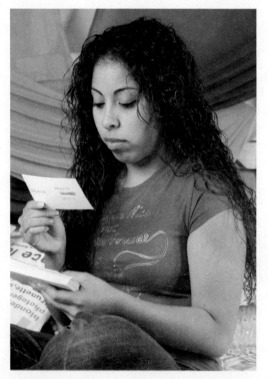

An effective outline can serve as notes to use during the delivery of your speech.

Tests Relevance of Supporting Ideas

Third, an outline helps the speaker test the relevance of supporting ideas. To understand how this works, assume that you have written the following portion of an outline for a speech on roller coasters:

I. Famous roller coasters
   A. Coney Island's "Cyclone"
   B. Montreal's "Le Monstre"
   C. Busch Gardens's "Kumba"
   D. New design technology

Notice that the fourth subpoint, "new design technology," is out of place because it is irrelevant to the main point. How do you solve this problem? One option is to make "new design technology" a separate main point if you can gather adequate supporting material on it; if you can't, eliminate it from your speech.

I. Famous roller coasters
   A. Coney Island's "Cyclone"
   B. Montreal's "Le Monstre"
   C. Busch Gardens's "Kumba"

II. New design technology

Speaking with Confidence

I have come to realize that outlining is an important part of the speech-making process. Having a clear and concise outline builds such self-confidence, not only in my ability to give the speech but in my knowledge of the topic as well. When I sit down to write my outline, all my thoughts seem to flow out onto the page in a step-by-step manner, so that my confidence in the subject builds up. Then, when I am finished with the outline, I feel as if I could give the speech right away because I have so much information down that I could expand on it as little or as much as I needed. Now that I realize how important outlining is, I will always be sure to make one for my speeches because of how much smoother it makes the speech-making process!

ALANA KWAST
San Antonio College

Checks Balance of Speech

A fourth function of outlining is to check the balance or proportion of the speech. Consider the outline on functions of service dogs. If the first main point has five subpoints and the second has four, the speech looks balanced, even though a speaker might spend more time on one of those main points than on the other. Yet if the main point "search functions" had five subpoints and "protection functions" had only two, the outline might not be balanced. This imbalance could be reflected in the speech.

How can you fix such an imbalance? One option is to focus just on those five search functions by making the subpoints into main points:

  I. Narcotics detection
 II. Bomb detection
III. Arson detection
 IV. Cadaver location
  V. Disease detection

As you can see, by testing the balance of your speech, an outline can lead you to alter your specific purpose.

Serves as Delivery Notes

Fifth and finally a special type of abbreviated outline can serve as notes for the speaker during the speech's delivery. The *speaking outline*, discussed later in this chapter, has only one rule: it must be brief. If you have prepared adequately for your speech, you should need only key words and phrases to remind you of each point you want to discuss. Moreover, having your notes in outline form rather than arranged randomly on notecards or sheets of paper will remind you of the importance of clear organization as you deliver your speech.

> **Key Points**
> **The Functions of Outlining**
> 1. Tests scope of content.
> 2. Tests logical relation of parts.
> 3. Tests relevance of supporting ideas.
> 4. Checks balance of speech.
> 5. Serves as delivery notes.

Principles of Outlining

11.2 Apply the five principles of outlining a speech.

Correct outlines take one of two possible forms: the **complete sentence outline** and the **key word or phrase outline**. In a complete sentence outline, each item is a sentence; each item in a key word or phrase outline is a word or group of words. These two forms of outlines should be kept consistent and distinct. Combine them only in the speaker's outline from which you deliver your speech. So far in this chapter, we have used only phrase outlines. More word or phrase outlines and an example of a complete sentence outline follow.

complete sentence outline

An outline in which all numbers and letters introduce complete sentences.

key word or phrase outline

An outline in which all numbers and letters introduce words or groups of words.

As you construct your outline, you will work more efficiently and produce a clearer outline if you follow a few rules, or principles.

Singularity

First, each number or letter in the outline should represent only one idea. A chief goal of outlining is to achieve a clear visual representation of the connections among parts of the speech. This is possible only if you separate the ideas. For example, suppose a speaker preparing a speech on color blindness has worded a key idea as "causes of and tests for color blindness." The phrase contains two distinct ideas, each requiring separate discussion and development. Instead, the speaker should divide the statement into two coordinate points: "causes of color blindness" and "tests for color blindness."

Consistency

Second, coordinate and subordinate points in the outline should be represented by a consistent system of numbers and letters. Main ideas are typically represented by Roman numerals: I, II, III, and so forth. Label subpoints under the main points with indented capital letters: A, B, C, and so forth. Beneath those, identify your supporting points with indented Arabic numerals: 1, 2, 3, and so on. Identify ideas subordinate to those with indented lowercase letters: a, b, c, and so on. Using this notation system, the labeling and indentation of a typical outline of the body of the speech would appear as follows:

I. Main point
   A. Subpoint
      1. Sub-subpoint
      2. Sub-subpoint
      3. Sub-subpoint
   B. Subpoint
      1. Sub-subpoint
      2. Sub-subpoint
         a. Sub-sub-subpoint
         b. Sub-sub-subpoint

II. Main point
   A. Subpoint
   B. Subpoint
      1. Sub-subpoint
      2. Sub-subpoint
   C. Subpoint

Adequacy

A third principle is that if any point has subpoints under it, there must be at least two. A basic law of physics is that you cannot divide something into only one part. If you have an A, you must also have a B. (You may, of course, also have subpoints C, D, and E.) If you have a 1, you must also have at least a 2.

Uniformity

Fourth, each symbol in a sentence outline should introduce a complete sentence. Each symbol in a word or phrase outline should introduce a word or phrase. Keep the form of the outline consistent. Sentences and phrases should be mixed only in your speaking outline.

Parallelism

Finally, coordinate points throughout the outline should have parallel grammatical construction. For example, a key phrase outline of a speech on how to write a résumé begins with a first main point labeled "Things to include." The second point should be "Things to omit," rather than "Leaving out unnecessary information." The first point is worded as a noun phrase; therefore, you should follow it with another noun phrase ("Things to omit") rather than a predicate phrase ("Leaving out unnecessary information"). This does not mean that you must choose noun phrases over verb phrases but rather that all points must match grammatically. In this next example, all coordinate points have parallel grammatical construction.

I. Including essential information
  A. Address
  B. Career objective
  C. Educational background
  D. Employment history
  E. References

II. Omitting unnecessary information
  A. Marital status
  B. Religious denomination
  C. Political affiliation

As you can see, coordinate main points I and II are verb phrases, while the coordinate subpoints are all nouns or noun phrases.

Stages of Outlining

11.3 Construct working, formal, and speaking outlines.

If you have difficulty generating or discovering the main points for a speech topic you have chosen, don't worry; you are not alone. Many people are intimidated by the prospect of selecting and organizing ideas, particularly for a first speech. Keep the following in mind when organizing and outlining your speech.

Key Points
Principles of Outlining

1. Each number or letter in the outline should represent only one idea.
2. Coordinate and subordinate points in the outline should be represented by a consistent system of numbers and letters.
3. If any point has subpoints under it, there must be at least two.
4. Each symbol in a sentence outline should introduce a complete sentence. Each symbol in a word or phrase outline should introduce a word or phrase.
5. Coordinate points throughout the outline should have parallel grammatical construction.

Ethical Decisions

FAIR AND BALANCED?

Carter, a member of State U's student government association, helped draft a proposal to reform its bylaws and streamline its operations. He is scheduled to give an informative speech in his public speaking class the week before the student body will vote on the proposal. Carter decides to inform his classmates about the plan's advantages and disadvantages.

As he outlines his speech using a pro–con pattern, Carter identifies three benefits of the change: equal representation of student constituencies, enhanced interaction between students and the SGA, and faster SGA response to campus problems. The only arguments he develops against the proposed change are minor transition problems as the SGA implements the new structure. Carter wants to empower students to make an informed decision and is concerned that his speech may appear self-serving and persuasive.

Which outlining principles can help Carter develop his organization and supporting materials? List and explain ethical guidelines that speakers should follow to ensure a fair and balanced discussion of issues.

First, there is no one right way of organizing all speeches on a particular topic. True, some topics logically lend themselves to certain patterns of organization. Speeches about processes often almost organize themselves chronologically. Speeches about people may be arranged chronologically or topically. Persuasive speeches on social issues are perhaps most logically organized according to a problem–solution format. Yet different speakers may use different structures. You must determine what works best for you, your topic, and your audience.

Second, the early stages of organizing and outlining a speech are filled with uncertainty. You may find yourself asking,

> Do I have enough main points, too many, or too few?
> Can I find adequate information to support all those main points?
> Am I overlooking other main points the audience would be interested in hearing me discuss?

Rather than feeling pressured by such questions, look on the early stages of outlining as a period of flexibility. The early, informal versions of your working outline are all provisional—temporary and open to change. Don't be afraid to experiment a little.

The Working Outline

The first step in preparing an outline is to construct a **working outline**, a list of aspects of your chosen topic. Such a list may result from research you have already done or some productive brainstorming. Once you have spent significant time researching the subject, you will notice topics that are repeated in different sources on the subject. If, for example, you had selected "super staph"—methicillin-resistant *Staphylococcus aureus* (MRSA)—as the topic for an informative speech and had conducted adequate research, your list of possible aspects of the topic might include its causes, symptoms, diagnosis, treatment, and prevention. Notice that these same topics could be applied to any disease, physical illness, or mental condition.

You can also generate topics by brainstorming. Brainstorming can help you generate topics and explore areas of your final topic.[2] Your creative brainstorming might even reveal interesting areas of your topic that have not been adequately treated in the existing research. This discovery provides you an opportunity to conduct original research or experimentation.

As you can see, at this stage, the term *outline* is very loose; the list of key ideas you are developing does not have any numbers or letters attached to it. That's fine, because these notes are for your benefit alone. This working outline is merely a record of the process you go through in thinking about a speech topic.

To illustrate these first steps in preparing an outline, consider one student's experience as he developed his speech about chewing gum. Our student Austin never enjoyed chewing gum. However, he saw many fellow students and friends chewing gum in various places, both on and off campus. Therefore, he became interested in why people chew gum and how it affects them. He started to talk with his fellow students and friends to get a general idea of why and how frequently they chew gum. Next, he conducted some preliminary research on gum chewing and reflected on the few times he had chewed gum himself.

At this point, Austin knew that he wanted to give an informative speech about chewing gum. He also knew from his preliminary research that he would have no trouble finding enough information about his topic. Just by brainstorming topics that might apply to any person chewing gum, Austin developed the following working outline:

I. Reasons people chew gum

II. Effects of chewing gum

III. Culture of gum chewers

working outline

An informal, initial outline recording a speaker's process of narrowing, focusing, and balancing a topic.

As Austin researched his topic further, he found some interesting information about the history of chewing gum. He also learned about potential benefits and drawbacks of chewing gum. He found several articles comparing sugar-free gum and regular gum with sugar, and added these topics to his working outline. Then, he added subtopics as he thought of them or encountered them in his research.

After completing his research, Austin realized that his information was too broad and several topics seemed to overlap. He also had a great deal of interesting information about the history of chewing gum: however, he could not include all this information within the time limit for his speech. As a result, he decided to develop three key ideas: history of chewing gum, pros of chewing gum, and cons of chewing gum. But when reviewing his key ideas, he concluded that the first key idea (history of chewing gum) did not seem to match well with the second (pros of chewing gum) and third (cons of chewing gum) key ideas. Therefore, he decided to focus on the pros and the cons in the body of his speech and to talk briefly about the history of chewing gum in his introduction (1) to spark his listeners' interest in the topic, (2) to establish importance of his topic, and (3) to establish speaker credibility. So, Austin's working outline of the body of his speech was revised as follows:

I. Pros of chewing gum

II. Cons of chewing gum

So was all the time spent learning the history of chewing gum, the reasons people chew gum, the effects of chewing gum, and the culture of gum chewers wasted? Not at all. Austin was able to extract relevant parts from all his readings as he prepared his speech. He included the most interesting parts of the history in his introduction. Next, he developed the pros and cons of chewing gum that he would include in his formal outline and speaking notes.

The Formal Outline

Your **formal outline** is a complete sentence outline reflecting the full content and organization of your speech. In its final form, it is the finished product of your research and planning for your speech. A stranger picking up your formal outline should be able to understand how you have organized and supported all your main points. If you keep that goal in mind, you should have no trouble deciding what to include.

If you are required to turn in an outline when you speak, find out if it should be a formal outline or if it can use key words or phrases. The actual outline should follow the accepted pattern of symbols and indentation that we showed you earlier in this chapter. Some instructors also ask students to label the superstructure of the speech—introduction, body, and conclusion—by inserting those words at the appropriate places in the outline but without any symbols attached to them.

Melissa Janoske developed and delivered her informative speech on Renaissance fairs. Below is a complete sentence outline of the body of her speech; a full transcript can be found in Chapter 15.

Speech title: Renaissance Fairs: The New Vaudeville
Specific purpose: To inform the audience about Renaissance fairs
Thesis statement: Imagining yourself as a Renaissance figure, affiliating with a Renaissance kingdom, and participating in a Renaissance fair are three ways to experience present-day Renaissance culture.

Body of Speech

    I. To experience Renaissance culture, you must imagine yourself to be part of the culture.

        A. You should suspend normal belief about who you are in your daily life.

        B. You should assume the role of someone from the Renaissance world.

            1. Select a traditional name and title.

Journal: Constructing a Working Outline

Suppose you are working on a speech on the topic of "Latin music" and you have come up with the below list of all the things you wish to cover. Which **four** of these entries would be the best choices for you to use as your key points, in order for you to be able to use all of the entries in your speech outline?

Mariachi	Romeo Santos
Small folk band	Countries
Cuba	*Merengue*
Styles	Shakira
Marc Anthony	*Salsa*
Artists	*Mariachi* band
Puerto Rico	Mexico
Rumba	Prince Royce
Latin big band	Elvis Crespo
Instrumentation	Brazil
Spain	*Mambo*

Melissa's well-crafted title not only gets attention but also hints at her speech topic. To check the goal of her speech, Melissa clearly states her specific purpose and thesis statement.

formal outline

A complete sentence outline written in sufficient detail that a person other than the speaker could understand it.

The three main points in the body of Melissa's speech match her thesis statement. Each item in the outline is a complete sentence. Coordinate and subordinate points are represented by a consistent system of numbers and letters. Each level in the outline has at least two headings, and coordinate points throughout have parallel grammatical construction.

2. Wear period clothing.
3. Learn about a profession in that time period.
C. You should attend a Renaissance fair and observe the diversity of the culture.

II. To experience Renaissance culture, you should affiliate with your local kingdom.
A. The Society for Creative Anachronism has divided the world into Renaissance kingdoms.
1. A map of these kingdoms can be found on its website, www.sca.org.
2. Virginia is located in the Kingdom of Atlantia.
3. Each kingdom has at least one university that is run by the kingdom officials.
B. Each kingdom offers classes to better understand Renaissance Europe.
1. You can learn how to be a goldsmith.
2. You can learn about the political methods of King Arthur.
3. You can learn how to joust, cook medieval delicacies, and shop for velvet gowns and leather boots.
C. You can become a member of a kingdom.

III. To experience Renaissance culture, you should participate in a Renaissance fair.
A. Fairs are the easiest and most fun way to practice Renaissance life.
B. There are different types of fair activities in which you can participate.
1. You can participate in jousting festivals, chain mail competitions, and cooking parties.
2. You can take classes on spinning and weaving.
3. You can participate in the annual St. Patty's Day Bloodbath.
C. Festivals are often held around present-day holidays such as Halloween and feasting days.
1. Renaissance Fright Night is held in Pennsylvania every year at Halloween.
2. Information about fairs in your area can be found on websites such as www.faires.com.

The Speaking Outline

The **speaking outline**, the one you actually use to deliver your speech, is a pared-down version of your full formal outline. You construct the formal outline for an interested reader having no necessary prior knowledge of your topic. However, you write the speaking outline for yourself. The only rule for the speaking outline is that it be brief.

Why is the speaking outline briefer than the formal outline? Chances are that your instructor will want most or all of your speeches delivered from notes rather than from a written manuscript. Your brief speaking outline, made up of essential words and phrases, serves as your speaking notes. If you spoke from a complete sentence outline, you might be tempted to read the speech, sacrificing eye contact and other vital interaction with your audience. Alternatively, you might try to memorize the formal outline, another dangerous tactic because you then risk forgetting part of the speech. If, instead, you speak using the outline having just key words and phrases to jog your memory, your delivery will seem more natural and conversational, and you will find yourself freer to interact with your audience.

Though the speaking outline leaves out a lot of what the formal outline includes, it also contains some important items not found in the formal outline. For example, you can include directions to yourself about the speech's delivery. A speaker with a tendency to speak too softly could write reminders in the margins, such as "Volume" or "Speak up!" You could also note places where you want to pause, slow down, or use presentational aids. Some speakers find it particularly helpful to make these delivery notes in a color of ink different from the rest of the outline.

Second, most speaking outlines include supporting materials you plan to use. Quotations and definitions should be written in complete sentences, even though the rest of the outline is in words and phrases. When you quote others, you must be exact.

speaking outline

A brief outline for the speaker's use alone, containing source citations and delivery prompts.

For that reason, insert notes about the exact sources you want to cite. Examples, illustrations, and statistics could be noted in only a few words or numbers. Any symbols or abbreviations you are comfortable with are likely appropriate in your speaking outline.

We believe that keeping your speaking notes in outline form will remind you of the importance of clear organization in the speech you deliver. Ultimately, though, they are *your* notes. As long as they help you without drawing attention to themselves, they are doing their job. If you tend to forget things under pressure, you may need a few more words in notes than some other people do. Resist the temptation to write out too much of the speech, however. If you write it, you'll want to read it. Instead, try the following suggestions:

- Use key words or phrases to remind you of each step in your introduction and conclusion. Then try to deliver those crucial parts of the speech without referring to your notes.

- In the body of the speech, your main ideas must be worded precisely and powerfully. Either write them in complete sentences or use a key word or phrase to remind you of the wording you practiced.

- Don't just read those main ideas when you deliver the speech. Use key words to remind yourself of supporting material and transitions; use numbers to remind you of statistics.

- Include just enough information to be able to cite each of your sources clearly.

- Write out any material you want to quote, using complete sentences. Insert delivery prompts using words, colors, or any other symbols that will jog your memory. We have even had students use a different colored notecard for each main point in the bodies of their speeches. It's an idea we might never have thought of, but it obviously reinforced the organization of the students' speeches. And that's what outlining and preparing speaking notes should do.

This chapter's "Theory Into Practice" feature shows you how our student, Austin, constructed his speaking notes. You can also read Austin's speech in Appendix D.

Theory Into Practice TIP

SAMPLE NOTECARDS FROM AUSTIN'S SPEECH

Austin Willis developed and delivered an informative speech on the organizing question "What does research tell us about the pros and cons of chewing gum?" He delivered his speech extemporaneously, and we asked him to share his speaking notes, which consisted of four notecards depicted below.[3]

Austin used "I" for the introduction, "II" for the body, and "III" for the conclusion of his speech. In his speaking notes, he recorded "II. First" and "II. Second" for pro and con divisions in the body of his speech. Although not correct for a formal outline, it's okay here. Speaking notes need only to make sense for the speaker. Also, someone who had not seen Austin's formal outline might be confused by the abbreviations FSM, PR, and JBNR on his notecards. See what these abbreviations mean as you read his notes.

Notecard #1

I. Introduction
    A. Question audience [PAUSE]
    B. Britt, Collins, and Cohen—"nearly 87% reported chewing gum at least occasionally."
    C. Wrigley (statisticbrain.com) "chewing gum is one of the oldest candies in the world [and] has grown to be a billion dollar industry in the U.S."
    D. Preview—positive effects and negative effects
[MOVE]

Delivery prompts are in capital letters so that Austin can see them at a glance and not confuse them with content prompts.

Notecard #2

II. First—Pros (FSM)

    A. Focus: Tänzer and colleagues (PR, 2009—8- to 9-year-old students remained focused).

        • Chewing gum "had a significant and positive effect on concentration performance."

        • Tucha and Simpson (2011) same for adults

    B. Stress: Zibell and Madansky—"56% of frequent gum chewers and 42% of infrequent gum chewers said that dealing with stress was a reason that they chewed gum."

    C. Memory: Tucha and Koerts (2012)—"an increase of learning performance of at least 30% was claimed following gum chewing."

        • Wilkinson & colleagues: *Immediate* vs. *delayed* memory [emphasize]

[MOVE]

This abbreviation reminds Austin to preview his key points focus, stress, memory.

PR is Austin's prompt to state the journal title Psychological Reports.

Notecard #3

II. Second—Cons (FSM)

    A. Focus: JBNR—"Alertness reaction time was significantly slower for a spearmint gum condition compared to not chewing [gum]"

        • Smith (2010)—mood and attention

    B. Stress: Torney, Johnson, and Miles (2009)—anagram, no change in stress; infrequent [gum] chewers said that dealing with stress was a reason that they chewed gum.

    C. Memory: Johnson & Miles (2008)—"Although flavorless gum and mint-flavored strips reported change in current mouth activity . . . they did not induce context-dependent memory."

        • *Poorer* recall [EMPHASIZE]

[MOVE]

JBNR is Austin's prompt to state his source, the Journal of Behavioral and Neuroscience Research.

Austin wrote out researchers' conclusions that he wanted to quote directly.

Notecard #4

III. Conclusion—Pros and cons (FSM)

    A. Unique perspective

    B. Keep on chewing [SMILE]

Austin Willis
Informative Speech: Gum Chewers
References: APA

Allen, A. P., & Smith, A. S. (2011). A review of the evidence that chewing gum affects stress, alertness, and cognition. *Journal of Behavioral and Neuroscience Research, 9*, 7–23.

Britt, D. M., Collins, F. L., & Cohen, L. M. (1999). Cigarette smoking and chewing-gum use among college students. *Journal of Applied Biobehavioral Research, 4*, 85-90.

Firestone, A. (n.d.). *Chew on this: Is gum addiction real?* Retrieved from www.divinecaroline.com/self/chew-gum-addiction-real

Statisticbrain.com (2013). *Chewing Gum Statistics*. Retrieved from www.statisticbrain.com/chewing-gum-statistics/

Tucha, L., & Koerts, J. (2012). Gum chewing and cognition: An overview. *Neuroscience & Medicine, 3*, 243–250.

Tucha, L., & Simpson, W. (2011). The role of time on task performance in modifying the effects of gum chewing on attention. *Appetite, 56*, 299–301.

Summary

Functions of Outlining

11.1 Apply the five functions of outlining a speech.

- Outlining serves five main purposes: (1) It allows the speaker to check the scope of the topic. Is the topic too broad? Are you trying to cover too much or too little? (2) It tests the logical relations between main points and subpoints. Are the points related and yet distinctive enough to qualify as separate ideas? (3) It checks the relevance of subpoints. Are supporting ideas all related to the main idea under which they are listed? (4) It gauges the balance of the speech. Does it look as though you will be spending too much time on one of your points and too little on others? Should you eliminate the points that have little support and reorganize those with a great deal of support? (5) It can function as speaking notes, jogging your memory with key words in correct order.

Principles of Outlining

11.2 Apply the five principles of outlining a speech.

- Effective outlining is greatly simplified if the speaker remembers these traditional principles: (1) Each symbol—number or letter—should represent only one idea. (2) Coordination and subordination should be represented by a consistent system of letters and numbers properly indented. (3) Any point divided into subpoints must have at least two. (4) Complete sentences and key words should be mixed only in the speaking outline. (5) Coordinate points throughout the outline should have simple, parallel grammatical construction.

Stages of Outlining

11.3 Construct working, formal, and speaking outlines.

- The first phase of outlining is a *working outline*, an informal list of different aspects of the selected speech topic. From there, the speaker should develop a complete sentence outline, or *formal outline*, that is clear and thorough enough to communicate the essence of the speech to any reader. Having checked the scope of the topic and the logical connections, relevance, and balance of the subpoints, the speaker can then select key words and phrases for a *speaking outline*. That outline may also include transitions, quotations, and source citations, as well as personal directions or prompts for the speech's delivery.

- While effective outlining does not guarantee clear organization in the delivered speech, chances are good that any well-organized speech has been carefully outlined at some stage in its development.

Chapter 12
Wording Your Speech

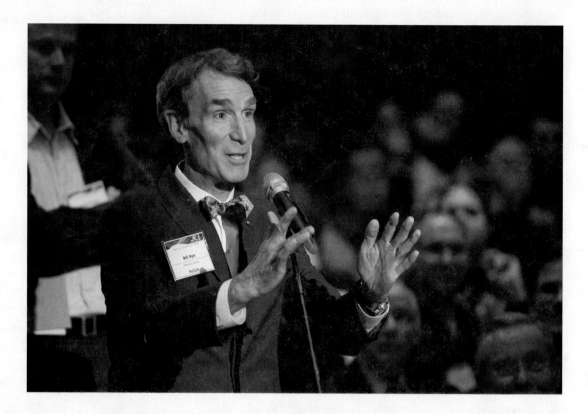

Learning Objectives

After studying this chapter, you should be able to

12.1 Word your speech using correct language.

12.2 Word your speech using clear language.

12.3 Use language that conveys your intended message.

12.4 Word your speech using vivid language.

12.5 Word your speech using inclusive language.

12.6 Word your speech using appropriate oral style.

Socrates was a famous Greek teacher who went around giving people advice. They killed him. Socrates died from an overdose of wedlock. After his death, his career suffered a dramatic decline.

— From a student paper[1]

Sisters Reunited after 18 Years in Checkout Line at Supermarket

—Newspaper headline[2]

Socrates died of an overdose of hemlock, not wedlock. We doubt that those sisters had to wait in the supermarket checkout line for 18 years, even if there were lots of double-coupon days! Examples of language abuse, both spoken and written, are all around us. Their effects can be comic or serious. A speaker's words communicate ideas to an audience, information about the speaker, and information about how the speaker perceives listeners. Thus, studying language is important because the more you know about it, the greater influence you will have.

Words can be compared to a tool belt used by a carpenter and, in a sense, you draw from that tool belt every time you speak. The words you choose help determine your success in informing, persuading, and entertaining your audience. In this chapter you will learn six principles for using language that is correct, is clear, conveys your intended message, is vivid, is inclusive, and is in an oral style.

Use Language Correctly

12.1 Word your speech using correct language.

When you use language incorrectly in your speech, you risk sending unintended messages and undermining your credibility. Poorly worded ideas are sometimes evaluated as poor ideas, although this may not be the case. For example, one student, concerned about the increase of sexually transmitted diseases, encouraged her listeners to commit to "long-term monotonous relationships." We hope she meant *monogamous*.

It is important for speakers to rid their speeches of all unnecessary intrusions. Speakers perceived to care about how they state their ideas are also perceived to care about what they say. The following examples illustrate some common language errors we have heard in student speeches:

1. The first criteria for selecting a good wine is to experience its bouquet. (The speaker should use the singular noun *criterion.*)

2. So, you may be thinking, "I could care less about student government elections. They don't affect me." (The speaker should say, "I *couldn't* care less. . . .")

3. Because they conduct most of their missions at night, a drug trafficker often alludes our understaffed border patrol. (*They* is plural, so the speaker should use *drug traffickers.* Also, the correct word is *elude*, not *allude*.)

4. Less than twenty students attended the lecture given by Dr. Hinojosa last Wednesday. (Use *fewer* for people or items that can be counted. Yes, those "10 Items or Less" supermarket checkout signs are wrong!)

Your language, like your physical and vocal delivery, should be free of all distractions. Errors in subject-verb agreement, misplaced modifiers, and incorrect word choice attract the attention of everyone who recognizes these errors. You won't upset anyone if your language is grammatically correct, but even small errors run the risk of monopolizing some people's attention. In turn, they stop listening carefully to *what* you say because they are paying attention to *how* you say it.

You can speak correctly if you follow a few simple guidelines. First, make a note of grammatical mistakes you hear yourself and other people make in casual conversation. Attentive listening is the first step to improving your use of language. Second, when you are unsure of a word's meaning, consult a dictionary. Third, if you have a question about proper grammar, refer to a handbook for writers. Fourth, when practicing your speech, record it and play it back, listening for mistakes you may not have noticed as you were practicing. Fifth, practice your speech in front of friends and ask them to point out mistakes. These strategies will help you detect and correct errors. Your speaking will improve, and you may save yourself some embarrassment.

Use Language Clearly

12.2 Word your speech using clear language.

To achieve clarity, a speaker should use language that is specific and familiar. If you sacrifice either criterion, your language may confuse your listeners.

Journal: Using Correct Language

Identify the error in the following sentence and rewrite the sentence to use correct language:

Any fan could tell that they were seeing the basketball player's final game before his retirement.

Use Specific Language

Many communication problems spring from the fact that there are always two messages involved when two people are communicating: the message that the speaker intends and the message that the listener infers or interprets. If you tell your instructor that you missed a deadline because you were "having some problems," you leave yourself open to a wide range of interpretations. Are they health problems, family troubles, or study and work schedule conflicts? These and other interpretations are possible because *problem* is an abstract term.

To clarify your ideas, use the lowest level of abstraction possible. Words are not either abstract or concrete but take on these qualities in relation to other words. Look at the following list of terms:

class
college class
college communication class
Communication Arts & Sciences 100: Effective Speech
CAS 100 at Penn State Hazleton
CAS 100 with Daniel H. Mansson at Penn State Hazleton

The term at the top of this list is more abstract than the phrase at the bottom. As we add those limiting, descriptive words, or *qualifiers*, the referent becomes increasingly specific. The lower the level of abstraction used, the more clearly the listener will understand the speaker.

Suppose you were giving a speech on how citizens can protect their homes from burglaries and you made the following statement:

> Crime is rampant in our city. Burglary alone has gone way up in the past year or so. So you can see that having the right kind of lock on your door is essential to your safety.

What's wrong with this statement? The language is vague. What does "rampant" mean? How much of an increase is "way up"—15 percent, 50 percent, 400 percent? Is "the past year or so" 1 year, 2 years, or more? What is "the right kind of lock"? As a speaker, you should help your audience by making these ideas more concrete. After some research, you might rephrase your argument like this:

> Last week I spoke with Captain James Winton, head of our City Police Department's Records Division. He told me that crime in our city has increased by 54 percent in the last year, and the number of burglaries has doubled. We can help deter crime by making our homes burglarproof, and one way of doing this is to make sure that all doors have solid locks. I brought one such lock with me: it's a double-keyed deadbolt lock.

Notice the improvement in the second paragraph. The message is clearer, and with that clarity you would gain credibility as a speaker.

Use Familiar Language

Your language may be specific but still not be clear. If listeners are not familiar with your words, communication is impaired.

Speakers sometimes try to impress listeners with their vocabularies. Phrases such as "the anathema of censorship" and "this obviates the need for" detract from rather than enhance the speaker's message. "We must ever be mindful to eschew verbosity and deprecate tautology" is good advice and fun to say. But if you are trying to communicate with another person, it's probably better to say simply, "Avoid wordiness."

The use of jargon can also undermine clarity. **Jargon** is the special language of a particular activity, business, or group of people. If you inform your classmates on the

jargon

The special language used by people in a particular activity, business, or group.

Ethical Decisions

DOUBLESPEAK OR CLEARSPEAK

In his book *The New Doublespeak*, William Lutz writes about the unclear and misleading language used in our society. In speeches and public statements, politicians have used phrases such as "revenue enhancement," "receipt proposals," and "wage-based premiums" when they mean taxes. Business leaders have referred to "laying off workers" as "work reengineering." Military spokespersons sometimes speak of "neutralizing the opposition" to avoid using the word *killing*.

Lutz argues that the use of such phrases is unethical because the "clearest possible language is essential for democracy to function, for it is only through clear language that we have any hope of defining, debating, and deciding the issues of public policy that confront us."

Do you agree with Lutz's position, or do you think it is legitimate for speakers to use this kind of language if it helps achieve their purposes? Can you think of a time when the use of such "doublespeak" would be appropriate? In general, what ethical guidelines should speakers use to govern their choice of language?

---

development of maglev trains, you will probably also need to tell them that *maglev* is short for "magnetic levitation" and then explain what that means.

If you are certain that the people you are addressing know such terms, jargon presents no problem. In fact, it is usually quite specific and can save a lot of time. Jargon can even increase your credibility by indicating that you are familiar with the subject matter. If you have any doubts about whether your listeners know the jargon, however, either avoid such terms or define each one the first time you use it.

Use Powerful Language

In order to enhance the clarity of your speech and to increase your perceived credibility, it is important that you avoid *powerless* language in your speeches. Powerless language refers to words and phrases that reduce the clarity and exactness of your message; it also decreases your perceived speaker credibility and ability to influence your audience members. Four common types of powerless language are disclaimers, hedges, hesitations, and tag questions.

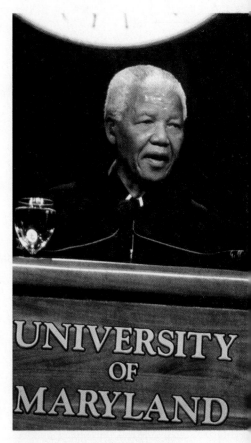

Nelson Mandela carefully crafted his language to urge his listeners to work toward a day when "we shall, together, rejoice in a common victory over racism."

- *Disclaimers* are words or phrases that preface your statements. Some examples of disclaimers are "Don't get me wrong, but . . ."; "I could be wrong, but . . ."; and "This may be a dumb question, but. . . ." If you use disclaimers in your speech, the audience members may think that you don't fully support your opinions or claims.

- *Hedges* are noncommittal words and phrases that reduce the exactness of your message. Some examples of hedges are "I guess," "I think," "kind of" "pretty much like," and "somewhat." If you use hedges in your speech, the audience members may get the impression that you lack confidence or that you question the accuracy of your message.

- *Hesitations* are filler words or filler sounds that are unintentionally added in a speech. Some examples of hesitations are "ah," "like," "umm," "well," and "you know." The use of hedges is often distracting to the audience members. To avoid hesitations, practice your use of pauses and take a moment to breathe before continuing to the next point in your speech.

- *Tag questions* are words and phrases at the end of a point, which suggest that the speaker needs to have her or his point confirmed or validated by the audience members. Some examples of tag questions are "don't you think?" "isn't it?" "right?" and "wouldn't it?" Speakers who use tag questions appear tentative and unsure about their message.

Key Points

Use Language Clearly

1. Use specific language.
2. Use familiar language.
3. Use powerful language.

Theory Into Practice TIP

AVOIDING POWERLESS LANGUAGE

	Powerless language: Instead of saying . . .	**Powerful language:** Say
Disclaimers	"I could be wrong about this, but if you . . ."	"If you . . ."
Hedges	"Bruce Springsteen is pretty much the best . . ."	"Bruce Springsteen is the best . . ."
Hesitations	"People should, you know, try to like, avoid . . ."	"People should avoid . . ."
Tag questions	"Earning good grades is important, isn't it?"	"Earning good grades is important."

Convey the Message You Intend

12.3   Use language that conveys your intended message.

Although public speaking is generally more formal than casual conversation, the precise level of language you use will depend on what you want your speech to accomplish.

Use Denotative Language

At times, we want our language to be "transparent," almost to disappear. In these instances, we focus on getting our meaning across to our listeners quickly and clearly. If you were reporting a fire, a gas leak, or some other emergency to a group of people and advising them to vacate their building, you would try to communicate that information directly, simply, and quickly, without causing panic. You would not waste time mentally editing and practicing the message to make it more clever or more memorable. Because your goal in these circumstances is getting your message across to a listener, you would use language with clear denotations. **Denotation** is the dictionary definition of a word.

Use Connotative Language

> **Journal: Denotative and Connotative Language**
>
> What is the denotative meaning of the word "feminism"? What are some connotative associations that listeners may have with this word?

On other occasions, you speak to get a message across and to convey it in an especially vivid way. At such times, you pay particular attention to the way you encode the message, choosing your words carefully. When your purpose is to signal your feelings about a subject, to strengthen the social bonds between you and your listeners, or to engage them in verbal play, you will likely use language that draws attention to itself and has strong connotations.[3]

Connotation is the emotional association that a particular word has for an individual listener. The word *fire* may have pleasant connotations for you if you spent some time around a campfire recently. The same word will have negative connotations for someone whose house has burned down.

denotation

The literal meaning or dictionary definition of a word or phrase.

connotation

The emotional association(s) that a word or phrase may evoke in individual listeners.

Your choice of language depends on the purpose of your speech. Usually, you will use a combination of denotative and connotative language. Whether the wording of your speech is straightforward or evocative, direct or highly embroidered, however, you must use language carefully.

Use Language Vividly

12.4 Word your speech using vivid language.

In addition to selecting language that is correct and clear, speakers should choose language that is colorful and picturesque. Vivid language engages the audience and makes the task of listening easier. Consider the following critiques of the speeches of the twenty-ninth U.S. president, Warren Harding:

1. Warren Harding was not an effective public speaker. His speeches often were confusing and uninspired. He did not make his points well.

2. "His speeches left the impression of an army of pompous phrases moving over the landscape in search of an idea; sometimes these meandering words would actually capture a straggling thought and bear it triumphantly a prisoner in their midst, until it died of servitude and overwork." William G. McAdoo, Democratic Party leader[4]

Poet, novelist, and educator, Maya Angelou made the written word come alive through vivid and picturesque language. Successful speakers use these same techniques to make the spoken word evoke vivid images.

Which of these two statements did you enjoy reading more? Which characterization of Harding's speaking did you find more colorful? Which paragraph contains the more vivid images? Which would you like to read again? We're fairly certain that you selected the second statement. Why?

The language of the first critique communicates an idea as simply and economically as possible without calling attention to it. Its language is transparent. It is also drab and colorless and displays little creativity. The language style is not nearly as lively as the second example. The language of the second statement calls attention to its sounds, textures, and rhythms. Vivid language helps listeners remember both your message and you.

One of the fiercest enemies of vivid language is the **cliché**, a once-colorful expression that has lost most of its impact through overuse. Many clichés involve comparisons. For example, complete the following phrases:

Like mother, like _____.

Truth is stranger than _____.

Between a rock and a _____.

Did you have any trouble completing these expressions? Probably not. In fact, *daughter*, *fiction*, and *hard place* most likely popped into your mind without much thought. Each of these sayings is a cliché, an overworked expression that doesn't require (or stimulate) much thinking. Clichés are bland and hackneyed. Avoid them!

Now that you have seen some of the effects of dull wording, what techniques can you use to make your language more vivid? The answer may be limited only by your imagination. Consider these options: (1) use active language and (2) use specific language techniques. Following these suggestions will give you a good start on making your speeches more colorful and thus more memorable.

Use Active Language

Which of the following statements is more forceful?

It was decided by the Student Government Association that the election would be delayed for a week.

The Student Government Association decided to delay the election for a week.

The second one, right? The first sentence uses passive voice, the second active. Active voice is more direct because it identifies the agent producing the action and places it first in the sentence. In addition, active voice is more economical than passive voice; the second sentence is shorter than the first by five words.

cliché
A once-colorful figure of speech that has lost impact from overuse.

Speaking with Confidence

SUZANNE L. HAMILTON
San Antonio College

Wording my speeches properly was a very high priority for me. I knew that if I did not effectively communicate my ideas, they would fall on deaf ears. I found it extremely important in my persuasive speech on college binge-drinking deaths. Since I was delivering this speech to an audience in a city that ranked in the top 10 for binge drinkers, I had to be sure that the language I used would grab their attention and keep it for the duration of the speech.

I used four techniques that aided in my success in this speech. First, I used language that appealed to the audience's emotions by painting vivid imagery. Second, when delivering quotes and statistics, I tried to use appropriate voice qualities to give them dramatic impact and to stress their logic. Third, I established my credibility by using my personal experiences and education in my field of study for an ethical appeal, while speaking on the audience's level and not using technical jargon. Finally, I imagined that I was speaking to each listener as "a friend." I just conversationally stated the facts and explained how I felt.

By employing these techniques and rehearsing several times, I felt more comfortable and confident in this speech and its delivery than I ever had before.

Active language, however, involves more than active voice. Active language has energy, vitality, and drive. It is not bogged down by filler phrases such as "you know," "like," "actually," and "stuff like that." Rather than being cliché-ridden, it may convert the commonplace into the unexpected. Language that is lively and active has impact.

In her persuasive speech, Cherie spoke of the injuries, even deaths, children suffer from playing baseball. After detailing ways to make the game safer, she twisted a familiar expression to create a dramatic conclusion: "Children may be dying to play baseball, but they should never die because of it."[5]

Active language is not your only option for enlivening your speech language. Public speaking gives you an opportunity to use some special language techniques that you may have studied in English classes.

Use Specific Language Techniques

Important ideas are easier to remember if they are memorably worded. Although there are hundreds of figures and structures of speech, we focus on a more manageable number to help you enliven the language of your speech. Seven of the most common techniques are simile, metaphor, personification, alliteration, parallelism, repetition, and antithesis.

Simile and **metaphor** are comparisons of two seemingly dissimilar things. In simile, the comparison is explicitly stated using the words *as* or *like*—for example, "Trying to pin the senator down on the issue is like trying to nail a poached egg to a tree."

In metaphor, the comparison is not explicitly stated but is implied, without using *as* or *like*. Metaphors help us accommodate the new in terms of the familiar. As a nation, we have moved from being "couch potatoes" to "channel surfers." At the same time, television executives and advertisers may conceive of us, remote controls in hand, as a nation of "grazers."

If we think of ourselves as channel surfers, perhaps we are compensating heavily for sitting in front of the television actually doing nothing. If the industry calls us grazers, perhaps they don't have too high an opinion of us. The metaphors people use give us insights into their conceptual and fantasy worlds. More than that, the metaphors shape how we perceive our "real world," and what we are doing in it.[6]

To produce metaphors is to extend meanings, to improvise, to let your imagination go.[7] Fresh metaphors have the power to surprise us into new ways of seeing

simile

A comparison of two things using the words *as* or *like*.

metaphor

An implied comparison of two things without the use of *as* or *like*.

things. Theodore Roosevelt created a memorable metaphor when he made the following comparison: "A good political speech is a poster, not an etching."[8]

Personification gives human qualities to objects, ideas, or organizations. "Blind justice," the "angry sea," and "jealousy rearing its ugly head" are all examples of personification.

Our student Amanda used personification in her speech on drummers. Notice how the drumbeat takes on human qualities as she introduces her topic:

> It's the catalyst to any gut wrenching rock song, the groove behind any rapper's flow, and the driving force behind any marching band. It's a drumbeat. No matter where or when you hear it, a drumbeat grabs you by the lapels, screams in your face, and then slams you back into your seat for the ride of your life.

Another student, Phillip, began his speech, "Nearly 8 years ago, a new neighbor moved to East Liverpool, Ohio. But residents of this low-income, minority town didn't greet the newcomer with welcoming signs." This "Unwanted Neighbor," the title of Phillip's speech, was just "400 yards from an elementary school site." The neighbor? A toxic waste incinerator. Using personification, Phillip made the incinerator an enemy, someone who needed to be turned away.[9]

Alliteration is the repetition of beginning sounds in adjacent or nearby words. A speaker who asks us "to dream, to dare, and to do" uses alliteration. The sounds of words give your speech impact. A student speaking on the topic of child abuse described the victims as "badly bruised and beaten." These words themselves convey a severe problem, and the repetition of the stern, forceful "b" sound vocally accentuates the violence of the act.

Holocaust survivor Elie Wiesel used alliteration in a speech entitled "The Shame of Hunger" when he spoke of "faith in the future," "complacency if not complicity," and "hunger and humiliation."[10]

Speakers use **parallelism** when they express two or more ideas in similar language structure. When they restate words, phrases, or sentences, they use **repetition**. Parallelism and repetition work in concert to emphasize an idea or a call for action. For example, Travis used an alarm clock image to summarize his persuasive speech on the dangers of sleep deprivation. He then used parallelism and repetition in his call to action and closure steps:

> Today, we've sounded the alarm about the harms of sleep deprivation, opened our eyes to the reasons this situation has developed, and finally awakened to the steps we must take to end this nightmare. Before we are all, literally, dead on our feet, let's take the easiest solution step of all. Tonight, turn off your alarm, turn down your covers, and turn in for a good night's sleep.[11]

Antithesis uses parallel construction to contrast ideas. You can probably quote from memory John F. Kennedy's challenge: "Ask not what your country can do for you, ask what you can do for your country." Dedicating a memorial for soldiers who had died in the Civil War battle at Gettysburg, Abraham Lincoln proclaimed, "The world will little note nor long remember what we say here, but it can never forget what they did here." The fact that we do remember both of these statements attests to the power of antithesis. Notice also that each speaker places what he wants the audience to do or remember at the end of the comparison. Antitheses are usually more powerful if they end positively.

Sarah Meinen of Bradley University won the national speech tournament of the Interstate Oratorical Association in 1999 with her speech "The Forgotten Four-Letter Word." She carefully researched and organized her speech on the problem of compassion fatigue, "the inability to care anymore about social issues." She crafted her language carefully, using the figures and structures of speech we have just discussed. Sarah's work paid off. She captured the attention and tapped the concern of her listeners, encouraging them to rekindle a passion for AIDS awareness and activism.

personification

A figure of speech that attributes human qualities to a concept or inanimate object.

alliteration

The repetition of beginning sounds in words that are adjacent, or near one another.

parallelism

The expression of ideas using similar grammatical structures.

repetition

Restating words, phrases, or sentences for emphasis.

antithesis

The use of parallel construction to contrast ideas.

Key Points

Specific Language Techniques

1. Simile
2. Metaphor
3. Personification
4. Alliteration
5. Parallelism
6. Repetition
7. Antithesis

Journal: Language Techniques

Listen to your favorite music artist or group. Try to identify examples of at least two of the following language devices in the song lyrics: alliteration, antithesis, metaphor, parallelism, personification, repetition, simile.

With statistics and expert opinions, Sarah reminded her listeners of the "savage spread" of this "vicious virus" [alliteration]. "AIDS has been too grim, too overwhelming, and it's been around too long" [parallelism and repetition]. She lamented that "despite our exposure to death and destruction, facts and figures, names and Quilt squares, AIDS has slowly faded from our national consciousness . . ." [alliteration and antithesis]. Sarah concluded, "Our well of compassion has run dry . . ." [metaphor].

Sarah urged her listeners to become advocates for change on a national and personal level. "Closing our eyes won't make a monster of this magnitude go away" [personification]. "We may be over AIDS, but AIDS is not over . . ." [antithesis]. "We may be immune to the stories and statistics, but none of us is safe from the reality of AIDS" [alliteration and antithesis]. Sarah exhorted her audience to do "whatever you have to do to be shocked, to be scared, to be involved, to be compassionate, and to keep this pandemic from being ignored, dismissed, and forgotten" [parallelism].[12]

Simile, metaphor, personification, alliteration, parallelism, repetition, and antithesis enable speakers to create vivid language and images. Remember, though, that your objective as a speaker is not to impress your listeners with your ability to create vivid language. Vivid language is not an end in itself but rather a means of achieving the larger objectives of the speech. As language expert William Safire notes, "A good speech is not a collection of crisp one-liners, workable metaphors, and effective rhetorical devices; a good speech truly reflects the thoughts and emotions of the speaker. . . ."[13]

Use Language Inclusively

12.5 Word your speech using inclusive language.

We have argued that ethics is a working philosophy that we apply to daily life and bring to all speaking situations. Nowhere is this more evident than in the words we select to address and describe others. Ethical communicators neither exclude nor demean others on the basis of their race, ethnicity, gender, sexual orientation, disability, age, or other characteristics. Their language is inclusive, unbiased, and respectful.

At least three principles should guide you as you become a more inclusive communicator.[14]

Use Appropriate Group Labels

In referring to individuals and groups of people, use the names they wish to be called. Ethical public speakers are audience-centered. Acceptable terms when referring to race or ethnicity include African American or black; Asian or Asian American; Native American or American Indian; white or Caucasian; and Hispanic, Latino, or Chicano. Refer to individuals' sexual orientations, not their sexual preferences. *Lesbians*, *gay men*, and *bisexual women and men* are acceptable terms. Address females and males who are over age 18 as *women* and *men*, not *girls* and *boys*. Not everyone with these characteristics favors the terms listed, and you should consider those preferences as you address a specific audience. Your goal, though, should be to respect individuals' rights to choose what they wish to be called.

Use People First Language

Use the "people first" rule when referring to individuals who have disabilities. As the name implies, we should place people before their disabilities. Avoid calling someone a disabled person, an epileptic, or a diabetic. Instead, refer to a person with disabilities, a person with epilepsy, or a person who has diabetes.

Use Nonsexist Language

Avoid using language that is sex-biased. The issue of sex bias is particularly pervasive and problematic. Language is sexist if it "promotes and maintains attitudes that stereotype people according to gender. It [**sexist language**] assumes that the male is the norm—the significant gender. **Nonsexist language** treats all people equally and either does not refer to a person's sex when it is irrelevant or refers to men and women in symmetrical ways when their gender is relevant."[15]

Sex bias occurs when language creates special categories for one sex, with no corresponding parallel category for the other sex. *Man* and *wife*, for example, are not parallel terms. *Man* and *woman* or *husband* and *wife* are parallel. Other examples of nonparallel language are nurse and male nurse, chairman and chairperson, and athletic team names such as *The Tigers* (the men's team) and *The Lady Tigers* (the women's team).

Perhaps the most common display of sexist language comes from the inappropriate use of a simple two-letter word: *he*. Sometimes called the "generic he," this word is used to refer to men and women alike, usually with the fallacious justification that there aren't acceptable alternatives without cluttering speech with intrusive phrases such as "he and she" and "him and her." This assumption is false.

Consider the following sentence: "A coach must be concerned with his players' motivation." Sexist, right, since both women and men are coaches? Now, consider how simple it is to remove this gender bias without changing the meaning of the sentence. First, use the plural form: "Coaches must be concerned with their players' motivation." Second, eliminate the pronoun: "A coach must be concerned with player motivation." A third way to avoid sex bias is to include both pronouns: "A coach must be concerned with her or his players' motivation." Although the use of "he and she" may seem wordy and intrusive, speakers sometimes use this double-pronoun construction strategically to remind listeners that both men and women perform the role being discussed.

Speakers exhibit fairness when they express their ideas and examples in language that treats others equally and fairly. The strategies discussed in this section should help you design, develop, and deliver a speech that uses inclusive language and respects your audience.

Speaking inclusively is an ethical obligation for those who value civil discourse. Maggio highlights both the limitations and possibilities of the role language can play in achieving tolerance, acceptance, and change:

> There can certainly be no solution to the problem of discrimination in society on the level of language alone. Replacing *handicap* with *disability* does not mean a person with disabilities will find a job more easily. Using *secretary* inclusively does not change the fact that fewer than 2 percent of U.S. secretaries are men. Replacing *black-and-white* in our vocabularies will not dislodge racism. However, research indicates that language powerfully influences attitudes, behavior, and perceptions. To ignore this factor in social change would be to hobble all other efforts.[16]

Use Appropriate Oral Style

12.6 Word your speech using appropriate oral style.

To speak appropriately, you must recognize that your oral style differs from your written style. Unless your instructor asks you to deliver some speeches from a manuscript, we believe it's better to think of "developing" speeches rather than "writing" them.

---

sexist language

Language that excludes one sex, creates special categories for one sex, or assigns roles based solely on sex.

nonsexist language

Language that treats both sexes fairly and avoids stereotyping either one.

Journal: Using Nonsexist Language

Decide on nonsexist words that could be substituted for each of the following examples:

a. Manpower
b. Salesmanship
c. Mother country
d. Man's best friend

EXPLORING ONLINE

Nonsexist Language

Conduct a search for "Pearson avoid sexist language" and access one publisher's suggestions for replacing sexist terms and labels with non sexist language.

Key Points

Use Language Inclusively

1. Use appropriate group labels.
2. Use people first language.
3. Use nonsexist language.

tone

The relationship established by language and grammar between speakers and their listeners.

Avoid writing your speeches for two reasons. First, you will likely try to memorize what you have written, and the fear of forgetting part of the speech will add to your nervousness and could make your delivery stiff and wooden.

Second, and more important, the act of writing itself often affects the tone of the communication. **Tone** is the relationship established by language and grammar between a writer or speaker and that person's readers or listeners. Many of us think of writing as something formal. For that reason, we tend not to write the way that we speak. Novelist and screenwriter Richard Price speaks from his experience about the crucial difference between the written and the spoken word:

> It's amazing how much stuff looks dazzlingly authentic and true and beautiful on the page, but dies in someone's mouth. That's the importance of a read-through for the writer and the director. Because when the actors at a big round table read all the parts of a script, what doesn't work is going to pop up so obviously. And there's no substitute for that. There's no other way you can learn that except to hear it in somebody's mouth.[17]

If you compose parts of a speech on paper, make certain that you read what's on the page out loud to see if it sounds oral rather than written. How can you tell the difference?

Our oral style differs from our written style in at least four important ways.

- First, *in speaking, we tend to use shorter sentences than we write.* Speakers who write their speeches often find themselves gasping for air when they try to deliver a long sentence in one breath.

- Second, *when we communicate orally, we tend to use more contractions, colloquial expressions, and slang.* Our speaking vocabulary is smaller than our writing vocabulary, so we tend to speak a simpler language than we write. Speakers who write out their speeches often draw from their larger written vocabularies. As a result, their presentational style seems formal and often creates a barrier between them and their listeners.

- Third, *oral style makes greater use of personal pronouns and references than written style does.* Speakers must acknowledge their listeners' presence. One way of doing this is by including them in the speech. Using the pronouns *I, we,* and *you* makes your speech more immediate and enhances your rapport with your listeners. You may even want to mention specific audience members by name: "Last week, John told us how to construct a power résumé. I'm going to tell you what to do once your résumé gets you a job interview." Notice how the name of the student, coupled with several personal pronouns, brings the speaker and audience together and sets up the possibility for lively interaction.

- A fourth difference is that *oral style uses more repetition.* Readers can slow down and reread the material in front of them. They control the pace. Listeners don't have that luxury. Speakers must take special care to reinforce their messages, and one way of accomplishing this is by using repetition. Refer to "Theory Into Practice: Keys to Effective Oral Style" for help in determining how to incorporate oral style into your speech.

No matter which of the world's nearly 7,000 languages you speak, the words you choose telegraph messages about your background, your involvement with your topic, and your relationship with your listeners.[18] Like the unique voice and body you use to deliver your speeches, your language is an extremely important part of your delivery. If you are conscientious, you must know when to speak simply and directly and when to embellish your language with specific language techniques. In short, you don't have to be a poet to agree with poet Robert Frost: "All the fun's in how you say a thing."[19]

Key Points

Principles of Effective Language Use

1. Use language correctly.
2. Use language clearly.
3. Convey your intended message.
4. Use language vividly.
5. Use language inclusively.
6. Use appropriate oral style.

Theory Into Practice TIP

KEYS TO EFFECTIVE ORAL STYLE

Oral style checklist	Instead of this:	Say this:
Use familiar language	Such an action would not be prudent at this juncture.	I don't think we should do that.
Use personal pronouns	People need to stand up and say, "Enough is enough."	We must stand up and say, "Enough is enough."
Use contractions	You will not find him in a library on a weekend if his personal computer is working.	You won't find him in a library on a weekend if his computer's working.
Use short sentences	According to Nigel Hawkes in his book *Structures: The Way Things Are Built*, an accidental discovery by well diggers in 1974 has led archaeologists in central China to unearth an army of possibly 8,000 terracotta figures of warriors and horses in the tomb of China's first emperor.	According to Nigel Hawkes in his book *Structures: The Way Things Are Built*, well diggers in central China discovered pieces of broken terracotta in 1974. Since then, archaeologists have unearthed what may be a total of 8,000 figures. They are terracotta figures of warriors and horses guarding the tomb of China's first emperor.
Use repetition	Several studies have estimated that approximately 80 percent of college students have talked on a cell phone or texted while driving.	Several studies have estimated that approximately 80 percent of college students have talked on a cell phone or texted while driving. That's eight out of ten students. And if our class is typical, approximately twenty of us are guilty.

Summary

Use Language Correctly

12.1 Word your speech using correct language.

- Your first obligation as a speaker is to use language *correctly*. To detect and correct language errors: (1) listen to the language you and others use, and focus on how it can be improved; (2) consult a dictionary when you are unsure of a word's meaning; (3) refer to a writer's handbook when you have a question about proper grammar; (4) use a recorder to detect incorrect language use; and (5) practice your speech in front of friends, and ask them to point out your mistakes.

Use Language Clearly

12.2 Word your speech using clear language.

- To use language *clearly*, use specific and familiar language. The more concrete your language, the more closely your referents will match those of your listeners. In addition to being specific, language must also be familiar. Listeners must know the meanings of the words you use. Lastly, use powerful language to enhance the clarity of your message and your speaker credibility.

Convey the Message You Intend

12.3 Use language that conveys your intended message.

- To convey the message you intend, use denotative and connotative language, or a combination of both, to achieve your intended purpose.

Use Language Vividly

12.4 Word your speech using vivid language.

- To use language vividly, incorporate active language and language techniques. Active language avoids clichés and filler phrases, using instead active voice, coined words, and well-turned phrases. Language techniques include simile, metaphor, personification, alliteration, parallelism, repetition, and antithesis.

Use Language Inclusively

12.5 Word your speech using inclusive language.

- To use language *inclusively*, consider audience diversity and avoid stereotypes about people based on characteristics such as race, ethnicity, age, and sex. Nonsexist language treats both females and males symmetrically and fairly, without creating special categories or assigning roles solely according to sex. Speakers who have difficulty selecting inclusive language should consult a dictionary of bias-free terms.

Use Effective Oral Style

12.6 Word your speech using effective oral style.

- To achieve effective *oral style*, use shorter sentences than you ordinarily write; use contractions, colloquial expressions, and slang when appropriate; use personal pronouns (*I, we, us, they*); and use more repetition than you normally would in writing.

Chapter 13
Delivering Your Speech

 Learning Objectives

After studying this chapter, you should be able to

13.1 Distinguish among the four methods of delivering speeches.

13.2 Apply qualities of effective delivery in your speech.

13.3 Incorporate the seven elements of effective vocal delivery into your speech.

13.4 Incorporate the six elements of physical delivery into your speech.

Communication scholar Karlyn Kohrs Campbell has said, "Ideas do not walk by themselves; they must be carried—expressed and voiced—by someone."[1] Each of us has a unique voice, body, and way of wording ideas. Your manner of presenting a speech—through your voice, body, and language—forms your style of delivery. In other words, *what* you say is your speech content and *how* you say it is your **delivery**. If you and a classmate presented a speech with the same words arranged in the same order (something we don't recommend), your listeners would still receive two different messages. This is because your delivery shapes your image as a speaker and changes your message in subtle ways.

This chapter is about the process of presenting your speech vocally and physically. Before we survey the individual elements that make up delivery, let's first consider four methods of delivering a speech.

Methods of Delivery

13.1 Distinguish among the four methods of delivering speeches.

The four basic ways you can deliver your public speech are: (1) impromptu, or with little or no advance preparation; (2) from memory; (3) from a manuscript; or (4) extemporaneously, or from notes.

Speaking Impromptu

We engage in **impromptu speaking** whenever someone calls on us to express an opinion or unexpectedly asks us to "say a few words" to a group. In these informal situations, other people may not necessarily expect us to be forceful or well organized, and we are probably somewhat comfortable speaking without preparation. The more important the speech, however, the less appropriate the impromptu method of delivery. Although impromptu speaking is excellent practice, no conscientious person should risk a grade, an important proposal, or professional advancement on an unprepared speech. To prepare yourself for impromptu speaking, consider the guidelines we discuss in "Theory Into Practice: The Impromptu Speech."

Speaking from Memory

Speaking from memory is appropriate only on rare occasions. We speak from memory when we prepare a written text and then memorize it word for word. At best, a memorized speech allows a smooth, almost effortless-looking delivery because the speaker has neither notes nor a manuscript and can concentrate on interacting with the audience. For most of us, however, memorizing takes a long time. Concentrating on the memory work we've done and our fear of forgetting part of the speech can also make us sound mechanical or programmed. For these reasons, speaking from memory is usually appropriate only for brief speeches, such as those introducing another speaker or presenting or accepting an award.

Speaking from Manuscript

Speaking from manuscript, or delivering a speech from a complete text prepared in advance, ensures that the speaker will not be at a loss for words and is essential in some situations. An address that will be quoted or later published in its entirety is typically delivered from a manuscript. Major foreign policy speeches and State of the Union addresses by U.S. presidents are always delivered from manuscript because it is important that the speaker be understood—and *not* misunderstood. Speeches of tribute and commencement addresses are often scripted. Manuscript delivery may be appropriate for any speaking situation calling for precise, well-worded communication.

delivery
The way a speaker presents a speech, through voice qualities, bodily actions, and language.

impromptu speaking
Speaking without advance preparation.

speaking from memory
Delivering a speech that is recalled word for word from a written text.

speaking from manuscript
Delivering a speech from a text written word for word and practiced in advance.

Theory Into Practice TIP

THE IMPROMPTU SPEECH

You are standing in the back of a crowded orientation session when, to your surprise, your supervisor introduces you and says, "Come up here and say a few words." Or you receive an award you didn't know you were being considered for. As people begin to applaud, you walk to the front of the room. These are but two situations in which you would deliver an impromptu speech.

The impromptu speech, one with limited or no advance preparation, can be intimidating. You have not had time to think about the ideas you want to communicate. You begin speaking without knowing the exact words you will use. You have not practiced delivering your speech. Don't panic! By now you have a pretty good understanding of how to organize, support, and deliver a speech. You will practice these skills in prepared speeches. All this practice will help you in your impromptu speech. If you follow these four guidelines, you should be ready for most impromptu speeches.

- If you have a choice, *speak on a topic you know well*. The more you know about your topic, the better you will be able to select relevant ideas, organize them, and explain them as you speak. In addition, your confidence will show in your delivery.

- *Make the most of the time you have*. Don't waste "walking time" from your seat to the front of the room worrying. Instead, ask yourself, "What do I want the audience to remember when I sit down? What two or three points will help them remember this?"

- *Focus on a single or a few key points*. If you have been asked to explain why you support building a new library instead of renovating the existing facility, think of two or three important reasons underlying your position. And remember to use the 4 S's as you present those reasons to your audience.

- *Be brief*. One public speaking axiom is, "Stand up! Speak up! Shut up! Sit down!" Although this can be carried to an extreme, it's probably good advice for the impromptu speaker. An impromptu speech is not the occasion for a long, rambling discourse. Say what you need to say, and then be seated.

Having every word of your speech scripted may boost your confidence, but it does not ensure effective delivery. You should write the speech in a conversational style. In other words, the manuscript must sound like something you would say in conversation. The text of your speech requires a good deal of time to prepare, edit, revise, and type for final delivery. In addition, if you do not also take time to practice delivering your speech in a fluent, conversational manner and with appropriate emphasis, well-placed pauses, and adequate eye contact, you are preparing to fail as an effective speaker.

Speaking Extemporaneously

The final method of delivery, and by far the most popular, is **speaking extemporaneously**, or from notes. Speaking from notes offers several advantages over other delivery methods. You need not worry about one particular way of wording your ideas because you have not scripted the speech. Neither do you have to worry that you will forget something you have memorized. With your notes in front of you, you are free to interact with the audience in a natural, conversational manner. If something you say confuses the audience, you can repeat it, explain it using other words, or use a better example to clarify it. Your language may not be as forceful or colorful as with a carefully prepared manuscript or a memorized speech, but speaking from notes helps ensure that you will be natural and spontaneous.

Former New York governor Mario Cuomo, skilled in various methods of delivery, reveals that he speaks extemporaneously whenever possible because "it's easier to engage the audience when you have both eyes in direct contact with the people you're addressing, both arms drawing pictures in the air, adding punctuation, fighting off the glaze."[3] The freedom, naturalness, and spontaneity of extemporaneous speaking make this method of delivery particularly attractive.

If a speech were a style of dress, it would be somewhere between a tuxedo and a flannel shirt. Not stiff. Not sloppy. . . . A speech is more like conversation than formal writing. Its phrasing is loose—but without the extremes of slang, the incomplete thoughts, the interruptions that flavor everyday speech.

—Elinor Donahue[2]

speaking extemporaneously

Delivering a speech from notes or from a memorized outline.

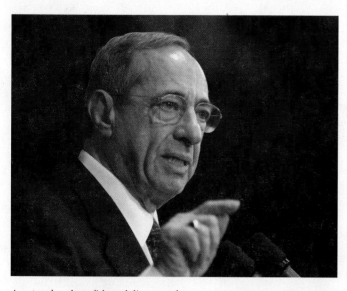

A natural and confident delivery style comes with practice. Record and view yourself on video or rehearse in front of friends to try out gestures and movements that will enhance your effectiveness.

When speaking either from notes or a manuscript, keep several practical points in mind:

1. *Practice with the notes or manuscript you will actually use in delivering the speech.* If you use sheets of paper, use a weight slightly heavier than bond so that it's easier to handle. Double- or even triple-space a speech manuscript and format text in a font size that's easy for you to see. Both of these strategies will make your words easier to read and help you keep your place. Type sentences on the upper two-thirds of each sheet of paper to help ensure better eye contact. You need to know where things are on the page so that you have to glance down only briefly.

2. *Number your notecards or the pages of your manuscript.* Check their order before you speak.

3. *Determine when you should and should not look at your notes.* Looking at your notes when you quote an authority or present statistics is acceptable. In fact, doing so may even convey to your audience your concern for getting supporting materials exactly right. However, do not look down while previewing, stating, or summarizing your key ideas. If you cannot remember your key points, what hope is there for your audience? Also, avoid looking down when you use personal pronouns such as *I*, *you*, and *we* or when you address audience members by name. A break in your eye contact at these points suddenly distances you from the audience and creates the impression that the speech is coming from a script rather than from you.

4. *Slide your notes or the pages of your manuscript rather than turning them.* To avoid picking them up and turning them over, do not write on the backs of your notes or manuscript. As a rule, if you use a lectern, do not let the audience see your notes after you place them in front of you. The less the audience is aware of your notes, the more direct and personal your communication with them will be.

5. *Devote extra practice time to your conclusion.* The last thing you say can make a deep impression, but not if you rush through it or deliver it while gathering your notes and walking back to your seat. Your goal at this critical point in the speech is the same as your goal for all your delivery: to eliminate distractions and to reinforce your message through your body, voice, and language.

The most satisfactory way of delivering your classroom speeches may combine all four of the methods we have discussed. To demonstrate that you are well prepared and to ensure eye contact with your audience, you may want to memorize your introduction and conclusion. If you deliver the body of your speech extemporaneously, look at your notes occasionally. Just don't look at your notes while you are stating or summarizing each main point. If you quote sources in your speech, you are, in effect, briefly using a manuscript. Finally, as an audience-centered speaker, you should be flexible enough to improvise a bit. You speak impromptu whenever you repeat an idea or think of a clearer or more persuasive example. If you are well prepared, this combination of delivery methods should look natural to your audience and feel comfortable to you.

Qualities of Effective Delivery

13.2   Apply qualities of effective delivery in your speech.

As you begin to think about the way you deliver a speech, keep in mind three characteristics of effective delivery. First, *effective delivery helps both listeners and speakers.*

Your audience has only one chance to receive your message. Just as clear organization makes your ideas easier to remember, effective delivery can underscore your key points, sell your ideas, or communicate your concern for the topic. Concentrate on your ideas and how the audience is receiving them. Pay attention to their interest in and understanding of your speech. If you notice listeners checking their watches, reading papers, text messaging, whispering to friends, or snoozing, they may be bored. At this point, enliven your delivery with movement and changes in your volume. Such relatively simple changes in your delivery may revive their interest. To make sure listeners understand the point you are making, you may want to slow your rate of delivery and use more pauses and descriptive gestures to reinforce your ideas.

Second, *the best delivery looks and feels natural, comfortable, and spontaneous.* Some occasions and audiences require you to be more formal than others. Speaking to a large audience through a stationary microphone, for example, will naturally restrict your movement. In other situations, you may find yourself moving, gesturing, and using presentational aids extensively. You want to orchestrate all these elements so that your presentation looks and feels relaxed and natural, not strained or awkward. You achieve spontaneous delivery such as this only through practice.

Third and finally, *delivery is best when nonverbal messages complement and reinforce the verbal messages.* We are reminded of the importance of nonverbal communication when someone breaks a nonverbal rule. Suppose Doris walks reluctantly to the front of the classroom, clutches the lectern, stands motionless, frowns, and says, "I'm absolutely delighted to be speaking to you today." Do you believe her? No. Why? Doris's speech began not with her first words, but with the many nonverbal messages that signaled her reluctance to speak. Nonverbal messages should complement and reinforce verbal ones. When they do not match, we tend to trust the nonverbal message.

Any prescription for effective delivery will include three basic elements: the *voice*, or vocal delivery; the *body*, or physical delivery; and *language*. Earlier we discussed how your language affects your delivery style. In this chapter, we focus on vocal and physical delivery.

> **Journal: Methods and Qualities of Delivery**
>
> Think of a recent presentation or lecture by one of your instructors. What method(s) of delivery did he or she use? Which of the qualities of effective delivery discussed in this text did the instructor follow? Based on these factors, how effective was the presentation overall?

Elements of Vocal Delivery

13.3 Incorporate the seven elements of effective vocal delivery in your speech.

Vocal delivery includes rate, pause, volume, pitch, inflection, articulation, and pronunciation.

Rate and Pause

You've probably heard the warning, "Look out for him; he's a fast talker," or words to that effect. Such a statement implies that someone who talks fast may be trying to put something over on us. At the other end of the spectrum, we often grow impatient with people who talk much slower than we do, even labeling them uncertain, dull, or dense. Though these stereotypes may be inaccurate, the impressions people form based on our nonverbal communication can become more important than anything we intend to communicate.

Your **rate**, or speed, of speaking can communicate something, intentionally or unintentionally, about your motives in speaking, your disposition, or your involvement with the topic. Your goal in a speech, therefore, should be to avoid delivery that is too fast or too slow. Instead, use a variety of rates to reinforce your purpose in speaking and make you seem conversational.

Although we can process information at rates faster than people speak, our comprehension depends on the type of material we are hearing. You should slow down, for example, when presenting detailed, highly complex information, particularly to

> **EXPLORING ONLINE**
>
> **Assessing Vocal Delivery**
>
> The History Channel's rich index of speeches and broadcasts that changed the world gives you a chance to appreciate the vocal deliveries of historical and contemporary figures. Just click on a category to browse the clips.

rate

The speed at which a speech is delivered.

Ethical Decisions

DELIVERY VERSUS CONTENT

A minister once wrote a delivery prompt in the margin of his speaking notes: "Shout here—argument weak!" Most of us would agree that using delivery to mask weak content is unethical. However, delivery can also demonstrate genuine confidence and enthusiasm for the topic.

As a member of Student Advocates for a Green Environment (SAGE), an organization promoting energy education, conservation, and efficiency across campus, you are selecting a spokesperson to represent SAGE to students, faculty, staff, and administrators. The individual will speak and answer questions in a series of public forums on campus.

Jones and Smith are the two best applicants, and you conclude that each would do a good job. However, you think Jones would be better at constructing the case for SAGE's agenda, but Smith would deliver her ideas with more enthusiasm and confidence.

All other factors being equal, which applicant would you select? What ethical obligations do you have to SAGE? To your audiences? To Jones and Smith? To yourself?

a group that knows little about your subject. This can work both ways, however. In some situations, speaking slightly faster than the rate of normal conversation may actually increase your persuasiveness by conveying the message that you know exactly what you want to say.

Pauses, or silences, can be an important element in your rate of delivery. You pause intentionally to allow the audience time to reflect on something you have just said or to heighten suspense about something you are going to say. Achim Nowak, author of *Power Speaking: The Art of the Exceptional Public Speaker*, contends that "a pause allows the listener to make a personal connection to the words she just heard. A pause invites the listener to relax into a presentation. A pause makes it possible for the speaker to sense the response of an audience to a presentation. Pauses are those beautiful moments when meaning happens and common ground emerges."[4] Pauses also mark important transitions in your speech, helping you and your audience shift gears. However, an unintentional pause at the wrong time may disrupt the flow of your speech and prevent your listeners from following the logic of your argument.

To test the importance of pauses, let's look at a sentence from a speech that President Barack Obama delivered. The president spoke at the memorial service for the victims of the 2011 shooting at a political gathering outside a Tucson, Arizona, supermarket. Try reading this passage without any internal punctuation or pauses:

> But at a time when our discourse has become so sharply polarized—at a time when we are far too eager to lay the blame for all that ails the world at the feet of those who happen to think differently than we do—it's important for us to pause for a moment and make sure that we're talking with each other in a way that heals, not in a way that wounds.

The sentences make sense only if you insert appropriate pauses. Speakers reading from a written text sometimes mark their manuscripts to help them pause appropriately. Now try reading Obama's sentence again, pausing a beat when you see one slash (/) and pausing a bit longer when you encounter two (//).

> But at a time when our discourse has become so sharply polarized // at a time when we are far too eager to lay the blame for all that ails the world / at the feet of those who think differently than we do // it's important for us to pause for a moment / and make sure that we're talking / with each other in a way that heals, // not a way that wounds.[5]

If the pauses marked were meaningful for you, the statement should have gained power. You may even disagree with the placement and length of the pauses we chose.

pause

An intentional or unintentional period of silence in a speaker's vocal delivery.

Accomplished speakers understand the importance of articulating clearly and adapting their volume to ensure that everyone in the audience can hear every word. If you are using a microphone, continue to speak in a conversational tone; let it do the work of amplifying your voice.

You might say the sentences differently, and that's fine. Public speaking is, after all, a creative and individual process. Remember, though, that to be effective in a speech, pauses must be used intentionally and selectively. If your speech is filled with too many awkwardly placed pauses—or too many **vocalized pauses**, such as "um" and "uh"—you will seem hesitant or unprepared, and your credibility will erode quickly.

Volume

Your audience must be able to hear you in order to listen to your ideas. **Volume** is simply how loudly or softly you speak. A person who speaks too loudly may be considered boisterous or obnoxious. In contrast, an inaudible speaker may be considered unsure or timid. Adapt your volume to the size of the room. In your classroom, you can probably use a volume just slightly louder than your usual conversational level.

When you speak before a large group, a microphone may be helpful or even essential. If possible, practice beforehand so that the sound of your amplified voice does not startle you. You may even be called on to speak before a large audience without a microphone. This is not as difficult as it sounds. In fact, your voice will carry well if you support your breathing from your diaphragm. To test your breathing, place your hand on your abdomen while repeating the sentence "Those old boats don't float" louder and louder. If you are breathing from the diaphragm, you should feel your abdominal muscles tightening. Without that support, you are probably trying to increase your volume from your throat, a mistake that could strain your voice.

At times, you may have to conquer a large space as well as external noise, such as the chattering of people in a hallway, the roar of nearby traffic, or the whoosh of an air-conditioning system. That may require hard work. If you can, use a microphone in such a situation, speak at normal volume, and let the public address system do the work for you. Don't use a microphone unless it is necessary; in a small room, a microphone distances you from the audience.

Pitch and Inflection

Pitch refers to the highness or lowness of vocal tones, similar to the notes on a musical staff. Every speaker has an optimal pitch range, or key. This is the range in which you are most comfortable speaking, and your voice is probably pleasant to hear in this range.

vocalized pause
Sounds or words such as *ah, like, okay, um, so,* and *you know* inserted to fill the silence between a speaker's words or thoughts.

volume
The relative loudness or softness of a speaker's voice.

pitch
The highness or lowness of a speaker's voice.

Speakers who are unusually nervous sometimes raise their pitch. Other speakers think that if they lower their pitch, they will seem more authoritative. In truth, speakers who do not use their normal pitch usually sound artificial.

The following practice technique may help you retain or recapture a natural, conversational tone in your delivery. Begin some of your practice sessions seated. Imagine a good friend sitting across from you, and pretend that she asks you what your speech is about. Answer her question by summarizing and paraphrasing your speech: "Mary, I'm going to talk about the advantages of consuming grass-fed rather than grain-fed beef. I've divided my speech into two main arguments. Grass-fed beef has half the saturated fat of grain-fed beef, and grass-fed cattle are treated more humanely than factory-farmed grain-fed beef." Listen closely to the tone of your voice as you speak. You are having a conversation with a friend. You're not tense; you feel comfortable.

Now, keeping this natural, conversational tone in mind, stand up, walk to the front of the room, and begin your speech. Your words will change, but the tone of your speech should be comfortable and conversational, as it was before. In a sense, you are merely having a conversation with a larger audience. We have found this technique helpful for students whose vocal delivery sounds artificial or mechanical. They find their natural pitch ranges and incorporate more meaningful pauses.

A problem more typical than an unusually high- or low-pitched voice is vocal delivery that lacks adequate **inflection**, or changes in pitch. Someone who speaks without changing pitch delivers sentences in a flat, uniform pitch that becomes monotonous. Indeed, the word *monotone* means "one tone," and you may have had instructors whose monotonous droning invited you to doze. Inflection is an essential tool for conveying meaning accurately. You can give a simple four-word sentence four distinct meanings by raising the pitch and volume of one word at a time:

"**She** is my friend." (Not the young woman standing with her.)

"She **is** my friend." (Don't try to tell me she isn't!)

"She is **my** friend." (Not yours.)

"She is my **friend**." (There's nothing more to our relationship than that.)

In public speaking, women can generally make wider use of their pitch ranges than men can without sounding affected or unnatural. For this reason, men often find that they need to vary other vocal and physical elements of delivery—volume, rate, and gestures, for example—to compensate for a limited pitch range.

Articulation and Pronunciation

The final elements of vocal delivery we will discuss are articulation and pronunciation. **Articulation** is the mechanical process of forming the sounds necessary to communicate in a particular language. Most articulation errors are made from habit and take four principal forms: deletion, addition, substitution, and transposition.

Deletion is leaving out sounds—for example, saying "libary" for "library" or "goverment" for "government." If you have heard someone say "athalete" for "athlete," you've heard an example of an articulation error caused by the *addition* of a sound. Examples of errors caused by the *substitution* of one sound for another are "kin" for "can" and "git" for "get." The final type of articulation error is one of *transposition*, or the reversal of two sounds that are close together. This error is the vocal equivalent of transposing two letters in a typed word. Saying "lectren" for "lectern" or "hunderd" for "hundred" are examples of transposition errors.

Articulation errors made as a result of habit may be so ingrained that you can no longer identify your mistakes. Your speech instructor, friends, and classmates can help you by pointing out articulation problems. You may need to listen to recordings of your speeches to locate problems and then practice the problem words or sounds to correct your articulation.

EXPLORING ONLINE

Checking Pronunciation
Use the Merriam-Webster website to check the pronunciations of unfamiliar words. Enter your query term and click the Search button. To hear the word pronounced correctly, just click the loudspeaker icon near the definition.

inflection
Patterns of change in a person's pitch while speaking.

articulation
The mechanical process of forming the sounds necessary to communicate in a particular language.

Pronunciation, in contrast to articulation, is simply a matter of knowing how the letters of a word sound and where the stress falls when that word is spoken. We all have two vocabularies: a speaking vocabulary and a reading vocabulary.

Most of us make errors in pronunciation primarily when we try to move a word from our reading vocabulary to our speaking vocabulary without consulting the dictionary. In a public speech, the resulting pronunciation error can be a minor distraction or a major disaster, depending on how far off your mispronunciation is and how many times you make the error. If you have any doubt about the pronunciation of a word you plan to use in a speech, look it up in a current dictionary and then practice the correct pronunciation out loud. Apply this rule to every word you select, including those in quotations. If you follow this simple rule, you will avoid embarrassing errors of pronunciation.

Pronunciation of proper nouns—the names of specific people, places, and things—can also pose difficulties. Proper nouns should be pronounced the way that the people who have the name (or who live in the place or who named the thing) pronounce them. For instance, the large city on the Texas Gulf coast is pronounced "HEWstun;" the street in New York City spelled the same way is pronounced "HOWstun." Decide on a reasonable pronunciation, practice it, and deliver it with confidence in your speech. For names of places, consult the *Pronouncing Gazetteer* or the list of geographical names found online or at the back of many dictionaries.

Once you have mastered these elements of vocal delivery, your speech will be free of articulation errors and mispronounced words. Your voice will be well modulated, with enough inflection to communicate your ideas clearly. You will speak loudly enough that all your listeners can hear you easily. You will adapt your rate to the content of your message, and you will pause to punctuate key ideas and major transitions. In short, your sound will be coming through loud and clear. Now let's consider the picture your listeners will see by examining the aspects of physical delivery.

> **EXPLORING ONLINE**
>
> **Pronouncing Proper Names**
> The National Library Service, a division of the Library of Congress, provides online pronunciation guides. Type "NLS pronunciation names" to access correct pronunciations of noted individuals. Type "NLS ABC Book" for brand names and acronyms.

> **Key Points**
> **Elements of Vocal Delivery**
> 1. Rate and pause
> 2. Volume
> 3. Pitch and inflection
> 4. Articulation and pronunciation

Elements of Physical Delivery

13.4 Incorporate the six elements of physical delivery into your speech.

Physical delivery includes appearance, posture, facial expression, eye contact, movement, and gestures.

Appearance

We all form quick impressions of people we meet based on subtle nonverbal signals. **Appearance**, in particular our grooming and the way we dress, is an important nonverbal signal that helps people judge us. Why is appearance so important?

Studies demonstrate that people we consider attractive can persuade us more easily than those we find unattractive. In addition, high-status clothing carries more authority than does low-status clothing. For example, studies show we are more likely to jaywalk behind a person dressed in a dark blue suit, a crisp white shirt, and a dark tie who is carrying an expensive black-leather briefcase than we would behind a person dressed in rags or even in jeans. We will also take orders more easily from that well-dressed person than we would from someone poorly dressed. These studies reinforce the adage that "clothes make the person," a saying any public speaker would do well to remember.

The safest advice on appearance that we can offer the public speaker is to be neat, to be clean, and to avoid extremes in dress and grooming. Use clothes to reinforce your purpose in speaking, not to draw attention. Every moment that the audience spends admiring your suit or wondering why you wore the torn T-shirt is a moment they are distracted from your message.

pronunciation

How the sounds of a word are to be said and which parts are to be stressed.

appearance

A speaker's physical features, including dress and grooming.

In selecting your attire, consider the occasion, audience, topic, and your image as a speaker.

1. *Consider the Occasion.* The speaking occasion dictates, in part, how formally or informally you can dress. A speech in your classroom probably permits you to be more informal than you would be delivering a business presentation to a board of directors or an acceptance speech at an awards ceremony.

2. *Consider Your Audience.* Some of your listeners dress more casually than others. In any audience, there is a range of attire. As a rule, dress at or near the top of that range. You should appear as nicely dressed as the best-dressed people in your audience.

3. *Consider Your Topic.* Your clothing can underscore or undermine the impact you want your speech to have. A hot-pink dress or a lime-green shirt might be entirely appropriate for a speech on Mardi Gras, but not for one on the high cost of funerals. On the other hand, you would look and feel silly wearing a business suit to demonstrate basic poses of Bikram yoga.

4. *Consider Your Image.* The clothing you select can shape—or even change—the image you want to create as a speaker. Darker colors convey authority and seriousness; lighter colors establish a friendlier image. A student perceived as the class clown may want to dress more formally to help dispel this image.

Clothing also shapes our self-perception. You probably have certain clothes that give you a sense of confidence or make you feel especially assertive or powerful when you wear them. Dressing "up" conveys your seriousness of purpose to your listeners. It also establishes this same positive attitude in your own mind.

Decide what you will wear before the day of your speech and practice at least once in those clothes. One of our students discovered that she was distracted during her presentation because when she moved her arms to gesture, her coat made a rustling sound. She could have eliminated this distraction if she had practiced in that suit coat before the day of her speech. Whatever the problems, it's best to encounter and fix them before the speech. You can then concentrate fully on the speech itself.

Posture

A public speaker should look comfortable, confident, and prepared to speak. You have the appropriate attire. Your next concern is your **posture**, the position or bearing of your body. The two extremes to avoid are rigidity and sloppiness. Don't hang onto or drape yourself across the lectern, if you are using one. Keep your weight balanced on both legs, and avoid shifting your weight back and forth. Equally distracting is standing on one leg and shuffling or tapping the other foot. You may not realize that you do those things. One student told us that she tied bells to her shoes when she practiced her speeches so that she would "hear what her feet were doing." If you practice in front of friends, ask them to point out delivery distractions. Remember that for your delivery to reinforce your message, it must be free of annoying mannerisms.

Facial Expression

Estimates of the number of possible human facial expressions range from 5,000 to 250,000.[6] Even if the actual number is closer to 5,000, that's still a significant amount of communication potential. Yet many people giving a speech for the first time put on a blank mask, limiting their **facial expression** to one neutral look. Inexperienced speakers are understandably nervous and may be more concerned with the way they look and sound than they are with the ideas they are trying to communicate.

Your facial expression must match what you are saying. The speaker who smiles and blushes self-consciously through a speech on date rape will simply not be taken

posture

The position or bearing of a speaker's body while delivering a speech.

facial expression

The tension and movement of various parts of a speaker's face.

seriously and may offend many listeners. If you detail the plight of earthquake victims, make sure your face reflects your concern. If you tell a joke and your listeners can't stop chuckling, break into a smile rather than a frown (unless your frown is part of the joke). In other words, your face should register the thoughts and feelings that motivate your words.

The way to use facial expression appropriately to bolster your message is simple: concentrate as much as possible on the ideas you present and the way your audience receives and responds to them. Try not to be overly conscious of how you look and sound. This takes practice, but your classroom speeches provide a good forum for such rehearsal. You will learn to interact with the audience, maintain eye contact, and respond with them to your own message. If you do those things, chances are your facial expression will be varied and appropriate and will reinforce your spoken words.

Eye Contact

We've all heard the challenge, "Look me in the eye and say that." We use direct eye contact as one gauge of a person's truthfulness. **Eye contact** can also carry many other messages: confidence, concern, sincerity, interest, and enthusiasm. A lack of eye contact, on the other hand, may signal deceit, disinterest, or insecurity.

Your face is the most important source of nonverbal cues as you deliver your speech, and your eyes carry more information than any other facial feature. As you speak, you will occasionally look at your notes or manuscript. You may even glance away from the audience briefly as you try to put your thoughts into words. Yet you must keep coming back to the eyes of your listeners to check their understanding, interest, and evaluation of your message.

As a public speaker, your goal is to make eye contact with as much of the audience as much of the time as possible. To do this, make sure that you take in your entire audience, from front to back and from left to right. Include all those boundaries in the scope of your eye contact, and look especially at those individuals who seem to be listening carefully and responding positively. Whether you actually make eye contact with each member of the audience is immaterial. You must create that impression. Again, this takes practice.

Movement

Effective **movement** benefits you, your audience, and your speech. First, place-to-place movement can actually help you relax. Moving to a visual aid, for example, can help you energize and loosen up physically. From the audience's perspective, movement adds visual variety to your speech, and appropriate movement can arouse or rekindle listeners' interest. Most important, though, physical movement serves your speech by guiding the audience's attention. Through movement, you can underscore key ideas, mark major transitions, or intensify an appeal for belief or action.

Remember that your speech starts the moment you enter your audience's presence. Your behavior, including your movement, sends signals about your attitudes toward the audience and your speech topic. When your time to speak arrives, approach your speaking position confidently, knowing that you have something important to say. If you use a lectern, don't automatically box yourself into one position behind it. Even the smallest lectern puts a physical barrier between you and your audience. Moving to the side or the front of it reduces both the physical and the psychological distance between you and your listeners and may be especially helpful when you conclude your speech with a persuasive appeal.

Make certain that your movement is selective and that it serves a purpose. Avoid random pacing. Movement to mark a transition should occur at the beginning or the end of a sentence, not in the middle. Finally, bring the speech to a satisfying

eye contact
Gaze behavior in which a speaker looks at listeners' eyes.

movement
A speaker's motion from place to place during speech delivery.

Speaking with Confidence

Delivery is an important part of the speech that is associated with speaker nervousness. For me, speaking extemporaneously helped me feel more confident because I didn't have to memorize my speeches. However, I still get nervous when delivering my speeches, which made me feel like I had extra energy flowing through my body. In this chapter, I learned that all that energy can be used to my advantage and actually make me speak more confidently. For example, I channeled my nervous energy to my voice by speaking loudly and clearly. Additionally, I managed my nervousness by walking when transitioning and using hand gestures, which reduced the nervous energy in my body. To ensure my delivery was effective and that it would help me feel more confident when delivering my speeches, I always practiced my delivery in front of my friends. My friends gave me suggestions about how to gesture and what words to emphasize and that made me less nervous when delivering my speeches in class.

LILIBETH FUENTES
Penn State Hazleton

psychological conclusion, and pause for a second or two before gathering your materials and moving toward your seat.

Gestures

gestures

Movements of a speaker's hands, arms, and head while delivering a speech.

Gestures—movements of a speaker's hands, arms, and head—seem to be as natural a part of human communication as spoken language. Gestures punctuate and emphasize verbal messages for the benefit of listeners and ease the process of encoding those messages for speakers. Studies show that people asked to communicate without gestures produce labored speech marked by increased hesitations and pauses. Such speakers also demonstrate decreased fluency and inflection, and they use fewer high-imagery words.[7] Hand gestures, then, seem to help speakers retrieve elusive words from their memories.[8]

Gestures are important adjuncts to our verbal messages; at times, they even replace words altogether. As a public speaker, you can use gestures to indicate the size of objects, to re-create some bodily motion, to emphasize or underscore key ideas, to point to things such as presentational aids, or to trace the flow of your ideas. If you don't normally gesture in conversation, force yourself to include some gestures as you practice your speech. At first you may feel self-conscious about gesturing. Keep practicing. Gestures that seem natural and spontaneous are well worth whatever time you spend practicing them. They reinforce your ideas and make you seem more confident and dynamic and, like movement, they can help you relax.

Effective speakers understand the importance of vocal and physical interaction with their audience. They talk to their listeners and not to their presentational aids.

To be effective, gestures must be coordinated with your words and must appear natural and spontaneous. Any gesture should be large enough for the audience to see it clearly. The speaker who gestures below the waist or whose gestures are barely visible over the top of a lectern may appear timid, unsure, or nervous. Speakers who gesture too much—who talk with their hands—may be perceived as nervous, flighty, or excitable. Therefore, the two extremes to avoid are the absence of gestures (hands clenched on the sides of the lectern) and excessive gestures (gestures emphasizing everything,

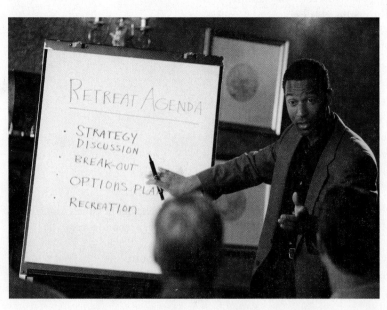

so that nothing stands out). Remember, if your audience is waiting for you to gesture or counting your many gestures, they are distracted from your message.

The following two generalizations from research on gestures are particularly helpful for the public speaker. First, people who are confident, relaxed, and have high status tend to expand into the space around them and use gestures that are wider than those of other people. Speakers who wish to emphasize their authority can do so by increasing the width of their gestures. Second, a wide, palms-up gesture creates an openness that is entirely appropriate when a speaker is appealing for a certain belief or urging the audience to some action. A palm-down gesture carries more force and authority and can be used to command an audience into action or to exhort them to a certain belief.

As a speaker, adapt the size of your gestures to the size of your audience. Before a crowd of several thousand, your gestures should be more expansive than when you stand at the front of a small classroom. In a cavernous auditorium, you must adjust your gestures, facial expressions, and eye contact so they will be clear to those in the back rows.

These, then, are the tools of vocal and physical delivery, from rate of speaking to hand gestures. Your goal throughout this class and in your future public speaking experience will be to eliminate distracting elements and then work toward delivery that is conversational, forceful, and as formal or informal as your audience and subject require.

One traditional saying is "If it's worth doing, it's worth doing well." That's wise counsel for the public speaker. Delivery is a vital part of your speech, and effective vocal and physical delivery are assets worth cultivating.

> **Key Points**
> **Elements of Physical Delivery**
> 1. Appearance
> 2. Posture
> 3. Facial expression
> 4. Eye contact
> 5. Movement
> 6. Gestures

> **Journal: Vocal and Physical Delivery**
> Name a famous person you find to be an exciting speaker. How does this individual's vocal and physical delivery add to his or her ideas? Which of these techniques could you adapt to make your speaking more dynamic?

Summary

Methods of Delivery

13.1 Distinguish among the four methods of delivering speeches.

- As a speaker, you can select one, or a combination, of four methods of delivery: *impromptu speaking*, or speaking without advance preparation; *speaking from memory*; *speaking from manuscript*; and *speaking extemporaneously*, or from notes.

Qualities of Effective Delivery

13.2 Apply qualities of effective delivery in your speech.

- As you begin to think about the way you deliver a speech, keep in mind three qualities. First, effective delivery helps both listeners and speakers. Second, your best delivery looks and feels natural,

comfortable, and spontaneous. And, third, delivery is best when nonverbal and verbal messages complement and reinforce each other.

Elements of Vocal Delivery

13.3 Incorporate the seven elements of effective vocal delivery in your speech.

- *Vocal delivery* includes your rate, use of pauses, volume, pitch, inflection, articulation, and pronunciation.

Elements of Physical Delivery

13.4 Incorporate the six elements of physical delivery into your speech.

- Your appearance, posture, facial expression, eye contact, movement, and gestures make up the elements of your *physical delivery*.

Chapter 14
Using Presentational Aids

Learning Objectives

After studying this chapter, you should be able to

14.1 Articulate four benefits of using presentational aids in speeches.

14.2 Describe, with examples, nine classifications of presentational aids.

14.3 Use the three types of projected presentational aids.

14.4 Apply the strategies for using presentational aids.

If you form a vivid mental image of any of the events described in the margin, you prove the haunting power of pictures.[1] We have all grown up in a visually oriented society. Even our language reflects the power of the visual message: "A picture is worth a thousand words." "I wouldn't have believed it if I hadn't seen it with my own eyes."

Today, our newspapers, magazines, and computer screens are filled with pictures—black-and-white or color. When the news is bad, we expect to see pictures or video of the airplane wreckage, the flooding, or the aftermath of the earthquake. When the news is good, we expect to see pictures of the winning team or the heroic rescue. We are, indeed, people for whom "seeing is believing." As a speaker, you need not rely only on words to communicate your ideas precisely and powerfully. You can add force and impact to many messages by incorporating a visual dimension.

A space shuttle exploding in a cloudless azure sky . . .

A Boeing 767 disappearing into the glass and steel frame of a 100-story building . . .

A wall of ocean water racing toward a tropical coastline . . .

Thirty-three Chilean miners rescued after more than 2 months underground . . .

World leaders and the citizens of South Africa gathering to commemorate the life of Nelson Rolihlahla Mandela . . .

The Importance of Using Presentational Aids

14.1 Articulate four benefits of using presentational aids in speeches.

A well-designed, appropriate presentational aid can add significantly to the effectiveness of the speech and the speaker. Consider the following four functions as you determine whether to include presentational aids in a particular speech.

Increases Message Clarity

First, presentational aids give your speech greater clarity. They can specify the demographic breakdown of voters in the past election, illustrate the structure of an online course, or explain the process of monitoring and controlling air traffic. You can convey detailed statistical information more clearly in a simplified line graph than by merely reciting the data. Speeches using a spatial organizational pattern often benefit particularly from visual reinforcement.

Reinforces Message Impact

Second, presentational aids give your speech greater impact. Seeing may encourage believing; certainly, it aids remembering. An Internet search for "effectiveness of visual aids" will enable you to access an abundance of research, expert opinion, and conjecture regarding the merits of using visual aids in a variety of contexts, including public speeches. Used wisely, visual aids can enhance the impact of your message. Because listeners both hear and see your message, they are more fully involved with your speech. This added sensory participation seems to appeal to audience members with various learning styles, lessen the opportunity for distractions, and increase message retention. Thus, a well-constructed presentational aid engages listeners to remember more of your speech for a longer period of time.

Increases Speaker Dynamism

Third, presentational aids increase your dynamism. Gestures are an important part of your delivery. Most speakers, unfortunately, have difficulty incorporating meaningful gestures into their delivery. Using presentational aids forces you to move, to point, and to become physically involved with your speech. Your gestures become motivated and meaningful, and, consequently, you appear more dynamic and forceful.

EXPLORING ONLINE

Using Presentational Aids

Search online for the University of Leicester's web page called "Using Visual Aids." Here you will find study guides and tips for creating and using visual aids in your presentations.

Enhances Speaker Confidence

A fourth benefit of using presentational aids in your speech is that it can increase your confidence as a public speaker. Clear, attractive presentational aids that you have practiced using can help you relax in three ways. First, knowing that your presentational aids will enhance the clarity and impact of your message should increase your confidence. Second, revealing your presentational aids gives purpose to your movement and gestures, and this will help burn off some of your nervous energy. Finally, if you become nervous when you see the listeners' eyes focused on you, you can use your presentational aids to divert their attention to your speech content. Just remember that the primary purpose of your presentational aids should not be to divert attention from you but to enhance the impact of your message.

Notice that in referring to the use of presentational aids, we have inserted words and phrases such as "well-constructed" and "used wisely." "Quite simply," as one professional speech coach notes, "the moment a visual appears on a screen, the audience will focus on the visual rather than listen to what you, the speaker, are saying. . . . [T]he visual always wins."[2] Remember that presentational aids are supplements to, not replacements for, your spoken words. As a speaker, you communicate; your presentational aids simply illustrate. As a speaker, you need to ask and answer several questions: Should I incorporate presentational aids in my speech? If so, what type should I select? How should I design these aids? When should I reveal them in my speech? How should I present them as I speak? We discuss these and other issues regarding this important speech component in this chapter.

> **Journal: Benefits of Presentational Aids**
>
> Suppose you are giving a speech to persuade your audience that a specific building on your campus should be torn down and replaced with another facility. Describe one possible presentational aid or image you might use. How would it benefit your speech?

Types of Presentational Aids

14.2 Describe, with examples, nine classifications of presentational aids.

Presentational aids come in many forms, but they can generally be divided into these classifications: objects, pictures, diagrams, graphs, charts, maps, film and video, handouts, and audio aids. You need to determine the type most appropriate to your presentation.

Objects

object
An actual item or three-dimensional model of an item used during the delivery of a speech.

Objects may be either actual size, such as a digital camera, or scaled, such as an architect's model. Other three-dimensional presentational aids are, for instance, a scuba diver's oxygen tank and breathing regulator, a deck of tarot cards, a replica of the Statue of Liberty, or an MP4 player.

Speaking with Confidence

Visual aids emphasize and stir interest in a speaker's topic. They can add dimension to the spoken word. My persuasive speech was on stem cell research. I knew that this topic was very controversial, and I didn't want my audience to get caught up in their own preconceived opinions. Using a visual aid that included a computer image of Christopher Reeve attached to a respirator in his wheelchair immediately captured the attention of my audience. I proceeded to explain all the possible medical advances and the thousands of individuals who could possibly be cured of their ailments by stem cell research. The visual image accompanied by my words left a lasting impression. Seeing the expressions on the audience's faces when they saw my visual aid helped me to feel more confident in my speaking ability.

LAUREN FISHMAN
Suffolk County Community
College, Selden

Also included in the category of objects are people or animals you employ in delivering a speech. You might enlist a volunteer to help you demonstrate tests for color blindness or, with your instructor's permission, bring in a Jack Russell terrier for a speech on that breed of dog. Objects used effectively give your speech immediacy and carry a great deal of impact.

Pictures

Pictures can make a speaker's oral presentation more concrete and vivid. It is difficult to imagine how a speech on the artistic styles of Georgia O'Keeffe or Edward Hopper could be effective without pictures or prints of some of their paintings. A speaker trying to persuade the audience that subliminal messages are common in advertising without showing some examples would be both vague and unconvincing.

Speakers can also use pictures to vivify a point. Our student Javier delivered a persuasive speech about wearing a helmet while riding a bicycle. A few years earlier, Javier had a serious bicycle accident and had to spend several days in a hospital. During that time, the doctors and Javier's family took several pictures of Javier's injuries. When delivering his speech, Javier displayed several of his pictures as a part of his PowerPoint presentation. The pictures were quite graphic and therefore enhanced the impact of his speech.

If you are not using your own photographs, you can locate pictures on the Internet in three different ways.[3] First, you can choose a search engine and enter the term you want, followed by the file format extension that you prefer (Eiffel Tower.jpg or roller coaster.gif, for example). Second, most popular search engines, such as Google, have a toolbar icon to let you limit your search to pictures, photos, or images. Third, you can use the photograph databases at special websites such as the ones mentioned in the "Exploring Online" feature on this page. Be sure to record information about the source of any photograph so that you can cite it appropriately in your speech and in a written bibliography.

When you use pictures, make sure that you select them with size and clarity in mind. A small snapshot of the Palace of Versailles or a picture from an encyclopedia held up for audience view detracts from, rather than reinforces, the speaker's purpose. Pictures used as presentational aids often must be enlarged. You can use a color copier at a copy shop or at your campus multimedia center to enlarge your pictures. If the room where you'll speak has a visual document camera, such as Elmo, you can project small pictures on a screen for easy audience viewing. These document cameras can project transparencies, video, computer slide shows, and computer animation as well as images of three-dimensional objects. Many models feature auto focus and power zoom magnification controlled by wireless remotes.

You can also scan or copy your picture and save it to a disk, a CD, or a flash drive. Then project your presentational aid from a computer.

Diagrams

Diagrams are graphics showing the parts of an object or organization or the steps in a process. A diagram could show the features of a commercial spacecraft design, the organizational structure of the U.S. judicial system, or the steps in the lost-wax method of casting jewelry. The best diagrams achieve their impact by simplifying and exaggerating key points. For example, no diagram of manageable size could illustrate all the parts of a hybrid, gas–electric car engine. However, a carefully constructed diagram, whether drawn on poster board or projected from the latest high-tech storage device, could isolate and label key parts of that engine design.

Graphs

Graphs can now be easily created using commonly available spreadsheet software and are effective presentational aids taking several forms.

EXPLORING ONLINE

Public Domain Photos
Public Domain Sherpa is an excellent website for researching photos and other public domain resources. An alphabetical listing of dozens of sites, with links, includes a brief introduction to "what's there" and "using the photos" for each site. Also instructive is background information regarding public domain, including a discussion of "10 Common Misconceptions about the Public Domain."

picture
A photograph, painting, drawing, or print used to make a point more vivid or convincing.

diagram
A graphic, usually designed on a computer or drawn on poster board, showing the parts of an object or organization or the steps in a process.

line graph

A diagram used to depict changes among variables over time.

bar graph

A diagram used to show quantitative comparisons among variables.

pie, or circle, graph

A diagram used to show the relative proportions of a whole.

LINE GRAPH.   A **line graph** is useful in depicting trends and developments over time. A speaker might convincingly use a line graph to illustrate the rising cost of a college education over the previous 20 years. Some line graphs trace two or more variables. For example, one of our students, Ashkira, used a two-line graph in which she displayed the changes in gasoline prices and the average annual income during the past 10 years. Her line graph was easy to interpret because she used two different colors (blue and red) and she provided a legend on her graph where she noted: blue = gasoline prices, red = annual income. This chapter's "Ethical Decisions" feature also includes examples of line graphs.

BAR GRAPH.   A **bar graph** is useful when comparing quantities or amounts. We can measure the economic health of an institution, a company, or a nation, for example, by learning whether it is "in the red" or "in the black." A bar graph contrasting deficits and profits, showing their relative size, provides a clear, visual indication of economic health, particularly when income is represented in black and deficits in red.

PIE, OR CIRCLE, GRAPH.   A third type of graph, the **pie, or circle, graph**, is helpful when you want to show relative portions of the various parts of a whole. If you are analyzing the federal budget, for example, a pie graph could illustrate the percentage allocated for defense. Pie graphs can show proportions that people spend in particular activities in a typical 24-hour day, the causes of cancer deaths, and the composition of your university according to declared majors. When using a pie graph, emphasize the pertinent "slice" of the graph with a contrasting color.

Edith used both bar and pie graphs to highlight key statistics in her speech. She had read and heard conflicting assertions about the amount of renewable energy produced in the United States. She decided to inform her audience of some "facts" about energy consumption so that they could better understand the context of the issue. In her speech, she displayed a pie graph (Figure 14.1) that she found on the U.S. Energy Information Administration's website; it showed that renewable energy was a source for 8 percent of energy consumption. Edith also read statistics that specified how much energy each of the seven types of renewable energy contributed. She reasoned that seven "slices" were too many in a pie graph, so she used a bar graph (Figure 14.2) to show how each source of energy compared to the others.

Figure 14.1 Sample Pie Graph

Pie graphs compare the percentages of a variable, here the sources of energy consumption.

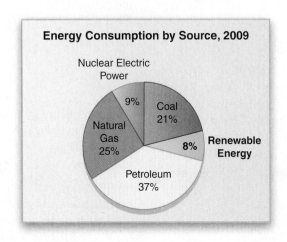

Figure 14.2 Sample Bar Graph

Bar graphs compare quantities or amounts, here the sources of renewable energy.

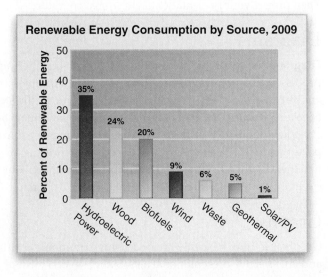

Ethical Decisions

IS SEEING BELIEVING?

Jayden chose involvement in student government as the topic for his persuasive speech. In his research, he discovered a decrease in the percentage of students voting in Student Government Association elections. He chose to focus on the past six years. He compiled the voting percentages, drew a rough draft of his intended visual aid, and asked his friend Leah to prepare a line graph on her computer. She produced the following graph:

Figure 14A

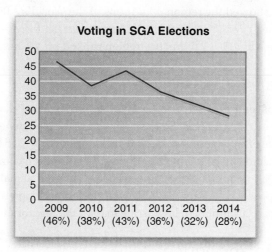

When Jayden evaluated the graph, he didn't think it sufficiently dramatized the decline in voting. He decided to include only the past four years when the percentage of students voting had decreased significantly. He increased the spacing in the vertical axis of his graph to emphasize the decline. Leah then produced the following graph:

Figure 14B

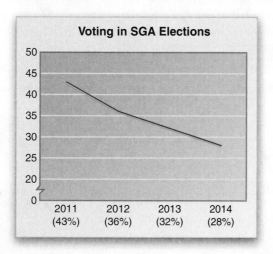

Do you think Jayden's second graph is an unethical manipulation of data? Why or why not? What ethical guidelines should speakers follow as they design presentational aids to be vivid and memorable? Provide some examples of presentational aids speakers might use that would be unethical.

Charts

Like diagrams and graphs, **charts** condense a large amount of information into a small space. Speakers introducing new terms will sometimes list those words on a chart. This strategy is particularly effective if the words can be uncovered one at a time in the order they are discussed. Using charts, you could list the top ten states in per capita lottery ticket sales or rank professional sports according to players' average salaries. A speaker detailing the solution phase of a problem–solution speech could list steps advocated on a chart and introduce them in the order they are discussed.

Joyce chose to inform her audience about how the Internet had facilitated greater global "connectedness." Early in her speech she presented a chart (Figure 14.3) that showed the regional locations of the World's 2,095,006,005 Internet users. Using PowerPoint, she "flew in" her numbered list from bottom to top, creating suspense as to where her classmates' region ranked on the list.

Maps

Maps lend themselves especially well to speeches discussing or referring to unfamiliar geographic areas. Speakers informing their listeners on the islands of Hawaii, the Battle of Gettysburg, or federal lands currently leased by oil companies would do well to include maps to illustrate their ideas. Although commercial maps are professionally prepared and look good, they may be either too small or too detailed for a speaker's purpose. If you cannot isolate and project a section of the map for a larger audience, prepare a simplified, large-scale map of the territory in question.

Film and Video

Films and videos are appropriate whenever action will enhance a visual presentation. Though videos carry with them possible distractions, their potential impact is undeniable. Many speeches on social problems are significantly more compelling if the audience not only hears about but also sees graphic evidence of the problem. You can find numerous video clips on the Internet using most search engines. Be sure to note the source of any film or video clip you plan to save for multimedia display in your speech so that you can cite them accurately. Moreover, with the widespread popularity of DVDs and updated technology in the classroom, this type of presentational aid

Figure 14.3 Sample Chart

Charts gather information into a convenient format, here the number of Internet users worldwide.

chart
A graphic used to condense a large amount of information, to list the steps in a process, or to introduce new terms.

map
A graphic representation of a real or imaginary geographic area.

film and video
Moving projections used to enhance a speaker's point.

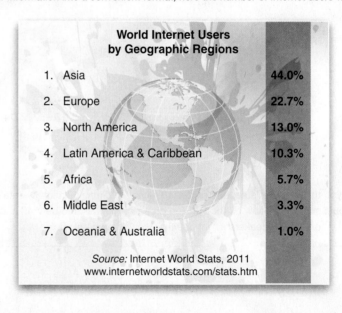

World Internet Users by Geographic Regions

1. Asia — 44.0%
2. Europe — 22.7%
3. North America — 13.0%
4. Latin America & Caribbean — 10.3%
5. Africa — 5.7%
6. Middle East — 3.3%
7. Oceania & Australia — 1.0%

Source: Internet World Stats, 2011
www.internetworldstats.com/stats.htm

is becoming easier and cheaper to use. However, it is important that you, not a presentational aid, organize and present the ideas of your speech. Use only short video clips to illustrate your key ideas.

One popular method for incorporating film clips into speeches is to use Internet-based video caches such as Yahoo!, Hulu, and YouTube. While YouTube and similar sites offer the distinct advantage of not having to buy or rent a DVD, your classroom must have reliable high-speed Internet access in order to smoothly present your clip. It is also somewhat precarious to rely on an Internet-stored video clip that can be removed from the site without notice. One solution to this problem is to use a software program allowing you to download the clips that can then be placed on a thumb drive or other storage devices, or inserted directly into a PowerPoint presentation.

Your imagination and your ability to limit yourself to brief clips are your primary obstacles. For example, using YouTube, Google Video, or any of the other video websites, you can show listeners gymnast Alexander Artemev's amazing moves on the pommel horse; vintage concert clips of singer/performer Nina Hagen; world-renowned mime Marcel Marceau's character Bip; or newsreel of the 1940 collapse of the Tacoma Narrows Bridge, known as Galloping Gertie. Video and film can also introduce viewers to aspects of various cultures. One of our students, Henry, delivered an informative speech on the topic of Sufism, an Islamic tradition that is both mystical and multicultural. He informed his listeners how this tradition combines dance and music to express spiritual ecstasy. He played a videotape of the "whirling dervishes" dances of the Mevlevi Order, pointing out the religious significance of the dancers' gestures and movements.

Handouts

A final method of visually presenting material is the **handout**. Copies of any presentational aid—pictures, diagrams, graphs, charts, or maps—may be handed out to individual audience members. Handouts are appropriately used when the information cannot be effectively displayed or projected or when the audience needs to study or refer to the information after the speech.

Gwen, a student presenting her speech "The Power Résumé," used a handout to great benefit. She distributed a sample power résumé and referred to it at key intervals in her speech: "If you look at line 15, you will see . . ." She had numbered the lines of the résumé in the margin so that the audience could find the references without fumbling. Not only could the audience refer to the résumé as Gwen discussed its key features, but many also probably saved it to use later as they prepared their own résumés. In a similar way, if you try to persuade your audience to contribute time and money to local charities, you will more likely achieve your goal if you distribute a handout with the name, address, and telephone number, and a brief description of each charity.

While working as a student assistant in the Financial Aid Office (FAO) in 2011, Jake revised and updated a chart of federal financial aid packages available for students (see Figure 14.4). Pleased with his efforts, the financial aid staff asked Jake to present his chart to a summer workshop for incoming first-year students and their parents. Because the chart contained many important details, it was too complex for projection; besides, students and their parents might want to refer to it later. So, at the workshop Jake previewed the four categories of aid, distributed his handout, and assisted the financial aid staff as they discussed and answered questions about various aid programs and how to apply for them.

If you are distributing handouts to listeners who are likely to receive handouts from other speakers on the same day you speak, use colored paper to distinguish your materials. If you are the only speaker and are distributing several handouts, consider putting each one on a different color paper. It's easier to identify which handout you want your listeners to look at if you can say, "On the blue sheet ...," for example.

handout
Any graphic visual aid distributed to individual audience members.

Figure 14.4 Sample Handout

FEDERAL STUDENT AID PROGRAMS, 2011			
CATEGORY OF AID	PROGRAM	QUALIFICATIONS	PAYBACK REQUIREMENT
Grants			
	Federal Pell Grant	Need based	none
	Federal Supplemental Educational Opportunity Grant (FSEOG)	Need based	none
	Teacher Education Assistance for College and Higher Education Grant (TEACH)	Must agree to teach	none
	Iraq and Afghanistan Service Grant	Child of deceased service man or woman	none
	Institutional Grants	Merit based	none
Campus-Based Aid			
	Federal Supplemental Educational Opportunity Grants (FSEOG)	Need based	none
	Federal Work-Study (FWS)	Need based	none
	Federal Perkins Loan	Need based	5% interest
Direct Stafford Loans			
	Direct Subsidized Loans	Need based	varies
	Direct Unsubsidized Loans	Not need based	varies
Direct PLUS Loans			
	Direct PLUS Loans for Parents	For parents of qualified students	7.9% interest

Source: Federal Student Aid Office. U.S. Dept. of Education.
https://studentaid.ed.gov/PORTALSWebApp/students/english/campusaid.jsp

Audio and Other Aids

Audio aids include records, tapes, compact discs, and MP4 files, as well as films and videos. Certain speech topics lend themselves to audio reinforcement of the message. A speech on Janis Joplin, for example, would be more vivid and informative if the audience could see and hear a videotaped clip of one of her performances. Lindahl began her speech on the savant syndrome by playing 30 seconds of a taped piano performance of Chopin's Polonaise no. 6 in A-Flat Major. Her first words were, "The person who was playing that music is considered handicapped, but he heard this piece of music for the first time only minutes before sitting down to play it." The audiotape was a compelling example of one form of the savant syndrome. A speech comparing the jazz styles of Branford and Wynton Marsalis could hardly be effective without letting listeners hear examples from each of those artists.

audio aid

A cassette tape, compact disc, record, or MP4 player used to clarify or prove a point by letting listeners hear an example.

Audio aids need not be confined to music topics, however. An audience listening to a speech on Winston Churchill could benefit from hearing his quiet eloquence as he addressed Great Britain's House of Commons and declared, "I have nothing to offer but blood, toil, tears, and sweat." And a speaker analyzing the persuasive appeals of radio and television advertisements could play pertinent examples.

You may want to appeal to senses other than sight and hearing. For example, a student of ours gave each audience member an envelope before her speech on aromatherapy. When she discussed the effects of certain scents on behavior, she had students open the envelopes and remove strips of lavender- and vanilla-scented paper, two of the scents she discussed. Think creatively and critically as you consider ways of supporting what you say.

Projection of Presentational Aids

14.3 Use the three types of projected presentational aids.

Once you have decided what type of presentational aids will best serve your audience, you must decide how to display them most effectively. **Projection** is especially appropriate when your audience is too large to see the presentational aid easily and clearly. In such a case, you may want to use projections such as transparencies, PowerPoint slides, or Breeze presentations.

A note of caution: As a beginning public speaker, you need to control and be the primary focus of the public speaking event. When you stand at the back of the room and narrate a slide show, you get little experience in speaking before an audience. Presentational aids must always support, not become, your speech.

PowerPoint

PowerPoint is a software program that enables speakers to supplement their presentations with text, graphics, images, audio, and video. Chances are that you have developed PowerPoint slides at some point in your education. The software's attractions are undeniable. PowerPoint can reassure an inexperienced speaker because in developing your slides you are predetermining your content and organization. Used well, PowerPoint can present a seamless blend of image, text, and spoken word.

Unfortunately, PowerPoint is not always used well. Two communication scholars surveyed research and concluded that "students are becoming less and less engaged by professors presenting with PowerPoint."[4] Some corporations have even restricted reliance on the use of PowerPoint in company presentations. Remember that *you* are the presenter—not PowerPoint, Keynote, OpenOffice Impress, or some other software program. Avoid the temptation to blend into the background and narrate a slide show.

Many excellent tutorials can help you learn PowerPoint or adapt to specific versions of the software. Your college may offer workshops or courses that teach PowerPoint. Additionally, most school libraries have ebooks with tutorials that can walk you through common features of the software.

Among the many display options PowerPoint provides, these are some things to keep in mind:

- Clear the screen when you want listeners to focus just on you. To replace any screen with solid black, just press B on the keyboard. Press the same key again to restore the PowerPoint image. Doing the same with the keyboard letter W replaces the image with a white screen.
- Be familiar with your slides so that you can skip ahead or go back if you need to. Print the Outline View of your slides and keep it handy as a reference. To skip to a slide, just type the number of the slide you want to go to.

projection

A manner of displaying presentational aids by casting their images onto a screen or other background.

PowerPoint

A software program that enables speakers to supplement their presentations with text, graphics, images, audio, and video.

- Limit or eliminate moving text. Transitions that have text flying or spiraling in make the audience wait until movement has stopped in order to read. Eliminate animations or sound effects that distract listeners' attention from you and your message.[5]

- While there are exceptions, we think that Guy Kawasaki's 10-20-30 rule establishes solid guidelines for most presentations. Kawasaki, former Apple chief evangelist, is well known for touting his 10-20-30 PowerPoint use guidelines. (1) Never use more than 10 slides; (2) Never speak for more than 20 minutes; (3) Never use a font smaller than 30 points. While all three rules may not apply to every speaking class, rule three helps to guard against the problem of too much text on slides. At 30-point font, you are helping ensure that those in the back row will actually see your slides, and you prevent the corresponding problem of reading your speech from a bulleted list crammed into your slides.[6]

There are some occasions when using PowerPoint is counterproductive: when you are trying to engage your audience's emotions or imaginations, when you are primarily interested in connecting with your listeners, when you want your listeners to be actively involved in creating the presentation with you, when your preparation time is limited, and when your audience suffers from PowerPoint fatigue.[7] Nick Morgan may have said it best: "You should use PowerPoint . . . sparingly. Don't think of it as wallpaper that's always there behind you, but a discrete moment in your talk when you turn to an illustration because it's too difficult to put the idea into mere words."[8]

Breeze Presentations

For many years, PowerPoint was the leading slideshow software used to aid speakers. Lately, however, Breeze Presenter has become increasingly popular. Breeze presentations, which are flash-based online presentations, can be created by converting existing PowerPoint presentations. You can also add narrations, audio files, video clips, pictures, and much more. Thus, because the general format of Breeze presentations is similar to that of PowerPoint presentations, we encourage you to follow the PowerPoint guidelines previously discussed when developing and using Breeze presentations.

Document Cameras

Presentational aids help listeners see as well as hear your message. Well-designed PowerPoint graphics, for example, can enhance the impact of your ideas.

Today's high-tech visual presenters such as Elmo offer the advantage of enlarging and projecting visual aids without the work of preparing transparencies. These document cameras can project transparencies, video, computer slide shows, and computer animation as well as images of three-dimensional objects. Many models feature autofocus and power zoom magnification controlled by wireless remotes.

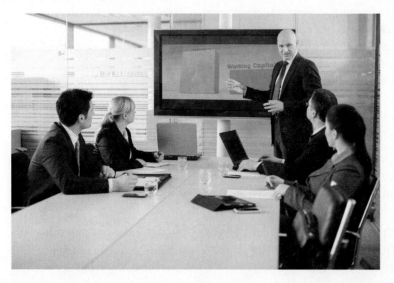

Strategies for Using Presentational Aids

14.4 Apply the strategies for using presentational aids.

Remember that even the most brilliant presentational aid cannot salvage a poorly planned, poorly delivered speech. Visuals can aid, but they cannot resuscitate, a weak speech. On the other hand, even the most carefully designed and professionally executed presentational aid can be spoiled by clumsy handling during a presentation. The effect of public speaking is cumulative, with each element contributing toward one final effect. The following section offers some practical guidelines on how to use presentational aids in your public speech.

Before the Speech

DETERMINE THE INFORMATION TO BE PRESENTED VISUALLY.   Sections of a presentation that are complex or detailed may be particularly appropriate for visualization. Be careful, however, not to use too many presentational aids. The premium in a speech is on the spoken word. Multimedia presentations can be exciting; they may also be extremely difficult to coordinate. Handling too many objects or charts quickly becomes cumbersome and distracting.

SELECT THE TYPE OF PRESENTATIONAL AID BEST SUITED TO YOUR RE-SOURCES AND SPEECH.   The information you need to present, the amount of preparation time you have, your technical expertise at producing the aid, and the cost involved will all influence the presentational aid you select. If preparing quality presentational aids to illustrate your speech will take more time, money, or expertise than you have, you are probably better off without them. A presentational aid that calls attention to its poor production is a handicap, no matter how important the information it contains.

ENSURE EASY VIEWING BY ALL AUDIENCE MEMBERS.   A speaker addressing an audience of 500 would not want to use a videotaped presentation displayed on a single television or computer monitor. A bar graph on poster board should be visible to more than just the first four rows of the audience. If possible, practice with your presentational aids in the room where you will speak. Position or project the aid and then sit in the farthest seat possible. (In an auditorium, make it the back row; people will not move forward unless forced to.) If you can read your presentational aid from that distance, it is sufficient in size. If you cannot, either enlarge or eliminate the aid.

MAKE SURE THAT THE PRESENTATIONAL AID COMMUNICATES THE INFOR-MATION CLEARLY.   Simplicity should be your guiding principle in constructing your presentational aid. Michael Talman, a graphic design consultant, compares a graphic in a presentation to "going by a highway billboard at 55 miles per hour. Its effectiveness can be judged by how quickly the viewer sees and understands its message."[9] Speakers sometimes construct PowerPoint presentations using all the special effects or posters and slides in Technicolor to make them lively and interesting. However, too many effects or too much color, like too much information, clutters and confuses. Limiting special effects and the range of colors, as well as muting secondary visual elements such as frames, grids, arrows, rules, and boxes, can clarify the primary information you want to convey.[10] Remember that the chief purpose of presentational aids is to inform—not to impress—the audience. You may want to use red to indicate a budget deficit, green to indicate growth, or other appropriate colors for a limited number of visual elements. However, as a rule, black or dark blue lettering on a light background is the most visually distinct color combination for text.

CONSTRUCT A PRESENTATIONAL AID THAT IS PROFESSIONAL IN APPEAR-ANCE.   In the business and professional world, a hand-lettered poster, no matter how neatly done, is inappropriate. Professionals understand the importance of a good impression and are willing to pay graphic designers to help them create polished presentational aids. Today, however, the computer puts a galaxy of inexpensive, professional-looking design options at the fingertips of anyone willing to learn the programs. If you are familiar with a computer graphics program that meets your needs, by all means use it. If you can't use a computer and doubt your freehand skills, another alternative is hiring an art student to draw and letter a presentational aid you have designed.

If you throw together a chart or graph the night before your speech, that is exactly what it will look like. Your hastily prepared work will undermine an image of careful and thorough preparation.

PRACTICE USING YOUR PRESENTATIONAL AID.   A conscientious speaker will spend hours preparing a speech; presentational aids are a part of that presentation. Just as you rehearse the words of your speech, you should rehearse referring to your aid, uncovering and covering charts, advancing slides, and writing on a whiteboard, a flip chart, or a sheet of paper projected by a document camera. In short, if you plan to use presentational aids, learn how *before* your speech; no audience will be impressed by how much you learn during the course of your presentation.

ARRANGE FOR SAFE TRANSPORTATION OF YOUR PRESENTATIONAL AIDS.   Aids worth using are worth transporting safely. The laptop computer you've bought or borrowed needs obvious care. Poster boards should be protected from moisture and bending. Cover your presentational aid with plastic to protect it from that freak rainstorm you encounter just before speech class. If you roll up paper or poster board charts, carry them to different classes, or leave them in a car trunk throughout the day, you cannot expect them to stay flat when you speak.

CARRY BACKUP SUPPLIES WITH YOU.   An exciting and informative presentation can be ruined when technology fails as you are preparing to speak. Make an inventory of equipment you may need—such as extension cords, bulbs, and batteries—and then take them with you.

POSITION THE PRESENTATIONAL AID PROPERLY.   Get to the place where you will speak *before* the audience arrives. Check out the equipment you will use. If you are using a computer, check to be sure your files are compatible, the projection equipment works, and that you can connect to the Internet, if needed. Check the height of the easel if you are using a flip chart or poster boards. If you are projecting text and images, make sure that the equipment works. Position or project your presentational aid in the most desirable location. Make sure that the maximum number of people will see it and that nothing obstructs the audience's view. If you are not to be the first speaker, have your presentational aid and any necessary equipment out of the way but readily located so that you can set up quickly and with little disruption.

TEST YOUR PRESENTATIONAL AID.   Finally, if you are using PowerPoint slides or documents projected by an overhead camera, make sure that they are in focus and in the correct order, and that any remote control you plan to use works. If possible, have any Internet-based videos ready to display to keep the audience from suffering lag time during your speech while you wait for a video to load. If there are people already in the room, you may not want to "give away" your topic by displaying one of your presentational aids. Some speakers prepare a test aid with the word Test on it. Although this keeps the audience from seeing part of the speech before you deliver it, it reveals little thought or creativity. A test aid with a creative title for your speech can create interest in your topic without revealing key information. In fact, it could motivate your audience to listen even before you utter your first word.

During the Speech

Not even the most careful preparation of a presentational aid guarantees that it will work for you as you deliver your speech. Keep the following commonsense guidelines in mind as you practice incorporating the aid into your delivery.

Key Points

Strategies for Using Presentational Aids before the Speech

1. Determine the information to be presented visually.
2. Select the type of aid best suited to your resources and speech.
3. Ensure easy viewing by all audience members.
4. Make sure that the aid communicates the information clearly.
5. Construct an aid that is professional in appearance.
6. Practice using your aid.
7. Arrange for safe transportation of your aid.
8. Carry backup supplies with you.
9. Properly position the aid.
10. Test your presentational aid.

Theory Into Practice TIP

DESIGNING VISUAL AIDS

Whether your visual aids will be slides projected from a computer, sheets of paper projected from a visual document camera, or charts displayed on poster board, these aids will have a positive impact only if they are clear and readable. Consider the following guidelines before preparing any visuals.[11]

Focus

- *Focus on a few key points.* Resist the temptation to present all your information visually. Select ideas that are the most important or that can best be made through the use of presentational aids.
- *Present ideas one at a time.* Don't let the audience get ahead of you. For example, if you are discussing the first of five solutions for road rage, keep steps 2 through 5 out of audience view. If you are using PowerPoint, build your list through a series of slides. If you display a list of steps using a document camera, cover the steps you have not yet discussed, revealing each when you get to it.

Layout

- *Use a landscape (horizontal) page format rather than a portrait (vertical) format.* Text displayed horizontally is easier to read and gives you a better chance of expressing an idea in a single line.
- *Use left-margin alignment.* It is easier to read than full- or right-margin justification.
- *Use bullets or numbers to highlight your key points.* If you have several key ideas, number them. Listeners can more readily focus on the appropriate part of the visual aid if they see a number when they hear you say, "My third suggestion. . . ."
- *Use no more than six words per line.* Longer sentences are more difficult to read and remember. Learning how to condense and simplify your message also hones your speaking skills.
- *Compose your text in the top half or two-thirds of your slide or document, with no more than six lines per page.* This ensures better viewing for those in the back of the room.

Fonts

- *Use strong, straight fonts.* Arial, Helvetica, and Times New Roman are good choices. Ornate fonts are more difficult to read.
- Use no more than two fonts per page or screen. Too many fonts can make your presentational aid more difficult to read.
- *Select a font size large enough to be read easily from the back row.* Minimum font size will vary according to room size and the distance between the projector and the screen. Check font size before your presentation.

Color and Art

- *Use color to enhance your presentational aids.* Research suggests that color can increase the audience's understanding and retention of information. Select colors that highlight the ideas you present. For example, a red line may reinforce a line graph showing a decline in student contributions to charitable organizations. Color can also complement the mood of a speech. A presentational aid for an informative speech on the celebration of Mardi Gras could use bright colors.
- *Limit the number of colors in your presentational aid.* Too many colors make reading a visual aid more difficult. Use no more than six colors per presentational aid and even fewer if the aid contains only text.
- Avoid "chartjunk."[12] Irrelevant graphics and art clutter and detract from your visual aid. An effective presentational aid draws the reader's attention to key points you are making in your speech.

Animations and Video Clips

- *Use the "insert" option in Microsoft PowerPoint and Adobe Breeze Presentations to add animations and video clips to your presentational aids.* If you have downloaded or recorded your own video clips, you can insert the video clips directly into your presentation. If you're using a video clip found online, you can insert the URL to the video clip. If so, we suggest you queue up the video clip before you begin your presentation to avoid delays while it is buffering.
- *Use brief animations and video clips that illustrate your point.* Remember that you, as the speaker, should be the focus of your presentation.

REVEAL THE PRESENTATIONAL AID ONLY WHEN YOU ARE READY FOR IT. A presentational aid is designed to attract attention and convey information. If it is visible at the beginning of the speech, the audience may focus on it, rather than on what you are saying. Your aid should be seen only when you are ready to discuss the point it illustrates.

If you are using projections, have someone cued to turn the lights off and the projector on at the appropriate time. If your presentational aid is on poster board, cover it with a blank poster board, or turn the blank side to the audience. At the appropriate time, expose the presentational aid.

Occasionally, a speaker will stop speaking, uncover a presentational aid, and then continue. This is where rehearsal can really help you. You want to avoid creating unnecessary breaks in the flow of your speech. With practice, you will be able to keep talking as you uncover or project your aid.

TALK TO YOUR AUDIENCE—NOT TO THE PRESENTATIONAL AID. Remember, eye contact is a speaker's most important nonverbal tool. Sustained visual interaction with your audience keeps their attention on you and allows you to monitor their feedback regarding your speech. Turning your back to your listeners undermines your impact. For this reason, use prepared graphics rather than a dry erase board.

REFER TO THE PRESENTATIONAL AID. Speakers sometimes stand at the lectern using their notes or reading their manuscript, relatively far from their presentational aid. This creates two lines of vision and can confuse your audience. It may also give the impression that you must rely on your notes because you do not fully understand what the presentational aid conveys.

Other speakers carry their notes with them as they move to the aid, referring to them as they point out key concepts. This is cumbersome and again reinforces the image of a speaker unsure of what he or she wants to say.

A well-constructed presentational aid should function as a set of notes. The key ideas represented on the aid should trigger the explanation you will provide. You should not need to refer to anything else as you discuss the point your presentational aid illustrates. When you practice using your presentational aid, use your aid as your notes.

If you use a computer mouse or a metal or wooden pointer to refer to the aid, have it easily accessible, use it only when pointing to the presentational aid, and set it down immediately after you are finished with it. Too many speakers pick up a pen to refer to their aid and end up playing with it during the rest of the speech.

Finally, point to your presentational aid with the hand closer to it. This keeps your body open and makes communication physically more direct with your audience.

KEEP YOUR PRESENTATIONAL AID IN VIEW UNTIL THE AUDIENCE UNDERSTANDS YOUR POINT. Remember that you are more familiar with your speech than your audience is. Too often, a speaker hurries through an explanation and covers or removes an aid before the audience fully comprehends its significance or the point it makes. Just as you should not reveal your aid too soon, do not cover it up too quickly. You will have invested time and effort in preparing the aid. Give your audience the time necessary to digest the information it conveys. As you discuss and describe the presentational aid, check your audience response. Many will likely signal their understanding of the presentational aid by nodding their heads or changing their posture.

CONCEAL THE PRESENTATIONAL AID AFTER YOU HAVE MADE YOUR POINT. Once you proceed to the next section of your speech, you do not want the audience to continue thinking about the presentational aid. If you are using projections, clear the computer screen or turn off the projector. If the aid is an object or poster board, cover it.

USE HANDOUTS WITH CAUTION. Of all the forms of presentational aids, the handout may be the most troublesome. If you distribute handouts before your remarks, the audience is already ahead of you. Passing out information during a presentation can be distracting, especially if you stop talking as you do so. In addition, the rustling of paper can distract the speaker and other audience members. Disseminating material after the presentation eliminates distractions but does not allow the listener to refer to the printed information as you are explaining it. In general, then, use handouts in a public speech only if that is the best way to clarify and give impact to your ideas.

You will encounter some speaking situations, such as a business presentation, that benefit from, and may demand, handout material. Those audiences are often decision-making groups. During an especially technical presentation, they may need to take notes. Afterward, they may need to study the information presented. Handouts provide a record of the presenter's remarks and supplementary information the speaker did not have time to explain.

Presentational aids—objects, graphics, film and video, handouts, and audio aids—can make your speech more effective. By seeing as well as hearing your message, the audience becomes more involved with your speech and more responsive to your appeals.

> **Key Points**
>
> **Strategies for Using Presentational Aids during the Speech**
>
> 1. Reveal the aid only when you are ready for it.
> 2. Talk to your audience—not to the aid.
> 3. Refer to the aid.
> 4. Keep your aid in view until the audience understands your point.
> 5. Conceal the aid after you have made your point.
> 6. Use handouts with caution.

Summary

The Importance of Using Presentational Aids

14.1 Articulate four benefits of using presentational aids in speeches.

- Presentational aids can add clarity and impact to a speaker's message, can make a speaker's delivery seem more dynamic, and can increase a speaker's confidence. By seeing as well as hearing your message, the audience becomes more involved with your speech and more responsive to your appeals.

Types of Presentational Aids

14.2 Describe with examples nine classifications of presentational aids.

- Presentational aids include objects, pictures, diagrams, graphs, charts, maps, film and video, handouts, and audio aids.

Projection of Presentational Aids

14.3 Use the three types of projected presentational aids.

- When using projected presentational aids (Power-Point, Breeze presentations, and document cameras), *focus* on just a few key points and present them one at a time. For graphics that contain text, use horizontal *layout*, with text placed in the top half or two-thirds and with the left margin aligned.

Graphics should have no more than six words per line, no more than six lines per page, with bullets or numbers highlighting key points. Use strong, straight *fonts*, with no more than two fonts on each graphic. Finally, select *color and art* that amplify the impact of the graphic without cluttering it.

Strategies for Using Presentational Aids

14.4 Apply the strategies for using presentational aids.

- To use these graphics or other presentational aids for maximum impact, take the following steps *before* the speech: (1) Determine the amount of information to be presented; (2) select the type of aid best suited to your resources and topic; (3) ensure easy viewing by all audience members; (4) ensure that the aid communicates its information clearly; (5) construct an aid that appears carefully or professionally done; (6) practice using the aid; (7) arrange for safe transportation of the aid; (8) carry backup supplies in case of equipment failure; (9) properly position the aid before beginning the speech; and (10) test the aid before using it.

- While delivering the speech, remember the following: (1) Reveal the aid only when ready to use it; (2) talk to the audience, not to the aid; (3) refer to the aid; (4) keep the aid in view until the audience understands the point it makes; (5) conceal the aid after making your point with it; and (6) use handouts with caution.

Chapter 15
Speaking to Inform

 Learning Objectives

After studying this chapter, you should be able to

15.1 Explain, with examples, the three characteristics of informative speeches.

15.2 Identify, with examples, the eight informative speech categories.

15.3 Apply the five guidelines for developing an effective informative speech.

Our thirst for knowledge and stimulation seems insatiable. It has also never been easier to satisfy. It is estimated that in June 2012 there were more than 2.4 billion Internet users in the world, a growth of 566 percent since 2000.[1] Users logged "onto the Internet to use email, get news, access government information, check out health and medical information, participate in auctions, book travel reservations, research their genealogy, gamble, seek out romantic partners, and engage in countless other activities."[2] Many who want to be connected—"plugged in"—find it amazingly easy to do so.

An informative speech assignment challenges you to take a small step toward building a sense of community within your classroom. Such an assignment also poses at least three challenges:

1. Choosing a topic you find interesting and that your listeners will find interesting or relevant

2. Finding adequate information to make you well informed about the topic

3. Organizing your information in the most fitting manner

These three tasks form the essence of informative speaking, the subject of this chapter.

Characteristics of a Speech to Inform

15.1 Explain with examples the three characteristics of informative speeches.

We seek knowledge for three reasons: we want to *know*, *understand*, and *use* information. The goals of anyone delivering a **speech to inform**, in turn, are to impart knowledge, enhance understanding, or enable application.

- *To impart knowledge.* Suppose you decided to prepare an informative speech on the general subject of advertising. Your specific purpose could be to inform the audience about advertising in ancient times. Your listeners probably know little about this topic, and you can readily assume that your speech would add to their knowledge.

- *To deepen understanding.* Alternatively, you could inform the audience about how effective advertising succeeds. Using examples your audience already is familiar with, you could deepen their understanding of advertising strategies and principles.

- *To enable application.* A third specific purpose could be to inform your listeners how to prepare effective, low-cost advertisements when they want to promote an event. In this instance, you would help the audience apply basic advertising principles.

When preparing an informative speech, you must make sure that you don't slip into giving a persuasive speech. This is often deceptively difficult. How can you avoid this problem? After all, a persuasive speech also conveys information. In fact, the best persuasive speeches usually include supporting material that is both expository and compelling.

Some topics are easy to classify as informative or persuasive. A speaker urging an audience not to text-message while driving is clearly trying to persuade; the speaker is attempting to intensify beliefs and either change or reinforce behavior. On the other hand, a speech charting the most recent options in cell phone technology can be a speech to inform. A speech describing different forms of alcohol addiction is informative, whereas a speech advocating the Alcoholics Anonymous program to overcome addiction is persuasive.

Sometimes speakers begin preparing a speech to inform, only to discover that during the speech construction process their objective has become persuasion. In other instances, speakers deliver what they intended to be an informative speech only to find that their listeners received it as a persuasive message. How can this happen? Let's look at the experience of one speaker, Sarah.

speech to inform

A speech to impart knowledge, enhance understanding, or facilitate application of information.

Journal: Maintaining an Informative Purpose

Write down an emotionally charged issue (political correctness, Internet filtering in public libraries, or legalization of drugs, for example). What are some aspects of the issue that would be appropriate for an informative speech?

Sarah designed a speech with the specific purpose of informing the audience of the arguments for and against allowing women to serve in military combat. She took care to represent each side's arguments accurately and objectively. After her speech, however, Sarah discovered that some listeners previously undecided on the issue found the pro arguments more persuasive than the con arguments and now supported permitting women to serve in combat roles. But Sarah also learned that others in the audience became more convinced that women should be excluded from such roles. Did Sarah's speech persuade? Apparently for some audience members the answer is yes; they changed their attitudes because of this speech. Yet Sarah's objective was to inform, not to persuade.

In determining the general purpose of your speech, remember that both speakers and listeners are active participants in the communication process. Listeners will interpret what they hear and integrate it into their frames of reference. Your objectivity as a speaker will not stop listeners from hearing with subjectivity. As a speaker, though, you determine *your* motive for speaking. In a speech to inform, it is not to advocate specific beliefs, attitudes, and behaviors on controversial issues. Your objective is to assist your listeners as they come to know, understand, or apply an idea or issue.

Informative Speech Topics

15.2 Identify, with examples, the eight informative speech categories.

Experts identify several ways of classifying informative speeches. We offer a topical pattern based on the types of topics you can choose for your speech. As you read about these topic categories, keep two guidelines in mind. First, approach each category of topics with the broadest possible perspective. Second, recognize that the categories overlap; the boundaries between them are not distinct. Whether you consider St. Peter's Basilica to be an object or a place, for example, is much less important than the fact that it's a fascinating informative speech topic. The purpose of our categories is to stimulate—not to limit—your topic selection and development. As you begin brainstorming, consider information you could provide your listeners regarding people, objects, places, activities, events, processes, concepts, conditions, and issues.

Speeches about People

People are an obvious and abundant source of topics for an informative speech. A speech about a person gives you the opportunity to expand your knowledge in a field that interests you while sharing those interests with your listeners. If you're an avid photographer, you could discover and communicate something about the life and accomplishments of Ansel Adams, Diane Arbus, or Annie Leibovitz. Of course, you don't need to confine your topic to individuals associated with your major or areas of interest. You could interest and inform audiences by discussing the lives and contributions of people such as Ray Charles, Cesar Chavez, Eric Greitens, Jimi Hendrix, Jay Z, Jackie Robinson, Nikola Tesla, or Mark Zuckerberg.

You may choose to discuss a group of people, such as the Four Horsemen of Notre Dame, the Red Hat Society, or the Capitol Steps, a political satirist troupe. You could even compare and contrast two or more individuals to highlight their philosophies and contributions, such as Rachel Carson and Ralph Nader, or Malcolm X and Martin Luther King, Jr.

In considering an informative speech about a person, you must decide what is important and what the audience will remember. Speeches about people organized so that they resemble biographical entries in an encyclopedia amount to lists of dates. Even the most attentive listener will remember few of the details in such a speech.

EXPLORING ONLINE

Online Biographies

Use the phrase "Biographies of Notable People" to access websites that introduce you to paragraph-length biographies of notable individuals. Particularly helpful is Fact Monster's searchable index of people from a variety of backgrounds.

Speeches about people are often organized chronologically or topically. In her speech about Mark Zuckerberg, cofounder and CEO of the online social network Facebook, Katherine used a chronological pattern to trace his life and accomplishments. She used parallel wording to help her listeners remember her three key points:

I. Growing Up

II. Building Up

III. Leading Up

First, Katherine discussed Zuckerberg's childhood, providing examples of his early predisposition toward technology. Second, she described how he cofounded Facebook during his sophomore year at Harvard University and then dropped out of school to build that enterprise. Finally, Katherine discussed how Zuckerberg's vision for the future of Facebook is reflected in his leadership style, relying not on top-down decision making but on encouraging openness, collaboration, and sharing of information. For example, when you walk into the Facebook headquarters, you see workstations but no individual offices; even Zuckerberg doesn't have a private office although there is a glass-enclosed room for meetings.

We read about, listen to, and watch people who fascinate us. Many of them have unique, interesting stories. Sharing this information with an audience can make an excellent speech.

Speeches about Objects

A second resource of informative topics is objects. Speeches about objects focus on what is concrete rather than on what is abstract. Again, consider objects from the broadest perspective possible so that you can generate a maximum number of topic ideas. Topics for this type of speech could include crop circles, electric cars, the Great Wall of China, performance clothing, smart roads, or volcanoes.

Speeches about objects can use any of several organizational patterns. A speech on the Catherine Palace of Tsarskoye Selo could be organized spatially. A speech tracing the development of cyclones and anticyclones evolves chronologically. A speech on the origins, types, and uses of pasta uses a topical division. If the speech focused only on the history of pasta, however, it might best be structured chronologically.

Kevin used a combination of topical and pro-con organization for his speech on genetically modified (GM) animals, sometimes called *designer animals*:

I. The process of designing animals

II. Benefits of GM animals

    A. Medical uses

    B. Commercial uses

III. Problems of GM animals

    A. Animal health issues

    B. Ethical issues

Speeches about Places

Places are an easily tapped resource for informative speech topics. These speeches introduce listeners to new locales or expand their knowledge of familiar places. Topics may include real places, such as historic sites, emerging nations, national parks, and

EXPLORING ONLINE

Researching Historical Topics

If you're interested in discussing an informative topic from a historical perspective, check out *American Memory*, historical collections maintained by the Library of Congress. Browse collections such as architecture, environment, folklife, immigration, religion, recreation, technology, war, and women's history. Each category provides additional links to more information.

EXPLORING ONLINE

Touring Places Online

Want to give a speech about a place? Conduct an Internet search by typing "virtual tours of" and then adding places of interest: museums, national parks, battlefields, caves, or some other category. You can read text, view pictures, and, occasionally, listen to audio or see a short movie as you enjoy online guided tours of places.

planets. Topics may also include fictitious places, such as the Land of Oz, the Island of the Lord of the Flies, and the Sea of Frozen Words. Speeches about places challenge speakers to select words that create vivid images.

To organize your speech about places, you would typically use one of three organizational patterns: spatial, chronological, or topical. A speech about the Nile, the world's longest river, is organized spatially if it discusses the upper, middle, and lower Nile. A presentation about your college could trace its development chronologically. A speech on Poplar Forest, Thomas Jefferson's getaway home, could use a topical pattern discussing Jefferson's architectural style.

If you selected as your informative speech topic Ellis Island, the site of the chief U.S. immigration center from 1892 to 1954, you could choose any of the following patterns of development:

Pattern: Spatial
Specific Purpose: To inform the audience about Ellis Island's Main Building
Key Ideas: I. The registry room
       II. The baggage room
      III. The oral history studio

Pattern: Chronological
Specific Purpose: To inform the audience of the history of Ellis Island
Key Ideas: I. Years of immigration, 1892–1954
      II. Years of dormancy, 1954–1984
      III. Years of remembrance, 1984–present

Pattern: Topical
Specific Purpose: To inform the audience of the history of Ellis Island
Key Ideas: I. The process of immigration
      II. The place of immigration
      III. The people who immigrated

Notice that each of these outlines is organized according to a distinct pattern. The key ideas in the first outline are organized spatially. Although the specific purposes of the second and third speeches are identical, the former is organized chronologically and the latter topically.

If you choose to speak about a place, avoid making your speech sound like a travelogue. Your speech should identify and develop ideas that contribute to the general education of your listeners.

Speeches about Activities and Events

Activities are things you do by yourself or with others to learn, relax, or accomplish a required task. Among the sources of speech topics are your hobbies, interests, and experiences. Topics that you already know well and are willing to explore more fully often enhance your credibility and energize your delivery.

If you're interested in dancing, a speech on krumping (sometimes called street dancing or clown dancing) could be lively and informative. You could use a topical pattern, informing your audience on these key points:

    I. The origins of krumping

    II. The purposes of krumping

    III. The style of krumping

    IV. The face-painting of krumping

Events are important or interesting occurrences. Examples of topics for this type of speech include the sinking of the *Titanic*, the Woodstock festival, and the rescue of 33 Chilean miners in 2010. For a speech assignment not requiring research, you could speak about an event in your life you consider important, funny, or instructive; for example, "the day I registered for my first semester in college," "the day my first child was born," or "my most embarrassing moment."

Speeches about events typically use a chronological or topical pattern. For example, if your topic is the daring Great Train Robbery that took place in Britain in 1963, you could organize your speech chronologically, describing what happened before, during, and after those famous 15 minutes.

The Woodstock Music and Art Fair, more commonly referred to as the Woodstock Festival or just Woodstock, was held on a dairy farm in Bethel, New York. A speech on this legendary event of August 15–18, 1969, could be divided into the topical categories of

    I. The organizers of Woodstock

   II. The audience at Woodstock

  III. The performers at Woodstock

If this topic is too broad, the speaker could focus on the performers or some other more limited topic.

Speeches about Processes

A process is a series of steps producing an outcome. Your informative speech about a process could explain or demonstrate how something works, functions, or is accomplished. Informative speeches could be on such how-to topics as suiting up and entering a "clean room," preventing identity theft, burglar-proofing your apartment, and making a good first impression. Speeches on global positioning systems, nuclear medicine, and cryptography (encoding and decoding messages) are also potentially good informative topics about processes.

Because a process is by definition a time-ordered sequence, speeches about processes commonly use chronological organization. For example, if your specific purpose is to inform your audience of the steps to a successful job interview, you could present these key ideas:

    I. Prepare thoroughly

   II. Arrive promptly

  III. Enter confidently

  IV. Communicate effectively

   V. Follow up immediately

Speeches about processes, however, are not confined to a chronological pattern. The best organization is the one that achieves the purpose of the speech. A student presenting a how-to speech on podcasting would likely choose a chronological pattern if the specific purpose was to explain the steps in the process. Another student might examine the process of podcasting more generally, using a topical pattern to discuss the equipment needed, the most popular file formats, the rapid growth of podcasts, or the effects on traditional broadcasters. Both speeches concern a process, but each uses an organizational pattern suitable for the speaker's specific purpose.

Speeches about Concepts

Speeches about concepts, or ideas, focus on what is abstract rather than on what is concrete. Whereas a speech about an object such as the Statue of Liberty may focus on the history or physical attributes of the statue itself, a speech about an idea may focus on the concept of liberty. Other topics suitable for informative speeches about concepts include ecotourism, objective music, pirate radio, artificial intelligence, endangered languages, and the bystander effect.

Speeches about concepts challenge you to make something abstract specific. These speeches typically rely on definitions and examples to support their explanations. Appropriate organizational patterns vary. A speech on Norse mythology could use a topical division and focus on key figures. Speeches about theories, particularly if they are controversial, sometimes use a pro–con division.

Drew, a student of ours, entertained his listeners with a speech on onomastics, or the study of names. Notice how his introduction personalizes his speech and quickly involves his listeners. You can also see from his preview statement that he used a topical organization for this speech about a concept:

> These are some actual names reported by John Train in his books *Remarkable Names of Real People* and *Even More Remarkable Names*. Let me repeat: These are actual names found in bureaus of vital statistics, public health services, newspaper articles, and hospital, church, and school records: E. Pluribus Eubanks, Loch Ness Hontas, Golden Pancake, Halloween Buggage, Odious Champagne, and Memory Leake.
>
> Train says in *Even More Remarkable Names* that "what one might call the free-form nutty name—Oldmouse Waltz, Cashmere Tango Obedience, Eucalyptus Yoho—is the one indigenous American art form."
>
> We're lucky. No one in here has a name as colorful as any of those. But we all have at least two names—a personal and a family name. Today, I'll tell you, first, why personal names developed, and second, the legal status of names. Finally, I have something to tell each of you about the origin of your name.

Speeches about Conditions

Conditions are particular situations: living conditions in a third-world country or social and political climates that give rise to movements such as McCarthyism, the women's movement, the civil rights movement, jihad, and national independence movements.

The word *condition* can also refer to a state of fitness or health. Speeches about conditions can focus on a person's health, and, indeed, medical topics are a popular source of student speeches. Informative speeches about obsessive-compulsive disorder, progressive supranuclear palsy, and seasonal affective disorder, for example, can educate listeners about these interesting conditions. A speaker could choose as a specific purpose "to inform the audience about the symptoms, causes, and treatment of preeclampsia." Topical organization is appropriate for many speeches about specific diseases or health conditions.

Jean became interested in the topic of autism. She gathered information from several organizations that conducted research and provided information on this developmental disability. Reviewing the FAQ links on several websites, Jean selected four questions to organize the body of her speech:

    I. What is autism?

    II. What causes autism?

    III. How do you treat autism?

    IV. Is there a cure for autism?

Although the fourth question is closed, requiring only a yes or no answer, Jean used it as an opportunity to discuss types of research being conducted in looking for a cure. At the conclusion of her speech, she referred the audience to the Autism Society of America and the Center for the Study of Autism websites so they could continue to learn more about this important topic.

States of health also characterize the economy, individual communities, and specific institutions. *Recession*, *depression*, and *full employment* are terms economists use to describe the health of the economy. Speakers inform their listeners about conditions when they describe the state of the arts in their communities, assess the financial situation of most college students, or illustrate how catch limits have affected the whale population.

Speeches about Issues

Speeches about issues deal with controversial ideas and policies. The word *controversial* may trigger the question: Isn't this category more appropriate for persuasive speeches? Many times it is; however, controversial topics can also be appropriate for informative speeches. Issues being debated in your school, community, state, or nation can be fruitful topics for a speech to inform.

This tour guide informs students of the issues, events, and leaders of the civil rights movement.

Suppose your school is considering moving from a letter-grade to a pass–fail grading system. You could give a persuasive speech in support of either approach. You also could deliver an informative speech so that your audience better understands the issue. For example, you could summarize the key arguments of proponents and opponents of the pass–fail approach, or you could discuss different types of pass–fail systems.

Two common organizational patterns for speeches about issues are the topical and pro–con divisions. Speakers predisposed toward one side of an issue sometimes may have difficulty presenting both sides objectively:

> Carl presented a speech on the issue of school uniforms for public schools. He presented four good reasons for them: uniforms (1) are more economical for parents, (2) reduce student bickering and fighting over designer clothes, (3) increase student attentiveness in the classroom, and (4) identify the school and promote school spirit. Carl's only argument against public school uniforms was that they limit students' freedom of expression. His speech seemed out of balance, and most of his classmates thought Carl favored school uniforms. Although the assignment was an informative speech, Carl's pro–con approach was ultimately persuasive.

If, like Carl, you feel strongly committed to one side of an issue, save that topic for a persuasive speech.

As you begin working on your informative speech, keep in mind this question: "How will the audience benefit from my topic?" What about topics such as the golden age of vaudeville, the origins of superstitions, the effect of music on livestock production, or the psychological aspects of aging? What about a truly bizarre topic like extreme ironing? Maybe you think that such topics are not relevant to your audience. But part of the process of becoming an educated individual is learning more about the world around you. We are committed to this perspective and believe it is one you should encourage in your listeners.

Ethical Decisions

MANAGING BIAS IN AN INFORMATIVE SPEECH

Leon serves as historian of his campus fraternity. He considers himself an expert on the subject of Greek life at his school, so he decides to use his observations and experiences as the basis for an informative speech on the pros and cons of joining fraternities and sororities. However, Leon fears that if he reveals that he is a fraternity officer, his listeners will assume that he is not presenting objective information—so he does not mention it.

Is it ethical for Leon to avoid mentioning his fraternity affiliation and position? Is it possible for him to give an unbiased presentation of both sides of the issue? What obligations does he have to his audience?

Theory Into Practice TIP

ORGANIZING INFORMATIVE SPEECHES

Speeches about	Use	If your purpose is to
People	Topical organization	Explain various aspects of the person's life
	Chronological organization	Survey events in the person's life
Objects	Topical organization	Explain various uses for the object
	Chronological organization	Explain how the object was created or made
	Spatial organization	Describe various parts of the object
Places	Topical organization	Emphasize various aspects of the place
	Chronological organization	Chart the history of, or developments in, the place
	Spatial organization	Describe the elements or parts of the place
Activities and Events	Topical organization	Explain the significance of the activity or event
	Chronological organization	Explain the sequence of the activity or event
	Causal organization	Explain how one event produced, or resulted from, another
Processes	Topical organization	Explain aspects of the process
	Chronological organization	Explain how something is done
	Pro–con organization	Explore the arguments for and against the procedure
	Causal organization	Discuss the causes and effects of the process
Concepts	Topical organization	Discuss aspects, definitions, or applications of the concept
Conditions	Topical organization	Explain aspects of the condition
	Chronological organization	Trace the stages or phases of the condition
	Causal organization	Show the causes and effects of the condition
Issues	Topical organization	Discuss aspects of the issue's significance
	Chronological organization	Show how the issue evolved over time
	Pro–con organization	Present opposing viewpoints on the issue

EXPLORING ONLINE

Choosing and Researching Informative Topics

Use the phrase "Voice of the Shuttle Humanities" to access this website. Whether you are generating ideas for informative speeches or researching a topic you've already chosen, look at this site if your subject is in the area of the humanities. The Voice of the Shuttle: Web Site for Humanities Research contains numerous links in areas from anthropology to science, technology, and culture.

After you select a topic, ask yourself the following three questions: (1) What does the audience already know about my topic? (2) What does the audience need to know to understand the topic? (3) Can I present this information in a way that is easy for the audience to understand and remember in the time allotted? If you are satisfied with your answers to these questions, your next step is to begin developing the most effective strategy for conveying that information. Use the "Theory Into Practice" feature to help you select an appropriate organizational pattern.

Guidelines for Speaking to Inform

15.3 Apply the five guidelines for developing an effective informative speech.

Before reading this chapter, you already knew several clusters of guidelines for developing excellent informative speeches. This is because some guidelines apply to all speeches: careful audience analysis, adequate research, clear organization, and dynamic delivery, to name a few. We've discussed how to construct an audience profile based on demographic and psychographic analysis of your listeners. We presented guidelines for collecting and evaluating information for supporting the ideas of your speech. We've detailed how to introduce your speech, how to develop the key ideas using the "4 S" strategy in the body of your speech, and how to conclude your speech. You've also learned ways to deliver your speech impressively using your words, your voice, and your body. We encourage you to review these sections of our book to assist you in preparing and presenting an excellent speech, be it informative or persuasive.

Yet there are some guidelines that apply specifically to an informative speech, and we discuss five of them in the remainder of this chapter.

Ethical decision making requires access to clear and accurate supporting materials. Speakers must consider multiple points of view as they research and evaluate their information.

Stress Your Informative Purpose

The primary objective of your informative speech is to inform, and it's important to be clear about this. Your topic may be controversial or related to other topics that are controversial. For example, if you are discussing the U.S. immigration policy, political correctness, or the role of women in religion, you must realize that some in your audience may already have some very strong feelings about your topic. Stress that your goal is to give additional information, not to change anyone's opinions.

Be Objective

An essential criterion for an informative speech is objectivity. Although both informative and persuasive speakers should support their ideas, informative speakers are committed to presenting a balanced view. Your research should take into account competing perspectives. If, as you develop and practice your speech, you find yourself becoming a proponent of a particular viewpoint, you may need to step back and assess whether your orientation has shifted from information to

Speaking with Confidence

Though informative speaking sounds like a simple concept, it is more complicated than it may first appear. It is all too easy to fall into the trap of biased speaking. I selected the hotly debated topic of standardized testing for my informative speech. I then began my research. Throughout the process I would write down notes, only to realize that the information could be interpreted as leaning toward one side of the debate. In order to remain objective, I made an outline to plot the main points that needed to be discussed. I carefully chose ideas that were purely informative, such as "What exactly is standardized testing?" and "When did standardized testing become widely used?" As I constructed my speech, I made sure to use reliable, objective websites that were not gung-ho for either side of the debate. Also, if I had a piece of information that had the slightest inclination to bias, I took it out and saved it for my persuasive speech. Researching an informative speech proved to be more challenging than I anticipated because it is human nature to be biased in any hotly debated issue. But all this work kept me focused. When I delivered my speech, I felt confident that it was strictly informative.

PATTY PAK
Virginia Tech University

Key Points
Guidelines for Informative Speaking
1. Stress your informative purpose.
2. Be objective.
3. Use an informative pattern for presenting your key ideas.
4. Limit your ideas and supporting materials.
5. Use descriptive language and nonverbal cues.

Journal: Apply Guidelines for Informative Speaking

Suppose you are asked to speak to a group of incoming students on the topic "Using the Campus Library." Your objective is to familiarize new students with the physical layout of the library so that they can research efficiently. What are the key ideas you would develop in your speech? What types of presentational aids would you use to reinforce your message?

persuasion. If you don't think you can make your speech objective, save the topic for a persuasive speech.

Use an Informative Pattern for Presenting Your Key Ideas

In this textbook, we have presented, discussed, and given examples of several patterns for dividing the body of your speech into key ideas. Topical, chronological, spatial, causal, and pro–con patterns are appropriate for informative speeches. There is no one best organizational pattern. Choose the pattern that is most appropriate to your topic and specific purpose. However, some patterns are inappropriate for an informative speech. While a pro–con approach is appropriate, a pro–con assessment strategy moves the speech into persuasion. Problem–solution and need–plan patterns are also inherently persuasive.

This chapter's "Theory Into Practice" feature offers suggestions for selecting an appropriate organizational pattern for informative speeches. If you have any doubt that your organization is informative rather than persuasive, check with your instructor.

Limit Your Ideas and Supporting Materials

Because this is a speech to inform, don't make the mistake of thinking that the more information you put into a speech, the more informative it will be. Listeners cannot process all, or even most, of what you present. If you overload your audience with too many facts, figures, and dates, they will stop listening. Remember the adage "less is more." Spending more time explaining and developing a few ideas will probably result in greater retention of these ideas by your listeners.

Use Descriptive Language and Nonverbal Cues

Nothing betrays the image of objectivity like the inappropriate use of language. For example, in an informative speech on the pros and cons of juvenile curfew laws, one of our students used language that telegraphed his opinion on the issue. Even when explaining the arguments for such laws, he described them as "silly," "costly," and "unenforceable." In an informative speech, your language should be descriptive, not evaluative or judgmental.

Some speakers have a misconception that vocal and physical delivery are more important for a persuasive speech than for an informative speech. Regardless of the type of speech, your voice and body should reinforce your interest in and enthusiasm for your topic. Your delivery should also reinforce your objectivity. If you find your gestures, body tension, or voice conveying an emotional urgency, you have likely slipped into persuasion. In an informative speech, you will probably use gestures that are more descriptive and less intense.

Annotated Sample Speech

After reading this chapter, you should know the principles and characteristics of informative speaking, understand how they contribute to effective speaking, and be able to apply them as you prepare your speeches. Our student Melissa Janoske understood and used these principles when she delivered the following speech to her classmates. As you read her transcript, notice how her supporting materials and organization of the introduction, body, and conclusion contributed to a seamless, organic whole. In the marginal annotations, we have indicated the major strengths of Melissa's speech.

Renaissance Fairs: The New Vaudeville[3]

Melissa Janoske, Radford University

1 Imagine you're walking down the street, minding your own business, about to go into a store, when suddenly, someone calls your name. You turn around, and the person advances toward you. Immediately, you find yourself in the middle of a sword fight—right in the middle of the street! As you fight for your life, a crowd gathers, watching and cheering. The fight is treacherous, and your opponent is worthy, but, finally, the fight ends when the gleaming edge of your sword pins your opponent onto the cobblestone path below him. Those who have gathered come up and congratulate you.

2 This seemingly outrageous scene is actually fairly commonplace in certain times and places. The year? Well, either 1521 or today. The place? Any busy street in Renaissance England, or your local Renaissance festival.

3 Elizabethan social historian Mike Bonk captures the excitement and fascination of this era on his current website, www.faires.com. He describes the Renaissance as "a period of intensity in all things: work, play, the arts, world exploration, religion, and superstition. Renaissance faires resurrect [these extremes], both as reenactment and as a way of life."

4 Some people live and die by their ability to re-create pre-seventeenth century Europe. They create elaborate costumes and have entire other personalities that they become on the weekends. Renaissance fairs are both exciting and educational, and anyone with curiosity and imagination can attend, observe, and even participate.

5 It's easy for you to experience present-day Renaissance culture through three easy acts: imagine yourself as a Renaissance figure, affiliate with your local kingdom, and participate in a local Renaissance festival or event.

6 To start on your journey into the Renaissance, imagine yourself becoming a part of the world of a Renaissance fair. This would mean becoming a person from the original world, letting that entire culture become part of who you are, and suspending normal belief about who you are in daily life. Renaissance fair enthusiast Mike Boar proclaims: "Monday through Friday, I'm Mike the Truck Driver. On the weekends, I'm the Barbarian King. Men fear me. Women can't get enough of me. Guess who I'd rather be?" And Mike isn't alone in his love of a personality switch for the weekend. According to Jules Smith, Sr., cofounder of International Renaissance Fairs Ltd., Renaissance fairs are the "new vaudeville," drawing a crowd of 193,000 people to the last fair he held in Maryland. That's a lot of people getting decked out in chain mail and corsets and going out for the weekend. Participants use traditional names and titles, wear period clothing, and even learn about a possible profession from that time period. Events are usually open to the public, and so even if you're not into wearing tights and riding horses, it's still fun to go and watch and learn about the diversity of the culture.

7 Learning how to do all of those character-altering activities is important, but the knowledge of all things Renaissance doesn't just come in a potion from the apothecary. It is instead often achieved through the second aspect of Renaissance life: affiliating with your local kingdom. The Society for Creative Anachronism, Inc., an international organization dedicated to Renaissance culture, has divided the world into sixteen kingdoms, spanning the entire globe and allowing everyone in the world in on the fun. A map of these divisions can be found on its website, www.sca.org. Many of these sixteen kingdoms have their divisions within the United States. Virginia is located in the Kingdom of Atlantia, and each kingdom has at least one university in a central location. These universities are run by kingdom officials and offer classes in how to become more immersed in the culture; how to be a goldsmith, or lessons in jousting; or even a lecture on the political methods of King Arthur. You can learn how to fence or ride a horse, cook medieval delicacies, or shop for velvet gowns and leather boots. Each kingdom also allows any of its subjects to gain membership, come to the annual events and fairs, and immerse themselves fully in any events or activities that might help them understand Renaissance Europe.

Melissa's opening comments arouse curiosity about her topic.

This early source citation builds Melissa's credibility on her topic.

Paragraph 5 previews the main points Melissa intends to discuss.

Here Melissa begins to apply the 4 S's to her first main point. She signposts ("To start") and states the point: becoming a part of the Renaissance world.

Melissa uses examples and testimony to support her point. Her sources (Boar and Smith) use narration, contrast, and statistics.

Melissa summarizes her first point by stressing the fun and educational value of becoming a Renaissance character.

A complementary transition links Melissa's first and second points. Notice Melissa's creativity in using the archaic phrase "potion from the apothecary."

Melissa signposts ("second") and states her next main point: affiliating with a local kingdom.

Melissa supports this point by providing examples of Renaissance activities.

Melissa summarizes this second point by reiterating the functions of Renaissance kingdoms.

Melissa signposts ("third") and states her final main point: participation in Renaissance fair culture.

Melissa provides examples of many fair activities and of particular fairs held annually.

Melissa summarizes the benefits of participation in Renaissance fairs.

Melissa clearly summarizes her three main points in the first sentence of her conclusion.

Melissa provides an easy-to-remember URL to help listeners extend their exploration of her topic.

Melissa's speech comes to a definite, satisfying close with this vivid, well-worded final image.

8 While each kingdom provides the learning opportunities for and access to these festivals, the actual participation in them is the third, and most important, aspect of Renaissance fair culture. Without this participation, all the character changes and kingdom knowledge don't mean nearly as much. It is the practice of Renaissance life that makes it worthwhile, and the actual Renaissance fairs are the easiest and most fun way to do that. There are lots of different types of fair activities to participate in, from jousting festivals to chain mail competitions to cooking parties. You can take classes on spinning and weaving and chain mail or participate in the annual Saint Patty's Day Bloodbath ($5 for a day of swordsmanship and excitement). All aspects of Renaissance culture are available and represented, and all you have to do is go out and look for it. Particular festivals are held around present-day holidays, such as Halloween and feasting days, or events that were important in Renaissance culture. There is a very popular fair held in Pennsylvania every year at Halloween called Renaissance Fright Night that includes renditions of "Frankenstein" and poetry from Poe, goblins and gargoyles that come alive, and street peasants, roasted chestnuts, and fighting for the plenty. This is just one example. There are many websites, such as www.faires .com, that offer detailed information about specific fairs in your area. These festivals are the culmination of the work that people do in learning about the way things were in Renaissance Europe. It's a chance to show off your costumes, present your new persona, showcase your work, or just go and be a part of the festivities. The festivals are a time to enjoy the culture and community that is created and to relax and bask in all the entertainment that is offered through a Renaissance fair.

9 Transforming yourself into a Renaissance figure, affiliating with your local kingdom, and participating in a Renaissance fair are three main ways to experience Renaissance culture today. To get started on your journey, visit www.faires.com. Just make sure you spell it the Renaissance way: f-a-i-r-E-s. Here you will find all sorts of suggestions on integrating Renaissance culture into your life in fun and exciting ways. So take the hint from Mike Boar, the truck driver: lose the college student in you for the weekend, and see how much you like being a Barbarian King with a penchant for chain mail.

Reprinted with permission of the speaker.

Summary

An informative speech requires you to choose a topic that you and your listeners will find interesting, to gather information about that topic, and to organize your information in the most fitting manner.

Characteristics of a Speech to Inform

15.1 Explain, with examples, the three characteristics of informative speeches.

- Your goals as an informative speaker are to expand listeners' knowledge, enhance their understanding, or help them apply the information you communicate.

Informative Speech Topics

15.2 Identify, with examples, the eight categories of informative speeches.

- Classifying informative speeches by subject gives you an idea of the range of possible topics and the patterns of organization each subject typically uses. Informative speeches can be about people, objects, places, activities and events, processes, concepts, conditions, and issues.

- As you begin to prepare an informative speech, ask yourself three questions: (1) What does the audience already know about this topic? (2) What does the audience need to know in order to understand this topic? (3) Can I present this information in the allotted time so that the audience will understand and remember it?

Guidelines for Speaking to Inform

15.3 Apply the five guidelines for developing an effective informative speech.

- To succeed in public speaking, you should review sections of this textbook that assist you in preparing and presenting an excellent speech, be it informative or persuasive.

- To capture the essence of informative speaking you should: (1) stress your informative purpose, (2) be objective in your approach to the topic, (3) use an informative pattern for arranging your key ideas, (4) limit the ideas and supporting material that you try to include, and (5) use descriptive language and nonverbal cues.

Chapter 16
The Strategy of Persuasion

Learning Objectives

After studying this chapter, you should be able to

16.1 Identify the benefits of participating in the persuasive process for speakers and listeners.

16.2 Define persuasion.

16.3 Describe, with examples, the three types of influences.

16.4 Differentiate among the three types of persuasive speeches.

16.5 Use the six strategies of developing your persuasive speeches.

Media specialist Tony Schwartz, producer of political commercials for presidential and other political candidates, combined *manipulation* and *participation* to create a new word: *partipulation*. He argues that voters are not simply manipulated by campaign and advertising strategists. Voters do, after all, have the option of rejecting the messages politicians present to them. So, Schwartz contends, "You have to participate in your own manipulation."[1]

Persuasion is similar to Schwartz's concept of partipulation. As a speaker, your goal should be to establish a common perspective and tap into values your listeners share. Your goal should not be to manipulate or trick them. As a critical listener, you have a right and an ethical responsibility to choose whether you are persuaded. Charles Larson echoes this speaker–listener orientation:

> [T]he focus of persuasion is not on the source, the message, or the receiver, but on *all* of them equally. They *all cooperate* to make a persuasive process. The idea of *co-creation* means that what is inside the receiver is just as important as the source's intent or the content of messages. In one sense, *all* persuasion is *self-persuasion*—we are rarely persuaded unless we participate in the process.[2]

In this chapter, we examine how source, message, and receiver interact to co-create persuasion, and we introduce you to the *strategy* of persuasion. Why is persuasive speaking important? How does the persuasive process work? What are some principles and strategies you can use as you prepare your message? The answers to these questions provide a blueprint for your speech. In the next chapter, "Speaking to Persuade," we introduce you to the *structure* of persuasion. You will use your blueprint as you build your persuasive speech. You will study how to organize and test the arguments of your speech. You will then discover how to integrate those arguments into a clear and convincing message.

The Importance of Persuasion

16.1 Identify the benefits of participating in the persuasive process for speakers and listeners.

Delivering a persuasive message will challenge and benefit you in several ways. First, it will require you to select an issue you think is important and to communicate your concern to your audience. Voicing your beliefs will demand that you confront their logic and support; in other words, you must test your ideas for their validity. Second, that process, in turn, will require that you gather supporting materials and draw valid inferences from them as you develop your arguments. Approached seriously and researched energetically, a persuasive speech assignment can develop both your critical thinking and speech-making skills. Finally, you may also use it as an opportunity to improve your school or community. Change can occur when people speak and audiences act.

As a listener, you also benefit by participating in the persuasive process. First, a speaker can make you aware of problems and can show you how to help solve them. Second, you hear other points of view and, consequently, may better understand why others have beliefs different from yours. A speech that challenges your beliefs often forces you to reevaluate your position. Third, participating as a listener also heightens your critical thinking and improves your ability to explain and defend your beliefs. Finally, as a listener, you have an opportunity to judge how others use persuasive speaking techniques, thus enabling you to improve your own persuasive speaking.

A Definition of Persuasion

16.2 Define persuasion.

Persuasion is the process of influencing another person's values, beliefs, attitudes, or behaviors. Persuasion does not necessarily require power. Power implies authority or control over another. For example, employers who want you to be on time will state that policy and then issue reprimands, withhold promotions, and even threaten to terminate your employment to ensure that you obey. They do not need to persuade you. Likewise, in this class, you probably speak on the days assigned because failing to do so would hurt your grade. In each instance, the power residing in some other person's position shapes your behavior, at least in part.

Persuasion, however, is more accurately equated with influence than with power. As a speaker, you try to influence the audience to adopt your position. You probably have little power over your listeners, and they have the freedom to reject your message. Suppose, for example, that your speech instructor wants your class to attend a lecture given on campus by author David Sedaris. You are not required to attend, and there is no penalty or reward. To influence you, however, your instructor emphasizes the importance of this opportunity by telling you about Sedaris's background and listing two of his best-known books: *Me Talk Pretty One Day* and *Dress Your Family in Corduroy and Denim*. Your instructor also mentions Sedaris's reputation as a lively, entertaining speaker and tells you that his sister is actress Amy Sedaris.

In this case, your instructor is using influence rather than power to persuade. The concept of persuasion as influence means that you can bring about change whether or not you are the more powerful party in a relationship. You can also see that compared to power, influence requires more effort, creativity, and sensitivity but in the long run is probably more effective. If persuasion is our attempt to influence others, let's look more closely at the types of influence we can achieve.

A persuasive speech provides you the opportunity to champion important causes, influence audience beliefs and attitudes, and motivate their behaviors.

Types of Influence

16.3 Describe, with examples, the three types of influences.

Persuasion can exert three types of influence. You can change, instill, or intensify your listeners' values, beliefs, attitudes, or behaviors. Your goal is to move your listeners closer to your position. It may help you to think of this process as a continuum.

Remember, when you speak to persuade, you are speaking to listeners who may oppose, be indifferent to, or support your position. If you've developed an audience profile, you will have a good idea of your target audience. The information you gather and the assumptions you make about your audience before your speech determine your strategy as you develop your remarks.

persuasion

The process of influencing another person's values, beliefs, attitudes, or behaviors.

Figure 16.1

Many students preparing persuasive speeches make the mistake of thinking that they must change their audiences' opinions from "oppose" to "favor," or vice versa. Take the example of Chris, who argued in his persuasive speech that the National Collegiate Athletic Association should adopt a play-off system to determine each year's college football champion. After his speech, only one classmate who opposed a play-off system said that Chris had persuaded her to support the proposal. Chris thought he had failed to persuade. Further class discussion, however, proved him wrong. A few listeners said they had moved their position from strong opposition to mild opposition. In addition, several who already supported the play-off system said that Chris's arguments had strengthened their opinion. Several other listeners who were neutral before the speech found that Chris persuaded them to agree with him. As you can see, even though Chris persuaded only one audience member to move from "oppose" to "favor," his speech was quite successful. Persuasion occurs any time you move a listener's opinion in the direction you advocate, even if that movement is slight.

Change

First, the most dramatic response you can request of your listeners is that they *change* a value, belief, attitude, or behavior. The response you seek is dramatic because you attempt to change opposition to support, or support to opposition. In terms of the continuum (see Figure 16.1), you are trying to move listeners from one side of zero to the other. For example, if you discover that the majority of your listeners eat high-cholesterol foods, your persuasive speech could encourage them to alter their diets. You would be trying to change their behavior.

Instill

Second, you can attempt to *instill* a value, an attitude, a belief, or a behavior. You instill when you address a particular problem about which your listeners are unaware or undecided. If you persuade your audience that a problem exists, you have instilled a belief. A speaker trying to persuade an audience that intensive care unit psychosis is a serious health problem would first need to define that term for listeners. Then, by documenting cases of "psychotic activity occurring specifically in the intensive care unit among patients . . . that can cause them to fall out of bed, pull out breathing tubes, or . . . pull out central [arterial] lines," the speaker could instill a belief in the audience.[3]

Intensify

Finally, you may try to *intensify* values, beliefs, attitudes, or behaviors. In this case, you must know before your speech that audience members agree with your position or behave as you will advocate. Your goal is to strengthen your listeners' positions and actions—to move them even slightly in the direction you advocate on the continuum. For example, your audience may already believe that recycling is desirable. If your persuasive speech causes your listeners to recycle more frequently, you have intensified their behavior. Your persuasive speech may even encourage them to persuade family and friends to adopt similar behavior. When you change believers into advocates and advocates into activists, you have intensified their attitudes and behavior.

Types of Persuasive Speeches

16.4 Differentiate among the three types of persuasive speeches.

Persuasive speeches are generally classified according to their objectives. An effective persuasive speech may change what people believe, what people do, or how people feel. Persuasive speeches, then, may be divided into speeches to convince, to actuate, or to inspire. Understanding these divisions can help you determine your primary objective as you work on your speech, but keep in mind that persuasive speeches often include two or more objectives. For example, if your purpose is to get your audience to boycott companies using sweatshop labor to produce their products, you must first convince them that your cause is right. We usually act or become inspired after we are convinced.

Leaders in business, government, religion, education, and other areas need to know when and how to convince, actuate, and inspire their audiences.

Speeches to Convince

In a **speech to convince**, your objective is to affect your listeners' beliefs or attitudes. Each of the following specific purpose statements expresses a belief the speaker wants the audience to accept:

- To convince the audience that "hate speech" is constitutionally protected.
- To convince the audience that hydrogen fuel-celled cars are commercially feasible.
- To convince the audience that there is a constitutional right to privacy.
- To convince the audience that sealed adoption is preferable to open adoption.

    The speaker's purpose in each of these speeches is to influence belief, not to secure action.

Speeches to Actuate

A **speech to actuate** may influence beliefs, but it always calls for the audience to act. The specific purpose statements listed here illustrate calls for action:

- To move, or actuate, the audience to donate nonperishable food to a local food bank.
- To move the class to sponsor a Relay for Life team to benefit the American Cancer Society.
- To move the audience to begin a low-impact aerobic workout program.

Speeches to Inspire

A third type of persuasive speech is the **speech to inspire**, one that attempts to change how listeners feel. Examples include pep talks and motivational speeches as well as special occasion speeches such as commencement addresses and eulogies. Some specific purposes of speeches to inspire are these:

- To inspire the audience to honor the service of fallen firefighters.
- To inspire the audience to appreciate those who made their education possible.
- To inspire listeners to give their best efforts to all college courses they take.

speech to convince

A persuasive speech designed to influence listeners' beliefs or attitudes.

speech to actuate

A persuasive speech designed to influence listeners' behaviors.

speech to inspire

A persuasive speech designed to influence listeners' feelings.

Speaking with Confidence

Rather than trying to convince my classmates to tackle a world problem, I wanted to motivate them to begin making simple but important choices to improve their health. I had noticed that some of them (and their friends) had the habit of wearing unsupportive, ill-fitting shoes, such a flip flops. So, I decided to speak on the health benefits of wearing properly fitting shoes. One of my concerns, though, was being taken seriously by my listeners, so I made sure to use sound arguments and credible sources. I presented the medical issues that could result, using expert sources and an accompanying visual aid. After securing agreement on the problems, I then asked my audience to consider healthy options the next time they bought shoes. By keeping my goals focused, limited, and practical, I felt confident that I had made a constructive contribution to the immediate and long-term health of my audience.

BRITTNEY HOWELL
Radford University

The purposes of inspiration are usually noble and uplifting. These speeches typically have neither the detailed supporting material nor the complex arguments characteristic of speeches to convince or actuate. Sometimes, speakers may ask their listeners to take a specific action to demonstrate their appreciation—for example, to donate to the National Fallen Firefighters Foundation. In this case, the speech to inspire transitions into a speech to actuate.

Thus far, we have seen the importance of audience involvement in the process of persuasion. We have provided a definition of *persuasion* and discussed the various goals that persuasive speakers can have. In the following section, we discuss six important strategies that apply to all persuasive speeches.

EXPLORING ONLINE

Readings on Rhetoric

If you want to know more about how to incorporate ethos, logos, and pathos into your persuasive appeals, conduct an Internet search for Arizona State University's rhetorical triangle website.

Persuasive Speaking Strategies

16.5 Use the six strategies of developing your persuasive speeches.

As far back as ancient Greece, there is evidence of people giving advice on how to be an effective persuasive speaker. Aristotle, for example, devoted much space to the subject in his classic work *The Rhetoric*. He discussed three modes of persuasion: ethos, logos, and pathos.[4] These three modes remain an important foundation today for our understanding of persuasive speaking. What do these terms mean, and how can they help you prepare a persuasive speech?

Ethos, or speaker credibility, derives from the character and reputation of the speaker. **Logos**, or logical appeal, relies on the form and substance of an argument. **Pathos**, or emotional appeal, taps the values and feelings of the audience. Each variable—speaker, message, and audience—affects the finished product. No two people will give the same speech on the same topic to the same audience. Your strategy for each speech must be based on your unique situation and on your own creativity. Nevertheless, we can give you some strategies, or guidelines, to follow as you prepare your persuasive speech.

ethos
Speaker credibility.

logos
Logical appeal.

pathos
Emotional appeal.

credibility
Listeners' perceptions of a speaker's competence, trustworthiness, and caring.

Establish Your Credibility

As a speaker, your first available source of persuasion is your own **credibility**, or ethos. Aristotle referred to credibility as a speaker's intelligence, character, and goodwill. More recent studies confirm these three components of credibility, although they are now named competence, trustworthiness, and caring.[5] Research indicates that the higher your perceived credibility, the more likely the audience is to believe you.[6]

Speaker credibility is fluid, varying according to your listeners. You possess only the credibility your listeners grant you. If you pepper your speaking with humor, for example, some listeners may see you as lively and interesting, while others may think you are frivolous. You probably have as many different images as you have audience members.

COMPONENTS OF CREDIBILITY.   Studies demonstrate that a highly credible speaker can more successfully persuade than a speaker having low credibility. Clearly, you need to pay careful attention to your credibility at each stage in order to deliver a successful persuasive speech. How do you enhance your image? Communication theorists agree that speakers who appear competent, trustworthy, and caring are viewed as credible.[7] So, if your audience perceives you to possess these attributes, you can be effective in persuading them.

Convey Competence.   The first component of speaker credibility is **competence**, your perceived expertise. This includes how knowledgeable, skilled, informed, and experienced you are with your topic. In this class, you are among peers, so your audience probably considers you a fellow student rather than an expert on your chosen topic. How can you get them to see you as knowledgeable and worthy of their trust? Four strategies will help you establish an image of competence on your subject.

1. *Know your subject.* To speak ethically, you must be well informed about your subject. The more you read and listen, the easier it is to construct a message that is both credible and compelling. You should comprehend both the content and the context of your persuasive message. Persuading your classmates to begin recycling low-density plastics (LDPs) does you little good if your area has no processing plant for LDPs and thus recyclers will not accept LDPs. A well-researched speech increases persuasion by contributing to your image as a well-informed individual. In a public speaking course such as this, the image-building you do is cumulative. Thorough, quality research enhances your credibility on the immediate topic and generates positive initial credibility for your next appearance before the same group.

2. *Document your ideas.* You document ideas by using clear, vivid, and credible supporting materials to illustrate them, as we discussed earlier in this textbook. Unsupported ideas are mere assertions. Though your listeners may not expect you to be an expert on your topic, they need assurance that facts and experts corroborate what you say. Providing documentation supports your statements and increases your believability.

3. *Cite your sources.* You need to tell your listeners the sources of your information. Remember, your audience is not going to have the opportunity to read your bibliography. Citing sources enhances the credibility of your ideas by demonstrating that experts support your position. It also requires that your sources be unbiased and of good quality.

4. *Acknowledge any personal involvement or experience with your subject.* Listeners will probably assume that you have an edge in understanding color blindness if you let them know you are color-blind. If you have worked with terminally ill patients and are speaking on hospice care, mentioning your experience will similarly add authority to your ideas.

Convey Trustworthiness.   A second criterion of speaker credibility is **trustworthiness**, and it tells your listeners that you are honest, moral, genuine, ethical, and objective in what you say. A speaker can demonstrate these attributes in two ways.

1. *Establish common ground with your audience.* If listeners know that you understand their values, experiences, and aspirations, they will be more receptive to

competence
Listeners' views of a speaker's qualifications to speak on a particular topic.

trustworthiness
Listeners' views of a speaker's honesty, morality, and objectivity.

Ethical Decisions

CREDIBILITY: CITING YOUR SOURCES

The competence component of credibility is, in part, dependent on speakers being able to document their ideas and cite their sources. When delivering their speeches, credible speakers cite their sources orally because the listeners don't have access to the speaker's bibliography.

Deciding on what supporting materials to use and what sources to cite in a speech may be quite difficult. For example, research informs us that there are health benefits to eating dark chocolate; there are even health benefits associated with moderate consumption of red wine. However, excessive consumption of either dark chocolate or red wine may be harmful to our health. So, if you are delivering a speech to actuate in which you encourage your listeners to eat more dark chocolate, how do you decide on what supporting materials to use and what sources to cite in your speech? Let's say that you find two excellent articles about dark chocolate consumption published in the *New England Journal of Medicine*. In the first study, the researchers concluded that eating dark chocolate enhances alertness, but it may make it more difficult to sleep. In the second study, the researchers concluded that dark chocolate consumption improves our moods, but it expedites tooth decay.

Would you cite these sources in your speech? Which supporting materials would you include to document your ideas? Will your decisions affect the perception of your character?

your arguments. You increase your persuasiveness when you identify with your listeners.

2. *Demonstrate your objectivity in approaching the topic.* The information and sources you include in your speech should demonstrate thorough, unbiased research. One student gave his speech on cigarette smoking, arguing that its harmful effects were greatly exaggerated. He relied on studies sponsored by the tobacco industry. Few in the audience were persuaded by his evidence. He undermined his image of trustworthiness because he limited his research to sources the audience considered biased.

Convey Caring. A third element of speaker credibility is **caring**, which refers to having the audience members' best interests at heart by being understanding, empathetic, and sensitive. As a speaker, you can enhance your perceived caring by tapping into your audience members' needs, conveying concern for your audience members, and conveying that your speech is intended to help or benefit your listeners in some way. Research shows that caring speakers are liked by their audience members and the audience members report that they learn a lot from caring speakers.[8] A speaker can demonstrate caring in two ways.

1. *Convey empathy.* Empathy is perceived favorably by listeners of persuasive messages. Being sensitive and understanding to your listeners' concerns and acknowledging their positions will enhance your perceived caring and ability to influence their values, beliefs, attitudes, and behaviors.

2. *Demonstrate that you have your listeners' best interest at heart.* Listeners prefer to be told how your speech can benefit them. As a caring speaker, you should emphasize that you are concerned with your listeners' physical and psychological well-being as well as their academic, financial, personal, and professional success. It is essential that your listeners do not think that you as the speaker will benefit from what you are proposing, but rather that your audience members will benefit from your speech.

caring

The extent to which listeners perceive a speaker as understanding, empathetic, and sensitive.

As a speaker, present a well-researched and well-documented message and communicate it in an honest and unbiased manner. Your verbal, vocal, and physical delivery should show you to be a fluent, forceful, and friendly individual serious about the issue you address. If listeners perceive you to be competent, trustworthy, and caring, you will have high source credibility and, hence, be an effective persuader.

STAGES OF CREDIBILITY.   Credibility varies over time. Your credibility before, during, and after your speech may change. These chronological divisions are sometimes referred to as *initial, derived,* and *terminal credibility*.[9]

Initial credibility is your image or reputation prior to speaking. The more the audience knows about you, the firmer your image. Even if your listeners don't know you personally, you can still bring varying images to the speaking occasion. For example, if you are a spokesperson for an organization, your audience may make certain assumptions about you based on what they know about that organization. If a representative from EMILY's List, the Family Research Council, the National Rifle Association, or the Sierra Club were to speak to you, you would probably make certain assumptions about the individual based on what you know about that organization. Just as you do with strangers, you form impressions of your classmates based on what they say in class, how they dress, whether they arrive to class on time, their age, and any organization to which they belong. They have also formed impressions of you, of course. Such images constitute your initial credibility.

Derived credibility is the image the audience develops of you as you speak. The moment you enter your listeners' presence, you provide stimuli from which they can evaluate you. As you begin your speech, the number of stimuli multiplies quickly. If you begin your speech with an offensive joke, listeners' images of you will become more negative. When you appeal to your listeners' values and present reasoned arguments to advance your position, you enhance your image. Your information helps your audience judge your credibility. Listeners will also judge your nonverbal behaviors, such as gestures, posture, eye contact, and appearance. If you convey confidence, authority, and a genuine concern for your listeners, you will enhance your credibility.

Terminal credibility is the image the audience has of you after your speech. Even this credibility is subject to change. The listener may be caught up in the excitement and emotion of your speech and end up with an elevated opinion of you. As time passes, that evaluation may moderate. As you can see, the process of generating and maintaining credibility is ongoing. In this class, for example, your credibility at the conclusion of one speech will shape your initial credibility for your next speech.

Focus Your Goals

A common mistake many beginning speakers make is to seek dramatic change in their listeners' values, beliefs, attitudes, and behaviors. The speaker who can accomplish this is rare—particularly if he or she seeks change on highly emotional and controversial issues such as abortion, gun control, capital punishment, religion, or politics. Keep in mind that the more firmly your audience is anchored to a position, the less likely you are to change their attitudes. It is unrealistic for you to expect dramatic change in a person's beliefs and values in a 5- to 10-minute speech. Instant conversions occur, but they are rare. Limiting your goals and arguing incrementally will help you focus your goals.

LIMIT YOUR GOALS.   Rather than trying to convince your audience to support (or oppose) the death penalty, try to convince them of a limited goal, a smaller aspect of the topic; for example, argue that capital punishment deters crime (or does not). Once a listener accepts that belief, you or another speaker can build on it and focus on a successive objective: support for (or opposition to) the death penalty.

Which specific purpose statement in the following pairs is the more limited and reasonable goal?

initial credibility

A speaker's image or reputation before speaking to a particular audience.

derived credibility

The image listeners develop of a speaker as he or she speaks.

terminal credibility

The image listeners develop of a speaker by the end of a speech and for a period of time after it.

To persuade the audience that exposure to violent video games promotes aggression, *or*

To persuade the audience that habitual exposure to violent video games promotes aggression in children

To persuade the audience that actively involving students in classroom learning is desirable, *or*

To persuade the audience that team learning is a cost-effective way to promote student learning

In both cases, the second statement is the more limited and potentially more persuasive. Remember the persuasive principle: *persuasion is more likely if your goals as a speaker are limited rather than global.*

ARGUE INCREMENTALLY.   The second principle builds on the first one: *persuasion is more permanent if you achieve it incrementally.* To be effective and long-lasting, persuasion should occur incrementally, or one step at a time. This principle becomes more important if your audience is likely to hear counterarguments to your argument. In any speech, you speak for a fixed amount of time. The greater the number of points you must prove, the less time you have to support and explain each. Because you must move through several steps, your limited time may force you to abbreviate your support of some of these steps. When your listeners hear another speaker attack one of those steps later, they may lack sufficient evidence to counter those attacks; as a result, what you accomplished may be only temporary. Your goal should be to "inoculate" your listeners against possible counterarguments. The stronger your arguments, the greater the likelihood that you will bring about enduring change in your audience's opinions. If you know your audience has been exposed to counterarguments, you may need to address those arguments before introducing your own.

Connect with Your Listeners

You are probably more easily persuaded by people similar to you than by those who are different. We may reason that individuals having backgrounds like ours will view situations and problems as we would. Furthermore, we believe that people who share our beliefs will investigate an issue and arrive at a judgment in the same manner we would if we had the time and the opportunity. Thus, *persuasion is more likely if a speaker establishes common ground with the audience.*

One way to increase your persuasion, then, is to identify with your listeners. Sonja, a weekend news anchor for a local television station, was asked to speak to a college television production class on employment opportunities in television. Notice how Sonja used the strategy of identification in her introduction as she focused on experiences she shared with her listeners.

> Seven years ago a timid freshman girl sat in a college classroom much like this. Just like you, she was taking a TV production class. And like some of you, I suspect, she dreamed of being in front of a camera someday, sitting at an anchor desk, reporting the news to thousands of families who would let her come into their homes through the magic of television.
>
> There was little reason to predict that this girl would achieve her dreams. In many ways she was rather ordinary. She didn't come from a wealthy family. She didn't have any connections that would get her a job in broadcasting. She was a B student who worked part-time in the university food service to help pay for her education. But she had a goal and was determined to attain it. And then one day, it happened. An instructor announced that a local TV station had an opening for a student intern. The instructor said the internship would involve long hours, menial work, and no pay. Hardly the opportunity of a lifetime! Nevertheless, after class, she approached the instructor, uncertain of what she was getting into. With her instructor's help, she applied for and

received the internship. It is because of that decision that I am now the weekend anchor of the city's largest television station.

The rest of Sonja's speech focused on the importance of student internships in learning about the reality of the broadcast media and making contacts for future references and employment. Her opening comments made Sonja a more believable speaker by bridging the gap between her and her listeners. Sonja's suggestions influenced her audience because she had established common ground with them.

Four principles of persuasion should guide how you establish common ground with your audience. Each principle requires you to analyze your audience carefully in order to understand your listeners.

ASSESS LISTENERS' KNOWLEDGE OF YOUR TOPIC.   *Persuasion is more likely if the audience lacks information on the topic.* In the absence of information, a single fact can be compelling. The more information your listeners possess about an issue, the less likely you are to alter their perceptions.

Arturo applied this principle in a speech to persuade his audience that auto insurance companies should not be allowed to set rates based on drivers' credit ratings. Few of his listeners knew that the practice occurred. Yet, by citing just a handful of credible sources, Arturo proved that the practice increased beginning in the mid-1990s, had been adopted by 92 percent of insurers by 2001, and was "nearly universal" by March 2002. As a result, drivers with the worst credit ratings paid rates that were, in some cases, 40 percent higher than those with the best ratings.

New and surprising information such as this can have great persuasive impact. Of course, this principle also has significant ethical implications. Ethical speakers will not exploit their listeners' lack of knowledge to advance positions they know are not logically supported.

ASSESS HOW IMPORTANT YOUR AUDIENCE CONSIDERS YOUR TOPIC

Ken, Andrea, and Brad gave their persuasive speeches on the same day. Ken's purpose was to persuade the audience to support the school's newly formed lacrosse team by attending the next home game. Andrea's topic concerned the increasing number of homeless adults and children in the city. She told the class about Project Hope, sponsored by the Student Government Association, and asked everyone to donate either a can of food or a dollar at designated collection centers in campus dining halls or in the Student Center. Finally, Brad advocated legalization of marijuana, citing the drug's medical and economic potential.

Which speaker do you think had the most difficult challenge? In answering this question, you must consider the audience. *Persuasion is related to how important the audience considers the topic.*

The perceived importance of a topic can increase the likelihood of persuasion. Audience members in the above example probably agreed with both Ken and Andrea, and both may have been successful persuaders. Listeners who viewed combating hunger as a more important goal than supporting the lacrosse team were probably more persuaded by Andrea and may have contributed to Project Hope.

Just as the importance of a topic can work for you as a persuasive speaker, it can also work against you and decrease the likelihood of persuasion. It is surely easier, for example, for someone to persuade you to change brands of toothpaste than to change your religion. The reason is simple: your religion is more important to you. Brad probably had a tougher time persuading his listeners than did either Ken or Andrea. Legalizing marijuana probably ran counter to some deeply held audience opinions, and the intensity of those beliefs and values may have made them more resistant to Brad's persuasive appeals. The importance of an issue will vary according to each audience member, and you need to take this into account as you prepare your persuasive appeal.

MOTIVATE YOUR LISTENERS. A third principle of persuasion is that *persuasion is more likely if the audience is motivated in the direction of the message.* People change their values, beliefs, attitudes, and behaviors because they are motivated to do so. To be an effective persuader, you must discover what motivates your listeners. This requires an understanding of their needs and desires. How can you do this? You can enhance your persuasive appeal by following three steps. First, identify as many of the needs and desires of your listeners as possible. Second, review your list, and select those that your speech satisfies. Third, as you prepare your speech, explain how the action you advocate fulfills audience needs. If you discover that your speech does not fulfill the needs or desires of your listeners, then you have probably failed to connect with the listeners. They may receive your speech with interest, but such listeners will probably not act on your message. What you intended as a persuasive speech may in fact be received as informative.

RELATE YOUR MESSAGE TO LISTENERS' VALUES. Finally, *persuasion is more likely if the speaker's message is consistent with listeners' values, beliefs, attitudes, and behaviors.* We expect our actions to match our beliefs. In fact, we will call someone a hypocrite who professes one set of values but acts according to another. Your ability to persuade is thus enhanced if you request an action that is consistent with your audience's values.

Use this principle of consistency in constructing your persuasive appeal. For example, we have had students who persuaded their classroom audience to oppose the use of animals in nonmedical product testing. They first identified the beliefs that would cause a person to challenge such tests—for example, product testing harms animals and is unnecessary. Next they showed their audience that they share these beliefs. Once they accomplished that, the speakers then asked their listeners to act in accordance with their beliefs and boycott companies that continue to test cosmetics on animals.

Organize Your Arguments

A poorly organized speech has little chance of surviving in the minds of audience members. Using the organizational strategies discussed earlier in this textbook can increase your listeners' retention of your message. This is especially important if you seek long-term changes in your audience's attitudes and behaviors. A well-organized speech in which the key points are presented in a logical manner taps into Aristotle's logos. (See Chapter 8, Learning Objectives 8.2 and 8.3, and Chapter 10, Learning Objectives 10.1 and 10.2, for a review of organizing a speech.)

In addition to what you've already learned about structuring your speech, we offer one more organizing principle: *persuasion is more likely if arguments are placed appropriately.* Once you have determined the key arguments in your speech, you must decide their order. To do that, you must know which of your arguments is the strongest. Assume for a moment that your persuasive speech argues that the public defender system must be reformed. Assume, too, that you are using a problem–solution organization (discussed in Chapter 8). Your first main point and the arguments supporting it could be:

The public defender system is stacked against the defendant.
A. Public defenders' caseloads are too heavy.
B. Public defenders have too little experience.
C. Public defenders have inadequate investigative staffs.

One of these three arguments will probably be stronger than the other two. You may have more evidence on one, you may have more recent evidence on it, or you may feel that one argument will be more compelling for your particular audience. Assume that you decide point B is the strongest. Where should you place it? Two theories of argument placement are the primacy and recency theories.

PRIMACY THEORY.   **Primacy theory** recommends that you put your strongest argument first in the body of your speech to establish a strong first impression. Because you are most likely to win over your listeners with your strongest argument, this theory suggests that you should win your listeners to your side as early as possible. Primacy theorists tell you to move your strongest argument to the position of point A.

RECENCY THEORY.   **Recency theory**, on the other hand, maintains that you should present your strongest argument last, thus leaving your listeners with your best argument. Recency theorists would have you build up to your strongest argument by making it point C.

If your listeners oppose what you advocate, you may want to present your strongest argument first. Moving them toward your position early in the speech may make them more receptive to your other ideas. If your audience already shares your beliefs and attitudes and your goal is to motivate them to action, you may want to end with your most compelling argument. Both the primacy and recency theorists generally agree that the middle position is the weakest. If you have three or more arguments, therefore, do not place your strongest argument in a middle position. When you sandwich a strong argument between weaker ones, you reduce its impact.

Aristotle argued that logos relies on the form and substance of argument. Organizing and supporting your ideas, the subjects of this and the following section, will help you develop the logical appeal of your speech.

Support Your Ideas

Well-supported ideas benefit your speech in two ways. First, they provide an ethical underpinning for your position. Ethical speakers test their ideas for validity and share that support with their listeners. Second, well-supported ideas enhance your credibility. Using quality evidence, citing your sources, and employing valid reasoning increase your credibility as a speaker.[10] By supporting your argument, you adhere to Aristotle's logos.

Two sections of this book will help you construct a convincing case for your position. In Chapter 9, we discussed the types of supporting material and tests of evidence that you can use to prove your arguments. You can use examples, definitions, narration, comparison, contrast, statistics, and testimony to give your ideas credibility. In Chapter 17, we will introduce you to the elements of an argument, describe five types of arguments you can use in your persuasive speaking, and define several categories of faulty reasoning you should avoid. (See Chapter 9, Learning Objectives 9.2 and 9.3, and Chapter 17, Learning Objectives 17.1, 17.2, and 17.3.)

Enhance Your Emotional Appeals

Pathos, Aristotle's third mode of persuasion, is the appeal to emotions. Among the emotions speakers can arouse are anger, envy, fear, hate, jealousy, joy, love, and pride. When speakers use these feelings to try to get you to believe something or to act in a particular way, they are using emotional appeals.

Because some of the feelings just listed seem negative, you may consider emotional appeals as unacceptable or inferior types of proof. Perhaps you have even heard someone say, "Don't be so emotional; use your head!" It is certainly possible to be emotional and illogical, but keep in mind that it is also possible to be both emotional and logical. Is it illogical, for example, to be angered by child abuse, to hate racism, or to fear chemical warfare? We don't think so. The strongest arguments combine reason with passion. Logos and pathos should not conflict; they should complement each other.

Jessica began her persuasive speech by relating a personal narrative she remembered from her childhood.

primacy theory
The assumption that a speaker should place the strongest argument at the beginning of the body of a speech.

recency theory
The assumption that a speaker should place the strongest argument at the end of the body of a speech.

I was 4 years old; my sister was only 2. It was not long after we reached my grandma's house that the phone rang. I could hear ambulance and police sirens head toward the highway as tears were forming in my mom's eyes. There had been a car accident. My dad was rushed to the hospital; his little Fiesta car was totaled. He had been hit on the passenger side by a man driving a station wagon, and, fortunately, both my dad and the other driver survived. Because the other driver fell asleep at the wheel, my dad went to the hospital instead of coming home that night to his family.

Jessica quoted several sources with examples and statistics related to driver fatigue, including these powerful statistics:

Drowsy driving is estimated to cause about 20 percent of [all vehicle] accidents, 1.2 million a year, more than drugs and alcohol combined. It accounts for an astonishing 5 percent of fatal crashes, and 30 percent of fatal crashes in rural areas.[11]

Did Jessica construct a logical argument? Yes. She presented examples and statistics to support her position. Did she construct an emotional argument? Again, yes. She tapped her listeners' need for safety and their compassion for those who have suffered because of drowsy drivers. Logos and pathos coalesced to form a compelling argument. You can use the guidelines in this chapter's "Theory Into Practice" feature to develop and enhance the pathos of your persuasive speech.

It is important to remember that these three modes of persuasion—ethos, logos, and pathos—all work to enhance your persuasive appeal. The best persuasive speeches combine all three. Effective persuaders are credible, present logically constructed and supported arguments, and tap their listeners' values.

Key Points

Persuasive Speaking Strategies

1. Establish your credibility.
2. Focus your goals.
3. Connect with your listeners.
4. Organize your arguments.
5. Support your ideas.
6. Enhance your emotional appeals.

Theory Into Practice TIP

DEVELOPING EMOTIONAL APPEALS

Thoughtful emotional appeals can engage listeners in both the content and delivery of your message. Use the following four guidelines to connect with your audience and enhance the pathos of your speech.

Tap Audience Values

This guideline requires, first, that you carefully analyze your audience to identify their beliefs, values, and needs. Then, as you construct and deliver your speech, show that what you advocate is consistent with your listeners' values.

Duncan's specific purpose was to persuade his classmates to become members of Amnesty International. He had joined this organization because he felt that, as an individual, he could do little to help end torture and executions of prisoners of conscience throughout the world. As part of a concerted worldwide effort, however, he saw the opportunity to further social and political justice. Duncan surveyed his classmates and discovered that although many of them knew little about Amnesty International, most strongly supported freedom of expression and opposed governments' actions to suppress this right. Duncan used these shared values to establish common ground with his listeners and to frame what he would propose.

Use Vivid Examples

Vivid, emotionally toned examples illustrate and enliven your message. After presenting testimony of persecution coupled with statistical estimates of the extent of the problem, Duncan paused and then announced, "I want you not only to hear of the plight of these victims but also to see it." He pushed a remote control button and proceeded to show five slides of people brutalized by their own governments. He did not speak but simply showed each slide for 10 seconds. After the last slide, he spoke again:

They say a picture is worth a thousand words. Well, these pictures speak volumes about human rights abuse. But these pictures should also speak to our consciences. Can we stand back, detached, and do nothing, knowing what fate befalls these individuals?

Duncan used dramatic visual examples to enhance the pathos of his speech.

Use Emotive Language

Nowhere can words be more powerful than when they work to generate emotional appeals. Near the end of his speech, Duncan told his listeners, "In the last 4 minutes you've heard about the anguish, the pain, the suffering, and the persecution experienced by thousands of people, simply because they want to be free and follow their consciences." *Anguish, pain, suffering*, and *persecution* are all words Duncan carefully chose to evoke strong feelings among the audience.

Use Effective Delivery

When a speaker's verbal and nonverbal messages conflict, we tend to trust the nonverbal message. For that reason, speakers who show little physical and vocal involvement with their speeches usually come across as uninterested or insincere. When you display emotion, you can sometimes generate audience emotion. Throughout his speech, Duncan made effective use of eye contact, gestures, pauses, and vocal emphasis to connect with his classmates. His speech had a powerful effect because his delivery demonstrated his concern for and commitment to his topic.

Summary

The Importance of Persuasion

16.1 Identify the benefits of participating in the persuasive process for speakers and listeners.

- As a speaker, persuasion challenges you to select topics important to your audience, evaluate possible supporting material, and construct valid and compelling arguments.

- As a listener, you should listen objectively, evaluate thoughtfully, and respond responsibly. Effective listening can enhance your ability to explain your beliefs and improve your own persuasive speaking.

A Definition of Persuasion

16.2 Define persuasion.

- Persuasion is the process of influencing another person's values, beliefs, attitudes, or behaviors.

Types of Influence

16.3 Describe, with examples, the three types of influences.

- Persuasive speakers must identify the type of influence they seek in their listeners. Do you want to *instill* values, beliefs, attitudes, or behaviors that your listeners may not already possess? Do you seek to *intensify* how your audience already thinks, feels, or acts? Do you want them to change their beliefs and behaviors, for example?

- How you answer these questions will determine your specific purpose and how you develop your persuasive speech.

Types of Persuasive Speeches

16.4 Differentiate among the three types of persuasive speeches.

- A persuasive speech aimed at changing beliefs and attitudes, but not requesting any overt behavior of listeners, is a *speech to convince*. A *speech to actuate* seeks to change behaviors. A *speech to inspire* encourages positive changes in the way listeners feel about their beliefs or actions.

Persuasive Speaking Strategies

16.5 Use the six strategies of developing your persuasive speeches.

- Three modes of persuasion, discussed at least as early as the time of Aristotle, are *ethos* (ethical appeal), *logos* (logical appeal), and *pathos* (emotional appeal).

- The higher your perceived credibility, the more likely the audience is to believe you. A starting point for persuasion, then, is to establish your credibility. Some speakers have *initial credibility* with a particular audience, based on the listeners' prior knowledge of the speakers. All speakers have *derived credibility*, developed from the ideas they present in their speech and their speech delivery, and *terminal credibility* based on the audience's evaluation of the speaker and the message after the speech.

- *Competence, trustworthiness*, and *caring* are three components of a speaker's credibility.

- You are more likely to persuade if your goals are limited rather than global. In addition, your persuasiveness with an audience will be more enduring if you achieve it incrementally, or step by step.

- Persuasion is more likely if you establish common ground with the audience. You are more likely to persuade listeners who lack information on your subject, who are self-motivated in the direction of your message, and whose values, beliefs, attitudes, and behaviors are consistent with your message.

- Persuasion is more likely if the speaker's arguments are appropriately placed within the speech. *Primacy theory* asserts that you should place your strongest argument first in the body of your speech. *Recency theory* maintains that you should build up to your strongest argument, placing it last in the body of

your speech. The lesson for public speakers is to avoid placing a strong argument between weaker ones.

- Provide solid support for your ideas. Well-supported ideas provide an ethical underpinning for your speech and enhance your ethos for the audience. Use a variety of quality supporting materials, cite your sources, and reason logically to increase your persuasiveness.

- Increase your persuasiveness by enhancing your message's emotional appeals. Tap audience values; use vivid, emotionally toned examples; use emotive language; and display emotion in the physical and vocal delivery of the speech.

Chapter 17
Speaking to Persuade

 Learning Objectives

After studying this chapter, you should be able to

17.1 Apply the three steps of making an argument and the four steps of refuting an argument.

17.2 Construct five types of arguments.

17.3 Explain, with examples, the ten fallacies of argument.

17.4 Develop speeches using three types of propositions.

17.5 Construct a speech using Monroe's motivated sequence.

Structuring sound arguments and detecting flawed reasoning are important skills for the public speaker. Thomas Gilovich, professor of psychology at Cornell University, explains:

> Thinking straight about the world is a precious and difficult process that must be carefully nurtured. . . . In the words of [paleontologist and evolutionary biologist] Stephen Jay Gould, "When people learn no tools of judgment and merely follow their hopes, the seeds of political manipulation are sown." As individuals and as society, we should be less accepting of superstition and sloppy thinking, and should strive to develop those "habits of mind" that promote a more accurate view of the world.[1]

In the previous chapter, we discussed the strategy of persuasion. You learned what persuasion is and strategies you can use to develop a convincing message. In this chapter, we will show you how to construct an argument, refute an argument, and detect faulty arguments. In addition, you will study characteristics and types of persuasive propositions and special organizational patterns you can use in persuasive speeches.

Making and Refuting Arguments

17.1 **Apply the three steps of making an argument and the four steps of refuting an argument.**

Aristotle argued the successful persuasive speaker has two basic goals: "you state an argument and you prove it."[2] Sounds simple, doesn't it? Well, an argument is more than an assertion or claim. **Argument** is the process of reasoning from evidence to *prove* a claim. Before you can prove your case, however, you must understand the structure of arguments and how those arguments are organized in your speech. Aristotle called this type of persuasive appeal logos, or logical appeal. Let's examine how all this works.

Steps of an Argument

Suppose you make the following statement: "I am more confident about public speaking now than I was at the beginning of this course." If someone asked you to justify your statement, you could respond in this way:

> I experience fewer symptoms of nervousness. I seem to worry less about facing an audience. The night before my speech, I sleep better than I used to. I establish eye contact with my audience now, rather than avoiding looking directly at them. I no longer nervously shift my weight from foot to foot, and I have started gesturing.

Together, your statement and response constitute an argument. You have made a claim ("I am more confident about public speaking now") and then supported it with evidence—in this case, examples from personal observation. Aristotle would be pleased.

At its simplest level, an argument includes three steps:

1. You make a claim.
2. You offer evidence.
3. You show how the evidence proves the claim.[3]

A *claim* is what you intend to prove. It is a statement you want your listeners to accept. Some examples of claims include:

> The influence of race undermines the accuracy of eyewitness testimony.
>
> The most important thing you can learn in college is how to learn.
>
> Visual aids make ideas easier to remember.

argument

The process of reasoning from evidence to prove a claim.

The **validity** of any claim depends on whether or not the evidence supports your statement. **Evidence** is the supporting material you use to prove a point. As an advocate, you have an obligation to support your position with valid arguments. Therefore, you must offer your listeners reasons to accept your claim.

Speakers may introduce a claim and then present supporting materials, or they may introduce evidence and show how that information leads to an inescapable claim. In her persuasive speech on the need to reform the organ donation system, Ali's first key idea was that an organ shortage existed. Notice how she gently introduced her claim and then presented statistical evidence and cited her sources. She let the evidence build to a more compelling claim—that "the demand for organs far outweighs the supply."

> First, let us examine the extent of the organ shortage in the United States.
>
> Every patient waiting for an organ transplant in the United States is registered with the United Network for Organ Sharing, or UNOS. The UNOS is a nonprofit organization established by Congress in 1984 that seeks to encourage organ donation. *U.S. News & World Report* of January 13, 2003, reports that every morning more than 83,000 people awaiting a new heart, liver, kidney, or other organ wake up to a brutal imbalance of supply and demand.
>
> During the next 24 hours, while it is likely that 66 of them will receive a transplant, 17 will die. And by the way, another 115 new names will be added to the waiting lists. Day by day, the human toll and the organ deficit grow. For example, the *Tulsa World* of August 18, 2003, reports that one of the most common organ transplants is the kidney. Approximately 13,000 kidney transplants are done each year in the United States, but there are almost 50,000 patients waiting for kidneys. There are also approximately 5,000 liver transplants done in the U.S. every year, but the waiting list for these organs is still about 15,000.
>
> Clearly the demand for organs is due to the low number of actual registered donors and a system unable to meet the exponentially growing demand for organ transplants in this country.[4]

Refuting an Argument

When you studied how to organize your speech, we suggested the "4 S" strategy for developing your key ideas in a speech. In a persuasive speech, you signpost your claim, state your claim, support your claim with quality evidence, and summarize, showing how your evidence proves your claim. But how do you refute another's argument? The question is relevant because topics you and your classmates select for your persuasive speeches will involve a spark of controversy. There is always another side, perhaps several sides, in addition to the one the speaker presents. You may even select a topic because you read or heard a statement with which you disagreed. Persuasive speakers and critical thinkers must know both how to prove arguments and how to refute them. For each argument you **refute**, you may want to use the following four-step **refutational strategy**:

1. State the position you are refuting.
2. State your position.
3. Support your position.
4. Show how your position undermines the opposing argument.

Seth selected his topic, the importance of language skills for career advancement, after hearing a comment by his roommate. He presented the following argument in his speech. The comments in the margin show how Seth used each of the four steps of refutation.

> Last week, my roommate stormed into the dorm room shaking a paper he just got back from his English composition teacher. He threw the paper on his bed

validity

The accuracy with which your supporting materials support your claim.

evidence

Supporting material a speaker uses to prove a point.

Ali has just stated her claim.

Ali then offers evidence for her claim.

Finally, Ali shows how the evidence proves the claim.

EXPLORING ONLINE

Constructing Arguments

The Purdue University Online Writing Lab website provides examples to help you understand logic and to practice constructing arguments. It also links to information on various types of logical fallacies. To learn more, conduct an Internet search for "Purdue University constructing an argument."

refute

To dispute; to counter one argument with another.

refutational strategy

A pattern of disputing an argument by (1) stating the position you are refuting, (2) stating your position, (3) supporting your position, and (4) showing how your position undermines the opposing argument.

and screamed, "I can't wait until I get out of college, away from teachers who are obsessed with grammar, and into the real world where people judge you on what you say, not how you say it!" Sound familiar? I bet many of us have felt the same way after getting back a paper with all those picky corrections marked in red ink. As my roommate says, "In the real world, you're not judged on your grammar."

Well, my roommate is wrong. Grammar is important in the business world just as it is here in the classroom. How we express our ideas *is* important to our success. At least that's the conclusion of Camille Wright Miller, and she ought to know. She has a Ph.D. and is a consultant on workplace issues. In her January 13, 2002, *Roanoke Times* column, she told about a candidate who was interviewed for an important position in a company, one that would pay more than $100,000. After the interview, one of the owners said, "How many times did he say 'I seen'"? Those two words cost him the job. And this isn't an isolated example. Dr. Miller says, "Many . . . organizations recognize the power of language and the negative impact of grammatically flawed language on their customers and employees." Employers evaluate grammar "in determining an individual's intelligence, capabilities, and fitness to be a manager."

Using incorrect language can keep us from landing a good job or getting promoted once we're hired. So, I'm going to tell my roommate that he probably should listen to what his English composition teacher says. And all of us should read those picky comments written in red on the papers we get back, too. Because there's some truth in the cliché "Good grammar never goes out of style."

The quality of your decisions—indeed, the quality of your life—depends on what you know and how you use that information.

Types of Argument

17.2 Construct five types of arguments.

Speakers can justify their claims by using any of five types of argument. You may offer proof by arguing from example, analogy, cause, deduction, or authority. The type of argument you select will depend on your topic, the available evidence, and your listeners. You may combine several types of argument in a single persuasive speech. Knowing how to construct and test arguments will also help as you listen to the speeches of others.

Argument by Example

Argument by example is an inductive form of proof. **Inductive argument** uses a few instances to assert a broader claim. For example, if you have struggled through calculus and analytic geometry, you may conclude that math is a difficult subject. We hear a few friends complain of electrical problems with a particular make of car and decide not to buy that model. A speaker relates several examples of corruption in city hall, and we conclude that political corruption is widespread. Those are all examples of inductive reasoning.

Patrick began his speech using a series of examples to suggest a larger problem. Only then did he ask his audience to consider the cause of the problem. See if you can guess his topic.

First came a report out of Alabama. The McMillan family found their tap water black, oily, and bubbling. Soon after came Texas. Three ranchers said their water smelled fouled, and two days later, seven of their animals were dead. Ohio. A gas buildup in the Payne family's basement well caused the house to explode, and testing found similar levels in the wells of 22 neighbors. Even

---

Seth states the position he plans to refute.

Seth states his position.

Seth supports his position.

Seth shows how his position undermines the opposing argument.

argument by example or inductive argument

Says that what is true of a few instances is true generally.

now, across the country folks are realizing that with just a match, they can light their tap water on fire.

As the reports mount, a shocking revelation is taking shape. For years, the drinking water of tens of millions of Americans has been systematically poisoned with chemicals like arsenic, formaldehyde, and sulfuric acid. But far from acts of terrorism, this sabotage is not only allowed by our government but subsidized. It's called hydraulic fracturing, a drilling technique that harnesses incredible amounts of natural gas, but at the cost of destroying our most precious resource: our drinking water.[5]

How can you test whether Patrick's or anyone's argument by example is sound? Argument by example is valid only if you can answer yes to each of the following four questions:

1. *Are the examples true?* When you studied supporting materials, you learned that hypothetical or imaginary examples can clarify a point, but they do not prove it. Only when verifiable examples are presented should you proceed to the next question.

2. *Are the examples relevant?* Suppose Susan presents the following evidence in her speech on homelessness: "According to police reports published in yesterday's *News Journal*, city police picked up three individuals who were found sleeping in the park this past weekend. So, you can see that even in our city homelessness is a serious problem." Do these examples really support the claim? Did these individuals not have homes? Had they passed out? Were they there for other reasons? Until you can answer these questions, you cannot assume that they were homeless. The examples must relate to the specific claim.

3. *Are the examples sufficient?* Susan must present enough examples to prove her assertion. In general, the greater the population for which you generalize, the more examples you need. Three examples of homelessness may be statistically significant in a small town, but that number is far below average for many large cities.

4. *Are the examples representative?* Was the weekend Susan reported typical? How did it compare with other weekends, weekdays, or seasons? To prove her argument, Susan must present examples that are true, relevant, sufficient, and representative.

Argument by Analogy

An analogy is a comparison. **Argument by analogy** links two objects or concepts and asserts that what is true of one will be true of the other. Argument by analogy

argument by analogy
Says that what is true in one case is or will be true in another.

Speaking with Confidence

I began drafting a persuasive speech on business ethics, targeting my peers as the next generation of business leaders. It quickly became clear, however, that I failed to research my audience. Many of them intended to pursue professions other than business, so I decided to show why it's important for *all* students to take ethics courses. I supported my claims with evidence from expert and unbiased sources. I gave examples of recent business scandals to show some of the problems created by unethical behavior. I shared what I learned in my ethical leadership class and quoted from the textbook. I argued that a better understanding of ethics would give all of us guidelines to use when we faced unexpected and difficult decisions in the future. Near the end of my speech, I provided my audience with specific ethics courses for all the majors in our class, and asked them to look into these classes for fall registration. Knowing that I had supported my claims well, I was confident that I had persuaded my audience to consider taking these ethics courses.

BRIAN DAVIS
Virginia Tech University

is appropriate when the program you advocate or oppose has been tried elsewhere. Some states have some form of "stand your ground" laws; others do not. Some colleges require SAT or ACT test scores for admission; others do not. Some public high schools offer magnet programs; others do not. A speech defending or disputing any of these programs could demonstrate success or failure elsewhere to establish its position.

Jon argued that pharmacists should not have the right to refuse to fill patients' prescriptions, even for moral or religious reasons. Notice how he used argument by analogy to support his position:

> The June 4, 2005, *Ledger Times* reminds us that in many ways pharmacists are like bus drivers and airline pilots. It would be outrageous for a pilot who disapproved of gambling to refuse to transport two Las Vegas–bound passengers who wanted to visit casinos. Or for a bus driver, disturbed [by] tax dollars [that] went to a lavish new football stadium rather than a decrepit public school, to refuse to let sports fans off at the arena. Professional pharmacists hold a state-conferred monopoly on medications. In that respect, they are public servants. Their role calls for neutrality on the job—whether they prefer it or not.[6]

Do you find Jon's argument persuasive? The key to this pattern of argument is the similarity between the two entities. In testing the validity of your argument by analogy, you need to answer this question: "Are the two entities sufficiently similar to justify my conclusion that what is true of one will be true of the other?" If not, your reasoning is faulty. This question can best be answered by dividing it into two questions.

1. *Are the similarities between the two cases relevant?* For example, suppose you used argument by analogy to advocate eliminating Friday classes during summer school on your campus as State U has done. The facts that both schools have similar library facilities and the same mascot would be irrelevant. Equivalent summer enrollments, numbers of commuting students, and energy needs are highly relevant and can be forceful evidence as you build your case.

2. *Are any of the differences between the two cases relevant?* If so, how do those differences affect your claim? If you discover that your college has far fewer commuting students than State U does, this difference is relevant to your topic and will undermine the validity of your claim.

Argument by Cause

Argument by cause connects two elements or events and claims that one is produced by the other. Causal reasoning takes two forms—reasoning from effect to cause and from cause to effect. The difference between the two is their chronological order. An *effect-to-cause argument* begins at a point of time (when the effects are evident) and moves back in time (to when the cause occurred). When you feel ill and go to the doctor, the doctor will usually identify the symptoms (the effects) of the problem and then diagnose the cause. The doctor is reasoning from effect to cause. In contrast, *cause-to-effect argument* begins at a point of time (when the cause occurred) and moves forward (to when the effects occurred or will occur). Doctors reason from cause to effect when they tell their patients who smoke that this habit may result in emphysema or lung cancer. If you choose to present an argument by cause, we encourage you to review the causal division strategy you learned earlier in the course.

In his persuasive speech "The Death of Reading," Nicholas used a book metaphor to organize and phrase his message. He previewed his key ideas: "Chapter 1: The Death of Reading; Chapter 2: The Autopsy; and Chapter 3: The Resurrection."

argument by cause

Says that one action or condition caused or will cause another.

Before presenting his solutions, Nicholas argued from effect to cause to explain why children today read less:

> Reading leisurely, whether newspapers, magazines, or books, has decreased over 50 percent in today's families since 1975. The American Psychological Association on December 17, 2003, argued that reading is essential to childhood imaginative growth. Modern entertainment, such as television and movies, leaves little room for creative interpretations. "A lack of reading invites Big Brother, preventing our children from being able to create the world themselves. When reading, the children are in control of the reality, not the films."

Effect

> Now that we have looked at the symptoms, we must next crack open the spine of today's books and run an autopsy to discuss the inherent causes of the death of reading. To children the answer is simple: reading isn't fun anymore. The December 28, 2003, *St. Petersburg Times* tells us that many children believe that the only motivation that they have to read is to pass tests. In 2002 alone, over 85,000 third graders were not allowed into the fourth grade due to an inability to pass their FCAT reading scores, and over 43,000 were forced into summer reading to pass. This form of education is known as "extrinsic motivation." This means that America's schools rely on external rewards, such as grades and test scores. Extrinsic motivation does not teach our children to think independently and critically about situations. Reading, it seems, has fallen prey to this school of thought, because children are taught to read to get good test scores, not because reading is entertaining and intellectual.[7]

Cause

Rachel used a cause-to-effect argument in her speech on the lack of safety in nursing homes:

> In 1965 the Fire Marshals Association of North America begged Congress to require sprinklers in all nursing homes. Forty years and 12 failed proposals later, Congress has yet to act. On December 16, 2005, *USA Today* reveals that there are 16,000 nursing homes that violate fire safety standards annually. Twenty-three thousand fires are reported every year. Four states—Massachusetts, Minnesota, Montana, and Hawaii—set no fire safety standards, only six states require fire sprinklers, and less than half require smoke alarms that alert authorities.

Cause

> These statistics lead up to an average of at least one fatal fire every month, much like the one that occurred just before the holidays as reported by the Associated Press on December 13, 2005, where two were killed in a Michigan fire and dozens more injured. Fires in nursing homes are all too common, and with more than 1.6 million residents in need of assisted-living arrangements, the danger is real.[8]

Effect

When you argue by cause, test the soundness of your reasoning by asking and answering the following three questions:

1. *Does a causal relationship exist?* For an argument from cause to effect or effect to cause to be valid, a causal relationship must exist between the two elements. Just because one event precedes another does not mean that the first caused the second. One of our students argued that the scholastic decline of American education began with and was caused by the Supreme Court's decision outlawing mandatory school prayer. We doubted the connection.

2. *Could the presumed cause produce the effect?* During a period of rising inflation, one of our students gave a speech arguing that various price hikes had contributed to the inflation rate. She provided three examples: the cost of postage stamps had increased 87.5 percent, chewing gum 100 percent, and downtown parking meter fees 150 percent. While she was able to document the dramatic percentage increase in the prices of these products, her examples had more interest than impact. They did not convince her audience that these increases could significantly influence the inflation rate by themselves.

Trial lawyers know that cases—and arguments—cannot be won by eloquent language alone. The validity of any claim depends on the quality of the evidence supporting that claim.

3. *Could the effect result from other causes?* A number of causes can converge to produce one effect. A student who argues that next year's increased tuition and fees are a result of the college president's fiscal mismanagement may have a point. But other factors may have made the tuition increase necessary: state revenue shortfalls, decreased enrollment, cutbacks in federal aid, and so on. Speakers strengthen their arguments when they prove that the alleged cause contributed substantively to producing the effect and that without the cause, the effect would not have occurred or the problem would have been much less severe.

Argument by Deduction

Ben began his speech on time management with the following statement:

> All of us are taking courses that require us to be in class and to study outside class. In addition, many of us are members of social, academic, religious, or career-oriented clubs and organizations. Some of us work. All of us like to party! Crowded into our school and work schedules are our responsibilities to friends and family members. In short, we're busy!
>
> College is a hectic time in our lives. Sometimes it seems that we're trying to cram 34 hours of activity into a 24-hour day. In order to survive this schedule and beat the stress, college students need to develop effective time-management skills. You are no exception! If you listen to my speech today, you will learn how to set realistic goals, meet them, and still have time to socialize with friends and get a good night's sleep. Sound impossible? Just listen closely for the next 8 minutes.

Ben used two types of argument in his introduction. He opened by arguing from example, providing several instances to make his case that college life is busy. He then used deductive reasoning to make the speech relevant to each member of the audience. A **deductive argument** moves from a general category to a specific instance. In this sense, deductive arguments are the reverse of argument by example. To see why that's true, consider the structure of a deductive argument.

Deductive arguments consist of a pattern of three statements: a major premise, a minor premise, and a conclusion. This pattern of deductive argument is called a **syllogism**. The **major premise** is a claim about a general group of people, events, or conditions. Ben's major premise was this: "College students need to develop effective

deductive argument

Says that what is true generally is or will be true in a specific instance.

syllogism

The pattern of a deductive argument, consisting of a major premise, a minor premise, and a conclusion.

major premise

A claim about a general group of people, events, or conditions.

time-management skills." The **minor premise** places a person, event, or condition into a general class. Ben's minor premise could be phrased like this: "You are a college student." The **conclusion** argues that what is true of the general class is true of the specific instance or individual. Ben concluded that each college student in his audience needed to develop effective time-management skills.

Use the following steps to check the structure of your deductive argument:

1. State your major premise.
2. Say "because," and then state your minor premise.
3. Say "therefore," and then state your conclusion.

The resulting two sentences should flow together easily and make sense. Ben could have said the following: "College students need to develop effective time-management skills. *Because* you are a college student, *therefore* you need to develop effective time-management skills." Notice that if the two premises are true and relate to each other, the conclusion must also be true. Should Ben have stated his argument that way in his speech? Probably not. The words *because* and *therefore* may sound forced, and his minor premise (You are a college student.) is obvious to his classmates. Nevertheless, using the because-therefore structure when preparing your speech allows you to check the logical flow of your argument.

For deductive arguments to be valid, they must meet certain tests. Whether you are listening to others' arguments or evaluating arguments in your own speech, keep in mind three questions.

1. *Are the premises related?* "All men are created equal. Equal is an artificial sweetener. Therefore, all men are artificial sweeteners." This statement doesn't make much sense, does it? The first sentence uses the word *equal* to mean "equivalent." The second uses *Equal* as a product name for a sugar substitute. For an argument to be valid, the premises must relate to each other. In this case, they clearly do not.

Let's construct another example. Suppose John prepares a speech trying to persuade his classmates to apply for a new academic scholarship named after his father, James Burke. In his speech, John makes the following statement:

> Any student enrolled in State U who is a U.S. citizen can apply for the Burke Scholarship. That includes everyone in this class. Just think, next year you could have your entire tuition and fees paid, and you can spend your money for something you've been wanting but were unable to afford. Maybe even that new laptop computer.

Before John convinces his classmates to apply for the scholarship, he first tells them that they are eligible. His argument may be depicted as follows:

Major premise: Any State U student who is a U.S. citizen can apply for the Burke Scholarship.
Minor premise: Every student in this class is a State U student who is a citizen of the United States.
Conclusion: Therefore, every student in this class can apply for the Burke Scholarship.

The terms in the minor premise fall within the scope of the major premise. The two premises are related, and the conclusion seems logical.

2. *Is the major premise true?* Before John's classmates begin filling out a scholarship application form, they should ask the question, "Is the major premise of the argument true?" Suppose two prerequisites for application are full-time student status and good academic standing. The statement "any State U student who is a U.S. citizen can apply for the Burke Scholarship" is then false. Part-time and

minor premise
A statement placing a person, an event, or a condition into a general class.

conclusion
The deductive argument that what is true of the general class is true of the specific instance.

Journal: Argument by Deduction

Identify the major premise, minor premise, and conclusion in the following group of statements:

Inquiring Minds should be aired on the Trashy Cable Network.
Inquiring Minds is a fluffy news show.
All fluffy news shows should be aired on the Trashy Cable Network.

probationary students cannot apply. The conclusion of the argument ("every student in this class can apply for the Burke Scholarship") would therefore not necessarily be true. You must be able to prove your major premise before you draw a conclusion.

3. Is the minor premise true? A false minor premise is just as damaging to an argument as a false major premise. Let's suppose that John's major premise is true and that any State U student who is a U.S. citizen can apply for the Burke Scholarship. What if his class includes some foreign students? His minor premise ("every student in this class is a State U student who is a citizen of the United States") is then false. Those students are not eligible for the scholarship, and John's conclusion is false. Arguing a position entails ethical considerations. You must know your facts and reason logically from them.

Argument by Authority

Argument by authority differs from the four other forms of argument we have discussed. To see how it is different, consider the following example from Lynn's speech:

> I believe that every student should be allowed to vote for Outstanding Professor on Campus rather than having the award determined by a select committee of the faculty. And I'm not alone in my opinion. Last year's recipient of the award, Dr. Linda Carter, agrees. The President of the Faculty Senate spoke out in favor of this proposal at last week's forum, and the Student Government Association passed a resolution supporting it.

Argument by authority uses testimony from an expert source to prove a speaker's claim; its validity depends on the credibility the authority has for the audience. In this example, Lynn did not offer arguments based on example, analogy, cause, or deduction to explain the validity of her position. Instead, she asserted that two distinguished professors and the SGA agreed with her. She asked her audience to believe her position based on the credentials of the authority figures who endorsed her claim. Her rationale was that her sources had access to sufficient information and had the expertise to interpret it accurately; thus, we should trust their conclusions.

An argument based on authority is only as valid as the source's credibility. To test your argument, ask and answer the following two questions:

1. Is the source an expert?
2. Is the source unbiased?

Our discussion of these questions and other tests of evidence in the supporting materials section of this book will help you select the best authority for your claim.

Testing the arguments you use and hear others use is crucial to effective, ethical speaking and listening. The "Theory Into Practice" feature summarizes these tests. When you analyze the arguments you use, you strengthen them and can save yourself the embarrassment of being caught using illogical or invalid proof. However, it is just as important to check the validity of persuasive arguments you hear. By doing this, you avoid being duped into misguided thoughts and actions.

In spite of these tests, persuasive speakers sometimes incorporate certain errors of proof into their speeches. These errors are so widely used that they have been named and studied. In the following section, we examine some of these arguments that appear—but only appear—to say something authoritative. If you can identify these errors, you can avoid them.

argument by authority

Uses testimony from an expert source to prove a speaker's claim.

Theory Into Practice TIP

TESTING YOUR ARGUMENTS

Mario Cuomo, noted speaker and former governor of New York, encouraged leaders to persuade others "not so much with speeches that sound good, as with speeches that are good and sound."[9] As you select and develop the arguments for your speeches, ask and answer the questions that we discussed in this chapter. Remember to use these same guidelines when you listen to the speeches of others.

To construct an *argument by example*, ask yourself:

- Are the examples true?
- Are the examples relevant?
- Are the examples sufficient?
- Are the examples representative?

To construct an *argument by analogy*, ask yourself:

- Are the similarities between the two cases relevant?
- Are the differences between the two cases relevant?

To construct an *argument by cause*, ask yourself:

- Does a causal relationship exist?
- Could the presumed cause produce the effect?
- Could the effect result from other causes?

To construct an *argument by deduction*, ask yourself:

- Are the premises related?
- Is the major premise true?
- Is the minor premise true?

To construct an *argument by authority*, ask yourself:

- Is the source an expert?
- Is the source unbiased?

Fallacies of Argument

17.3 Explain, with examples, the ten fallacies of argument.

A **fallacy** is "any defect in reasoning which destroys its validity."[10] Fallacies can be dangerous and persuasive for the same reason: because they resemble valid reasoning, we often accept them as legitimate. They can produce bad decisions leading to harmful consequences.

Fallacies are flawed patterns of reasoning. Speakers who value civility respect the credibility of their ideas and the welfare of their listeners. As you construct your persuasive speech, make sure that the arguments you encounter in your research are valid. Then, use your research to develop sound arguments to support the ideas in your speech. As a listener, you have an ethical responsibility to evaluate critically the ideas other speakers present to you. Be alert for those arguments based on sound versus flawed reasoning. Consider the valid arguments and reject fallacious ones.

How can you tell the difference? We will discuss ten of the most common fallacies. As you read them, notice how many resemble the patterns of argument we have just discussed.

fallacy

A flaw in the logic of an argument.

hasty generalization

A fallacy that makes claims from insufficient or unrepresentative examples.

false analogy

A fallacy that occurs when an argument by analogy compares entities that have critical differences.

post hoc

A chronological fallacy that says that a prior event caused a subsequent event.

Hasty Generalization

People who jump to conclusions commit the fallacy of **hasty generalization**, a faulty form of argument by example. What distinguishes valid from fallacious inductive proof is the quantity and quality of examples. When speakers make claims based on insufficient or unrepresentative instances, their reasoning is usually flawed. For example, a speaker uses examples of three students convicted of plagiarism and concludes that cheating is widespread on campus. An advertisement shows a dentist recommending a particular brand of toothbrush, and the consumer assumes that it carries the endorsement of dentists in general. People who rely too much on first impressions, who do not read widely, or who spend little time researching are prime candidates for reasoning from hasty generalization. They often develop beliefs and opinions that later prove erroneous.

False Analogy

Speakers argue by analogy when they link two items and assert that what is true of one will be true of the other. If the two items are sufficiently similar, the speaker's claim may be valid. However, if the items differ in critical ways, the persuader may be guilty of using a **false analogy**, and the claim may be fallacious. You've probably heard someone respond to an argument by saying, "That's like comparing apples and oranges." That person just detected a faulty comparison. Consider some of the arguments we've heard in students' speeches and see if you can detect some faulty reasoning:

> We license drivers; why shouldn't we license parents? You can't take to the road until you learn how to drive and pass a test. Aren't children more important than cars?

> Investing in the stock market is no different than playing the lottery. Each is risky and there's no guarantee you won't lose money.

What do you think of these arguments? Which comparisons are valid arguments by analogy? Which are fallacies? You need to exercise your critical thinking skills as you read, listen to, and develop arguments by analogy.

Post Hoc Ergo Propter Hoc

This fallacy uses the Latin title and literally means "after this, therefore because of this." A chronological fallacy, **post hoc** (as it is usually called) assumes that because one event preceded another, the first caused the second; it is an improper application of the argument by cause. Perhaps you have heard a friend comment, "I knew it would rain; I just washed my car!" Your friend is probably making a joke based on the post hoc fallacy. People exhibit post hoc reasoning when they expect something good to happen if they carry a lucky charm while gambling, wear a lucky shirt to a football game, or cross their fingers as a teacher returns an exam.

These defects in reasoning may seem obvious. Yet other examples of confusing coincidence with causation are more subtle and potentially more damaging. For instance, a person rejects medical treatment, relying instead on a cure, that has not yet been researched, because someone else tried it and subsequently got well. An incumbent mayor takes credit for every city improvement that occurred since she took office; her opponent blames her for everything bad that happened during this time. An event may have more than one cause. It is also preceded by occurrences having no effect on it whatsoever. As a result, determining the relationship between two events or conditions is often difficult. You must examine that relationship if you are to avoid the post hoc fallacy.

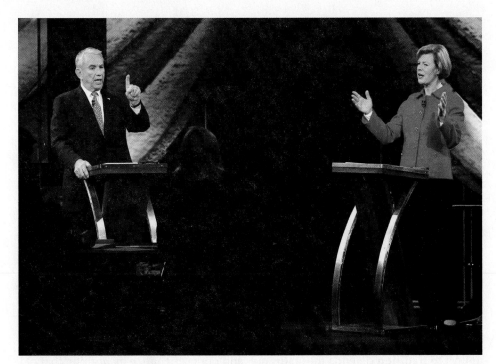

Participants in a political debate are judged on the quality of their arguments as well as their manner of presentation.

Slippery Slope

Envision yourself at the top of a hill on a wintry day. You take one step, slip on a patch of ice, lose your footing, and begin sliding down the hill. You try to regain your balance, but you continue your slide, stopping only when you reach the bottom of the hill. This visual image depicts the slippery slope fallacy. **Slippery slope** asserts that one action inevitably sets in motion a chain of events or indicates a trend; it is an example of the faulty use of argument by cause. This defect in reasoning is exemplified in the following two arguments:

> If you amend the Constitution to prohibit flag burning, you open the door to other amendments to our Bill of Rights. Ultimately, you destroy the freedoms upon which our nation is based.

> If we begin to control the sale of guns by restricting the purchase of handguns, where will it end? Will shotguns be next? And then hunting rifles? Soon the right to bear arms will disappear from the Constitution, and sportsmen and sportswomen will be denied one of their basic freedoms.

These speakers' arguments imply that a single act will set in motion a series of events that no one will be able to stop, but that's not necessarily the case. Just because legislators support one constitutional amendment or one law doesn't mean that they must support subsequent reforms. Usually, a slide down the slope is preventable. Each journey involves a series of decisions, and it is possible to retain or regain your footing.

Red Herring

The name of the **red herring** fallacy apparently originated with the English fox hunt. When the hunt was over, the hunt master would drag a red herring—a type of fish that is smoked and salted—across the path of the hounds. The pungent scent would divert the dogs from their pursuit of the fox, and they could then be rounded up. If you love to read murder mysteries, you may have trained yourself to be on guard for some incidental twist in the plot that seems to be there just to throw less attentive readers off track. Such devices have come to be called *red herrings*.

slippery slope
A fallacy of causation stating that one action inevitably sets a chain of events in motion.

red herring
A fallacy that introduces irrelevant issues to deflect attention from the subject under discussion.

A red herring fallacy is an example of a faulty argument by deduction. An arguer makes a claim based on an irrelevant premise. In essence, a speaker guilty of the red herring fallacy introduces an irrelevant issue to deflect attention from the subject under discussion. Both of the following speakers attempted to divert discussion from germane issues to irrelevant concerns:

> A politician answers charges that she accepted illegal campaign contributions by noting her service on the state's ethics advisory board.
>
> A student responds to a charge of plagiarism with the statement, "I was a Boy Scout throughout high school."

When you present a persuasive speech, you are an advocate for the position you present. As such, you have an ethical responsibility to defend your arguments. Answer criticisms of your argument with evidence and logic; don't deflect criticism by diverting your audience to another track.

Appeal to Tradition

This fallacy is grounded in a respect for traditional ways of doing things. On the surface, respect for tradition seems reasonable. But the fallacy commonly called **appeal to tradition** defends the status quo and opposes change by arguing that old ways are superior to new ways; it is an improper use of an argument by authority. A speaker who argues against admitting men to her college because of the school's history as a women's school commits this fallacy unless she offers additional support for the claim. Its most common form of expression—"We've always done it that way"—is merely descriptive. It discourages discussion and reevaluation of our traditions.

As important as many traditions are to us, they should not be used to thwart needed change. The Constitution of the United States gave people many of the freedoms they enjoy. Yet it also precluded non-European Americans and women from full participation in society. The fight to secure the right to vote for all citizens challenged that tradition. Old ways are not always the best ways.

False Dilemma

When forced to choose between two alternatives, you face a dilemma. Dilemmas can be actual or false. In an actual dilemma, the alternatives you face are real; there is no room for compromise. Suppose you are asked to choose between going to a movie with friends and attending a review session for an upcoming test. If the review and theater hours coincide, your dilemma is real and you must forfeit either entertainment or study.

A **false dilemma** presents only two options when, in reality, there are more. For example, if there is a late showing of the movie, perhaps you can convince your friends to meet you at the theater after you attend the review. In this instance, the dilemma is false because you do not have to choose between studying and seeing the movie; you can do both.

The fallacy of false dilemma is sometimes called the *either–or fallacy*. The dilemma usually polarizes issues into two mutually exclusive categories, such as "Stand with America or stand for terrorism" and "When guns are outlawed, only outlaws will have guns!" Neither slogan allows for middle-ground positions.

Listeners should be especially attentive to all "either–or" and "if–then" statements they hear. These grammatical constructions lend themselves to the fallacy of false dilemma, as in the following examples:

appeal to tradition

A fallacy that opposes change by arguing that old ways are always superior to new ways.

false dilemma

A fallacy that confronts listeners with two choices when, in reality, more options exist.

A person is either a Republican or a Democrat. Because I know Carolyn isn't a Republican, she must be a Democrat.

The issue is very simple: Either you support the Constitution on which this nation was founded, or you're not a patriotic American.

I don't support a cutback in defense spending. I don't want to see a weakening of America's strength.

Each of these examples presents the listener with only two choices. However, they disregard other legitimate options. Carolyn may be a Libertarian, a Socialist, an Independent, or a member of some other political party. We can exhibit patriotism and still question a nation's laws and policies. Eliminating unnecessary defense spending does not necessarily weaken the country. Using that money for other important projects—like major road and bridge repair—may make America stronger.

False Authority

The fallacy of **false authority** is an invalid form of argument by authority. This fallacy occurs when advocates support their ideas with the testimony of people who have apparent but not real expertise. Before deciding to accept someone's opinion or testimony, ask the question, "Is the person an objective expert on this topic?" Celebrity endorsements of commercial products frequently illustrate this fallacy. Advertisers often use celebrities more for their popularity than their credibility.

It is important to exercise your critical thinking skills to avoid using the fallacy of false authority. If you cite information from a website without checking its authority and accuracy or if you quote from authors without knowing their credentials, you have used the fallacy of false authority, most likely unintentionally. The statement "I couldn't find any information about the author" is a recipe for irresponsibility. You can avoid the fallacy of false authority by using only information from experts and credible sources.

Bandwagon

In the 1800s and early 1900s, political candidates held parades to meet the people. A band rode on a wagon leading the parade through town. As the wagon passed, local leaders would jump on the bandwagon to show their support. The number of people on board was considered a barometer of the candidate's popularity and political strength.

The **bandwagon** fallacy is also a faulty argument by authority. It assumes that popular opinion is an accurate measure of truth and wisdom. Frequently referred to as the "everybody's doing it" fallacy, bandwagon arguments commonly use phrases such as "everyone knows" or "most people agree." Door-to-door salespeople or intrusive phone solicitors who tell you that all your friends and neighbors are purchasing their products use the bandwagon appeal. They base their sales pitch on the product's popularity, not on its merits.

Speakers who defend the rightness of their positions by pointing to polls showing popular support similarly exploit the bandwagon fallacy. While agreement regarding a belief or action may be reassuring, it is no guarantee of accuracy or truth. "Truth is not always democratic."[11] History is cluttered with popularly held misconceptions. Remember, most people once believed that the world was flat and that the sun revolved around Earth. You should decide the validity of an argument by its form and substance, not merely by how many people agree on it.

Ad Hominem

Ad hominem, literally meaning "to the man," arguments ask listeners to reject an idea because of the allegedly poor character of the person voicing it. Political speeches often are peppered with ad hominem arguments. These statements may evoke applause,

false authority

A fallacy that uses testimony from sources who have no expertise on the topic in question.

bandwagon

A fallacy that determines truth, goodness, or wisdom by popular opinion.

ad hominem

A fallacy that urges listeners to reject an idea because of the allegedly poor character of the person voicing it; name-calling.

Key Points

Fallacies of Argument

1. Hasty generalization
2. False analogy
3. Post hoc ergo propter hoc
4. Slippery slope
5. Red herring
6. Appeal to tradition
7. False dilemma
8. False authority
9. Bandwagon
10. Ad hominem

Journal: Fallacies

Corey tells his audience the incident of Chicago firefighters who discovered sacks of undelivered mail in the home of a mail carrier. From this example, he argues that there is a need for national reform of the U.S. Postal Service. Identify the fallacy that is illustrated by Corey's argument and explain your answer.

cheers, and laughter, but they provide little insight into issues. When Rush Limbaugh refers to feminists as "feminazis," he is making an ad hominem attack rather than engaging in reasoned discourse. A club member commits this fallacy when he argues that Bryan's proposal for an alcohol-free party should not be taken seriously because Bryan has two DUI (driving under the influence) convictions.

In its most obvious form, this fallacy is name-calling. For some people, simply knowing that a speaker is liberal, conservative, feminist, or fundamentalist is sufficient to close their minds. They disregard the merits of an idea because of the person giving the message. An ethical listener has a responsibility to give all ideas a fair hearing.

To speak ethically and with civility, you must know how to construct valid arguments and avoid defective ones such as those we have just discussed. Once you have mastered this ability, you can use your arguments to achieve the overall goal of your speech. In the remainder of this chapter, we will show you how to develop a persuasive proposition and how to organize your arguments effectively.

Selecting Propositions for Persuasive Speeches

17.4 Develop speeches using three types of propositions.

Earlier, you learned that your first steps in constructing a speech are to select your topic, focus or narrow it, determine your general purpose, formulate your specific purpose, and construct a thesis statement. In persuasive speaking, you can add one additional step: state your proposition.

A **proposition** is a declarative sentence expressing a judgment you want the audience to accept. If you speak on the topic of improving education, you may narrow this broad subject and select as your specific purpose to persuade the audience that teacher salaries should be increased. Your basic position—"teacher salaries should be increased"—can be thought of as a proposition. Notice that this proposition *expresses a judgment* that *is debatable* and that *requires proof*. We will discuss these three characteristics of propositions in the next section.

Your thesis statement, in contrast, lists the reasons you offer to prove your proposition. In the preceding example, your thesis statement could be: higher teacher salaries would recruit better teachers, retain better teachers, and improve student learning. The following example illustrates the similarities and differences among the proposition, specific purpose, thesis statement, and key ideas of a speech.

> *Proposition:* The new campus classroom building should be named Richter Hall.
> *Specific Purpose:* To persuade the audience that the new classroom building should be named for Louise Richter
> *Thesis Statement:* The new classroom building should be named for Louise Richter, an outstanding teacher, advisor, and friend.
> *Key Ideas:* I. The name of the new classroom building should honor an outstanding educator.
> II. Louise Richter deserves this recognition.
> A. She was an outstanding teacher.
> B. She was an outstanding advisor to student organizations.
> C. She was a cherished friend.

proposition

A declarative sentence expressing a judgment or an opinion a speaker wants listeners to accept.

Notice that this proposition expresses a judgment, while the thesis statement includes the reasons the speaker will offer to prove the proposition.

Characteristics of Propositions

If you formulate a well-worded proposition early in preparing your persuasive speech, you will be sure of your persuasive goal and can keep it firmly in mind. Your proposition also helps you focus your persuasive speech and test the relevance of supporting ideas as you develop them. Devising your proposition can be relatively easy. Propositions are marked by three characteristics.

PROPOSITIONS EXPRESS A JUDGMENT.   A proposition for a persuasive speech states the position you will defend. Consequently, it should be worded as a declarative sentence expressing your position. If you advocate statehood for Puerto Rico, your proposition could be worded like this: "The United States should grant Puerto Rico statehood." This simple declarative sentence clearly states your position on the issue.

Sometimes, however, you may be interested in a topic but lack enough information to have developed a position on it. In this case, you may first want to phrase a question to guide your research. Once you answer the question, you can then develop your proposition.

Mark, a criminal justice major, worded the following question to guide his research: "Is the death penalty for juveniles cruel and unusual punishment?" He researched the topic, reading articles by scholars and jurists on both sides of the issue. He made a list of arguments for and against capital punishment for juveniles. Although Mark supported capital punishment for adult offenders, his research convinced him to oppose it for juveniles. The proposition he subsequently decided to defend was "The death penalty for juveniles is cruel and unusual punishment." By phrasing his position statement, writing it out, and keeping it in front of him as he continued researching and assembling his arguments, Mark was able to keep his speech focused on arguments against capital punishment for juveniles.

PROPOSITIONS ARE DEBATABLE.   Propositions are appropriate for persuasive speeches only if they are debatable. In other words, the judgment must include some degree of controversy. The proposition "Earth revolves around the sun" is not a good proposition for a persuasive speech because you are unlikely to find any qualified authority today opposing that statement. We now accept it as fact. Once we accept a proposition as fact, it ceases to be an appropriate topic for persuasive speeches.

PROPOSITIONS REQUIRE PROOF.   A proposition is an assertion, and assertions are statements that have not yet been proved. Your objective as a persuasive speaker is to offer compelling reasons for listeners to accept your proposition. As we discussed earlier in this chapter, you may support your proposition with arguments from example, analogy, cause, deduction, or authority.

> **Key Points**
> **Requirements of Propositions**
> 1. Propositions express a judgment.
> 2. Propositions are debatable.
> 3. Propositions require proof.

The power of persuasion can mobilize speakers to debate issues, combining logic with passion.

Types of Propositions

Propositions for persuasive speeches are of three types: fact, value, and policy. The type of organization and supporting materials you will use depends on the type of proposition you defend.

proposition of fact

An assertion about the truth or falsity of a statement.

proposition of value

An assertion about the relative worth of an idea or action.

proposition of policy

A statement requesting support for a course of action.

PROPOSITIONS OF FACT. A **proposition of fact** focuses on belief. You ask the audience to affirm the truth or falsity of a statement. The following are examples of propositions of fact:

> Access to math tutors increases students' grades in mathematics courses.
>
> An aspirin a day can reduce the risk of heart disease.
>
> Antimatter-powered space travel is technologically feasible.

In her speech on random drug testing, Jennifer defended this proposition: "Random drug testing on the job decreases workplace drug use." Her specific purpose and key ideas were as follows:

> *Specific Purpose*: To convince the audience that random drug testing decreases workplace drug use
> *Key Ideas*: I. Random drug testing deters casual drug use.
> II. Random drug testing helps decrease drug addiction.
>   A. It identifies users.
>   B. It encourages users to seek therapy.

PROPOSITIONS OF VALUE. A **proposition of value** requires a judgment on the worth of an idea or action. You ask the audience to determine the "goodness" or "badness" of something, as in this proposition: "Corporal punishment in schools is wrong." Propositions of value can also ask you to compare two items and determine which is better, as in Sir William Blackstone's statement, "It is better that ten guilty persons escape than one innocent suffer." Other propositions of value include the following:

> Deterrence is a more important goal of criminal justice than rehabilitation.
>
> Censorship is a greater evil than pornography.
>
> Minority rule is morally indefensible.

Suppose you decided to persuade your audience that free agency is bad for professional sports. You could develop your speech on this value proposition as follows:

> *Specific Purpose*: To persuade the audience that free agency is hurting professional sports
> *Key Ideas*: I. It destroys the competitive balance of teams.
> II. It undermines the financial solvency of teams.
> III. It creates bad role models for kids.

PROPOSITIONS OF POLICY. A **proposition of policy** advocates a course of action. You ask the audience to endorse a policy or to commit themselves to some action. These statements usually include the word *should*. Here are some examples of policy propositions:

> College athletes should be paid.
>
> Nonviolent offenders should be excluded from "three strikes and you're out" sentencing.
>
> Students should be able to repay student loans through community service.

Duane wanted to persuade his audience to support the student government association's proposal to change from a quarter to a semester academic calendar. Organizing his speech topically, he presented three benefits of a semester system.

> *Specific Purpose*: To persuade the audience that this college should adopt a semester calendar
> *Key Ideas*: I. Semesters allow more time for research in theory courses.
> II. Semesters allow more time for skill development in performance courses.
> III. Semester credits are easier to transfer to other institutions.

Journal: Types of Propositions

Determine whether the following statement is a proposition of fact, value, or policy and explain your answer:

"The FDA should reduce required testing for experimental drugs to fight life-threatening illnesses."

Monroe's Motivated Sequence

17.5 Construct a speech using Monroe's motivated sequence.

In this textbook we have presented, discussed, and given examples of seven patterns for dividing the body of your speech into key ideas. Topical, chronological, spatial, and causal patterns are appropriate for both persuasive and informative speeches. The pro–con pattern, appropriate for an informative speech, can become a persuasive pattern by adding one step: pro–con assessment. Problem–solution and need–plan patterns are appropriate, almost exclusively, for persuasive speeches. You should review these seven patterns before you develop a persuasive speech. (See Chapter 8, Learning Objective 8.2, to learn more about these seven patterns of organization.)

In this chapter, we offer an eighth organizational option. One type of persuasive speech, the speech to actuate, provides an interesting challenge to speakers. In the 1930s, Alan Monroe developed one of the most popular patterns for organizing the superstructure of a speech to actuate.[12] Called "the motivated sequence," this pattern is particularly appropriate when you discuss a well-known or easily established problem. Monroe drew from the conclusions of educator and philosopher John Dewey that persuasion is best accomplished if a speaker moves a listener sequentially through a series of steps. **Monroe's motivated sequence** includes five steps, or stages: attention, need, satisfaction, visualization, and action.

ATTENTION.   Monroe argued that speakers must first command the *attention* of their listeners. Suppose your geographic area is experiencing a summer drought. You could begin your speech with a description of the landscape as you approached your campus a year ago, describing in detail the green grass, the verdant foliage, and the colorful, fragrant flowers. You then contrast the landscape of a year ago with its look now: bland, brown, and blossomless. With these contrasting visual images, you try to capture your audience's attention and interest.

NEED.   Your second objective is to establish a *need*. This step is similar to the problem and need steps in the problem–solution and the need–plan patterns of organizing a speech. For example, your speech on the drought situation could illustrate how an inadequate water supply hurts not only the beauty of the landscape but also agricultural production, certain industrial processes, and, ultimately, the economy of the entire region.

SATISFACTION.   When you dramatize a problem, you create an urgency to redress it. In the *satisfaction* step of the motivated sequence, you propose a way to solve or at least minimize the problem. You may suggest voluntary or mandatory conservation as a short-term solution to the water shortage crisis. As a longer-range solution, you might ask your audience to consider the merits of planting grasses, shrubs, and other plants that require less water. You could advocate that the city adopt and enforce stricter regulations of water use by businesses or that it develop alternative water sources.

VISUALIZATION.   Monroe argued that simply proposing a solution is seldom sufficient to bring about change. Through *visualization*, Monroe's fourth step, you seek to intensify your audience's desire to adopt and implement the proposed solution. You could direct the audience to look out the window at their campus and then ask if that is the scenery they want. More often, though, you create word pictures for the audience to visualize. Without adequate water, you could argue, crops will die, family farms will fail, industries will not relocate to the area, and the quality of life for everyone in the area will be depressed. In contrast, you could refer to the landscape of a year ago, the image you depicted as you began your speech. The future can be colored in green, red, yellow, and blue, representing growth and vitality.

Monroe's motivated sequence
A persuasive pattern composed of (1) getting the audience's attention, (2) establishing a need, (3) offering a proposal to satisfy the need, (4) inviting listeners to visualize the results, and (5) requesting action.

ACTION. The final step of the motivated sequence is the *action* you request of your listeners. It is not enough to know that something must be done; the audience must know what you want them to do, and your request must be within their power to act. Do you want them to join you in voluntary conservation by watering their lawns in the evening when less water will evaporate or by washing their cars less frequently? Are you asking them to sign petitions pressuring the city council to adopt mandatory conservation measures when the water table sinks to a designated level? Conclude your speech with a strong appeal for specific, reasonable action.

Dolly decided that her final speech would be a speech to actuate; she wanted her classmates to study a foreign language. She researched articles she found in the library and on the Internet. She interviewed a professor in the foreign languages department and borrowed some brochures published by the Modern Language Association. After taking extensive notes, she opened a new computer file and typed five phrases: Attention Step, Need Step, Satisfaction Step, Visualization Step, and Action Step. She then began to draft the framework for her speech. Using the motivated sequence helped Dolly move her listeners step by step to her final request for action.

Attention Step

In January 1997 Diane Crispell, executive editor of *American Demographics*, observed that "America is a linguistic paradox. Even as it boasts a richly diverse population speaking a host of languages, it encourages immigrants to forsake their mother tongues and doesn't encourage native English speakers to acquire foreign-language skills." Those who reject opportunities to connect with other cultures do so at their personal and professional peril. Studying a foreign language can give you a competitive edge. Learning a foreign language develops your communication skills, your analytical skills, and your employment opportunities.

Need Step

College students need a variety of competencies for personal, academic, and career success.
A. Communication skills are essential in each of these areas.
B. Problem-solving skills are necessary to function successfully in life.
C. An understanding of other cultures is increasingly important in a global society.

Satisfaction Step

Studying a foreign language can give you a competitive edge.
A. It improves your communication skills.
B. It develops your analytical skills.
C. It provides employment advantages.

Visualization Step

Wouldn't it be nice to take a friend to a romantic French movie and be able to understand the dialogue without having to read the translation? Or, when visiting another country, to be able to pick up a newspaper and to read the headlines? Or, when you land that dream job, to be able to negotiate an important business deal with a client from another country, in part because you spoke her language and understood the customs of her culture?

Action Step

Before the semester is over, I want you to take a step that will give you a competitive edge in your personal, academic, and professional life.
A. Enroll in a foreign language class while you are in college.
B. Visit the International Programs Office, and sign up for a study abroad program.
C. Buy some foreign language self-study learning tapes or CDs.
D. Begin learning a foreign language from a friend from another culture.

Annotated Sample Speech

Daniel Hinderliter delivered the following persuasive speech and placed fourth at the 2013 Interstate Oratorical Association National Speech Contest. As you read his speech, notice the use of elements of Monroe's motivated sequence to frame his problem-solution discussion of reducing food waste by creating a more sustainable food culture.

Eating Better through Reducing Food Waste[13]

Daniel Hinderliter, West Chester University, Pennsylvania

1 On October 19, 2012, journalist and Bucknell University expert-in-residence Jonathan Bloom performed an experiment: using a large scale, he calculated the amount of food waste thrown out by students in a two-hour lunch period. As reported in his Wastedfood.com blog post of the same day, 1,000 students wasted almost 100 pounds of food *in two hours*. This food waste becomes more staggering when considering the nation as a whole: an August 2012 report from the Natural Resources Defense Council, or NRDC, disclosed that 25 percent of all household food purchases are wasted. That's four slices in the average loaf of bread, one quart of every gallon of milk, three eggs out of each dozen. Ours is a food culture pervaded by waste.

2 It's important at this point to acknowledge that farmers and the food industry suffer from their own wasteful practices. That waste, however, is designed to protect us; consumer waste is not. As a nation, we are attempting to shift to a more sustainable future. Sustainability, however, cannot be legislated or technologically innovated. It takes our own committed collective efforts. In order to truly embody sustainable living, we must make necessary changes in our own individual habits. With over 11 million tons of wasted food in the U.S. since the beginning of 2013, according to the running counter on endhunger.org, something must be done to dramatically curtail our shameful amount of waste.

3 Today, we will grasp the problem of food waste, isolate the causes, and advocate for concrete solutions, to create a more sustainable food culture.

4 Our level of food waste is staggering. The U.S. Environmental Protection Agency estimated on their website epa.gov, last updated April 15, 2010, Americans generated 34 million tons of food scraps. Despite our frequent discounting of this waste through offhanded statements like, "Our wasted food wouldn't be sent to starving children anyway," while true, this everyday behavior of wasting food can have drastic consequences. Effects of food waste are twofold: first, economic and second, environmental.

5 First, our misuse of food has economic consequences in the store and at home. Food waste watchdog Leanpath.com estimates on October 1, 2012, that food prices have risen 42 percent in the past ten years, including an 8 percent price rise in 2011 alone. This means the amount of money we waste in our homes on discarded food rises as well. An Economic News Release dated September 25, 2012, from the U.S. Bureau of Labor Statistics reveals that each dwelling in the U.S. spends $6,500 per year on food. Extrapolating from that number, this means we invest roughly $790 billion in food annually. If the aforementioned National Resources Defense Council is to be believed, roughly $200 billion is to be thrown away.

6 As if the [economic] effects of this food waste are not enough, personal food waste has environmental effects as well, in meal preparation and food disposal. CNN on June 27, 2012, laments that North Americans waste, on average, 230 pounds of food a year per person. In the same report, Richard Swannell, waste prevention director for the Waste and Resources Action Program, warns on CNN of June 27, 2012, "A significant percentage of the household food that is wasted ends up in landfill where it produces CO_2 and methane. Methane is 23 times more potent than CO_2 as a greenhouse gas." Moreover, the previously cited NRDC report opines that 25 percent of the fresh water used for food production is squandered through available food

waste. The EPA exposed on their previously cited website that the United States uses 230 billion gallons of water daily for food production, which means we waste 80 billion gallons of water *every single day*.

7 Jonathan Bloom illustrated through his experiment that students perpetuate the wasted food problem, but why do they waste in the first place? A closer look at personal food waste reveals two causes: the Costco effect and the commoditization of food.

8 First, big bulk food supermarkets such as Costco, Sam's Club, and BJ's can have a huge effect on the way we purchase food. Defined by an April 2012 CNBC documentary as "the routine tendency of its members to succumb to the store's discount-chic allure and spend more than they expect, often buying more than they need," the Costco effect encourages patrons to purchase far more food than they can consume before the food goes bad and needs to be thrown out. In the name of big savings, we end up overbuying big time.

9 Second, the commoditization of food has contributed to our waste of food as well. From the farm to the fork, food has become not a dietary staple, but rather a designer accessory. Food has become a commodity, meaning it's one among any number of products to be merely bought and sold. In our culture we like to buy new. Leftovers are viewed as used food to be thrown away to make room for new food. The January 2012 *Monthly Review* agrees that this commodification means "the farmers producing the bulk of food … have become greatly separated from the public that finally purchases their products, not just physically, but also by the long chain of intermediaries between farms and people's tables." We have lost the relationship of producer-consumer and, thus, have lost the ability to see food for what it is—a basic human necessity.

10 With such overarching causes resulting in our wasteful habits, the future does seem bleak. After his experiment, Jonathan Bloom disagrees. Bloom's experiment leads us to see solutions on two levels: the institutional and the individual.

11 First, institutions such as public schools and universities can enact programs to cut down on food waste. Many have started waste collection calculators similar to Bloom's experiment in their cafeterias. University of Notre Dame started a waste calculator in their lunchroom. Program chairperson Anna Gorman explains in an October 30, 2012, article from the *Notre Dame Observer*: "It's mainly just being conscious of what you're picking up," she said. "It's all about making a conscious effort to reduce waste." Programs like these highlight the relationship people have with their food. Ask your own universities about programs you may have in your cafeterias, and inquire about starting them if such programs do not exist.

12 Second, on a personal level, we can all take steps to reduce our own personal food waste in purchase and consumption. When shopping, look for "half price" sales instead of "buy one get one" sales, meaning you get the proper amount of food for a reduced cost instead of twice the amount of food for the regular cost.

13 On the consumer level, Jonathan Bloom admits in his 2011 book *American Wasteland* solutions are easy: the biggest step to take is just to plan. By knowing what we have in our cabinets and refrigerators, we eliminate the need to go grocery shopping for new and redundant foods. Use websites such as supercook.com and myfridgefood.com or comparable phone apps that allow you to scan food on hand, which they convert into tasty recipes. Preserve perishables through proper canning or freezing to increase shelf life and edibility of foods long term. Finally, just eat your leftovers. If you haven't chewed it, it's not used food.

14 Bloom's experiment may have been skewed by an uncontrolled variable: terrible cafeteria food. But this cannot be an excuse for all of us. We have a profound problem. We waste food at an unconscionable level. Yes, part of it is systemic and we can't directly affect that. But every day we each can make a difference that can significantly curtail this shameful waste of our most basic resource.

15 Today, after confronting the problems, isolating the causes, and advocating essential solutions, we understand the magnitude of our waste as well as the magnitude of our ability to change.

Satisfaction

In paragraphs 10–13, Daniel seeks to *satisfy* the need for a change by presenting a two-step solution of institutional and individual action.

Visualization

In paragraph 11, the first sentence uses *satisfaction* by introducing one solution to the problem. Daniel then uses *visualization* as he describes one university's program to reducing waste. His last sentence moves to the *action* step by encouraging classmates to ask for a similar program at their university.

Action

In paragraphs 11–15, Daniel tells his audience how they can *act* to implement a solution. He lists steps students can take "to reduce our own personal food waste" in paragraphs 12 and 13.

Summary

Making and Refuting Arguments

17.1 Apply the three steps of making an argument and the four steps of refuting an argument.

- Persuasion is the art of influencing other people's values, beliefs, attitudes, or behaviors. To be an effective persuader, you must know how to structure a valid argument, detect flaws in reasoning, and word propositions.

- The three steps of structuring an *argument* are to (1) make a claim you want the audience to accept, (2) supply evidence supporting that claim, and (3) explain how the evidence proves your claim.

- The act of countering one argument with another is called *refutation*. To refute an argument, follow this *refutational strategy*: (1) state the position you are refuting, (2) state your own position, (3) support your position with evidence, and (4) show how your position undermines the argument you oppose.

Types of Argument

17.2 Construct five types of arguments.

- To give listeners a reason to accept a persuasive claim, speakers may use any of five types of argument: (1) *argument by example*, which uses specific instances to support a general claim; (2) *argument by analogy*, which links two concepts, conditions, or experiences and claims that what is true of one will be true of the other; (3) *argument by cause*, which links two concepts, conditions, or experiences and claims that one causes the other; (4) *deductive argument*, which employs a pattern called a *syllogism*, which consists of a major premise, a minor premise, and a conclusion; and (5) *argument by authority*, which uses testimony from an expert source to prove a speaker's claim.

Fallacies of Argument

17.3 Explain, with examples, the ten fallacies of argument.

- Fallacious arguments are dangerous because they may resemble sound reasoning.

- Ten fallacies of argument are common. (1) The *fallacy of hasty generalization* makes claims based on insufficient or unrepresentative examples. (2) *False analogy* compares entities that have critical differences. (3) *Post hoc ergo propter hoc* falsely confuses chronology with causation, arguing that because event A preceded event B, A caused B. (4) The *slippery slope* fallacy asserts that one event inevitably unleashes a series of events. (5) *Red herring* introduces irrelevant issues to deflect attention from the true question under discussion. (6) *Appeal to tradition* asserts that old ways of doing things are correct or best, simply because they are traditional. (7) *False dilemma* argues that we must choose between two alternatives, when in reality we may have a range of options. (8) *False authority* uses testimony from sources who have no real expertise on the topic in question. (9) The *bandwagon* fallacy argues that we should behave or think a particular way because most people do. (10) Finally, *ad hominem* urges listeners to reject an idea because of allegations about the character, politics, religion, or lifestyle of the person voicing the idea.

Selecting Propositions for Persuasive Speeches

17.4 Develop speeches using three types of propositions.

- All persuasive speeches advocate *propositions*, position statements the speaker wants listeners to accept. A persuasive proposition must be stated as a declarative sentence that expresses a judgment, is debatable, and requires proof in order to be accepted. The three types of persuasive propositions are propositions of fact, value, and policy.

Monroe's Motivated Sequence

17.5 Construct a speech using Monroe's motivated sequence.

- A persuasive speech must move listeners through a series of steps. *Monroe's motivated sequence* is a formal, five-step pattern for moving listeners to belief or action: (1) get the attention of your listeners, (2) clarify the need, (3) show how to satisfy that need, (4) visualize the solution, and (5) request action.

Chapter 18
Speaking on Special Occasions

 Learning Objectives

After studying this chapter, you should be able to

18.1 Apply the five guidelines for a speech of introduction.

18.2 Apply the four guidelines for a speech of presentation.

18.3 Apply the four guidelines for an acceptance speech.

18.4 Apply the five guidelines for a speech of tribute.

18.5 Apply the five guidelines for a speech to entertain.

18.6 Apply the four steps of answering a question from the audience.

We can all count on being called on to deliver a speech on some special occasion—for example, introducing a guest speaker at a club meeting, accepting an award from a civic group, or delivering a eulogy at the memorial service of a relative or friend. To speak your best on any of these occasions, you must consider the customs and audience expectations in each case.

In this chapter, we discuss six special occasions or special circumstances for public speaking: the speech of introduction, the speech of presentation, the acceptance speech, the speech of tribute, and the speech to entertain. We also discuss the question–answer period, which gives you the opportunity to interact with your audience after a speech or a team presentation. You will learn guidelines for and read examples of these types of speeches. This information can serve you well beyond the classroom and prepare you for any occasion when you are requested, invited, or expected to speak.

The Speech of Introduction

18.1 Apply the five guidelines for a speech of introduction.

One of the most common types of special-occasion speech is the **speech of introduction**. Some people use that phrase to indicate speeches by people introducing themselves to an audience. We use the phrase in this chapter to mean a speech introducing a featured speaker. The following five guidelines will help you prepare a speech of introduction:

- *Keep the focus on the person being introduced.* The audience has not gathered to hear you, so don't upstage the featured speaker. Keep your remarks short, simple, and sincere.

- *Be brief.* If you can, request and get a copy of the speaker's résumé or vita. This will give you information to select from when preparing your introductory remarks. The key word in that last sentence is *select*. Your listeners will tune out quickly if your introduction is a lengthy chronology of jobs or events in a person's life. Highlight key information only.

- *Establish the speaker's credibility on the topic.* You do this by presenting the speaker's credentials. As you prepare, ask and answer questions such as these: What qualifies the speaker to speak on the subject? What education and experiences make the speaker's insights worthy of our belief?

- *Create realistic expectations.* Genuine praise is commendable; just be careful not to oversell the speaker. Can you imagine walking to the microphone after the following introduction? "Our speaker tonight is one of the great speakers in this country. I heard her last year, and she had us laughing until our sides hurt. Get ready for the best speech you've heard in your entire life!"

- *Establish a tone consistent with the speaker's presentation.* Would you give a humorous introduction for a speaker whose topic is "The Grieving Process: What to Do When a Loved One Dies"? Of course not. On the other hand, if the evening is designed for merriment, your introduction should help set that mood.

Communication professors should certainly know how to introduce a featured speaker. In the following example, Professor Don Ochs of the University of Iowa did an exemplary job of introducing his longtime colleague Professor Samuel L. Becker, the keynote speaker at a Central States Communication Association convention. You'll see that Ochs uses some communication jargon because he was speaking to a group of communication professionals. Notice, though, how Ochs's brief, cordial remarks focus on Becker, establishing his credibility and setting the tone for Becker's informative and inspirational speech.

> **Key Points**
>
> **Guidelines for the Speech of Introduction**
> 1. Focus on the featured speaker.
> 2. Be brief.
> 3. Establish the speaker's credibility.
> 4. Create realistic expectations.
> 5. Set the tone for the speech.

speech of introduction

A speech introducing a featured speaker to an audience.

Sample Speeches

"Gifts of Speech" is an ongoing project from Sweet Briar College in Virginia. Conduct an Internet search for this site, which offers access to texts of speeches by influential women from around the world. You can search this collection alphabetically by speakers or chronologically by year. The site also lists the "Top 100 American Speeches of the 20th Century," with transcripts of some of those speeches.

Journal: The Speech of Introduction

Imagine you will be introducing your best friend as a speaker on a topic you feel he or she is very knowledgeable about. What would that topic be? Write a sentence or two that would help you establish your friend's credibility for speaking on that topic.

speech of presentation

A speech conferring an award, a prize, or some other recognition on an individual or group.

Thirty years ago I walked out of an Iowa City store onto the main street and noticed Sam Becker walking about 20 feet ahead of me. His youngest daughter was alongside Sam but she was terribly upset about something, crying, and obviously hurt about something. Sam put his arm around his daughter and, in the space of two blocks, said something that comforted and fixed the problem. She was smiling when they parted company.

I share this snapshot of Sam with you because, for me, it captures Sam's approach to life, higher education, scholarship, and our profession.

Sam Becker has figuratively put his arm around difficulties and problems for his entire career. He's made all of us as teachers and scholars better persons and better professionals with his intellect, his vision, his energy, and his instinctive willingness to help.

As a rhetorician, I would much prefer to introduce Sam with figures and tropes, with synecdoche, litotes, and hyperbole. But Sam is a social scientist, so I will be quantitative instead.

How much has Sam helped us? Sam has taught at four universities, written six books, been active in eight professional associations, authored 10 monographs, served on 12 editorial boards, worked on evaluation teams for 32 colleges and universities, served on 36 university committees, lectured at 50 colleges and universities, directed 55 Ph.D.s, and authored 105 articles. Without doubt, he has helped and assisted and supported all of us. Our speaker today, Sam Becker.[1]

The Speech of Presentation

18.2 Apply the four guidelines for a speech of presentation.

The **speech of presentation** confers an award, a prize, or some other form of special recognition on an individual or a group. Such speeches are typically made on special occasions: after banquets or parties, as parts of business meetings or sessions of a convention, or at awards ceremonies.

When you give a speech of presentation, let the nature and importance of the award being presented as well as the occasion on which it is being presented shape your remarks. The following four guidelines will help you plan this special-occasion speech:

Ethical Decisions

HOW (AND WHETHER) TO POLISH A BAD APPLE

Russell King is president of the Porridge Players, an organization that stages musical comedies on his campus. This season, the Players have performed *South Pacific*, and the actress who played Nelly Forbush is Maria MacIntosh, an enormously talented singer, dancer, and actress with a horrible temper and an insufferably arrogant attitude. As president of the Players, King has been called on time after time to mediate disputes between this woman and other members of the cast and crew. By the time the season is over, he has little respect for her, despite her considerable talents.

At the end of each season, the faculty advisory board for the Players votes on awards for the best performers, director, technical people, and so forth. No one is very surprised when Maria is chosen to receive the award for best actress. King, however, is dismayed to learn that he has to present it, along with a short introductory speech. He wonders what to do.

Should King simply praise Maria's performance and not mention the difficulties she caused, or is it his responsibility to make the faculty board aware of her flaws and negative impact on the company? What kind of information do you think King should include in his speech?

- *State the purpose of the award or recognition*. If the audience is unfamiliar with the award or the organization making the award, begin by briefly explaining the nature of the award or the rationale for presenting it. This is especially important if you represent the organization sponsoring the award. In contrast, an award having a long history probably needs little if any explanation.

- *Focus your speech on the achievements for which the award is being made*. Don't attempt a detailed biography of the recipient. Because you are merely highlighting the honoree's accomplishments, the speech of presentation will be brief, rarely more than 5 minutes long and frequently much shorter.

- *Organize a speech of presentation primarily according to whether your listeners know the name of the recipient in advance*. If they do not know the honoree, capitalize on their curiosity. Begin by making general comments that could refer to several or many people; as the speech progresses, let your comments become more specific. Use gender-neutral descriptions ("this person" or "our honoree"), rather than using "he" or "she." In this way, you keep your audience guessing and allow them the pleasure of solving a puzzle. If the audience knows in advance the name of the person being recognized, begin the speech with specifics and end with more general statements that summarize the reasons for the presentation.

- *Compliment all finalists for the award*. If a group of individuals has been nominated and you are announcing the winner with your speech of presentation, briefly compliment the entire group of people who have been nominated for the award.

> **Key Points**
> Guidelines for the Speech of Presentation
> 1. State the purpose of the award or recognition.
> 2. State the recipient's qualifications.
> 3. Adapt your speech's organization to audience knowledge.
> 4. Compliment finalists for the award.

We asked Josh McNair, a graduate teaching assistant, to create and present an award for the graduate student selected to follow him. Notice how he focuses on the reasons for the award and the honoree's qualifications. Josh also uses imagery and quotations appropriate to the occasion.

> Laurent A. Daloz, a twentieth-century educator, once observed, "In the end, good teaching lies in a willingness to attend and care for what happens in our students, ourselves, and the space between us." I couldn't agree more. Teaching is the dynamic process of filling the space between teacher and student through authentic and open communication.
>
> As part of a new tradition at Radford University, graduate students who have completed their teaching responsibilities are given the opportunity to recognize Graduate Teaching Fellows (GTFs), who will soon begin their teaching journey as communication instructors. The Great Teaching Future Award recognizes graduate students in the Department of Communication who have demonstrated academic excellence, teaching aptitude, and commitment to higher education. This year's honoree has shown all these qualities and now begins his journey to fill the space between himself and his students with knowledge, skills, and the desire for learning. It is both a privilege and pleasure to present the first Great Teaching Future Award to Mr. Zach Henning.
>
> This year's award recipient has demonstrated a unique commitment to teaching speech communication. This past year he independently sought out academic and applied opportunities for training as a college instructor. Last fall he successfully designed and delivered a public speaking teaching module in a graduate seminar in communication education. As an intern in Dr. George Grice's undergraduate persuasion class, Zach used multimedia and email to actively engage students in learning both in and out of the classroom. He completed his instructor training over the summer when, on a volunteer basis, he assisted Dr. Bill Kennan in teaching two sections of public speaking. Under Dr. Kennan's tutelage, Zach listened to and critiqued more than a hundred student speeches.
>
> Those of us who know Zach have witnessed his commitment to filling the space between himself and his students. First, Zach fills the space with knowledge of what to teach. The public speaking teaching module he developed includes clear teaching objectives that emphasize both the critical thinking and

experiential components of constructing and delivering speeches. Second, Zach fills the space with skills on how to teach. In Dr. Grice's persuasion class, he successfully incorporated communication technology, traditional lecture, and small-group formats to motivate students. Finally, Zach fills the space with humor and his unique wit to foster in his students a desire for learning.

As our teaching mentor, Dr. Grice, states in his teaching philosophy, "Understanding and applying knowledge comes from discovering relationships through communication, imagination, and invention." The Great Teaching Future Award follows this teaching philosophy and recognizes Graduate Teaching Fellows who have demonstrated excellence in attending to and caring for the space between themselves and their students. It is with great pleasure, then, that I present Zach Henning with this year's Great Teaching Future Award.[2]

The Acceptance Speech

18.3 Apply the four guidelines for an acceptance speech.

At some point in your life, you may be commended publicly for service you have given to a cause or an organization. You may be presented a farewell or retirement gift from your friends or coworkers. You may receive an award for winning a sporting event, an essay contest, or a speech contest. Although these are different occasions, they have at least one thing in common—each requires a response. To accept a gift or an award without expressing appreciation is socially unacceptable. An **acceptance speech**, then, is a response to a speech of presentation. When a recipient acknowledges the award or tribute, he or she provides closure to the process. A gracious acceptance speech usually includes four steps:

- *Thank the person or organization bestowing the award.* You may wish to name the group sponsoring the award and the person who made the speech of presentation. In addition, you may want to commend what the award represents. Your respect for the award and its donor authenticates your statement of appreciation.

- *Compliment your peers as a group rather than individually.* If you are accepting a competitively selected award and especially if your competitors are in the audience, acknowledge their qualifications and compliment them.

- *Thank those who helped you achieve the honor.* Whether you are an accomplished pianist, vocalist, artist, athlete, or writer, you have usually had someone—parents, teachers, or coaches—who invested time, money, and expertise to help you achieve your best.

- *Accept your award graciously.* Whether you are a novice or an experienced award winner, you should emphasize how valuable the award is to you and how honored you are to receive it.

In response to Josh's speech of presentation, graduate student Zach Henning delivered the following acceptance speech. Notice how he incorporates the four guidelines we've discussed.

> Thank you, Josh, for your kind words and for your support. It is with great honor that I accept this award. I realize that I have big shoes to fill and I will do my best to follow your example.
>
> When I think about teaching, I'm reminded of what the great philosopher Aristotle said, "Teaching is the highest form of understanding." Through my internship and volunteer work with the communication department, I've learned more about who I am and how I can help others succeed. My understanding started with the feelings I experienced when I noticed thirty-four students looking up and paying attention to my words and thoughts. Their eagerness to learn inspired me to be the best instructor I can.

Key Points

Guidelines for the Acceptance Speech

1. Thank those who bestowed the award.
2. Compliment the competition.
3. Thank those who helped you attain the award.
4. Accept the award graciously.

acceptance speech

A speech responding to a speech of presentation by acknowledging an award, a tribute, or recognition.

I know many qualified candidates who share my beliefs and feelings about teaching. Each could easily take my place with the experiences they bring to this department. I'm sure they would agree that teaching is more than a chore or an occupation. Instead, it's an art that is mastered through experience and guidance.

For that guidance, I turned to Dr. George Grice and Dr. William Kennan. They taught me about classroom logistics, lesson plans, and practical knowledge about the mechanics of teaching. More importantly, however, they taught me how to be passionate about what I am doing and how to positively influence the lives of students beyond the textbook and lecture material. For this I thank you both for your patience and generosity in offering me the opportunity to share in that passion.

I would also like to thank Dr. Gwen Brown, the director of our graduate program. Last year, new to the program and this university, I came to her wanting to know how I could become a graduate teaching fellow. Though there were no positions available at that time, Dr. Brown guided me to curricular and extracurricular opportunities that would heighten my interest in teaching. Her advice gave me the opportunity to reapply and accept this honor today.

And, most importantly, I would like to thank my students for their hard work and dedication. It is my goal not only to teach you about how to succeed in the classroom, but also to teach you about how to succeed in life. I am a firm believer in Dr. Martin Luther King, Jr.'s challenge that "the function of education is to teach one to think intensively and to think critically." I share this goal of education to teach both knowledge and character to prepare you for the challenges and opportunities you will encounter in your professional lives.

I hope that I never stop learning and understanding. There are always new challenges and new ways of thinking and teaching. I hope to continue to grow and change as I gain more experience and knowledge. Thank you for this first step to a lifetime of teaching and learning.[3]

The Speech of Tribute

18.4 Apply the five guidelines for a speech of tribute.

A **speech of tribute**, or commemorative speech, honors a person, a group, or an event, and it can be one of the most moving forms of public address. A special form of this speech is the **eulogy**, a tribute to someone who has recently died. Vivid and memorable examples include Abraham Lincoln's Gettysburg Address, Ronald Reagan's tribute to the crew of the *Challenger* after the shuttle explosion in 1986, and Barack Obama's eulogy for human rights advocate and former South African President Nelson Mandela on a rainy Tuesday in December 2013 in Johannesburg, South Africa.

Peggy Noonan, presidential speechwriter, captures the power of eulogies:

> They are the most moving kind of speech because they attempt to pluck meaning from the fog, and on short order, when the emotions are still ragged and raw and susceptible to leaps. It is a challenge to look at a life and organize our thoughts about it and try to explain to ourselves what it meant, and the most moving part is the element of implicit celebration. Most people aren't appreciated enough, and the bravest things we do in our lives are usually known only to ourselves. No one throws

speech of tribute
A speech honoring a person, group, or event.

eulogy
A speech of tribute praising a person who has recently died.

On June 7, 2014, at Wake Forest University's Wait Chapel, Michelle Obama delivered a eulogy for poet, author, and civil rights activist Maya Angelou. The First Lady spoke of how Angelou had "gathered so many of us under her wing" and shared "her wisdom, her genius, and her boundless love."

ticker tape on the man who chose to be faithful to his wife, on the lawyer who didn't take the drug money, or the daughter who held her tongue again and again. All this anonymous heroism. A eulogy gives us a chance to celebrate it.[4]

The following five guidelines will help develop a eulogy or any other speech of tribute:

- *Establish noble themes.* As you begin developing a speech of tribute, ask, "Why is this person worthy of my respect and praise?" Answer this question by developing themes you want the audience to remember. Focus on the positive. A speech of tribute celebrates what is good about a person; it is not an occasion for a warts-and-all biography. You must be careful, however, not to exaggerate a person's accomplishments. To do so may undermine your speech by making it seem insincere or unbelievable.

  Our student Stuart delivered a speech of tribute for one of his childhood heroes: Hall of Fame baseball player Ted Williams. He avoided the trap of organizing his speech as a biographical listing in an encyclopedia. Instead, he highlighted three lessons that all audience members, whether baseball fans or not, could learn from studying Williams's life. Stuart introduced these themes as he previewed his key ideas:

  > He was given many eloquent nicknames by his teammates and the news media: The Splendid Splinter, The Kid, and Teddy Ballgame. All portray his amazing baseball talent, but all fail to capture the values that directed his life. *Ted Williams taught us a lesson in patriotism, a lesson in perseverance, and a lesson in charity.* And he did so not by lecturing or preaching, but by powerfully leading by example.

- *Provide vivid examples.* Anecdotes, stories, and personal testimony are excellent ways of making your speech more vivid, humane, and memorable.

- *Express the feelings of the audience assembled or those whom you represent.* The audience needs to be a part of the occasion for any speech of tribute. If you are honoring Mr. Crenshaw, a former teacher, you may speak for yourself and for all students who studied under him. The honoree should feel that the tribute expresses more than one person's view.

- Your use of noble themes, vivid examples, and audience feelings should combine to *create a memorable image of the person being honored.* Your speech not only honors someone but also helps audience members focus on that person's importance to them.

- *Be genuine.* If you are asked to deliver a speech of tribute about someone you do not know, you may want to decline respectfully. The personal bond and interaction you develop in getting to know someone well is essential for a speech of tribute. Also, the person being honored may find the tribute more meaningful if it comes from a person he or she knows well.

Oprah Winfrey delivered a moving eulogy of Rosa Parks at a memorial service in the Metropolitan AME Church in Washington, D.C., on October 31, 2005. You can read about Winfrey's speech (and how to find it online) in Appendix D. As you read or listen to the speech, notice how she applied the guidelines discussed above.

The Speech to Entertain

18.5 Apply the five guidelines for a speech to entertain.

The **speech to entertain** seeks to make a point through the creative, organized use of the speaker's humor. The distinguishing characteristic of this speech is the entertainment value of its supporting materials. It is usually delivered on an occasion when people are in a light mood: after a banquet, as part of an awards ceremony, or on other festive occasions.

Key Points

Guidelines for the Speech of Tribute

1. Establish noble themes.
2. Provide vivid examples.
3. Express audience feelings.
4. Create a memorable image.
5. Be genuine.

Journal: The Speech of Tribute

Imagine that you are to give a speech of tribute for someone you admire who is known to your class. This person may be a campus, local, national, or international figure. What are two or three noble themes you could develop about this person in your speech? What is one story or anecdote you might develop into a vivid example about the person?

speech to entertain

A speech designed to make a point through the creative, organized use of humorous supporting materials.

A *speech to entertain* is different from *speaking to entertain*. In their opening monologues, Jimmy Fallon, Ellen DeGeneres, and Conan O'Brien speak to entertain. Their purpose is to relax the audience, establish some interaction with them, and set the mood for the rest of the show. Their remarks are usually not organized around a central theme, something essential to a speech to entertain.

The following five guidelines along with what you already know about developing a public speech will enable you to construct a speech to entertain:

- *Make a point.* Frequently, the person delivering a speech to entertain is trying to make the audience aware of conditions, experiences, or habits that they take for granted. The following are examples of topics on which we have heard students present successful speeches to entertain:

    The imprecision and incorrectness of language, especially that used in some advertisements

    Many doctors' failure to speak language that their patients can understand and many patients' failure to ask their doctors the right questions

    Our interest in or curiosity about tabloid news stories

    The routine, expensive date versus creative, less expensive dating options

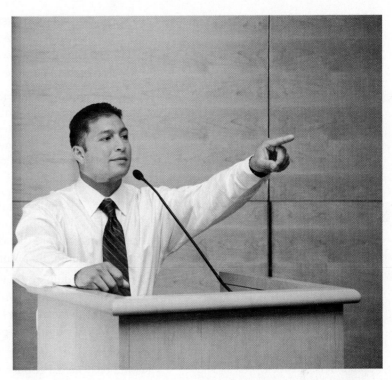

Having the opportunity to field questions from the audience following your speech gives you an excellent opportunity to adapt to your audience. You know what your listeners want to hear because they ask the questions.

In some of these speeches, the speaker had stated the main point fairly bluntly by the end of the speech: Look carefully at the language used to sell you things; you owe it to your health to ask questions of your doctor; you do not have to spend a fortune to have an interesting time on a date. In other speeches, speakers simply implied their thesis.

- *Be creative.* To be creative, your speech to entertain must be your product and not simply a replay of an Ellen DeGeneres or a Jimmy Kimmel monologue. A replay is not creative, even if you do a great job of delivering the other person's lines. Moreover, if you copy other people's words and don't credit them, you are plagiarizing. Your speech to entertain should give your audience a glimpse of your unique view of the world.

- *Be organized.* Your speech must have an introduction, a body, and a conclusion, just as informative and persuasive speeches do. The speech to entertain must convey a sense of moving toward some logical point and achieving closure after adequately developing that point. Failure to organize your materials will cause you to ramble, embarrassing both you and your audience. You will feel like the novice comic caught without a finish, a sure-fire joke that makes a good exit line. The audience will sense that you are struggling and will have trouble relaxing and enjoying your humor.

- *Use appropriate humor.* The speech to entertain is difficult to do well for a simple reason: most people associate entertainment with lots of laughter and feel that if the audience is not laughing, they are not responding favorably to the speech. But consider the range of things that entertain you, from outrageous antics to quiet, pointed barbs. Your humor should be adapted to your topic, your audience, the occasion, and your personal style. The following four suggestions should guide your use of humor:

    ○ *Be relevant.* Good humor is relevant to your general purpose and makes the main ideas of your speech memorable. Michael's speech to entertain discussed

Key Points

Guidelines for the Speech to Entertain

1. Make a point.
2. Be creative.
3. Be organized.
4. Use appropriate humor.
5. Use spirited delivery.

EXPLORING ONLINE

Commencement Speeches

The graduation commencement address is another type of special-occasion speech. Conduct an Internet search for The Humanity Initiative's webpage titled "Commencement Speeches." Browse transcripts of commencement addresses ranging from Theodor Geisel (Dr. Seuss) to Bill Gates and covering the years from 1936 to the present. You can also read an essay offering suggestions on writing a commencement speech.

the ways we label products and people. One of his points was that the product warnings printed on packaging tell us about various companies' views of their customers. His examples were relevant to that main idea and added humor to his speech by helping him show the absurdity of many product labels.

> For example, the first thing I saw on the box my toaster came in was a warning. Warning—do not submerge in water, especially when the plug is connected to an electrical outlet. Now just at a practical level, I'm pretty sure that almost anyone should be able to figure out that the chances of getting your Pop-Tart to turn brown at the bottom of a Jacuzzi are pretty slim to begin with.[5]

○ *Be tasteful.* Audience analysis is vital for a speech to entertain. Taste is subjective. What delights some listeners may offend others. Do your best in analyzing your audience, but when in doubt, err on the side of caution. Remember, humor that is off-color is off-limits.

○ *Be tactful.* Avoid humor that generates laughter at the expense of others. There may be times when good-natured ribbing is appropriate, but humor intended to belittle or demean a person or group is unethical and unacceptable. For that reason, sexist and inappropriate ethnic humor is also off-limits.

○ *Be positive.* The tone for most occasions featuring speeches to entertain should be festive. People have come together to relax and enjoy one another's company. Dark, negative humor is usually inappropriate, as it casts a somber tone on the situation.

• *Use spirited delivery.* We have often heard good speeches to entertain and looked forward to reading transcripts of them later. We were usually disappointed. The personality, timing, and interaction with the audience that made the speech lively and unforgettable could not be captured on paper. We have also read manuscripts of speeches to entertain that promised to be dynamic when presented, only to see them diminished by a monotonous, colorless, and lifeless delivery.

The Question–Answer Period

18.6 Apply the four steps of answering a question from the audience.

Theory Into Practice TIP

THE QUESTION–ANSWER PERIOD

Holding a question–answer period following your speech gives you the opportunity to interact directly with your audience. This usually results in a natural, lively delivery and makes for better speaker–listener rapport.

   If questions are friendly, that is a high compliment: the audience is genuinely interested in you and your topic. If questions stem from audience confusion about your presentation, you have an opportunity to clarify. If someone asks you a combative and contentious question, you've just been given a second chance to win this person over to your point of view.

   You will find the following guidelines helpful when you stand in front of an audience and ask, "Are there any questions?"

1. *Restate or clarify the question.* This is important for three reasons. First, repetition makes sure that the entire audience has heard the question. Second, repeating the question gives the questioner the opportunity to correct you if you misstate it, saving you the embarrassment of beginning to answer a different question. Third, if the question seems confusing to you or somehow misses the point, you can rephrase the question to make it clearer, more focused, and more relevant. Never answer a question you don't understand.

2. *Compliment the question whenever possible*. We have all heard speakers say, "I'm glad you asked that." Of course, you cannot repeat that same remark after each question. But you can say, "That's a good (or perceptive or interesting) question" or "I was hoping someone would ask that." This applies even to hostile questions. Sincerely complimenting a hostile questioner can defuse a tense situation and focus attention on issues rather than on personal antagonism.

3. *Answer the question*. Of course, the content and the form of your answers depend on the specific questions; nevertheless, the following suggestions may be helpful:

   - *Know your topic thoroughly*. Your success during the question–answer period will depend in large part on your research and preparation for your speech. You should always know more than you include in your speech. Most of the time, poor answers reflect poor preparation.
   - *Be as brief as possible*. Obviously, some questions require longer, more thoughtful answers than others. The question, "How much did you say it will cost to complete Phase II of the new library?" can be answered simply, "Two and a half million dollars." The question, "What will that $2.5 million provide?" will require a much longer answer.
   - *Be methodical in giving lengthy answers*. When you need to give a detailed answer, use the organizational strategies that you've already learned and practiced: Signpost, state, and explain what you want the audience to remember.
   - *If you don't know an answer, admit it*. Making up an answer is unethical. Fabricated answers can not only undermine your credibility, but the audience may also act on incorrect information you have provided. There is nothing wrong with saying, "I don't know" or "I don't know, but I'll check on it and let you know." If you give the second response, make sure you follow up promptly.
   - *Be careful about what you say publicly*. Remember that in a public gathering there is no such thing as an off-the-record statement. If the press is present, what you say may indeed be reported. As a rule, never say anything that would embarrass you or slander others if it were to appear in the next morning's paper.

4. *Check the response with the questioner*. Did you answer the question to her or his satisfaction? Is there a follow-up question? Remember two drawbacks to this approach, however. If each person is allowed a question and a follow-up, you will be able to answer fewer people's questions. Second, if questioners are argumentative, asking them if you answered the question to their satisfaction gives them an opportunity to keep the floor and turn the question–answer period into a debate.

On a practical level, the question–answer period is one sure test of how well you know the topic of your speech. Handled effectively, a question–answer period gives you a final chance to clarify questions audience members might have, to reinforce your main points, and to cultivate the image you want to leave with your listeners.

Summary

The Speech of Introduction

18.1 Apply the five guidelines for a speech of introduction.

- The *speech of introduction* presents a featured speaker to an audience. Be brief, focus your remarks on the featured speaker, establish that person's credibility, create positive but realistic audience expectations, and match the tone of the featured speech.

The Speech of Presentation

18.2 Apply the four guidelines for a speech of presentation.

- The *speech of presentation* confers an award, prize, or special recognition on an individual or group. Such a speech should state the purpose of the award or recognition, particularly if it is new or unfamiliar to the audience. Reveal why the person deserves the award. If the audience does not know the name of the recipient in advance, create suspense, revealing the recipient's name only late in the speech. If the person being honored has been selected from nominees known to the audience, compliment those other individuals.

The Acceptance Speech

18.3 Apply the four guidelines for an acceptance speech.

- The *acceptance speech* is an honoree's response to a speech of presentation. In accepting an award, thank the people bestowing it. You should also compliment your competitors if you know them. Then thank those who helped you attain the award, and accept the award graciously.

The Speech of Tribute

18.4 Apply the five guidelines for a speech of tribute.

- The *speech of tribute*, or commemorative speech, honors an individual, a group, or a significant event. A eulogy, spoken to honor a person who has recently died, is one of the most familiar speeches of tribute. In delivering a speech of tribute, you should establish noble themes built on vivid examples from the subject's life. In addition you should express the collective feelings of the audience, create a memorable image of the subject, and be genuine.

The Speech to Entertain

18.5 Apply the five guidelines for a speech to entertain.

- The *speech to entertain* seeks to make a point through the creative, organized use of the speaker's humor.

Usually delivered on a light, festive occasion, your speech to entertain should make a point, be creative, be well organized, use appropriate humor, and be delivered in a spirited manner. The humor you use should be relevant to your point, tasteful, tactful, and positive.

The Question–Answer Period

18.6 Apply the four steps of answering a question from the audience.

- The *question–answer period* after your speech gives you the opportunity to interact with your audience. Restate or clarify what is asked, compliment the question or the questioner, answer the question, and check your response with the person who asked the question.

Appendix A
Giving and Receiving Feedback

Learning Objectives

After studying this appendix, you should be able to

A.1 Use the model of criticism by articulating judgments, reasons, and norms.

A.2 Apply the ten guidelines for critiquing speeches.

A.3 Apply the four guidelines for acting on feedback to improve your speeches.

Appropriate feedback is crucial to your development as a public speaker. What you learn from your instructor and classmates about distractions caused by language, voice, or body will help you polish your speaking skills. You, in turn, want to be an incisive and sensitive critic when you write or speak about others' speeches. **Criticism** is information given to others in a way that enables them to use it for self-improvement.[1]

This information includes both positive comments that reinforce what a speaker did well and negative comments that point to areas for improvement. If you say, "Your speech was well within the 7-minute time limit," you spotlight a positive aspect of the speech. If you write or say, "I liked your speech," you are also providing feedback. This last comment, however, doesn't really teach the speaker anything. There is nothing wrong with saying, "I enjoyed your speech," or "I didn't care for this speech as much as your last one." Just don't stop there. Explain why.

Question: What's the shortest word in the English language that contains the letters a, b, c, d, e, and f?
Answer: Feedback

A Model of Criticism

LO A.1 Use the model of criticism by articulating judgments, reasons, and norms.

All criticism contains three parts: *judgments, reasons,* and *norms.*[2] Figure A.1 illustrates the relationships between these parts. The most familiar and superficial level of criticism consists of **judgments**. We make them frequently about many different subjects: "I loved the movie *Last Vegas*," "Dr. Venkat is an excellent teacher," or "I always enjoy your speeches."

criticism

Feedback offered for the purpose of improving a speaker's speech.

judgments

A critic's opinions about the relative merits of a speech; the most common and superficial level of speech criticism.

Figure A.1 A Model of Criticism

Underlying those judgments, whether we voice them or not, are **reasons**: "*Last Vegas* had a great cast and I really liked the relational bonds depicted in the movie, but I thought it was too predictable at the end." "Dr. Venkat is an excellent teacher because her lectures make a course I dreaded lively and interesting," or "I always enjoy your speeches because you choose such unusual topics." Statements such as these specify reasons for the critics' judgments.

The statements in the preceding paragraph are instructive and useful because they help others infer your **norms**—the values you believe make something good or effective or desirable. Such statements tell us that the critics dislike predictability in movies, appreciate liveliness in class lectures, and like unusual topics in public speeches. We may, of course, argue with the critics about whether these norms are valid. That's healthy and productive. As speech critics we must provide reasons for our judgments; only by doing so do we tell the speaker the basis of our reactions.

Here are some examples of helpful comments made by students about their classmates' speeches:

> Karen, your concern for children certainly shows in this speech on rating day care centers. Your personal examples really helped make the speech interesting.

> John, your speech on how to improve study habits was the best I heard. It was appropriate and beneficial to everyone in the class. Your language was simple and coherent. You explained just what we needed to know in the time you had.

reasons

Statements that justify a critic's judgments.

norms

The values a critic believes necessary to make any speech good, effective, or desirable.

Lettie, one problem I saw was your use of visual aids. Once you have finished with the visual aid, you should put it away rather than leave it where the audience can see it. That way, the audience will focus their attention on you rather than on the object.

One value of receiving well-written or thoughtful oral comments about your speeches is that repetition of feedback will reinforce it. If one person tells you that you need to speak louder, you may dismiss the advice. If twelve people say that they had trouble hearing you, however, you are more likely to pay attention.

A second value of receiving feedback from many people, especially people from various cultures, is that different people value different aspects of a speech. Some may put a premium on delivery, others on speech content, and still others on organization. With such a variety of perspectives and values, it would be a shame if all feedback were reduced to "Good job!" or "I liked it." To provide the best feedback you can, remember to specify the reasons for your judgments; ask yourself why a speech affects you and then try to communicate those reasons to the speaker.

We should also make a final note about the spirit in which you give feedback in this class. You should never make criticisms that are designed to belittle or hurt the speaker. *Target the speech, not the speaker*. Focus on specific behaviors rather than the person exhibiting those behaviors. You will probably never hear a speech so fine that the speaker could not make some improvement, and you will never hear a speech so inept or ill prepared that it does not have some redeeming value. *Listen evaluatively* and then *respond empathetically*, putting yourself in the speaker's place, and you should make truly helpful comments about your classmates' speeches.

Critiquing Speeches

LO A.2 Apply the ten guidelines for critiquing speeches.

To help you become a better critic, we offer ten guidelines you can use as you evaluate speeches. One of our students, Susan, delivered an informative speech on three major tenets of the Amish faith. We asked some students to critique Susan's speech, and we have used their comments to illustrate our suggestions.

Begin with a Positive Statement

Do you remember being told, "If you can't say something nice, don't say anything at all"? Well, that's good advice to follow when you critique your classmates' speeches. Public speaking is a personal experience. You stand in front of an audience expressing *your* thoughts in *your* words with *your* voice and *your* body. When you affirm the positive, you establish a healthy climate for constructive criticism. Demonstrate to speakers that what they said or how they said it was worthy. Fortunately, you can always find something helpful to say if you think about it. Be positive—and sincere!

Two of our students began their critiques of Susan's speech with these opening statements:

> I found your speech on the Amish to be very interesting; their beliefs are fascinating. They seem very simple but very committed to their group—what a unique way of living.
>
> I have lived near the Amish in Pennsylvania. Your speech explained the reasons for their behavior. You clearly explained why they do what they do.

Notice that while both critics compliment the speaker, the second critic also demonstrates her involvement in the topic.

Target a Few Key Areas for Improvement

Imagine how you would react if you were told, "There are seventeen areas you need to work on for your next speech." You'd probably feel overwhelmed. *How can I possibly do all that in time for my next speech? Which of the seventeen suggestions should I focus on first?* Susan's critics focused on the most important strengths and areas of improvement of her speech. In doing so, they provided her with manageable goals for her next speech. After accomplishing them, she could begin to improve other aspects of future speeches.

Organize Your Comments

A critique, just like a speech, is easier to follow if it is well organized. You can select from several options to frame your comments, and you should select the one that is most appropriate to you, the speaker, and the speech.

For example, you can organize your comments topically into the categories of speech *content*, *delivery*, and *organization*. A second option is chronologically; you can discuss the speech's *introduction*, *body*, and *conclusion*. A third option is to divide your comments into speaking *strengths* and *areas of improvement* (remember, give positive comments first). You could even combine these options. You could discuss the speaker's introduction, body, and conclusion and within each category discuss first the strengths and then areas for improvement.

Be Specific

Suppose, instead of this list of ten guidelines for offering feedback, we simply said, "When you critique your classmates' speeches, be as helpful as possible so that they can improve their speaking." Although that is good advice, it's not very helpful. By being more specific, we hope to provide you with tools to improve your critiquing skills. Similarly, you will help speakers if you provide them with specific suggestions for improvement.

For speakers to become more proficient, they need to know *what* and *how* to improve. One student told Susan, "I liked the way you presented the speech as a whole." That statement provides a nice pat on the back, but it doesn't give Susan much direction. The qualifying phrase "as a whole" seems to suggest that the listener noticed small problems that were minimized by the generally positive effect of Susan's speech. What were those problems, and what could Susan have done to minimize them? Remember to provide reasons for your judgments. In the two statements below, the listeners' comments are specific.

> I was really impressed with the fact that you did not use your note-cards while you delivered the introduction or the conclusion. That suggests that you were confident and well prepared.

> Susan, you used good transitional phrases or words to move from subtopic to subtopic within each main point. An example of this was when you said, "Not only do the Amish have simple ways of dressing, but they also provide very simple toys for their children."

Be Honest but Tactful

Phrasing suggestions for improvement tests your interpersonal skills. At times you may be reluctant to offer criticism because you think it may offend the speaker. If you are not honest, the speaker may not know that the topic was dull, the content superficial, and the delivery uninspiring. Still, you must respect the speaker's feelings. The statement "Your speech was dull, superficial, and uninspiring" may be honest, but it is hardly tactful. It may provoke resistance to your suggestions or damage the speaker's self-esteem.

One student thought Susan's speech content and organization were excellent but that her delivery was mechanical and lifeless. The student could have said, "Your delivery lacked excitement." Instead, she wrote, "The only problem I saw with your speech was a lack of enthusiasm. Maybe the speech was too rehearsed. It sounded kind of like a newscast. I think it needed some humor to break the monotony."

Personalize Your Comments

The more interest and involvement your critique conveys, the more likely the speaker is to believe in and act on your advice. You can personalize your comments in three ways. First, use the speaker's name occasionally, as in "Susan, your hand gestures would be more effective if you used them less. I found myself being distracted by them."

A second way of reducing a speaker's defensiveness and establishing speaker–critic rapport is by using I-statements in place of you-statements. Explain how the speech affected you. Instead of saying, "Your organization was weak," say, "I had trouble following your key ideas," and then give some examples of places where you got lost. The following is an example of what one of our students could have said and what she actually did say in her critique of Susan's speech:

> *She could have said:* "You lost my attention during the first part of your speech because you spoke so fast that I couldn't keep up with you."

> *Instead, she said:* "I had difficulty following your words at first because your rate seemed fast to me. After you settled down into the speech, though, I could listen with more attention."

A third way of personalizing your comments is by stating how you have benefited from hearing the speech. The following statement from a student critique let Susan know that her use of visual aids to illustrate Amish artifacts was interesting and helpful:

> Your speech . . . especially caught my attention when you showed the toys, the quilt, and the artwork. And putting the visual aids down after explaining them helped in keeping me interested in the next area.

Reinforce the Positive

Sometimes we want so much to help someone improve that we focus on what the speaker did wrong and forget to mention what the speaker did well. As you enumerate how speakers can improve, don't forget the things they did well and should continue doing. One student, impressed with Susan's language and vocal delivery, made the following comment:

> Susan, your delivery was excellent. You used your voice to emotionally color your message. I really felt as if I was living in the pictures that your descriptions created.

Problem-Solve the Negative

If you are serious about wanting to improve your speaking, you will want to recognize areas of improvement for your speech. Only then can you improve. As a critic, you have a responsibility to help others become better speakers. Don't be afraid to let them know what went wrong with a speech.

As a rule, though, do not criticize behaviors that the speaker cannot correct. On the day she spoke, Susan was suffering an allergic reaction. As a result of antihistamines she was taking, her throat was dry. Even if this had detracted significantly from her message, it would have been inappropriate for a student to comment, "I had trouble listening to what you said because your mouth seemed dry. Avoid that in your next speech." Such a request may be beyond the speaker's control. On the other hand, it would be useful to suggest that Susan take a drink of water immediately before speaking.

You will help speakers improve their speaking skills if you follow two steps in your feedback. First, point out a specific problem and, second, suggest ways to correct it.

One student was impressed with Susan's visual aids but offered her the following advice about one of them:

> You said that the Amish don't like to have their pictures taken, and yet you used a picture of an Amish man as a visual aid. Next time, if you'd explain how or where you got the picture, it wouldn't leave picky people like me wondering during the rest of your speech how you got that picture.

Provide the Speaker with a Plan of Action

When you give your comments, include a plan of action for the speaker. What should the speaker concentrate on when presenting the next speech?

One student focused Susan's attention on her next speaking experience by suggesting the following action plan:

> Susan, your overall speech and style of presentation were very good. However, I detected two minor things that could be improved. First, except when you were moving toward or away from a visual aid, you remained in one place. I believe that taking a few steps when you begin a subtopic would emphasize your transitions and enhance your message. Second, take more time to demonstrate and talk about the boy's toy that you showed us. You said, "It has marbles and fun moving parts," but I didn't really get a chance to see how it operates. Your organization, your vocal emphasis and inflection, your eye contact, and your knowledge of the topic were all terrific. You're an effective speaker, and if you use these suggestions for your next speech, you will be even more effective.

End with a Positive Statement

Conclude your critique on a positive note. Remind speakers that both you and they benefited from this experience. One of the best compliments you can give a speaker is that you learned something from the speech. Two of our students concluded their critiques of Susan's speech as follows:

> Great job, Susan! You were very specific and enthusiastic about your subject, and your visual aids reinforced what was already thorough.

> Susan, you did an outstanding job. Your speech was well organized and very informative. You showed some signs of nervousness, but more practice will alleviate most of them. Whenever and wherever you will be speaking next, I'd like to be there.

Acting on Feedback

LO A.3 **Apply the four guidelines for acting on feedback to improve your speeches.**

Many of us dislike receiving criticism, yet such feedback is important to our development and success as public speakers. If you want to communicate more effectively, you must seek feedback from your listeners. Ethical speakers respect their audiences. Consideration for the audience means, in part, trusting their opinions and advice. If you respect your listeners, you will value their questions and advice about your speech. The following guidelines will enable you to get the most out of this process.

Focus on *What* Your Critics Say, Not *How* They Say It

Listen to the content of the feedback, not the way it is presented. Too often, we become defensive when someone critiques us. Remember that offering criticism is not easy, and your critic may not have mastered the guidelines we've presented in the previous section. Avoid reacting emotionally to feedback, even if it is poorly worded and insensitive. Instead, focus on the content of the suggestions you receive.

Seek Clear and Specific Feedback

To improve your speaking, you must be aware of specific areas for improvement. Suppose a critic says, "Your organization could be improved." That may be an honest and valid statement, but it isn't very helpful because it lacks specific areas for improvement. Ask the critic to be more specific. Is the problem with the introduction, body, or conclusion? What specific strategies could you use to improve your organization? It may take some good interpersonal communication to elicit the feedback you need to become a better public speaker.

Sometimes you may receive conflicting feedback. Don't dismiss criticisms simply because they seem contradictory. For example, one critic may comment that your eye contact was good, another that it was poor. Both may be right. Perhaps you spoke only to those in the center of the room; they may have liked your eye contact, while others felt excluded. Or a critic's reaction may have been based on cultural norms; some cultures value eye contact more than others. It's important to learn the reasons behind a critic's judgment before you can improve your public speaking.

Evaluate the Feedback You Receive

It's not enough just to receive and understand feedback. You must use your critical thinking skills to analyze and evaluate that feedback. Repetition is one standard of judgment. If only one classmate thought your attention-getting step was weak, don't be too concerned. However, if your instructor and the majority of your classmates thought it was deficient, you should target that as an area for improvement.

Develop a Plan of Action

After receiving feedback, summarize and record those comments. Then rank those areas needing improvement according to their importance. Rather than tackling every criticism, select a few to work on for your next speech. Write a plan of action that states your goals and the strategies you will use to achieve them.

Remember that your goal as you move from one speech to the next is not consistency but consistent improvement. So, rather than defending what you said or did in your speech, listen carefully and act on those suggestions for improvement that you receive most frequently. If you have doubts about the validity of suggestions your classmates are making, discuss the matter with your instructor. You will make the most accelerated improvement if you graciously accept the compliments of your peers and your instructor and then work quickly to eliminate problems that they bring to your attention.

Key Points

Guidelines for Acting on Feedback

1. Focus on *what* your critics say, not *how* they say it.
2. Seek clear and specific feedback.
3. Evaluate the feedback you receive.
4. Develop a plan of action.

Appendix B
Using an Audience Questionnaire

Learning Objectives

After studying this appendix, you should be able to

B.1 Design a questionnaire to elicit information about your audience and their views on your topic.

B.2 Gather your data in a manner that ensures anonymous and confidential responses.

B.3 Interpret questionnaire responses as you develop the supporting materials in your speech.

A **questionnaire** is a set of written questions designed to elicit information about your listeners' knowledge, beliefs, attitudes, or behaviors regarding your specific speech topic.[1] If you're unable to learn enough about your listeners through informal means such as observation and discussion, you have another option. If you need precise, measurable information and have the luxury of ample time and opportunity to collect it, consider administering a questionnaire. When you administer a questionnaire, you conduct *survey research*. The following guidelines will help you construct and administer a questionnaire and then interpret the responses.

Construct a Questionnaire

B.1 Design a questionnaire to elicit information about your audience and their views on your topic.

First, determine what you need to know about your audience. Do not ask unnecessary questions. What do they already know about your topic? If you're trying to persuade them, do they agree or disagree with you, or are they undecided? How strongly do they hold these positions?

Second, construct your questions depending on the type and amount of information you seek, how long respondents will have to complete your questionnaire, and how you plan to compile and use the information you gather.

You can ask two types of questions in your questionnaire: closed questions and open-ended questions. *Closed questions,* which are ideal for

questionnaire

A set of written questions designed to elicit information about listeners' knowledge, beliefs, attitudes, or behaviors regarding your specific speech topic.

gathering demographic information offer respondents a finite set of responses that are either categorical or in a scale format that asks people to place themselves along a continuum. The following are examples of demographic questions using a closed categorical response format.

- What is your sex?   [ ] Female   [ ] Male
- Are you currently employed?   [ ] Yes   [ ] No
- What's your academic status?   [ ] First-year student   [ ] Sophomore
  [ ] Junior   [ ] Senior   [ ] Other

Closed questions that are scaled ask respondents to place themselves at a particular point along a continuum. This type of question is useful when assessing attitudes, beliefs, values, and frequency of behaviors. Generally, ratings for scaled questions ascend from left to right or move from lowest to highest ratings. The following are examples of scaled closed questions that assess attitudes, beliefs, values, and frequency of behaviors.

- I enjoy watching college football games on TV. (Attitude)

  [ ] Strongly disagree   [ ] Disagree   [ ] Neutral   [ ] Agree
  [ ] Strongly agree

- The honor code at our school is too strict. (Belief)

  [ ] Strongly disagree   [ ] Disagree   [ ] Neutral   [ ] Agree
  [ ] Strongly agree

- It is important to earn a college degree. (Value)

  [ ] Strongly disagree   [ ] Disagree   [ ] Neutral   [ ] Agree
  [ ] Strongly agree

- I talk to my instructors to get clarification on assignments. (Frequency of behavior)
- [ ] Almost never   [ ] Rarely   [ ] Sometimes   [ ] Often
  [ ] Almost always

Open-ended questions invite respondents to answer questions about their attitudes, beliefs, values, and behaviors in their own words. Though they take more time to answer, compile, and interpret, open-ended questions often provide unexpected, helpful information, or specific examples a speaker may include in a speech. The following are examples of open-ended questions.

- What do you think are the qualities of a good supervisor? (Belief)
- How do you feel about the general education requirements at our school? (Attitude)
- What are some activities in which you participate that contribute to a healthy lifestyle? (Behavior)
- What are some important attributes of a good friend? (Value)

Your questions, whether open-ended or closed, should be clear, objective, and focused. Each question should focus on one item or issue. Avoid emotional language that may "lead" respondents to a particular response.

Figure B.1. James's Audience Questionnaire

Please take a few minutes to answer the following questions. The information gathered will be used to assist me in preparing for my persuasive speech. To maintain anonymity, do not include your name. Thank you for your assistance.

1. What is your sex?   [ ] Female   [ ] Male

2. Do you live on or off campus? [ ] On campus   [ ] Off campus

3. How would you describe your current state of health?
   [ ] Very healthy   [ ] Unhealthy   [ ] Neutral   [ ] Healthy   [ ] Very unhealthy

4. How would you describe your eating habits?
   [ ] Very healthy   [ ] Unhealthy   [ ] Neutral   [ ] Healthy   [ ] Very unhealthy

5. I believe that eating animals is unethical.
   [ ] Strongly disagree   [ ] Disagree   [ ] Neutral   [ ] Agree   [ ] Strongly agree

6. Would you consider changing your eating habits if it would improve your health?
   [ ] Yes   [ ] Maybe   [ ] No

7. A vegetarian diet is a healthy diet.
   [ ] Strongly disagree   [ ] Disagree   [ ] Neutral   [ ] Agree   [ ] Strongly agree

8. Are you a vegetarian? [ ] Yes   [ ] No

9. What do you think are the benefits of a vegetarian diet? (Please explain your answer.)

10. What do you think are the drawbacks of a vegetarian diet? (Please explain your answer.)

Pilot test your questionnaire on friends who are similar to your intended audience. Time how long it takes to complete the questionnaire. Ask for clarity and objectivity of your questions, and then revise your questions accordingly.

During his sophomore year in college, James enrolled in an ethics class that required him to write a midterm paper on a current ethical issue. James had seen a televised news story about People for the Ethical Treatment of Animals (PETA) and decided to research the issue of animal rights. Always an animal lover, James was shocked when he accessed PETA's website and read accounts of how beef cattle and poultry are housed, injected with hormones, and slaughtered. During his junior year, James started to attend PETA meetings on campus and decided to stop eating meat products and become a vegetarian. For his persuasive speech, James wanted to convince his classmates that it was unethical to eat meat products and to persuade them to become vegetarians. To help him learn more about his audience, he constructed the questionnaire shown in Figure B.1.

Administer a Questionnaire

B.2   Gather your data in a manner that ensures anonymous and confidential responses.

After you have constructed your questionnaire, you need to give it to your intended audience. Because the information you gather will shape your speech, administer any questionnaire at least a week before your speech is due. Your written and oral directions should ensure respondent anonymity and confidentiality; people are more likely to provide truthful responses if they think the information cannot be used to embarrass them. You have an ethical responsibility to consider your listeners' interests, respect their privacy, and not mislead them. Remember, asking people to reveal their values, beliefs, attitudes, or behaviors implies an ethical commitment on your part. James ensured respondent anonymity and confidentiality, and he also thanked his classmates for their participation, both orally and on his written questionnaire. To ensure that you do not violate any ethical guidelines, ask your instructor or search your campus's website for information about your school's Office of Research Compliance.

Interpret Questionnaire Responses

B.3 **Interpret questionnaire responses as you develop the supporting materials in your speech.**

After you have administered your questionnaire, you will need to analyze the responses and interpret the results so that you can incorporate the information into your speech. The first step is to organize the responses to each question. For closed questions, simply count the number in each response category. This is called a *frequency count*. James tallied responses for Question 3 (How would you describe your current state of health?) as follows:

> How would you describe your current state of health?
>
> Very healthy = 2
>
> Healthy = 16
>
> Neutral = 1
>
> Unhealthy = 5
>
> Very unhealthy = 0

Compiling responses to open-ended questions is more subjective and time consuming. One method is to summarize responses on separate pieces of paper and then tabulate those according to common themes. For example, James identified poor taste, inconvenience, and a lack of protein as common responses to the open question concerning the drawbacks of a vegetarian diet (Question 10).

Once you have organized the questionnaire responses, you are ready to answer the important question: *What does all this information tell me?* Do your listeners agree or disagree with your position on the topic, or are they neutral? Do their attitudes, beliefs, values, and behaviors vary widely? Do these differences vary according to age, sex, ethnicity, or academic classification? Are there well-worded answers to open questions that you can attribute to the anonymous respondent and use as supporting material?

The payoff for all the work you put into constructing, administering, analyzing, and interpreting the results of your questionnaire is that you have specific information about your audience to help you construct your speech.

Before he administered his questionnaire, James had planned to persuade his audience to become vegetarians by arguing that eating meat supports and sustains poor treatment of animals. After compiling and analyzing his classmates' responses, James discovered that only two students believed that eating animals is unethical; however, twenty said they would consider changing their eating habits if it would improve their health. James used this information to adapt his speech to his audience. Instead of focusing on the ethical issue of eating meat, he emphasized the health benefits of a vegetarian diet. Because a slight majority had listed the lack of protein as a drawback of a vegetarian diet, James explained how protein-rich foods such as beans and tofu could ensure proper nutrition. Next, he outlined some simple steps for selecting tasty vegetarian foods. Because three-fourths of the class lived on campus, he provided several menu selections available in the dining halls and fast-food venues on campus.

James's hard work paid off. He delivered a speech that was adapted to his specific audience, and his classmates were impressed that he made the effort to include them in his speech.

Appendix C
Developing and Delivering
Team Presentations

Learning Objectives

After studying this appendix, you should be able to

C.1 Apply the ten individual and collaborative steps of preparing a team presentation.

C.2 Apply the ten strategies for delivering a team presentation.

Successful athletic teams recognize the importance of working together as a group to accomplish their goals. Business and professional organizations are increasingly using work teams to accomplish their objectives. Communication scholars Thomas Harris and John Sherblom argue that "teams differ substantially from many small groups, because the teams, rather than the leader, control the group process." Teams rely on individual responsibility and shared leadership.[1]

For most of your work in this public speaking class, you have operated alone. You have selected, researched, and organized your speech topics. You have practiced and delivered these speeches standing alone in front of your classmates. Team presentations will tap many of the skills you have already learned while also testing your ability to work productively with others toward a shared goal. International management consultant Ken Blanchard offers a simple, compelling benefit of working in teams: "None of us is as smart as all of us."[2] To be successful, team members must interact and support one another as they prepare and deliver cohesive team presentations.

Preparing a Team Presentation

C.1 Apply the ten individual and collaborative steps of preparing a team presentation.

Although there is no one correct way to prepare for a team presentation, the following ten suggestions will help you work efficiently and produce an effective product. The symbol "•" denotes those steps requiring team interaction; the other steps can be completed individually.

- **Brainstorm about the topic.** Through brainstorming, you will discover what team members already know, and you will uncover numerous ideas for further research. In addition to providing content, brainstorming also serves a relationship function. By giving all members an opportunity to participate, brainstorming gives you a glimpse of your peers' personalities and their approaches to team interactions. You get to know them, and they get to know you. Maintaining an atmosphere of openness and respect during this first meeting gets the team off to a good start. Once you have generated a list of areas concerning your topic, you are ready for the second step.

  Conduct exploratory research. The second phase of your team process is individual research. While there may be some merit in each person selecting a different topic to research, your research roles should not be too rigid. Rather than limiting yourself by topic, you may wish to divide your research by resources. One member may search the Internet, another the library's databases, while a third may interview a professor who is knowledgeable on the topic, and so forth. It is important that you not restrict your discovery to the list of topics you have generated. Exploratory research is also a form of brainstorming. As you look in indexes and read articles, you will uncover more topics. Each team member should try to find a few good sources that are diverse in scope.

- **Discuss and divide the topic into areas of responsibility.** After exploratory research, your team should reconvene to discuss what each member found. Which expectations did your research confirm? Which were contradicted? What topics did you find that you had not anticipated? Your objective at this stage of the team process is to decide on the key areas you wish to investigate. Each person should probably be given primary responsibility for researching a particular area. That person becomes the content expert in that area. While this approach makes research more efficient, it has a drawback. If one person serves as a specialist, the team gambles that he or she will research thoroughly and report findings objectively. If either assumption is not valid, the quantity of information may be insufficient and its quality contaminated. An alternative approach is to assign more than one person to a specific area.

  Research your specific topic area. Your focus should be on the quality of the sources you discover, not on quantity. While your primary goal should be to gather information on your topic, you should also note information related to your colleagues' topics. Jot down sources that may help another team member. If you are researching a relevant Internet source that could benefit another team member, email her or him the URL. Team members who support one another in these and other ways make the process more efficient and, hence, more enjoyable. This usually results in a better product.

Draft an outline of your content area. After you have concluded your initial research but before you meet again with your team, construct an outline of the ideas and information you've found. This step is important because it requires you to make sense of all the information you have collected, and it will expedite the next step when you will share information with the team.

- **Discuss how all the information interrelates.** You are now ready to meet with your team. Members should summarize briefly what they have discovered through their research. After team members have shared their ideas, they should decide which ideas are most important and how these ideas are related. There should be a natural development of the topic that can be divided among team members.

- **Finalize the team presentation format.** The speaking order should already be determined. There are, nevertheless, certain procedural details that the team must decide. Will the first speaker introduce all presenters or will each person introduce the next speaker? Where will the participants sit when they are not speaking: facing the audience or in the front row? The more details you decide beforehand, the fewer distractions you will have on the day you speak.

- **Plan the introduction and conclusion of the presentation.** As previously stated, a presentation should appear to be that of a team and not that of four or five individuals. Consequently, you must work on introducing and concluding the team's comments, and you must incorporate smooth transitions from one speaker's topic to the next. An introduction should state the topic, define important terms, and establish the importance of the subject. A conclusion should summarize what has been presented and end with a strong final statement.

Prepare and practice your presentation. By this time, you know the requirements of an excellent speech and have had the opportunity to deliver a few speeches. Most of our earlier suggestions also apply to your speech in your team's presentation. Some differences are worth noting, however. For example, as part of a team presentation, you will need to refer to your colleagues' comments and perhaps even use some of their supporting materials. The team presentation may also impose physical requirements you have not encountered as a classroom speaker, such as speaking to those seated around you in addition to making direct eye-contact with the audience, or speaking from a seated position.

- **Rehearse and revise the presentation.** Independent practice of your portion of the presentation is important, but that is only one part of rehearsal. The team should practice its entire presentation. Team rehearsal will make participants more confident about their individual presentations and will give the team a feeling of cohesion, meaning "togetherness."

Delivering a Team Presentation

C.2 Apply the ten strategies for delivering a team presentation.

A team presentation is more than just a collection of individual speeches on the same topic. By coordinating your team's content and delivery, you will enhance your collective credibility and message impact. Consider the following ten guidelines to create a polished and proficient team presentation.

Dress appropriately. All presenters should be well groomed and dressed up, rather than dressed too casually. To enhance your team's cohesiveness, you should consider dressing similarly. When athletic teams travel to tournaments and games, they dress alike to bolster the athletes' team spirit.

Introduce the presentation and team members. Provide an agenda for your presentation. What will listeners learn and who will present each section? Will one person introduce all team members at the beginning, or will each person introduce the next presenter?

Organize and deliver the team's ideas. Throughout the presentation, use all the strategies you've learned in this class.

Incorporate smooth transitions from one person to the next. A seamless presentation requires planning and practice. Just as you used transition statements to enhance the flow of your individual speeches, it is essential that the transitions from one speaker to the next are smooth in your team presentation.

Have one person design and produce all presentational aids. This will ensure that their design and appearance are consistent.

Have one person display all presentational aids except when he or she is speaking. Assigning one person to handle and project all the aids will help make the presentation flow smoothly and consistently.

Assign someone to keep time and provide other signals to the team. Use subtle but clear time signals so that team members do not exceed their time limits. This person may also signal when presenters are speaking too softly or too rapidly.

Conclude the main part of your presentation. Often the person who introduced the presentation also concludes the presentation.

Conduct a question-and-answer session. If you are allowed a Q & A period, decide who will manage it. Will one person or several answer questions from the audience? Who will recognize those who want to ask questions? Review the guidelines discussed in the "Theory Into Practice" box in Chapter 18.

And, of course, practice, practice, practice. Successful team presentations require that you practice both individually and as a team. Practicing may not guarantee perfection, but it can enhance your mastery of public speaking, both in this class and in the future.

Following the procedures we have described should result in a carefully planned, conscientiously researched, adequately supported, and well-delivered team presentation. More than that, however, your presentation should also demonstrate the spontaneity, goodwill, and camaraderie that will likely have developed if members of your team have functioned effectively and productively together.

Appendix D
Sample Speeches

Flash Mobs[1]

Jennell Chu, San Antonio College

Jennell Chu delivered the following classroom speech in the spring of 2011. Notice her simple structure and her use of examples that would be familiar to many of her listeners.

1 On June 3, 2003, over 100 people gathered in New York City's Macy's department store, on the ninth floor, around an expensive rug. When asked what they were doing, they would each respond that they all lived together on the outskirts of town and were buying a rug. Then they just left. Later that day about 200 people gathered in the lobby of the Grand Hyatt New York and clapped for 15 seconds. Then, once again, they just dispersed.

2 According to Kenneth Baldauf, who studied these and other such occasions for his ebook *Emerge with Computer Concepts*, these are part of a growing trend called flash mobs, which is what I will be talking about today.

3 According to Baldauf, a flash mob is a group of people who assemble suddenly in a public place, do something unusual, and then disperse in order to gain attention or to create confusion and sometimes amusement. Now, I've actually participated in a few flash mobs myself and they have always been a lot of fun without any ill intent behind them. And as flash mobs are a trend that you're seeing more and more today, it is good to know common types of flash mobs and why these occasions are becoming so common.

4 Now, first I will be speaking about the common types of flash mobs. Dance flash mobs are one of the most common types of flash mobs that you will see. And what happens in them is that a group of people get together and learn how to do choreography to set to music. And a lot of the times these are done as tributes to the artists themselves, such as the group Flash Amsterdam who does Michael Jackson tributes. So they would go out and do things to his classic songs such as "Beat It" and "Billie Jean" and so many others.

5 Now freeze flash mobs are another type of common flash mob. These began when the group Improv Everywhere started, filmed at the Grand Central Station in New York. You can read more about this at their website www.improveverywhere .com underneath "Frozen Grand Central." What they did [was] a group of people just went to the station and then they just froze. It didn't matter if they were talking, whether they were taking a picture, or even one man I remember dropped his notes on the floor and was starting to pick them up. They just froze and did not move for a certain amount of time. Then, afterwards, by some certain signal, they just once again started going on with their daily lives. Now according to Baldauf, the largest freeze flash mob ever done was in Paris, where over 3,000 people participated.

6 And another type of common flash mob that you've seen doesn't have a set method, as [do] dance and freeze flash mobs; it's more general, one that you can come up with for yourself. These flash mobs are done in support [of] or opposition to a certain idea. The World News Network picked up on a flash mob done by a group, United Way, in Washington Station. What this group did [was] they went into the station and then they just began undressing. And when they undressed, you could see across their T-shirts a slogan that said, "Live United." This was to show support of how all people in the world should live together in harmony, without any prejudice. So whether it's a dance flash mob, a freeze flash mob, or a flash mob to show your support for or opposition [to] something, these are just some of the common types that you will see today.

7 Now the second thing I will be speaking about is why flash mobs are becoming so common in today's society. The Internet is a big reason why flash mobs are so common nowadays. Thanks to the Internet we have social networking sites such as Facebook, Twitter, MySpace, and so many others that it is just so easy for a large group of people to come together for one purpose. And of course there's also YouTube. With YouTube, if you search the words "flash mob," you can come up with thousands of videos that you just spend hours watching because [they are] very entertaining to watch. And once on to these videos, people watch them, think they're fun, then they eventually want to be part of one or they want to start their own. And that, of course, just helps spread the trend all over the world.

8 Cell phones are another big reason why flash mobs are so common. Nowadays, cell phones are basically mini-computers. Everywhere you go, you have the Internet, so once again you have those social networking sites. Then you also have your instant access to your email, and there's also text messaging. So now it's just so easy to get the news spread out to everyone. And you can even make [a flash mob] up as soon as [you] get the idea because you can just send it out to everyone in your phone book, and they can send it out to more people [who can send it on to] more people. And you can just have a huge group.

9 And, of course, flash mobs are themselves just becoming more mainstream these days. There are businesses around the world [that] are using flash mobs as a way of advertising. And then, of course, there are television shows which are becoming more used to the idea of flash mobs and are incorporating them in [their programs]. Erica Futterman even stated in the *Rolling Stone*'s February 9th edition that the popular show "Glee" used a flash mob in order for one of the show's characters to attempt to get a date on the Valentine's episode. So as you can see, the Internet, cell phones, and just by flash mobs becoming more mainstream [are] reason[s] why these occurrences are becoming so much more common in today's society.

10 So by now you should know some of the common types of flash mobs and why they are becoming so common. And, like I said, flash mobs can be anything—they can be complex like a dance flash mob, where you have hundreds of people learning choreography. Or, you can just get people to start a pillow fight in a random street. Or, if you're like me, you'll wind up downtown with a group of girls and start singing the "Sailor Moon" theme song. But any way you start, while each individual flash mob will appear and then quickly disappear, the trend of flash mobs themselves doesn't appear to be disappearing quite as quickly.

Gum Chewers[2]

Austin Willis, Penn State Hazleton

Austin delivered this informative speech in a Communication Arts & Sciences class at Penn State Hazleton. Notice Austin's use of a pro-con division strategy and internal signposts within each key idea.

1 By a show of hands, how many of you in this room chew gum? [20 of 23 students raised their hands] Now, how many of you don't chew gum? [3 students raised their hands] My point exactly.

2 In fact, researchers Britt, Collins, and Cohen confirmed that this class is similar to the rest of the college student population. In a survey consisting of American undergraduate students, "nearly 87 percent confirmed that they chew gum at least occasionally." Based on this research, it is no surprise that chewing gum has grown into a popular pastime, as stated by the International Chewing Gum Association. Yes, there really is an International Chewing Gum Association.

3 "[C]hewing gum has grown into being one of the world's oldest candies [and] has even become a billion dollar industry" as stated by Wrigley, a leading gum production company, in a statement on Statisticbrain.com.

4 Today, I will inform you first on the positive effects of chewing gum, and second, I will inform you on the negative effects of gum chewing.

5 First, let's uncover the positive effects of chewing gum. Specifically, we will focus on the ideas that chewing gum can help enhance persons' ability to focus, maintain their stress, and even enhance their memory.

6 First, we'll consider the notion that chewing gum helps us focus. In *Psychological Reports* 2009, Tänzer and colleagues reported the results of their study of gum chewing and the abilities of 8- to 9-year-old students to maintain focus during a 16-minute test. Although students who chewed gum didn't perform so well in the first 12 minutes, they outperformed the no-gum control group in the last 4 minutes. The authors concluded that chewing gum "had a significant and positive effect on concentration performance." Similar results have been reported in more recent studies. Specifically, in 2011, Tucha and Simpson reported that chewing gum has a positive effect on healthy adults' abilities in maintaining focus during extended periods of time. After understanding how gum affects our ability to focus, let us go over how chewing gum may positively impact our stress levels.

7 Second, let's review how chewing gum may help us manage our stress. Chewing gum is believed to relax the mind. When it comes to dealing with stress, two studies were conducted by researchers Zibell and Madansky [who] compared frequent and infrequent gum chewers to see how both manage their stress. "Fifty-six percent of frequent gum chewers and 42 percent of infrequent [gum] chewers stated that managing their stress is a reason why they chew gum." Following this survey, the State-Trait Anxiety Inventory was administered, which is one approach of assessing stress. Studies revealed that in abstaining of chewing gum resulted in higher levels of anxiety and stress among all participants. Not only may chewing gum relieve stress, it may also enhance our memory.

8 Third, chewing gum may enhance our memory. While studying, chewing gum can help people focus, and apparently, if people chew the same flavor of gum during an exam as when they studied, it can even boost their memory. In fact, "an increase of learning performance of at least 30 percent was claimed following chewing gum" as stated in an August of 2012 article titled "Gum Chewing and Cognition: An Overview" by researchers Tucha and Koerts. Moreover, there's a difference between *immediate* and *delayed memory*. Researchers Wilkinson and colleagues published a study revealing significant improvements in both immediate and delayed memory. In order to test this study, participants had to remember a list of 15 words, and the delayed recall was within less than an hour. This study indicated that a recall of information improved when people chew[ed] gum during the learning period. In addition to the positive effects of chewing gum, it should be noted that chewing gum has also been found to have negative effects on people, or even no effects at all.

9 Second, let's discuss the negative implications of chewing gum.

10 First, let's go over the questionable belief that chewing gum has the ability to enhance our abilities to focus. A plethora of experiments found no connection between chewing gum and people's ability to focus. According to a *Journal of Behavioral and Neuroscience Research* article titled "A Review of the Evidence that Chewing Gum Affects Stress, Alertness and Cognition," two experiments found "alertness reaction time was significantly slower for a spearmint gum control group compared to not chewing [gum]" at all, indicating that chewing gum slows down and inhibits a person's full potential to focus. Researcher Smith in 2010 challenged this claim by concluding that gum led to a prolonged attention rate by using a choice reaction time task. Unfortunately, studies only showed the relationship between a person's positive mood and their attention spans rather than the physicality of chewing gum and their attention rates. Not only has chewing gum been found to have no impact on a person's ability to focus, but it also showed no improvement on controlling stress.

11 Second, I will discuss the inconsistent relationships found between chewing gum and stress. Stress has become a major reason why people chew gum, but how much stress does this habit truly relieve? The answer to this question could be none at all. For instance, in 2009, researchers Torney, Johnson, and Miles were unable to find a benefit of chewing gum related to self-reported stress. In order to test this, they utilized an anagram in which participants had to solve and were hoping that this would cause stress through embarrassment if participants were unable to solve the anagram. However, no increased stress was found, which suggests that gum has no effect on the different levels of acute stress. After discussing the relationship between chewing gum and stress, we can continue by discussing how gum affects our memory.

12 Third, does chewing gum really enhance our memory? Researchers Johnson and Miles conducted two separate experiments in 2008 to test the effects of chewing gum on people's memory. Their results included the following statement: "Although flavorless gum and mint-flavored strips reported change in current mouth activity . . . [t]hey didn't [show signs] that induce context-dependent memory." This indicates that neither the type of gum nor the sensation of chewing aids a person's ability to recall information. Further research showed that chewing gum during a learning period actually may cause *poorer* recall. Researchers are continually attempting to discover connections between chewing gum and maintaining our memory. However, the phenomenon of gum chewing is very robust and it is unclear to determine whether or not chewing gum is actually beneficial.

13 Today, I have talked about both the positive and possibly the negative effects that gum chewing can have on people's ability to focus, maintain their stress, and even strengthen their memory. I hope I provided all of you with a unique perspective on the contradicting beliefs of gum chewing.

14 With the difficulty of proving whether or not the pros or cons of gum chewing are stronger, researchers will continue to study the effects of chewing gum. But in the meantime, for those of you who are fans of the product, if you desire to, keep on chewing.

The New Catch-22: Unemployment Discrimination[3]

Michael Kelley, Kansas State University

Michael delivered this persuasive speech and placed second at the 2012 Interstate Oratorical Association contest. Notice how he used a problem–solution format to frame his discussion of jobless discrimination.

1 In Joseph Heller's classic novel *Catch-22*, a group of fighter pilots serving during World War II search desperately for a way out. They can say that they are insane and be removed from combat, but in admitting that they're insane, they prove that they are in fact sane and must continue fighting. That is the famous [c]atch-22 that keeps them locked into jobs they don't want.

2 Unfortunately, there is a new [c]atch-22 that keeps people from getting the jobs they so desperately seek. As ABC news reported on March 4, 2011, more and more employers are saying that in order to have a job you must already be employed somewhere else. So if you have a job, you can apply, but if you are unemployed, you can't? Welcome to the newest [c]atch-22: jobless discrimination.

3 According to *Time* magazine on May 23, 2011, "Companies are denying job searchers interviews on the basis of their unemployment at a time when unemployment is the highest it's been in decades." According to the National Employment Law Project of July 12, 2011, jobless discrimination occurs when a company or business refuses to employ individuals unless they are already employed elsewhere.

4 This should alarm us for several reasons. Now even though the economy is beginning to show signs of recovery, the Bureau of Labor Statistics of April 6, 2012, still points out there are 5.3 million Americans who have been unemployed for seven months or more because of the recession. It's not fair to discriminate against them. Second, many of us at this tournament will soon be looking for jobs in the "real world." And I'm guessing we won't have an employment track record either—unless you count the fast food industry. Jobless discrimination threatens us as well. We need to make jobless discrimination just as illegal as refusing to hire people because of their sex, race, or religion.

5 In order to do so, we must first reveal the damage created by this discrimination, second refute its reasoning, and finally provide the specific steps to solve what the National Employment Law Project's executive director Christine Owens fears "is becoming business as usual."

6 You might think that jobless discrimination only affects the unemployed, but you have to understand that it's creating damage for all of us in two ways: those out of work are going to have a tougher time even applying for a job, and ultimately this prolongs the recession as a whole.

7 First, employers are refusing to even interview potential employees because they've been out of work. The *National Law Review* of March 16, 2011, explains that employment organizations have reported job postings that specifically exclude the unemployed. "These postings ranged from requirements that the

person has been employed in the last six months to specific announcements that no unemployed candidates will be considered at all." In this instance and countless others, job seekers are being told not to apply for a job because they don't have a job already. This is not a rare instance either. *The New York Times* of July 26, 2011, explains that a recent review of job searching sites, such as Monster.com, Career Builder, and Craigslist had hundreds of job listings that specifically excluded the unemployed from consideration. It's the same story for 46-year-old Kim Keough, who has been looking for another position since losing her previous job in human resources back in 2008. She explains to the *Wall Street Journal* of February 24, 2012, "Recruiters have told me not to bother sending a résumé if I'm not currently employed. It's damned if you do, damned if you don't."

8 Second, even if you do have a job, we have to consider the damage jobless discrimination creates for our overall economy. Because, with so many job seekers turned away, the pace and strength of the recovery are called into question. The *Los Angeles Times* of June 3, 2011, puts it like this: When the unemployed can't buy more than what they actually need, those who are employed are paid less. With less money in hand, consumers have less purchasing power, which ultimately pushes companies to be even more selective when hiring new recruits. This creates a terrible cycle that could have a profoundly negative effect on Americans for generations.

9 So if jobless discrimination creates so much damage, the reasonable question is why do employers pursue this policy? To explain, there are two reasons for this shortsighted strategy: it's legal, and the unemployed are considered subpar applicants.

10 Initially, employers practice jobless discrimination because they can. The jobless as a group are not protected from employment discrimination. As *The New York Times* of February 19, 2011, reveals, no current legislation specifically protects the rights of those without a job. This is why the EEOC [Equal Employment Opportunity Commission] has said that while they are keeping an eye on jobless discrimination complaints, they can't actually do anything about it.

11 And without legal protection, the unemployed face the second reason. As Professor Helen Norton of the University of Colorado explained in a February 16, 2011, news release from the Equal Employment Opportunity Commission, the rationale for jobless discrimination is that employers believe that those who've been out of work are not good employees and that their job skills are not up to par. What's especially damaging is the assumption that if you don't already have a job, you must be some sort of trouble-maker. Reeve Zimmerman, a hospitality management recruiter for Goodwin and Associates, explained in the *Huffington Post* on October 8, 2010, an individual without a job raises red flags because employers wonder if that person was let go because of improper conduct or something of that nature. As a result, employers regard their unemployment as something caused by the employee even without any hard evidence to support the claim.

12 Now in a robust economy, that argument might hold merit, but when millions of people have lost their jobs because of a recession that according to *Reuters* on July 15, 2011, threatens to rival the Great Depression, the assumption that the unemployed are bad options just doesn't make sense. Obviously, some people did lose their jobs because they were bad employees. But when a nation is facing the rate of unemployment we see in the United States, it's just as obvious that a good number of the unemployed are victims of an economy gone badly. Job discrimination is a legal way to unfairly punish those people. If we're going to legally limit job

applications to those who already have jobs, then we're allowing a [c]atch-22 even Joseph Heller could never have imagined.

13 Now, you're probably thinking that if the economy's beginning to recover, won't this problem just go away? But because our economy will always cycle through patches of good and bad fortune, we will inevitably have periods of high unemployment. While we can't do much about that, we can take steps to ensure that jobless discrimination is no longer a legal option. So let's finally look to how we [can] solve the employment [c]atch-22. We need to do two things: First, make jobless discrimination illegal and second, put pressure on the businesses that have this misguided policy.

14 Initially, the simple answer is for our government to pass legislation regarding the issue. Now the Fair Employment Opportunity Act of 2011, which would prohibit this sort of discrimination, was introduced on July 12, 2011, but is stuck in committee. While I strongly urge you to write [to] your congressional representative on this matter, a more feasible solution may be to get a similar measure passed on the state level. According to the *Los Angeles Times* of January 7, 2012, New Jersey's governor Chris Christie signed a bill into law last March that prohibits openly requiring current employment for applicants. California and several other states are also considering similar measures. Contact your state representative to get a similar measure passed in your state, because if enough states pass this, our national legislators will realize the need for this protection at a federal level.

15 But what do we do until these various pieces of legislation become law? This is where our second responsibility applies. We need to boycott the employers that continue to refuse applications from those who are currently unemployed. In the previously cited National Employment Law Project's briefing, it named several organizations that have listed job postings that explicitly bar those who are out of work, such as: Allstate Insurance, Johns Hopkins University, and the Los Angeles Bar Career Center. I have business cards with a link to the site and my contact email if you'd like a form letter to send to these companies, available after the round. By boycotting these companies and supporting those that don't participate in this heinous practice, we can send a clear message that refusing to hire those who are without a job will not be tolerated by the American consumer.

16 Being unemployed is hard enough, but today we can understand why it's become that much more difficult by understanding the damage, reasons, and solutions to jobless discrimination.

17 In Joseph Heller's book, a few lucky pilots were able to find a way around the [c]atch-22. However, I continue to deliver this speech for my mother and father, and the millions of others still trapped in this new [c]atch-22. It is imperative that this problem be adequately addressed in order to preserve an equal playing field and give all Americans looking for work a fighting chance.

Steganography: Hidden Messages[4]

Julian Petrin Fray, San Antonio College

Julian found her informative speech topic during the flurry of Internet communication about national security following the tragedy of 9/11. She heightened listener interest in this novel topic by showing its ancient origins. Julian won first place in informative speaking at the Texas Community College Speech and Theater Association state tournament in the spring of 2002.

1 In the movie *Along Came a Spider*, students of influential Washington politicians attend an elite, private school. The classrooms in this school don't look like what you might see in an ordinary public school. Here, students are assigned their own computers, all of which are networked together. As the instructor proceeds through his lesson, the students are prompted to follow along on their own screens. The use of this kind of technology may suggest wisdom beyond their years, but these students are still very much like other fourth graders. When the character Megan Rose wants to pass a note in class, she doesn't resort to the conventional folded-up piece of paper. Instead, she uses her computer to send an innocent-looking picture of a tiger to her friend, Dimitri. Dimitri then takes the picture and applies a simple program, thereby revealing a hidden message.

2 These students are using the very complex technology of steganography to accomplish a very simple goal. Steganography has existed throughout history, but just recently it has been given new attention. In fact, this old technique has been given new applications due to today's technology. This new use allows messages to pass, undetected, through many different media, including video, email, and digital photographs. This means that every image you view on your computer has the potential to contain a hidden message. This message can come in many different formats, including as a virus that can interfere with the files on your hard drive.

3 So today, we'll first discuss what steganography is and how it came into existence. Second, we will see exactly how steganography works. Finally, we'll look at its current uses and possible future applications.

4 First, then, what is steganography? As defined by Richard Lewis, of the System Administration, Networking, and Security Institute, steganography literally means "covered writing" and is the art of concealing the very existence of a message. The purpose of steganography is to hide a message within another form of communication in such a way that prevents an observer from learning that anything unusual is taking place.

5 Steganography has a long and rich history in warfare. One of the first recorded instances of its use is written in the *History of Herodotus*. In ancient Greece, messages were conveyed using wax tablets. In one story, Demeratus wanted to notify his hometown of Sparta that Xerxes was intending to invade the Peloponnesus. To ensure that the message would not be intercepted, he scraped the wax off of the tablets and wrote his message on the underlying wood. He recovered the tablets with wax so that they appeared to be blank. In this form, they could pass undetected back to Sparta. Once in Sparta, the wax was melted off, revealing the hidden message.

6 Another method of steganography is to use invisible inks. According to Declan McCullagh, in the February 2, 2001, edition of *Wired News,* these inks were used as recently as World War II. A covert message could be written between the lines of a seemingly innocuous letter. The most common inks used were milk, vinegar, fruit juices, and even urine. These liquids would darken when heated, thereby revealing the hidden messages. Later, with the use of other chemicals, the invisible ink became even harder to detect.

7 Just as Demeratus hid his message, we can now hide a message in an electronic format so that it's almost undetectable. The wax tablet has given way to the electronic file, but the goal remains the same: to obscure the message to all but the intended viewer. So, second, let's take a closer look at how steganography works.

8 In his article on steganography at the Johnson and Johnson Technology Consultants website, www.jjtc.com, last accessed on September 16, 2001, Neil F. Johnson, a professor at George Mason University, explains how these messages are embedded. In every computer file, there is a large amount of "empty" space, or space that is not integral to the file. These "low-order" bits can be changed slightly without alerting the human senses. Steganography takes advantage of this by embedding the digital message in these bits. You see, in a computer, an image is simply an array of numbers that represents light intensities at various points called pixels. Each pixel can contain up to three bytes of information, but most images do not require that amount of memory. So the steganographic program can simply utilize the "extra" bytes in those pixels. This creates a slight degradation in the quality of the photograph. Look at this picture of a chapel [Julian shows Photograph 1]. Now, take a look at this picture [Julian shows Photograph 2]. While they initially appear to be identical, you might notice the slight degradation in the second photograph. The reason for this is that Photograph 2 actually contains an aerial view of the Pentagon, encoded using steganography [Julian shows Photograph 3]. The degradation, noted previously, is somewhat helpful in detecting a hidden message, but it's not a very effective tool. The degradation is so slight that most people won't even notice it, even when compared side by side with the original.

9 After hiding, then sending the message, the next step is to extract it. This is the easiest step because it's done by the computer. According to Dr. Johnson, using a steganalysis program, your computer can pull out the message and display it. Each day, many of us receive emails from various friends, family, and co-workers. Many of these contain jokes or images. These images are perfect vessels for steganographic messages. Much like the U.S. postal workers were unwitting couriers of the anthrax virus, you too might just be propagating covert information without your knowledge.

10 Now that we understand how steganography works, let's look, finally, at some of its applications. One of the most unsettling aspects about this technology is its very nature: the sending and receiving of covert messages. Consider this example, given by Robert Vamosi, in the June 27, 2001, edition of the *ZDNet News:* You work for the National Security Agency monitoring terrorist activities. In the past week, you have recorded a large increase in the number of encrypted emails being sent. This may tip you off to a forthcoming event, or terrorist activity. At the very least, your suspicions will be aroused and cause you to take a closer look at those emails. Then consider that, instead of being able to monitor obviously encrypted emails, you had to monitor the subtle patterns of every single image on the Internet. This is the exact reason terrorists, including the infamous Osama bin Laden, use steganography to communicate. Because these embedded images can be posted to free websites, terrorists can convey their messages around the world without ever tipping off major security officials. Jack Kelley, in his June 6, 2001, article in *USA Today*, states that steganography has become so fundamental to the operations of these groups that bin Laden and other Muslim extremists are teaching it at their camps in Afghanistan and the Sudan.

11 On a more local level, steganography can be a very important tool for businesses. For example, let's say you work in New York City for a large software firm. You've just written a breakthrough program that has immense possibilities. The source code for this program needs to be sent to the parent company, located in California, but you're afraid that it may be intercepted. Prior to copyrighting the program, the only thing that keeps your program from being used by another developer is that they don't have access to your source code. Keeping this source code protected is very important and shouldn't be trusted to a simple encrypted email. So, you can embed the source code using steganography and send the email without worrying about its interception.

12 For the future, we can expect to see an increase in this type of communication. The technologies allowing messages to be hidden will increase in sophistication to reduce the amount of degradation, thereby making it even more difficult to detect these messages.

13 Today we have explored a new technology that can change the way we communicate. We have examined what steganography is and how it works. We have also explored current and future applications for this technology.

14 Current steganography is a new and exciting twist on an old form of communication. The uses I have shown you today are but a small portion of the possibilities for this technology. From terrorists to CEOs, this technology has a wide range of applications. So next time you open an email and see a picture of a family member or a familiar scene, you might think about what may be in the image that you're just not seeing.

The Problem with Food Aid[5]

Chiwoneso Beverley Tinago, William Carey University

Chiwoneso placed second at the 2009 Interstate Oratorical Association contest. Notice how she reveals her personal commitment and connection to the topic near the end of her persuasive speech.

1 Muna is an eight-year-old girl from Mulonda, Zambia. Every morning she walks to a food distribution point set up by the World Food Program at a nearby hospital. She holds tightly to her battered tin cup as she waits in line for hours to receive the mixture of corn and soy powder, but the stocks are running low and like every other day, she walks home empty-handed.

2 Muna's reality is that she is an AIDS orphan who struggles to stay alive, but she will not die from AIDS; more than likely she will die of hunger. This story is becoming all too common and was taken from *The New York Times* of January 17, 2009. The latest estimates from the UN Food and Agriculture Organization (FAO) show that another 40 million people were pushed into hunger in 2008 as a result of higher food prices. The FAO warned that the ongoing economic crisis could tip even more people into hunger and poverty.

3 Since the late 1960s, wealthy countries have been obligated by the Food Aid Convention to feed the hungry. However, a major part of the problem that the hungry face today is the nature of the food aid itself. This is not a new issue, but as the world's remaining arable farmland comes under increasing pressure from climate change and the development of biofuels, it is an issue that policy makers, humanitarian workers, and politicians need to resolve if widespread world hunger is ever to be alleviated.

4 Today, we will reveal the current problems inherent in the global food aid policy, then examine some of the causes before finally providing some workable and desperately needed solutions.

5 In August 2007, one of the biggest and well-known American charity organizations, CARE, announced that it was turning down $45 million a year in

food from the U.S. government. According to the USAID [United States Agency for International Development] website updated daily, the U.S. provides nearly 60 percent of the world's food aid—that's nearly double the amount provided by European countries combined. Until this day, CARE claims that the way U.S. aid is structured causes, rather than reduces, hunger in the countries where it is received. Let's assess their claims by revealing the current problems in the food aid policy. These problems are threefold: ineffective use of aid money, monetization, and undercutting of local economies.

6 First. Transporting thousands of tons of food from the United States is a costly and timely process. The *Bloomberg News* of December 8, 2008, told the story of how a bag of corn stamped "US Aid from the American people" took more than 6 months to reach Ethiopian native Haylar Ayako. The corn had traveled more than 12,000 miles by rail, ship, and truck. Warehouse-stays punctuated each leg of the journey until the corn finally arrived in the village of Shala-Luka. But by that time Haylar had buried seven of his grandchildren. According to the *World Politics Review* of December 19, 2008, transporting the food drains needed funds from the actual provision of food aid. By the time all the costs are figured in, it's like every dollar worth of food ends up costing three dollars to get [the food] to the people who need it.

7 Second. Most of us view food aid as simply free food given to needy people. This is not entirely true. The *Seattle Times* of November 11, 2008, states that some food that is transported falls into the hands of aid agencies who in turn sell the grain to local communities and use the revenue to finance their development programs. This means that a large portion—even a majority—of food donated as project food aid is not used as food at all but is converted to cash. This is known as monetization. More than likely, food ends up going to those who can afford it instead of whose who desperately need it.

8 Third. The introduction of imported food in certain regions removes farmers' incentives to produce. According to the WTO [World Trade Organization] website updated daily, the grain that the agencies are selling is undercutting local farming since the aid grain is cheaper than the local grain. This puts local farmers out of business and deeper into poverty and, in the long run, becomes part of a process by which those countries lose the means to develop.

9 Now, the U.S. does not stand alone in the food aid problem. Countries like Canada and South Korea also sell food aid; however, more attention has been placed on the U.S. because it has a larger sphere of influence since it provides the most food aid. So with that in mind, having outlined the problem, let us move on and examine some of the causes. These problems are twofold: current U.S. legislation and lack of regulation.

10 First. According to the aforementioned *Seattle Times* article, U.S. legislation requires that 75 percent of all food aid shipments be sent aboard U.S.–flagged carriers. The U.S. also buys grain used for food aid from U.S. farms. But these are far from being family farms. A U.S. Government Accountability Office study released last year in April noted that just 18 U.S. companies were deemed eligible to bid for food aid contracts, with two of the country's largest agribusinesses, Cargill and Kalama Export Company, earning $28 million in food aid contracts in March and April 2008 alone.

11 Second. Another cause is [the] lack of regulation. The Food Aid Convention is the main international agreement governing food aid. According to the WFP website updated daily, the convention has no mechanism for determining food

aid effectiveness or for evaluating performance of individual donors. Moreover, it operates with little transparency, providing remarkably little public information on its deliberations. Thus, this lack of effectiveness and transparency allows for practices like monetization to take place.

12 By no means are we denying the positive accomplishments of food aid programs, but it is obvious that the current policy on food aid is both self-interested and politicized; thus, action needs to be taken on the international, governmental, and personal levels. First and most important, donor countries need to negotiate a new global food aid compact to replace the languishing Food Aid Convention. The new agreement would strengthen effectiveness and accountability by officially doing away with monetization of food aid and requiring that donors purchase food aid locally or closer to the needy region whenever possible. Programs like Purchase for Progress, which was formed by the World Food Program and the Bill and Melinda Gates Foundation in September 2008, now buy 70 percent of all their food aid in developing countries like Malawi and India. This allows countries to develop their own agriculture economies and allows food to move more quickly and cost-effectively to the people who need it most.

13 Second. Change is needed in the current U.S. food aid legislation. In January 2008, American growers, processors, and transporters fought off a proposal before Congress that would speed deliveries of food aid by buying at least 25 percent more food closer to needy regions. This proposal must be reconsidered under the new Obama administration, and it is essential to point out that the proposal does not ask for more money, but rather, asks that the 2 billion dollars that is currently available for food aid be utilized wisely in order to feed the most people.

14 Finally, on a more personal level, if you donate money to any aid organizations, be more aware of how your money is being used. I recently started an initiative on campus called students turning hunger into hope, which encourages the other 44 organizations on campus to use the 2008–2009 school year as a food aid platform by supporting organizations that use cost-effective food aid programs. At the end of my speech, I will be handing out a card with a list of some of these organizations. Now if you are unable to donate money, then I encourage you to visit www.thehungersite.com. Click on the orange Give box on the main page, and the site sponsors led by Mercy Corps International will pay for cups of food to be given to children at numerous schools in developing countries at no cost to you. Last year the site fed over 72 million children.

15 Today, we have revealed the current problems inherent in the global food policy, then examined some of the causes before finally providing some solutions. The plight of the hungry is sometimes difficult to fathom. I have been a recipient of food aid after my country suffered a severe drought in the 90s, but unlike Muna, Haylar, and the other 25,000 people who die from hunger every day, the food arrived just in time. When President John F. Kennedy named the Food for Peace program in 1961, he said, "Food is strength, and food is freedom, and food is a helping to people around the world whose goodwill and friendship we want." That may be true, but it would be imprudent of us to forget that food is food. As governments and aid agencies worry about losing money if an overhaul of the global food aid policy is achieved, it is essential to remember now more than ever that losing once had a kinder, nobler name—giving.

Discussion of Oprah Winfrey's Eulogy for Rosa Parks

On the evening of December 1, 1955, a seamstress in Montgomery, Alabama, was going home after work. Sitting in a seat on a public bus, this black woman was told by the driver to give up her seat to a white man. She paused and quietly refused to move to the back of the bus. Rosa Parks was arrested and later convicted of violating a law that enforced this segregation. These events, combined with others, precipitated the 381-day Montgomery Bus Boycott to challenge segregated public transportation laws. The boycott was led, in large part, by a young black minister, Martin Luther King, Jr.

On October 31, 2005, in the Metropolitan AME Church in Washington, D.C., Oprah Winfrey delivered a eulogy at a memorial service for Rosa Parks. Oprah reflected on the courage and character of the woman often called the first lady of the civil rights movement. You can find this eulogy in print and on the Internet. It's interesting to read the eulogy, then hear it on audio, and then see it on video. You will observe how each of these channels shapes your interpretation of this speech of tribute.

We invite you to explore more of the history and significance of Rosa Parks. Oprah Winfrey's eulogy is her tribute for a seamstress who sat on a bus and refused to be moved and, in doing so, "made life better for us all."

Discussion of Martin Luther King, Jr.'s "I Have a Dream" Speech

Speaking from the steps of the Lincoln Memorial on August 28, 1963, Martin Luther King, Jr., delivered the keynote address of the March on Washington, D.C., for civil rights. Many scholars consider this the greatest American speech of the twentieth century.

You can access a transcript, the audio, the video, and commentary of the Reverend King's address by typing "I Have a Dream speech" into an Internet search. Our Google search generated more than 80 million hits in .28 seconds, so select carefully and wisely. Three of our favorite sites are the following.

American Rhetoric provides free full text, audio, and pay-for-play video of Dr. King's speech.

You can also listen to the speech—as well as other speeches—and read selected papers at The Martin Luther King, Jr. Research and Education Institute, located at Stanford University. Click on "I Have a Dream" and "March on Washington" for excellent background information.

Coretta Scott King established The Martin Luther King, Jr. Center for Nonviolent Social Change as a "definitive source for accurate information on the life, legacy, and teachings of Dr. and Mrs. Martin Luther King, Jr." Click on links to Dr. King's speeches, sermons, quotations, and additional resources.

Endnotes

Chapter 1

1. For excellent discussions of the benefits of public speaking, consult the following three sources: Stephen K. Hunt, Cheri J. Simonds, and Brent K. Simonds, "Uniquely Qualified, Distinctively Competent: Delivering 21st Century Skills in the Basic Course," *Basic Communication Course Annual* 1, no. 1 (2009), 1–29; Sherwyn P. Morreale, Michael M. Osborn, and Judy C. Pearson, "Why Communication is Important: A Rationale for the Centrality of the Study of Communication," *Journal of the Association for Communication Administration* 29, no. 1 (2000): 1–25; Sherwyn P. Morreale and Judy C. Pearson, "Why Communication Education is Important: The Centrality of the Discipline for the 21st Century," *Communication Education* 57, no. 2 (2008): 224–240.

2. Thomas M. Scheidel, *Persuasive Speaking* (Glenview, IL: Scott, Foresman, 1967), 2.

3. C. K. Ogden and I. A. Richards, *The Meaning of Meaning*, 9th ed. (New York: Harcourt, Brace, 1953), 10–12. Chapter 1, "Thoughts, Words and Things" (pp. 1–23), explains in detail the relationships among symbols, referents, and interpreters.

4. HNN Staff, "So What Does Jihad Really Mean?" *History News Network,* accessed June 18, 2002, www.historynewsnetwork.org/articles/article.html?id=774.

5. "'Jihad' Dropped from Harvard Student's Speech," *CNN.com,* accessed June 18, 2002, wysiwyg://153/http://fyi.cnn.com/2002/f...dnews/05/31/harvard.jihad.ap/index.html.

6. Karlyn Kohrs Campbell, *The Rhetorical Act*, 2nd ed. (Belmont, CA: Wadsworth, 1996), 119.

7. National Center for Educational Statistics, *National Assessment of College Student Learning: Identifying College Graduates' Essential Skills in Writing, Speech and Listening, and Critical Thinking,* NCES 95-001 (Washington, DC: GPO, May 1995), 122.

8. Robert Ennis, "A Taxonomy of Critical Thinking Dispositions and Abilities," in *Teaching Thinking Skills: Theory and Practice*, ed. Joan Boykoff Baron and Robert Sternberg (New York: W. H. Freeman, 1987), 10.

9. June Stark, "Critical Thinking: Taking the Road Less Traveled," *Nursing* 95 (November 1995): 55.

10. National Assessment of Educational Progress, *Reading, Writing and Thinking: Results from the 1979–80 National Assessment of Reading and Literature*, Report No. 11-L-01 (Washington, DC: GPO, October 1981), 5.

Chapter 2

1. Mark M. Monmonier, *Mapping It Out: Expository Cartography for the Humanities and Social Sciences* (Chicago: University of Chicago Press, 1993), 140. We are grateful to Professor Jeremy Crampton of George Mason University for directing us to this source.

2. Fabien A. P. Petitcolas, "Digital Watermarking and Steganography," *The Information Hiding Homepage*, last modified January 28, 2002, www.cl.cam.ac.uk/~fapp2/steganography. We are grateful to Jolinda Ramsey and her student Julian Petrin Fray for first introducing us to the field of steganography.

3. Donald K. Smith, *Man Speaking: A Rhetoric of Public Speech* (New York: Dodd, Mead & Co., 1969), 228.

4. Kenneth Blanchard and Norman Vincent Peale, *The Power of Ethical Management* (New York: Fawcett-Ballantine, 1988), 9.

5. Mary Cunningham, "What Price 'Good Copy'?" *Newsweek* (November 29, 1982): 15.

6. James C. McCroskey, *An Introduction to Rhetorical Communication* (Englewood Cliffs, NJ: Prentice-Hall, 1968), 237.

7. Alexander Lindey, *Plagiarism and Originality* (New York: Harper & Brothers, 1952), 2.

8. John L. Waltman, "Plagiarism: Preventing It in Formal Research Reports," *ABCA Bulletin* (June 1980): 37.

9. Michael T. O'Neill, "Plagiarism: Writing Responsibly," *ABCA Bulletin* (June, 1980): 34, 36.

10. Erik Vance, "Genetically Modified Conservation," *Conservation Magazine* (July/September 2010): Reprinted as "Genetic Engineering for Good: A Researcher Modifies Crops to Feed the Hungry and Cut Pesticide Use," *Utne Reader* (January/February 2011): 23.

11. *Paraphrase: Write It in Your Own Words*, Purdue OWL (Online Writing Lab), Purdue U Writing Lab, accessed June 16, 2005, http://owl.english.purdue.edu/handouts/print/research/rphr.html.

12. *Copyright and Fair Use in the Classroom, on the Internet, and the World Wide Web*, Information and Library Sciences, University of Maryland University College, accessed June 30, 2011, www.umuc.edu/library/copy.shtml.

13. U.S. Copyright Office, *Limitation on Exclusive Rights: Fair Use*, accessed June 30, 2011, www.copyright.gov/title17/92chap1.html#107.

14. Georgia Harper, "Using the Four Factor Fair Use Test," *Fair Use of Copyrighted Materials*, University of Texas, Austin, last modified August 10, 2001, www.utsystem.edu/ogc/intellectualproperty/copypol2.htm.

15. "Copyright Exceptions," Purdue University Copyright Office, accessed June 29, 2011, www.lib.purdue.edu/uco/CopyrightBasics/fair_use.html.

16. These guidelines have been shaped and reinforced by several excellent sources, including Harper, "Using the Four Factor Fair Use Test"; Georgia Harper, "Copyright Crash Course: Fair Use of Copyrighted Materials," University of Texas Libraries, accessed June 29, 2011, http://copyright.lib.utexas.edu/copypol2.html; "Copyright Exceptions," Purdue University Copyright Office; "Chapter 9, Fair Use," Stanford University Libraries, accessed April 26, 2011, http://fairuse.stanford.edu/Copyright_and_Fair_Use_Overview/chapter9/index.html.

17. Institute for Civility in Government, "Reclaiming Civility in the Public Square: 10 Rules That Work," September 21, 2008, www.instituteforcivility.org/what-we-do/reclaiming-civility-in-the-public-square-book.aspx.

18. Rod L. Troester and Cathy Sargent Mester, *Civility in Business and Professional Communication* (New York: Peter Lang, 2007), 10.

19. Rona Marech, "Thanks for the Civility: Mannerly Campaign Spread Nationwide," *Baltimoresun.com*, November 1, 2007, www.choosecivilitymc.org/published/dat/baltimore_sun.pdf.

20. Institute for Civility in Government.

Chapter 3

1. Wendy Wasserstein, "Streeping Beauty: A Rare Interview with Cinema's First Lady, *Interview* (December 1988): 90.

2. Virginia P. Richmond and James C. McCroskey, *Communication: Apprehension, Avoidance, and Effectiveness*, 5th ed. (Boston: Allyn & Bacon, 1998), 41.

3. Karen K. Dwyer and Marlina M. Davidson, "Is Public Speaking Really More Feared Than Death?" *Communication Research Reports* 29 (2012): 107.

4. Christopher Turk, *Effective Speaking: Communicating in Speech* (London: E. & F. N. Spon, 1985).

5. Chia-Fang Hsu, "Sources of Differences in Communication Apprehension between Taiwanese and Americans," *Communication Quarterly* 52 (2004): 370.

6. Nadene N. Vevea, Judy C. Pearson, Jeffrey T. Child, and Julie L. Semiak, "The Only Thing to Fear is. . . Public Speaking? Exploring Predictors of Communication in the Public Speaking Classroom," *Journal of the Communication, Speech, & Theatre Association of North Dakota* 22 (2009): 1.

7. Matthew M. Martin and Scott A. Myers, "Students' Communication Traits and Their Out-of-Class Communication with Their Instructors," *Communication Research Reports* 23 (2006): 155.

8. Daniel H. Mansson and Scott A. Myers, "A Reexamination of Swedish and American

College Students' Communicative Attributes," *Journal of Intercultural Communication Research* 38 (2009): 9.

9. Richmond and McCroskey, 45.

10. James A. Belasco and Ralph C. Stayer, *Flight of the Buffalo* (New York: Warner, 1993), 327–28.

11. Belasco and Stayer, 328.

12. Petri Laukka, Clas Linnman, Fredrik Åhs, Anna Pissiota, Örjan Frans, Vanda Faria, Åsa Michaelgård, Lieuwe Appel, Mats Fredrikson, and Tomas Furmark, "In a Nervous Voice: Acoustic Analysis and Perception of Anxiety in Social Phobics' Speech," *Journal of Nonverbal Behavior* 32 (2008): 195.

13. Joe Ayres and Theodore S. Hopf, "Visualization: A Means of Reducing Speech Anxiety," *Communication Education* 34 (1985): 321.

14. Daryl J. Bem, *Belief, Attitudes, and Human Affairs* (Belmont, CA: Brooks/Cole, 1970), 57.

15. Jack Valenti, *Speak Up with Confidence* (New York: William Morrow, 1982), 19.

Chapter 4

1. Larry Barker, Renee Edwards, Connie Gaines, Karen Gladney, and Frances Holley, "An Investigation of Proportional Time Spent in Various Communication Activities by College Students," *Journal of Applied Communication Research* 8 (1980): 101–9.

2. Robert L. Montgomery, *Listening Made Easy* (New York: AMACOM, 1981), n.p.

3. Lyle V. Mayer, *Fundamentals of Voice and Diction*, 8th ed. (Dubuque, IA: William C. Brown, 1988), 178. Laura Janusik, "Listening Facts," *International Listening Association*, accessed June 27, 2011, http://d1025403.site.myhosting.com/files.listen.org/Facts.htm.

Chapter 5

1. Mary Raymond Shipman Andrews, *The Perfect Tribute* (New York: Charles Scribner's Sons, 1906), 1–9.

2. Thomas M. Scheidel, *Persuasive Speaking* (Glenview, IL: Scott Foresman, 1967), 97. For a fuller account, see Mark E. Neely, *The Last Best Hope of Earth: Abraham Lincoln and the Promise of*

America (Cambridge, MA: Harvard University Press, 1993), 154–55. Neely notes that Lincoln made these remarks to acknowledge a serenade celebrating recent Union victories at Gettysburg and Vicksburg.

3. Carl Sandburg, *Abraham Lincoln: The Prairie Years and the War Years* (New York: Harcourt, Brace & Co., 1954), 443–44.

4. Newspaper reporters the next day began to reflect widely different public views of the president's surprisingly brief speech. *The Chicago Times* referred to "the silly, flat, and dish-watery utterances" of Lincoln; the *Harrisburg* [Pennsylvania] *Patriot and Union* simply reported, "We pass over the silly remarks of the President . . ." (Sandburg, 445). Other newspapers, however, made entirely positive evaluations of Lincoln's speech. *The Chicago Tribune* predicted, "The dedicatory remarks of President Lincoln will live among the annals of man" (Sandburg, 445). *The Philadelphia Evening Bulletin* noted that thousands who would not wade through Everett's elaborate oration would read Lincoln's brief remarks, "and not many will do it without a moistening of the eye and a swelling of the heart" (Sandburg, 446). *The Providence Journal* reminded its readers of the adage that the hardest thing in the world is to make a good 5-minute speech and said, "We know not where to look for a more admirable speech than the brief one which the President made at the close of Mr. Everett's oration" (Sandburg, 446).

5. Jeffrey F. Milem, "Why Race Matters," *Academe* (September–October 2000): 28.

6. Abraham H. Maslow, *Motivation and Personality*, 2nd ed. (New York: Random House, 1970), 35–47.

7. Maslow, 38.

8. Maslow, 41.

9. Ari Posner, "The Culture of Plagiarism," *New Republic* (April 18, 1988): 19.

Chapter 6

1. Leonard J. Rosen and Laurence Behrens, *The Allyn & Bacon Handbook*, 4th ed. (Boston: Allyn & Bacon, 2000): 68.

Chapter 7

1. Patricia Senn Breivik, *Student Learning in the Information Age* (Phoenix, AZ: Oryx Press, 1998), 2.

2. Wayne C. Booth, Gregory G. Colomb, and Joseph M. Williams, *The Craft of Research* (Chicago: University of Chicago Press, 1995), 35.

3. Robert C. Jeffrey and Owen Peterson, *Speech: A Text with Adapted Readings*, 2nd ed. (New York: Harper & Row, 1983), 169.

4. "How Academic Librarians Can Influence Students' Web-based Information Choices," *OCLC [Online College Learning Center] White Paper on the Information Habits of College Students*, June 2002, accessed August 7, 2002, www2.oclc.org/oclc/pdf/printondemand/informationhabits.pdf.

5. Frederick J. Friend, "Google Scholar: Potentially Good for Users of Academic Information," *The Journal of Electronic Publishing*, 9, no. 1 (2006). doi:10.3998/3336451.0009.105.

6. "Google Scholar," Lehigh University, Library & Technology Services, last modified April 14, 2005, www.lehigh.edu/helpdesk/docs/google/.

7. Michael K. Bergman, "White Paper: The Deep Web: Surfacing Hidden Value," *The Journal of Electronic Publishing*, 7, no. 1 (August 2001), accessed August 19, 2011, http://hdl.handle.net/2027/spo.3336451.0007.104.

8. Stephen Dingman, email to the authors, September 2, 2005.

9. Bergman, 1.

10. Alison J. Head and Michael Eisenberg. "How Today's College Students Use Wikipedia for Course-related Research," *First Monday* 15, no. 3 (March 2010), accessed July 25, 2011, www.uic.edu/htbin/cgiwrap/bin/ojs/index.php/fm/article/view/2830/2476.

11. "Wikipedia FAQ/Schools," Wikipedia, last modified June 10, 2011, http://en.wikipedia.org/wiki/Wikipedia:FAQ/Schools.

12. We adapted this checklist from Serena Fenton and Grace Reposa, "Evaluating the Goods," *Technology & Learning* (September 1998): 28–32; "Module IX: Evaluating Information Sources," McConnell Library, Radford University, accessed September 2, 2002, http://lib.runet.edu/highlanderguide/evaluation/intro.html; Esther Grassian, "Thinking Critically about Web 2.0 and Beyond," UCLA College Library, last modified November 4, 2006, www.sscnet.ucla.edu/library/modules/Judge/CLThinkWeb20.pdf; and Keith Stanger, "Criteria for Evaluating Internet Resources," University Library, Eastern Michigan University, accessed August 30, 2002, http://online.emich.edu/~lib_stanger/ineteval.htm.

13. "Preface," *Ulrich's Periodicals Directory 2009*, serials dir. Laurie Kaplan (New Providence, NJ: ProQuest, 2008), vii.

14. Joann Keyton, *Communication Research: Asking Questions, Finding Answers*, 3rd ed. (Boston: McGraw-Hill Higher Education, 2011).

15. Lawrence R. Frey, Carl H. Botan, and Gary L. Kreps, *Investigating Communication: An Introduction to Research Methods*, 2nd ed. (Boston, MA: Allyn & Bacon, 2000), 1–507.

16. Frey, Botan, and Kreps.

17. Alden Todd, *Finding Facts Fast*, 2nd ed. (Berkeley: Ten Speed, 1979), 14.

Chapter 8

1. Robert Half, "Memomania," *American Way* (November 1, 1987): 21.

2. Matthew Whitley, "Involuntary Commitment Laws," *Video User's Guide for the Allyn & Bacon/AFA Student Speeches Video I* (Boston: Allyn & Bacon, 1997), 43–45.

3. B. Scott Titsworth, "Students' Notetaking: The Effects of Teacher Immediacy and Clarity," *Communication Education* (October 2004): 317.

4. Glenn Leggett, C. David Mead, Melinda Kramer, and Richard S. Beal, *Prentice Hall Handbook for Writers*, 11th ed. (Englewood Cliffs, NJ: Prentice-Hall, 1991), 417–18. We have drawn on examples these authors use in their excellent section on connecting language.

5. Robert DiYanni and Pat C. Hoy, *The Scribner Handbook for Writers*, 3rd ed. (New York: Longman, 2001), 196.

6. DiYanni and Hoy, 197.

Chapter 9

1. Ross Petras and Kathryn Petras, *The 365 Stupidest Things Ever Said* (New York: Workman, 1999), n.p.

2. Joseph J. Chesebro and Melissa Bekelja Wanzer, "Instructional Message Variables," in *Handbook of Instructional Communication: Relational and Rhetorical Perspectives 2006*, eds. Timothy P. Mottet, Virginia P. Richmond, and James C. McCroskey (Boston: Pearson, 2006), 89–116.

3. Kyle Zrenchik, "9/11 Rescue Workers: The Forsaken Heroes," *Winning Orations, 2007* (Mankato, MN: Interstate Oratorical Association, 2007), 42. Coached by Ray Quiel.

4. *Encarta World English Dictionary* (New York: St. Martin's, 1999), 1600.

5. Chiwoneso Beverley Tinago, "The Problem with Food Aid," *Winning Orations, 2009* (Mankato, MN: Interstate Oratorical Association, 2009), 38–39. Coached by Jennifer Talbert.

6. Paul Starbuck, "Exercise Anorexia: The Deadly Regimen," *Winning Orations, 2007* (Mankato, MN: Interstate Oratorical Association, 2007), 5. Coached by Ana Petero.

7. Zrenchik, 42.

8. C. Everett Koop, address, National Press Club, Washington, DC, September 8, 1998.

9. Tony Martinet, "Ribbons: Function or Fashion," *Winning Orations, 2004* (Mankato, MN: Interstate Oratorical Association, 2004), 79. Coached by Christina Ellis.

10. Tasha Carlson, "License to Save," *Winning Orations, 2009* (Mankato, MN: Interstate Oratorical Association, 2009), 34. Coached by Kristofer Kracht.

Chapter 10

1. Angela Wnek, Untitled Speech, *Winning Orations, 2012* (Mankato, MN: Interstate Oratorical Association, 2012), 143. Coached by Scott Placke.

2. Hillary Rodham Clinton, "Remarks on the Working Women's Forum," Speech, Working Women's Forum, Chennai, India, July 20, 2011, accessed September 29, 2011, www.state.gov/secretary/rm/2011/07/168835.htm.

3. Michael Kelley, "The New Catch-22: Unemployment Discrimination," *Winning Orations, 2012* (Mankato, MN: Interstate Oratorical Association, 2012), 56. Coached by Craig Brown and Darren Epping.

4. Jake Gruber, "Heart Disease in Women," *Winning Orations, 2001* (Mankato, MN: Interstate Oratorical Association, 2001), 16. Coached by Judy Santacaterina.

5. Jayme Meyer, Untitled Speech (University of Texas at Austin, 2001–2002).

6. Tess Drager, "Clostridium Difficile: The Killer Bacterium," *Winning Orations, 2013* (Mankato, MN: Interstate Oratorical Association, 2013), 79. Coached by Brian Klosa.

7. Kimberly Paine, "Red Light Running," *Winning Orations, 2001* (Mankato, MN: Interstate Oratorical Association, 2001), 41. Coached by Susan Miskelly.

8. Paine, 42.

9. Viqar Mohammad, "Ovarian Cancer," *Winning Orations, 2007* (Mankato, MN: Interstate Oratorical Association, 2007), 17. Coached by Judy Santacaterina.

10. Mohammad, 19.

Chapter 11

1. E. D. Hirsch, Jr., *Cultural Literacy: What Every American Needs to Know* (New York: Vintage Books, 1988), 34.

2. Many people who teach creative writing prefer visual brainstorming, or "branching," to the traditional linear outlines such as the ones we illustrate. For interesting discussions of how outlining by visual brainstorming draws on both sides of the brain, see Henriette Anne Klauser, *Writing on Both Sides of the Brain: Breakthrough Techniques for People Who Write* (San Francisco: HarperSanFrancisco, 1987), 47–55, and Gabriele Lusser Rico, *Writing the Natural Way: Using Right-Brain Techniques to Release Your Expressive Powers* (New York: Tarcher/Putnam, 2000).

3. Austin Willis, "Gum Chewers," Speech Delivered at Penn State Hazleton, Hazleton, Pennsylvania, Fall 2013. Used with permission.

Chapter 12

1. Richard Lederer, *Anguished English: An Anthology of Accidental Assaults upon Our Language* (Charleston, SC: Wyrick, 1987), 8.

2. Gloria Cooper, ed., *Red Tape Holds up New Bridge, and More Flubs from the Nation's Press* (New York: Perigee, 1987), n.p.

3. This discussion of two ways of responding to language is based on Louise M. Rosenblatt, *The Reader, the Text, the Poem: The Transactional Theory of the Literary Work* (Carbondale: Southern Illinois University Press, 1978), particularly Chapter 3, "Efferent and Aesthetic Reading."

4. Miriam Ringo, *Nobody Said It Better!* (Chicago: Rand, 1980), 201.

5. Cherie Spurling, "Batter Up—Batter Down," *Winning Orations, 1992* (Mankato, MN: Interstate Oratorical Association, 1992), 12. Coached by Janet Hunn.

6. Raymond Gozzi, "Metaphors around the TV Remote Control," *ETC: A Review of General Semantics* (Winter 1998): 441.

7. Gozzi, 438.

8. Elyse Sommer and Dorrie Weiss, eds., *Metaphors Dictionary* (Detroit: Gale, 1995), xi.

9. Phillip J. Wininger, "The Unwanted Neighbor," *Winning Orations, 2001* (Mankato, MN: Interstate Oratorical Association, 2001), 36, 38. Coached by Judy Woodring.

10. Elie Wiesel, "The Shame of Hunger," in *Representative American Speeches: 1990–1991*, ed. Owen Peterson (New York: Wilson, 1991), 70–74.

11. Travis Kirchhefer, "The Deprived," *Winning Orations, 2000* (Mankato, MN: Interstate Oratorical Association, 2000), 151. Coached by Ron Krikac.

12. Sarah Meinen, "The Forgotten Four-Letter Word," *Winning Orations, 1999* (Mankato, MN: Interstate Oratorical Association, 1999), 26–29. Coached by Dan Smith.

13. William Safire, "On Language: Marking Bush's Inaugural," *New York Times Magazine* (February 5, 1989): 12.

14. Our guidelines have been shaped and reinforced by suggestions in these two excellent publications: *Publication Manual of the American Psychological Association*, 6th ed. (Washington, DC: American Psychological Association, 2010), 70–77, and Rosalie Maggio, *Talking about People: A Guide to Fair and Accurate Language* (Phoenix, AZ: Oryx, 1997)

15. Rosalie Maggio, *The Bias-Free Word Finder: A Dictionary of Nondiscriminatory Language* (Boston: Beacon, 1991), 7.

16. Maggio, *Talking about People*, 1.

17. Richard Price, interview with Terry Gross, *Fresh Air*, National Public Radio, WHYY, Philadelphia, May 9, 1995.

18. Lewis, M. Paul, ed., *Ethnologue: Languages of the World*, 16th ed. (Dallas, TX: SIL International, 2009), online version accessed August 10, 2011, www.ethnologue.com/.

19. Quoted in George Plimpton, ed., *The Writer's Chapbook: A Compendium of Fact, Opinion, Wit, and Advice from the 20th Century's Preeminent Writers* (New York: Viking, 1989), 176.

Chapter 13

1. Karlyn Kohrs Campbell, *The Rhetorical Act*, 2nd ed. (Belmont, CA: Wadsworth, 1996), 119.

2. Elinor Donahue, "Writing Your Own Speeches," *Fund Raising Management*, accessed July 7, 1999, http://web4.infotrac.galegroup.com/itw/i...5!xrn_49_0_A18711219?sw_aep=viva_radford.

3. Mario Cuomo, "Introduction," in *More Than Words: The Speeches of Mario Cuomo* (New York: St. Martin's, 1993), xiv–xv.

4. Achim Nowak, *Power Speaking: The Art of the Exceptional Speaker* (New York: Allworth, 2004), 11.

5. Barack Obama, "Remarks by the President at a Memorial Service for the Victims of the Shooting in Tucson, Arizona," Speech Delivered in Tuscon, Arizona, January 12, 2011, www.whitehouse.gov/the-press-office/2011/01/12/remarks-president-barack-obama--memorial-service-victims-shooting-tucson.

6. Deborah Blum, "Face It! Facial Expressions Are Crucial to Emotional Health," *Psychology Today* (September 19, 1998): 32. Blum uses Paul Ekman's estimate of 5,000 facial expressions. Ray Birdwhistell posited the number 250,000 in

his *Kinesics and Context: Essays on Body Motion Communication* (Philadelphia: University of Pennsylvania Press, 1970), 8.

7. Donna Frick-Horbury and Robert E. Guttentag, "The Effects of Restricting Hand Gesture Production on Lexical Retrieval and Free Recall," *American Journal of Psychology* (Spring 1998): 45–46.

8. "Gestures May Trigger Ability to Recall Words," *Roanoke Times*, June 10, 2005, A12. See also Sharon Begley, "Living Hand to Mouth," *Newsweek* (November 2, 1999): 69.

Chapter 14

1. We adapted this chapter opening from four images described in an effective Nikon advertisement we saw for the first time in *American Photo* (March/April 1991): 19.

2. Achim Nowak, *Power Speaking: The Art of the Exceptional Public Speaker* (New York: Allworth, 2004), 192.

3. Elizabeth Downs and Judi Repman, "Picture Perfect!" *Library Journal*, September/October, 2001, 39.

4. Chris Gurrie and Brandy Fair, "(Re) Discovering PowerPoint: Retooling the PowerPoint Pedagogy for 2009 and Beyond," National Communication Association Convention, Chicago, November 12, 2009, 1.

5. Dave Paradi, "Ten Secrets for Using PowerPoint Effectively," accessed April 27, 2009, www.thinkoutsidetheslide.com/articles.ten_secrets_for_usingpowerpoint.htm.

6. Guy Kawasaki, "How to Change the World: A Practical Blog for Impractical People," December 30, 2005, http://blog.guykawasaki.com/2005/12/the_102030_rule.html#axzz1F4K0TMii.

7. These guidelines were part of a handout, "When Not to Use PowerPoint," distributed by Prof. Barbara Strain and Prof. Karen Wilking during a workshop at San Antonio College, Spring 2008. Used with permission.

8. Nick Morgan, *Give Your Speech, Change the World* (Boston: Harvard Business School, 2005), 139.

9. Michael Talman, *Understanding Presentation Graphics* (San Francisco: SYBEX, 1992), 270.

10. Edward R. Tufte, *Visual Explanations: Images and Quantities, Evidence and Narrative* (Cheshire, CT: Graphics Press, 1997), 74.

11. We adapted this list of guidelines from multiple sources, including Ann Luck, *Visual Aid Checklist for Interactive Video Presentation* (1997). Used with permission of the author. Also from Joyce Kupsch and Pat R. Graves, *Create High Impact Business Presentations* (Lincolnwood, IL: NTC Learning Works—NTC/Contemporary, 1998), 89–90, 95–96, 107–09.

12. Edward R. Tufte, *The Visual Display of Quantitative Information* (Cheshire, CT: Graphics Press, 1983), 121. See also Tufte's richly illustrated later works: *Envisioning Information* (Cheshire, CT: Graphics Press, 1990) and *Visual Explanations*.

Chapter 15

1. Internet World Stats, "Internet Users in the World," last modified June 30, 2012, www.internetworldstats.com/stats.htm.

2. Pew Internet & American Life Report, "Internet Evolution," accessed July 2, 2005, www.pewinternet.org/PPF/r/148/report_display.asp.

3. Melissa Janoske, "Renaissance Fairs: The New Vaudeville," Speech Delivered at Radford University, Radford, VA, spring 2002. Used with permission.

Chapter 16

1. "The 30-Second President," narr. Bill Moyers, *A Walk through the 20th Century with Bill Moyers*, PBS, 1984.

2. Charles U. Larson, *Persuasion: Reception and Responsibility*, 9th ed. (Belmont, CA: Wadsworth, 2001), 10.

3. Neel Bhatt, Untitled Speech, *Winning Orations, 2004* (Mankato, MN: Interstate Oratorical Association, 2004), 21. Coached by David Moscovitz.

4. *The Rhetoric of Aristotle*, trans. Lane Cooper (New York: Appleton, 1960), 8.

5. Paul Schrodt and Amber N. Finn, "Students' Perceived Understanding: An Alternative Measure and Its Association with Perceived

Teacher Confirmation, Verbal Aggressiveness, and Credibility," *Communication Education* 60 (2011): 231.

6. James Benjamin, *Principles, Elements, and Types of Persuasion* (Fort Worth, TX: Harcourt Brace, 1997), 122, 124.

7. James C. McCroskey and Jason J. Teven, "Goodwill: A Reexamination of the Construct and its Measurement." *Communication Monographs* 66 (1999): 66.

8. Paul Schrodt, Paul L. Witt, and Paul D. Turman, "Instructor Credibility as a Mediator of Instructors' Prosocial Communication Behaviors and Students' Learning Outcomes," *Communication Education* 58 (2009): 350.

9. James C. McCroskey, *An Introduction to Rhetorical Communication*, 7th ed. (Boston: Allyn, 1997), 87–88.

10. Benjamin, 129. See also Robert H. Gass and John S. Seiter, *Persuasion, Social Influence, and Compliance Gaining* (Boston: Allyn & Bacon, 1999), 89.

11. Jessica J. Jones, "Are You Guilty?" *Winning Orations, 2004* (Mankato, MN: Interstate Oratorical Association, 2004), 93. Coached by Barbara F. Sims.

Chapter 17

1. Thomas Gilovich, *How We Know What Isn't So* (New York: Free Press, 1991), 6.

2. Aristotle, *The Rhetoric of Aristotle*, trans. Lane Cooper (New York: Appleton, 1932), 220.

3. For a more elaborate discussion of the structure of an argument, see Stephen Toulmin, *The Uses of Argument* (New York: Cambridge University Press, 1974).

4. Ali Heidarpour, "Organ Donation Reform," *Winning Orations, 2004* (Mankato, MN: Interstate Oratorical Association, 2004), 69. Coached by Stacy Schrank and Thomas Bartl.

5. Patrick Martin, "The Energy Cure that Kills: Hydraulic Fracturing for Natural Gas," *Winning Orations, 2011* (Mankato, MN: Interstate Oratorical Association, 2011), 147. Coached by Karen Morris.

6. Jon Meinen, Untitled Speech, *Winning Orations, 2006* (Mankato, MN: Interstate Oratorical Association, 2006), 17. Coached by Dan Smith.

7. Nicholas Barton, "The Death of Reading," *Winning Orations, 2004* (Mankato, MN: Interstate Oratorical Association, 2004), 32. Coached by Craig Brown and Robert F. Imbody III.

8. Rachel Resnick, "The Nursing Home Catastrophe," *Winning Orations, 2006* (Mankato, MN: Interstate Oratorical Association, 2006), 1. Coached by Josh Miller.

9. Mario Cuomo, Keynote Address, Democratic National Convention, *Vital Speeches of the Day* (August 15, 1984): 647.

10. John M. Ericson and James J. Murphy with Raymond Bud Zeuschner, *The Debater's Guide*, rev. ed. (Carbondale, IL: Southern Illinois University Press, 1987), 139.

11. W. Ward Fearnside and William B. Holther, *Fallacy—The Counterfeit of Argument* (Englewood Cliffs, NJ: Prentice-Hall, 1959), 92.

12. Raymie E. McKerrow, Bruce E. Gronbeck, Douglas Ehninger, and Alan H. Monroe, *Principles and Types of Speech Communication*, 14th ed. (New York: Addison-Longman, 2000), 153–61. See also: Alan H. Monroe, *Principles and Types of Speech* (Chicago: Scott, Foresman & Company 1935).

13. Daniel Hinderliter, "Eating Better Through Reducing Food Waste," *Winning Orations, 2013* (Mankato, MN: Interstate Oratorical Association, 2013), 109–11. Coached by Mark Hickman.

Chapter 18

1. Donald Ochs, "Introduction of Samuel L. Becker, Central States Communication Association Convention, April 12, 1991," *The CSCA News* (Spring 1991): 2.

2. Josh McNair, Speech of Presentation, Radford University, VA, Summer 2002. Reprinted with permission of the author.

3. Zachary Henning, Acceptance Speech, Radford University, VA, Summer 2002. Reprinted with permission of the author.

4. Peggy Noonan, *What I Saw at the Revolution* (New York: Random House, 1990), 253.

5. Michael McDonough, Untitled Speech, *1990 Championship Debates and Speeches* (Annandale, VA: Speech Communication Association, 1990), 86.

Appendix A

1. This definition is adapted from Hendrie Weisinger and Norman M. Lobsenz, *Nobody's Perfect: How to Give Criticism and Get Results* (New York: Warner, 1981), 9–10.

2. This model of criticism is adapted from Beverly Whitaker Long, "Evaluating Performed Literature," *Studies in Interpretation*, vol. 2, eds. Esther M. Doyle and Virginia Hastings Floyd (Amsterdam: Rodopi, 1977), 267–81. See also her earlier article: Beverly Whitaker, "Critical Reasons and Literature in Performance," *The Speech Teacher* 18 (November 1969): 191–93. Long attributes this three-part model of criticism to Arnold Isenberg, "Critical Communication," *The Philosophical Review* (July 1949): 330–44.

Appendix B

1. In constructing our suggestions regarding audience questionnaires, we drew from advice in two excellent texts: Lawrence R. Frey, Carl H. Botan, and Gary L. Kreps, *Investigating Communication: An Introduction to Research Methods*, 2nd ed. (Boston: Allyn & Bacon, 2000). Joann Keyton. *Communication Research: Asking Questions, Finding Answers*, 4th ed. (New York: McGraw-Hill, 2014).

Appendix C

1. Thomas E. Harris and John C. Sherblom, *Small Group and Team Communication*, 3rd ed. (Boston: Allyn & Bacon, 2005), 156.

2. "Kenneth Blanchard Quotes," *Famous Inspirational Quotes* 23 May 2009 <http://www.inspirationalquotes4u.com/blanchardquotes/index.html>.

Appendix D

1. Jennell Chu, "Flash Mobs," Speech Delivered at San Antonio College, San Antonio, Texas, Spring 2011. Used with permission.

2. Austin Willis, "Gum Chewers," Speech Delivered at Penn State Hazleton, Hazleton, Pennsylvania, Fall 2013. Used with permission.

3. Michael Kelley, "The New Catch-22: Unemployment Discrimination," *Winning Orations, 2012* (Mankato, MN: Interstate Oratorical Association, 2012), 56-58. Coached by Craig Brown and Darren Epping.

4. Julian Petrin Fray, "Steganography: Hidden Messages," Speech Delivered at the Texas Community College Speech and Theater Association State Tournament, Spring 2002. Coached by Jolinda Ramsey. Used with permission.

5. Chiwoneso Beverley Tinago, "The Problem with Food Aid," *Winning Orations, 2009* (Mankato, MN: Interstate Oratorical Association, 2009), 38–39. Coached by Jennifer Talbert.

Glossary

Consult the pages on which these terms are defined and discussed for a fuller, contextual understanding of the term's use and the definition's origins.

acceptance speech   A speech responding to a speech of presentation by acknowledging an award, a tribute, or recognition. (p. 250)

actual example   A true instance or illustration. (p. 115)

ad hominem   A fallacy that urges listeners to reject an idea because of the allegedly poor character of the person voicing it; name-calling. (p. 237)

alliteration   The repetition of beginning sounds in words that are adjacent, or near one another. (p. 159)

antithesis   The use of parallel construction to *contrast* ideas. (p. 159)

appeal to tradition   A fallacy that opposes change by arguing that old ways are always superior to new ways. (p. 236)

appearance   A speaker's physical features, including dress and grooming. (p. 173)

argument   The process of reasoning from evidence to prove a claim. (p. 224)

argument by analogy   Says that what is true in one case is or will be true in another. (p. 227)

argument by authority   Uses testimony from an expert source to prove a speaker's claim. (p. 232)

argument by cause   Says that one action or condition caused or will cause another. (p. 228)

argument by example or inductive argument   Says that what is true of a few instances is true generally. (p. 226)

articulation   The mechanical process of forming the sounds necessary to communicate in a particular language. (p. 172)

attitude   A statement expressing an individual's approval or disapproval, like or dislike. (p. 59)

audience disposition   Listeners' feelings of like, dislike, or neutrality toward a speaker, the speaker's topic, or the occasion for a speech. (p. 62)

audience profile   A descriptive sketch of listeners' characteristics, values, beliefs, attitudes, and/or actions. (p. 64)

audience segmentation   The strategy of dividing an audience into various subgroups based on their demographic and psychographic profiles. (p. 56)

audience targeting   The strategy of directing a speech primarily toward one or more portions of the entire audience. (p. 56)

audience-generated topics   Speech subjects geared to the interests and needs of a speaker's listeners. (p. 70)

audio aid   A cassette tape, compact disc, record, or MP4 player used to clarify or prove a point by letting listeners hear an example. (p. 186)

bandwagon   A fallacy that determines truth, goodness, or wisdom by popular opinion. (p. 237)

bar graph   A diagram used to show quantitative comparisons among variables. (p. 182)

behavior   An individual's observable action. (p. 59)

belief   A statement that people accept as true. (p. 58)

brainstorming   Noncritical free association to generate as many ideas as possible in a short time. (p. 68)

caring   The extent to which listeners perceive a speaker as understanding, empathetic, and sensitive. (p. 214)

causal division   Organization of a speech from cause to effect, or from effect to cause. (p. 99)

causal transition   Establishes a cause-effect relationship between two ideas. (p. 108)

channel   The way a message is sent. (p. 8)

chart   A graphic used to condense a large amount of information, to list the steps in a process, or to introduce new terms. (p. 184)

chronological division   Organization of a speech according to a time sequence. (p. 98)

chronological transition   Shows how one idea precedes or follows another in time. (p. 108)

circular conclusion   A conclusion that repeats or refers to material used in the attention-getting step of the introduction. (p. 137)

civility   Communication behaviors that reflect respect for others and foster harmonious and productive relationships. (p. 24)

cliché   A once-colorful figure of speech that has lost impact from overuse. (p. 157)

cognitive restructuring   A strategy for reducing communication anxiety by replacing negative thoughts and statements with positive ones. (p. 33)

communication   The process of sharing meaning by sending and receiving symbolic cues. (p. 4)

communication apprehension   The fear or anxiety associated with real or anticipated communication with another person or persons. (p. 28)

comparison   The process of associating two items by pointing out their similarities. (p. 118)

competence   Listeners' views of a speaker's qualifications to speak on a particular topic. (p. 213)

complementary transition   Adds one idea to another. (p. 108)

complete sentence outline   An outline in which all numbers and letters introduce complete sentences. (p. 143)

conclusion   The deductive argument that what is true of the general class is true of the specific instance. (p. 231)

connotation   The emotional association(s) that a word or phrase may evoke in individual listeners. (p. 156)

contrast   The process of distinguishing two items by pointing out their differences. (p. 118)

contrasting transition   Shows how two ideas differ. (p. 108)

coordinate ideas   Ideas that have equal value in a speech. (p. 141)

credibility   The believability or dependability of speakers and their sources. Listeners' perceptions of a speaker's competence, trustworthiness, and caring. (pp. 113, 212)

critical thinking   The logical, reflective examination of information and ideas to determine what to believe or do. (p. 10)

criticism   Feedback offered for the purpose of improving a speaker's speech. (p. 259)

database   A huge collection of information arranged for quick retrieval by computer using key words stipulated by a researcher. (p. 85)

decoding   The process of attaching meanings to symbols received. (p. 7)

deductive argument   Says that what is true generally is or will be true in a specific instance. (p. 230)

deep Web   Huge databases of Internet information posted by public, government, corporate, and private agencies and available only by specific queries. (p. 82)

definition   An explanation of the meaning of a word, phrase, or concept. (p. 116)

definition by etymology   Explanation of the origin of the word being defined. (p. 116)

definition by example   Providing an instance or illustration of the word being defined. (p. 116)

definition by operation   Explanation of how the object or concept being defined works, what it does, or what it was designed to do. (p. 117)

definition by synonym   Substitution of a word having similar meaning for the word being defined. (p. 116)

delivery   The way a speaker presents a speech, through voice qualities, bodily actions, and language. (p. 166)

demographics   Characteristics of the audience, such as age, sex, ethnicity, education, religion, economic status, and group membership. (p. 56)

denotation   The literal meaning or dictionary definition of a word or phrase. (p. 156)

derived credibility   The image listeners develop of a speaker as he or she speaks. (p. 215)

diagram   A graphic, usually designed on a computer or drawn on poster board, showing the parts of an object or organization or the steps in a process. (p. 181)

direct question   A question that asks for an overt response from listeners. (p. 128)

encoding   The process of selecting symbols to carry a message. (p. 7)

environment   The occasion, social context, and physical setting for communication. (p. 8)

ethics   Standards used to discriminate between right and wrong, good and bad, in thought and action. (p. 14)

ethos   Speaker credibility. (p. 212)

eulogy   A speech of tribute praising a person who has recently died. (p. 251)

evaluate   Judging the merits of the stimuli you received; the fifth step of the process of listening. (p. 46)

evidence   Supporting material a speaker uses to prove a point. (p. 225)

example   A sample or illustration of a category of people, places, objects, actions, experiences, or conditions. (p. 114)

eye contact   Gaze behavior in which a speaker looks at listeners' eyes. (p. 175)

facial expression   The tension and movement of various parts of a speaker's face. (p. 174)

factual distractions   Listening disturbances caused by attempts to recall minute details of what is being communicated. (p. 47)

fair use provision   Section 107 of U.S. copyright law allowing limited noncommercial use of copyrighted materials for teaching, criticism, scholarship, research, or commentary. (p. 23)

fallacy   A flaw in the logic of an argument. (p. 233)

false analogy   A fallacy that occurs when an argument by analogy compares entities that have critical differences. (p. 234)

false authority   A fallacy that uses testimony from sources who have no expertise on the topic in question. (p. 237)

false dilemma   A fallacy that confronts listeners with two choices when, in reality, more options exist. (p. 236)

feedback   Verbal and nonverbal responses between communicators about the clarity or acceptability of messages. (p. 8)

figurative comparison   Associations between two items that do not share actual similarities. (p. 118)

figurative contrast   Distinctions between two items that do not have actual differences. (p. 118)

film and video   Moving projections used to enhance a speaker's point. (p. 184)

formal outline   A complete sentence outline written in sufficient detail that a person other than the speaker could understand it. (p. 147)

general purpose   The broad goal of a speech, such as to inform, to persuade, or to entertain. (p. 76)

gestures   Movements of a speaker's hands, arms, and head while delivering a speech. (p. 176)

group communication   Three or more people interacting and hoping to influence one another to pursue a common goal. (p. 6)

handout   Any graphic visual aid distributed to individual audience members. (p. 185)

hasty generalization   A fallacy that makes claims from insufficient or unrepresentative examples. (p. 234)

hearing   The continuous, natural, and passive process of receiving aural stimuli. (p. 44)

hypothetical example   An imaginary or fictitious instance or illustration. (p. 115)

impromptu speaking   Speaking without advance preparation. (p. 166)

inductive argument   Says that what is true of a few instances is true generally. (p. 226)

inflection   Patterns of change in a person's pitch while speaking. (p. 172)

initial credibility   A speaker's image or reputation before speaking to a particular audience. (p. 215)

intentional plagiarism   The deliberate, unattributed use of another's ideas, words, or pattern of organization. (p. 21)

interpersonal communication   Communication between individuals in pairs; also called dyadic communication. (p. 6)

interpret   Decoding, or attaching meaning to the stimuli; the third step of the process of listening. (p. 45)

interpreter   Any person using symbols to send or receive messages. (p. 4)

intrapersonal communication   Cognition or thought; communicating with oneself. (p. 6)

jargon   The special language used by people in a particular activity, business, or group. (p. 154)

judgments   A critic's opinions about the relative merits of a speech; the most common and superficial level of speech criticism. (p. 259)

key word or phrase outline   An outline in which all numbers and letters introduce words or groups of words. (p. 143)

line graph   A diagram used to depict changes among variables over time. (p. 182)

listener   The receiver, or decoder, of the message. (p. 7)

listening   The intermittent, learned, and active process of giving attention to aural stimuli. (p. 44)

literal comparison   Associations between two items that share actual similarities. (p. 118)

literal contrast   Distinctions between two items that share actual differences. (p. 118)

logos   Logical appeal. (p. 212)

major premise   A claim about a general group of people, events, or conditions. (p. 230)

map   A graphic representation of a real or imaginary geographic area. (p. 184)

Maslow's hierarchy   A model of five basic human needs—physiological, safety, belongingness, esteem, and self-actualization—in an ordered arrangement. (p. 60)

mass communication   One person or group communicating to a large audience through some print or electronic medium. (p. 6)

message   Ideas communicated verbally and nonverbally. (p. 7)

metaphor   An implied comparison of two things without the use of *as* or *like*. (p. 158)

minor premise   A statement placing a person, an event, or a condition into a general class. (p. 231)

Monroe's motivated sequence   A persuasive pattern composed of (1) getting the audience's attention, (2) establishing a need, (3) offering a proposal to satisfy the need, (4) inviting listeners to visualize the results, and (5) requesting action. (p. 241)

movement   A speaker's motion from place to place during speech delivery. (p. 175)

narration   The process of describing an action or series of occurrences; storytelling. (p. 117)

need–plan division   A variation of problem–solution organization that (1) establishes a need or deficiency, (2) offers a proposal to meet the need, (3) shows how the plan satisfies the need, and (4) suggests a plan for implementing the proposal. (p. 102)

noise   Anything that distracts from effective communication. (p. 9)

nonsexist language   Language that treats both sexes fairly and avoids stereotyping either one. (p. 161)

norms   The values a critic believes necessary to make any speech good, effective, or desirable. (p. 260)

object   An actual item or three-dimensional model of an item used during the delivery of a speech. (p. 180)

occasion-generated topics   Speech subjects derived from particular circumstances, seasons, holidays, or life events. (p. 71)

organizing question   A question that, when answered, indicates the ideas and information necessary to develop your topic. (p. 96)

parallelism   The expression of ideas using similar grammatical structures. (p. 159)

paraplage   Plagiarism consisting of half original writing and half quotation from an unattributed source. (p. 21)

pathos   Emotional appeal. (p. 212)

pause   An intentional or unintentional period of silence in a speaker's vocal delivery. (p. 170)

personal narrative   A story told from the viewpoint of a participant in the action and using the pronouns *I* or *we*. (p. 117)

personification   A figure of speech that attributes human qualities to a concept or inanimate object. (p. 159)

persuasion   The process of influencing another person's values, beliefs, attitudes, or behaviors. (p. 209)

physical distractions   Listening disturbances that originate in the physical environment and are perceived by the listener's senses. (p. 46)

physical noise   Distractions originating in the physical environment. (p. 9)

physiological distractions   Listening disturbances that originate in a listener's illness, fatigue, or unusual bodily stress. (p. 47)

physiological noise   Distractions originating in the bodies of communicators. (p. 9)

picture   A photograph, painting, drawing, or print used to make a point more vivid or convincing. (p. 181)

pie, or circle, graph   A diagram used to show the relative proportions of a whole. (p. 182)

pitch   The highness or lowness of a speaker's voice. (p. 171)

plagiarism   The unattributed use of another's ideas, words, or pattern of organization. (p. 20)

post hoc   A chronological fallacy that says that a prior event caused a subsequent event. (p. 234)

posture   The position or bearing of a speaker's body while delivering a speech. (p. 174)

PowerPoint   A software program that enables speakers to supplement their presentations with text, graphics, images, audio, and video. (p. 187)

preview   A statement that orients the audience by revealing how the speaker has organized the body of a speech. (p. 134)

primacy theory   The assumption that a speaker should place the strongest argument at the beginning of the body of a speech. (p. 219)

problem–solution division   A rigid organizational pattern that establishes a compelling problem and offers one or more convincing solutions. (p. 101)

pro–con division   Organization of a speech according to arguments for and against some policy, position, or action. (p. 100)

projection   A manner of displaying presentational aids by casting their images onto a screen or other background. (p. 187)

pronunciation   How the sounds of a word are to be said and which parts are to be stressed. (p. 173)

proposition   A declarative sentence expressing a judgment or an opinion a speaker wants listeners to accept. (p. 238)

proposition of fact   An assertion about the truth or falsity of a statement. (p. 240)

proposition of policy   A statement requesting support for a course of action. (p. 240)

proposition of value   An assertion about the relative worth of an idea or action. (p. 240)

psychographics   Characteristics of the audience, such as values, beliefs, and attitudes, which influence behaviors. (p. 58)

psychological distractions   Listening disturbances that originate in the listener's attitudes, preoccupations, or worries. (p. 47)

psychological noise   Distractions originating in the thoughts of communicators. (p. 9)

public communication   One person communicating face to face with an audience. (p. 6)

questionnaire   A set of written questions designed to elicit information about listeners' knowledge, beliefs, attitudes, or behaviors regarding your specific speech topic. (p. 269)

rate   The speed at which a speech is delivered. (p. 169)

reasons   Statements that justify a critic's judgments. (p. 260)

receive   Getting auditory stimuli; the first step of the process of listening. (p. 45)

recency theory   The assumption that a speaker should place the strongest argument at the end of the body of a speech. (p. 219)

red herring   A fallacy that introduces irrelevant issues to deflect attention from the subject under discussion. (p. 235)

referent   The object or idea each interpreter attaches to a symbol. (p. 4)

refutational strategy   A pattern of disputing an argument by (1) stating the position you are refuting, (2) stating your position, (3) supporting your position, and (4) showing how your position undermines the opposing argument. (p. 225)

refute   To dispute; to counter one argument with another. (p. 225)

repetition   Restating words, phrases, or sentences for emphasis. (p. 159)

research   The process of gathering evidence and arguments to understand, develop, and explain a speech topic. (p. 80)

research-generated topics   Speech subjects discovered by investigating a variety of sources. (p. 71)

resolve   Deciding what to do with the stimuli you received or how to respond; the sixth step of the process of listening. (p. 46)

rhetorical question   A question designed to stimulate thought without demanding an overt response. (p. 128)

search engine   A tool for locating information on the Internet by matching items in a search string with pages that the engine indexes. (p. 82)

select   Choosing which stimuli to focus on; the second step of the process of listening. (p. 45)

self-generated topics   Speech subjects based on the speaker's interests, experiences, and knowledge. (p. 69)

semantic distractions   Listening disturbances caused by confusion over the meanings of words. (p. 47)

sexist language   Language that excludes one sex, creates special categories for one sex, or assigns roles based solely on sex. (p. 161)

signpost   Numbers (*one*, *two*, and *three*) or words (*initially*, *second*, or *finally*) that signal the listener of the speaker's place in the speech. (p. 103)

simile   A comparison of two things using the words *as* or *like*. (p. 158)

slippery slope   A fallacy of causation stating that one action inevitably sets a chain of events in motion. (p. 235)

spatial division   Organization of a speech according to the geography or physical structure of the subject. (p. 99)

speaker   The sender, source, or encoder of the message. (p. 7)

speaking extemporaneously   Delivering a speech from notes or from a memorized outline. (p. 167)

speaking from manuscript   Delivering a speech from a text written word for word and practiced in advance. (p. 166)

speaking from memory   Delivering a speech that is recalled word for word from a written text. (p. 166)

speaking outline   A brief outline for the speaker's use alone, containing source citations and delivery prompts. (p. 148)

specific purpose   A statement of the general purpose of the speech, the speaker's intended audience, and the limited goal or outcome. (p. 76)

speech of introduction A speech introducing a featured speaker to an audience. (p. 247)

speech of presentation A speech conferring an award, a prize, or some other recognition on an individual or group. (p. 248)

speech of tribute A speech honoring a person, group, or event. (p. 251)

speech to actuate A persuasive speech designed to influence audience behaviors. (pp. 76, 210)

speech to convince A persuasive speech designed to influence audience beliefs and attitudes rather than behaviors. (pp. 76, 211)

speech to entertain A speech designed to make a point through the creative, organized use of humorous supporting materials. (pp. 76, 252)

speech to inform A speech designed to convey new or useful information in a balanced, objective way. A speech to impart knowledge, enhance understanding, or facilitate application of information. (pp. 75, 195)

speech to inspire A persuasive speech designed to influence listeners' feelings. (p. 211)

speech to persuade A speech designed to influence listeners' beliefs or actions. (p. 76)

statistics Data collected in the form of numbers (p. 119)

subordinate ideas Ideas that support more general or more important points in a speech. (p. 141)

syllogism The pattern of a deductive argument, consisting of a major premise, a minor premise, and a conclusion. (p. 230)

symbol Anything to which people attach meaning. (p. 4)

terminal credibility The image listeners develop of a speaker by the end of a speech and for a period of time after it. (p. 215)

testimony Quotations or paraphrases of an authoritative source to clarify or prove a point. (p. 120)

thesis statement A one-sentence synopsis of a speaker's message. (p. 77)

third-person narrative A story told from the viewpoint of a witness and using the pronouns *he, she,* or *they.* (p. 117)

tone The relationship established by language and grammar between speakers and their listeners. (p. 162)

topical division Organization of a speech according to aspects, or subtopics, of the subject. (p. 97)

transition A statement that connects parts of the speech and indicates the nature of their connection. (p. 108)

trustworthiness Listeners' views of a speaker's honesty, morality, and objectivity. (p. 213)

understand Integrating the stimuli into your frame of reference by considering both the content and context of the stimuli; the fourth step of the process of listening. (p. 46)

unintentional plagiarism The careless or unconscious unattributed use of another's ideas, words, or pattern of organization. (p. 21)

validity The accuracy with which your supporting materials support your claim. (p. 225)

value Judgment of what is right or wrong, desirable or undesirable, usually expressed as words or phrases. (p. 58)

visual brainstorming Informal written outline achieved by free associating around a key word or idea. (p. 72)

visualization A strategy for reducing communication anxiety by picturing yourself delivering a successful speech. (p. 33)

vocalized pause Sounds or words such as *ah, like, okay, um, so,* and *you know* inserted to fill the silence between a speaker's words or thoughts. (p. 171)

volume The relative loudness or softness of a speaker's voice. (p. 171)

working outline An informal, initial outline recording a speaker's process of narrowing, focusing, and balancing a topic. (p. 146)

Credits

Name Index

Name Index

Note: Page numbers followed by *t* indicate tables; those followed by *f* indicate figures.

Subject Index

Note: Page numbers followed by *t* indicate tables; those followed by *f* indicate figures. Boldface page numbers indicate marginal glossary entries.

Notes

Notes

Notes

Notes

Notes

Notes

Notes